Reasoning Aptitude

For Banking Prelims Exams

Latest Edition
Practice Kit

25 Tests
25 Topic-Wise Test

Topic Wise Chapters with Questions

✓ Thoroughly Revised and Updated

✓ Detailed Analysis of all MCQs

Title	: Reasoning Aptitude For Banking Prelims Exams
Author Name	: Mr. Rohit Manglik
Published By	: EduGorilla Community Pvt. Ltd.
Publishers Address	: 12/651, First Floor Opp. Arvindo Park, Near Jama Masjid, Indira Nagar, Lucknow, Uttar Pradesh-226016, India

Copyright EduGorilla

ISBN : 978-93-91464-93-6

Second Edition

Disclaimer EduGorilla

Compiled and created by EduGorilla Community Pvt. Ltd

Printed By EduGorilla Community Pvt. Ltd.

ROHIT MANGLIK
CEO, EduGorilla

Dear Applicants,

People say *"Success comes to those who work hard."* But I've seen people working hard for their exams day in and day out for marginal success. While others succeed in their examinations by putting in just half the work. So are they God Gifted? No! I believe that it's because they work *smart* and not just *hard*. Similarly, for your exams, you should strategize your preparation so as to increase the likelihood of success. Well with EduGorilla get ready to increase your *chances of selection* in your exam by *16x*.

EduGorilla helps you in not only working *hard* but also working in a *smart and strategic* manner. With EduGorilla's preparation package, you get a chance to make your exam preparation easy, and a fun learning path towards selection. Finding the right path to your preparations can be difficult if you don't know in which direction to head. Don't worry, we have you covered! EduGorilla will be your guide to success in your journey. With our Preparation Package, you can prepare strategically and beat the exam in just one attempt.

EduGorilla's Preparation Package includes-

- **Test Series**
- **Books**

Our preparation package is handcrafted as per the latest changes, expert opinions, and students' discretion. Thus, enabling you to get through each stage of the selection process for your exam.

Our Books are designed by the teachers and experts of the respective exam with a combined 150+ years of experience; to provide you with easy, efficient, and effective learning. Our books are smart, in the sense that not only do they give you the answers to the questions but also provide similar questions for practice.

EduGorilla's competent Test Series gives you real-time experience and confidence through which you can clear your offline or online exam in just one attempt. We currently host 83,000+ mock tests for 1,440+ competitive and academic exams.

Thus, EduGorilla misses no chance to assist you in your preparation and covers all stages of the exam, so that you don't have to look anywhere else.

We provide complete preparation packages for defense, banking, teaching, and other National & State-Level exams. Hence, it doesn't matter which exam you aspire to because you will reach your success.

ALL THE BEST !

Let EduGorilla be your Guide to Success.

Rohit Manglik,
Founder and CEO, EduGorilla

INTRODUCTION

EduGorilla focuses on guiding students to succeed in their examinations. With that in mind, our book, titled "Reasoning Aptitude : For Banking Prelims Exams", has been drafted through the collective efforts of our distinguished experts with 150+ years of combined experience. This book consists of questions that are created following the latest changes in the syllabus and exam pattern. We compiled the book on the basis of questions that are most likely to appear in the Banking Exams. Through EduGorilla's "Reasoning Aptitude : For Banking Prelims Exams" your chances of success will increase 16x.

EduGorilla does this through our Complete Preparation Package. This package consists of well-conceptualized and structured content in the form of questions that are tailor-made according to your needs and will help you practice for exams in a smart way by pinpointing all the necessary information. It also provides hints and solutions, along with a smart answer sheet for your self-evaluation. You can assess your shortcomings and work accordingly on areas that may require more of your attention.

EduGorilla promises to help you succeed in your examination and accomplish your dream goals. We believe in our aspirants and see them at the top of the merit list. And the first step towards the top is to start preparing with us. EduGorilla's "Reasoning Aptitude : For Banking Prelims Exams" includes the following attributes.

➤ Well-Researched Content

➤ Top-Notch Quality

➤ Detailed Answers and Analysis

➤ Smart Answer Sheet

➤ Exam Relevant Questions

Therefore, EduGorilla fortifies your preparation and makes it durable enough to help you stand tall and beat the examination.

TABLE OF CONTENTS

Q.1 Direction: In the following question consists of a statement followed by two arguments I and II. You have to decide which of the arguments is a strong argument and which is a weak Argument.

Statement: Should there be a ban on product advertising?

Arguments :

I. No. It is an age of advertising. Unless your advertisement is better than your other competitors, the product will not be sold.

II. Yes. The money spent on advertising is very huge and it inflates the cost of the product.

A. Only argument I is strong.

B. Only argument II is strong.

C. Either I or II is strong.

D. Neither I nor II is strong.

E. Both I and II are strong.

Q.2 Direction: In the following question consists of a statement followed by two arguments I and II. You have to decide which of the arguments is a strong argument and which is a weak Argument.

Statement: Should luxury hotels be banned in India?

Arguments :

I. Yes. They are places from where international criminals operate.

II. No. Affluent foreign tourists will have no place to stay.

A. Only argument I is strong.

B. Only argument II is strong.

C. Either I or II is strong.

D. Neither I nor II is strong.

E. Both I and II are strong.

Q.3 Direction: In the following question consists of a statement followed by two arguments I and II. You have to decide which of the arguments is a strong argument and which is a weak Argument.

Statement: Should shifting agriculture be practised?

Arguments :

I. No. It is a wasteful practice.

II. Yes. Modern methods of farming are too expensive.

A. Only argument I is strong.

B. Only argument II is strong.

C. Either I or II is strong.

D. Neither I nor II is strong.

E. Both I and II are strong.

Q.4 Direction: In the following question consists of a statement followed by two arguments I and II. You have to decide which of the arguments is a strong argument and which is a weak Argument.

Statement : Should our country extend generous behaviour and goodwill to our erring and nagging neighbours?

Arguments :

I. Yes. Goodwill always pays dividend.

II. No. Our generous behaviour and goodwill will be considered as our weakness.

A. Only argument I is strong.

B. Only argument II is strong.

C. Either I or II is strong.

D. Neither I nor II is strong.

E. Both I and II are strong.

Q.5 Direction: In the following question consists of a statement followed by two arguments I and II. You have to decide which of the arguments is a strong argument and which is a weak Argument.

Statement: Is the pen mightier than a sword?

Arguments :

I. Yes. Writers influence the thinking of the people.

II. No. With the help of physical force, one can conquer all.

A. Only argument I is strong.

B. Only argument II is strong.

C. Either I or II is strong.

D. Neither I nor II is strong.

E. Both I and II are strong.

Q.6 Direction: In the following question consists of a statement followed by two arguments I and II. You have to decide which of the arguments is a strong argument and which is a weak Argument.

Statement: Should the sex determination test during pregnancy be completely banned?

Arguments :

I. Yes. This leads to indiscriminate female foeticide and eventually will lead to social imbalance.

II. No. People have a right to know about their unborn child.

A. Only argument I is strong.

B. Only argument II is strong.

C. Either I or II is strong.

D. Neither I nor II is strong.

E. Both I and II are strong.

Q.7 Direction: In the following question consists of a statement followed by two arguments I and II. You have to decide which of the arguments is a strong argument and which is a weak Argument.

Statement: Should persons convicted of criminal offenses in the past be allowed to contest elections in India?

Arguments :

I. No. Such persons cannot serve the cause of the people and country.

II. Yes. It is democracy - let people decide whom to vote.

A. Only argument I is strong.

B. Only argument II is strong.

C. Either I or II is strong.
D. Neither I nor II is strong.
E. Both I and II are strong.

Q.8 Direction: In the following question consists of a statement followed by two arguments I and II. You have to decide which of the arguments is a strong argument and which is a weak Argument.

Statement: Should officers accepting bribe be punished?

Arguments :

I. No. Certain circumstances may have compelled them to take bribe.

II. Yes. They should do the job they are entrusted with, honestly.

A. Only argument I is strong.
B. Only argument II is strong.
C. Either I or II is strong.
D. Neither I nor II is strong.
E. Both I and II are strong.

Q.9 Direction: In the following question consists of a statement followed by two arguments I and II. You have to decide which of the arguments is a strong argument and which is a weak Argument.

Statement: Should there be a complete ban on use of all types of chemical pesticides in India?

Arguments :

I. No. The pests will destroy all the crops and the farmers will have nothing to harvest.

II. Yes. The chemical pesticides used in agriculture pollute the water underground and this has become a serious health hazard.

A. Only argument I is strong.
B. Only argument II is strong.
C. Either I or II is strong.
D. Neither I nor II is strong.
E. Both I and II are strong.

Q.10 Direction: In the following question consists of a statement followed by two arguments I and II. You have to decide which of the arguments is a strong argument and which is a weak Argument.

Statement: Should cutting of trees be banned altogether?

Arguments :

I. Yes. It is very much necessary to do so to restore ecological balance.

II. No. A total ban would harm timber-based industries.

A. Only argument I is strong.
B. Only argument II is strong.
C. Either I or II is strong.
D. Neither I nor II is strong.
E. Both I and II are strong.

Q.11 Direction: In the following question consists of a statement followed by two arguments I and II. You have to decide which of the arguments is a strong argument and which is a weak Argument.

Statement : Should all refugees, who make unauthorized entry into a country, be forced to go back to their homeland?

Arguments :

I. Yes. They make their colonies and occupy a lot of land.

II. No. They leave their homes because of hunger or some terror and on human grounds, should not be forced to go back.

A. Only argument I is strong.
B. Only argument II is strong.
C. Either I or II is strong.
D. Neither I nor II is strong.
E. Both I and II are strong.

Q.12 Direction: In the following question consists of a statement followed by two arguments I and II. You have to decide which of the arguments is a strong argument and which is a weak Argument.

Statement: Should India create a huge oil reserve like some Western countries to face difficult situations in the future?

Arguments :

I. No. There is no need to block huge amount of foreign exchange and keep the money idle.

II. Yes. This will help India withstand shocks of sudden rise in oil prices due to unforeseen circumstances.

A. Only argument I is strong.
B. Only argument II is strong.
C. Either I or II is strong.
D. Neither I nor II is strong.
E. Both I and II are strong.

Q.13 Direction: In the following question consists of a statement followed by two arguments I and II. You have to decide which of the arguments is a strong argument and which is a weak Argument.

Statement: Should there be more than one High Court in each state in India?

Arguments :

I. No. This will be sheer wastage of taxpayers' money.

II. Yes. This will help reduce the backlog of cases pending for a very long time.

A. Only argument I is strong.
B. Only argument II is strong.
C. Either I or II is strong.
D. Neither I nor II is strong.
E. Both I and II are strong.

Q.14 Direction: In the following question consists of a statement followed by two arguments I and II. You have to decide which of the arguments is a strong argument and which is a weak Argument.

Statement: Should the judiciary be independent of the executive?

Arguments :

I. Yes. This would help curb the unlawful activities of the executive.

II. No. The executive would not be able to take bold measures.

A. Only argument I is strong.
B. Only argument II is strong.

C. Either I or II is strong.

D. Neither I nor II is strong.

E. Both I and II are strong.

Q.15 Direction: In the following question consists of a statement followed by two arguments I and II. You have to decide which of the arguments is a strong argument and which is a weak Argument.

Statement: Should all the practicing doctors be brought under Government control so that they get salaries from the Government and treat patients free of cost?

Arguments :

I. No. How can any country do such an undemocratic thing?

II. Yes. Despite many problems, it will certainly help minimize, if not eradicate, unethical medical practices.

A. Only argument I is strong.

B. Only argument II is strong.

C. Either I or II is strong.

D. Neither I nor II is strong.

E. Both I and II are strong.

Q.16 Direction: In the following question consists of a statement followed by two arguments I and II. You have to decide which of the arguments is a strong argument and which is a weak Argument.

Statement: Should students take part in politics?

Arguments :

I. Yes. It inculcates in them qualities of leadership.

II. No. They should study and build up their career.

A. Only argument I is strong.

B. Only argument II is strong.

C. Either I or II is strong.

D. Neither I nor II is strong.

E. Both I and II are strong.

Q.17 Direction: In the following question consists of a statement followed by two arguments I and II. You have to decide which of the arguments is a strong argument and which is a weak Argument.

Statement : Should the opinion polls predicting outcome of elections before the elections be banned in India?

Arguments :

I. Yes. This may affect the voters mind and may affect the outcome.

II. No. Such polls are conducted all over the world.

A. Only argument I is strong.

B. Only argument II is strong.

C. Either I or II is strong.

D. Neither I nor II is strong.

E. Both I and II are strong.

Q.18 Direction: In the following question consists of a statement followed by two arguments I and II. You have to decide which of the arguments is a strong argument and which is a weak Argument.

Statement: Should the political parties be banned?

Arguments :

I. Yes. It is necessary to teach a lesson to the politicians.

II. No. It will lead to an end of democracy.

A. Only argument I is strong.

B. Only argument II is strong.

C. Either I or II is strong.

D. Neither I nor II is strong.

E. Both I and II are strong.

Q.19 Direction: In the following question consists of a statement followed by two arguments I and II. You have to decide which of the arguments is a strong argument and which is a weak Argument.

Statement: Should the system of offering jobs only to the wards of government employees be introduced in all government offices in India?

Arguments :

I. No. It denies opportunity to many deserving individuals and government may stand to lose in the long run.

II. No. It is against the principle of equality, does not government owe its responsibility to all its citizens?

A. Only argument I is strong.

B. Only argument II is strong.

C. Either I or II is strong.

D. Neither I nor II is strong.

E. Both I and II are strong.

Q.20 Direction: In the following question consists of a statement followed by two arguments I and II. You have to decide which of the arguments is a strong argument and which is a weak Argument.

Statement: Should vehicles older than 15 years be rejected in metros in India?

Arguments :

I. Yes. This is a significant step to lower down the pollution level in metros.

II. No. It will be very difficult for vehicle owners to shift to other parts in country because they will not get suitable job for their very existence.

A. Only argument I is strong.

B. Only argument II is strong.

C. Either I or II is strong.

D. Neither I nor II is strong.

E. Both I and II are strong.

Q.21 Direction: In the following question consists of a statement followed by two arguments I and II. You have to decide which of the arguments is a strong argument and which is a weak Argument.

Statement: Should the tuition fees in all post-graduate courses be hiked considerably?

Arguments :

I. Yes. This will bring in some sense of seriousness among the students and will improve the quality.

II. No. This will force the meritorious poor students to stay away from post-graduate courses.

A. Only argument I is strong.

B. Only argument II is strong.

C. Either I or II is strong.
D. Neither I nor II is strong.
E. Both I and II are strong.

Q.22 Direction: In the following question consists of a statement followed by two arguments I and II. You have to decide which of the arguments is a strong argument and which is a weak Argument.

Statement: Should persons below the age of 18 years be allowed to join armed forces?

Arguments :

I. No. Persons below the age of 18 do not attain both physical and mental maturity to shoulder such burden.

II. Yes. This will help the country develop its armed forces which will serve the country for a longer time.

A. Only argument I is strong.
B. Only argument II is strong.
C. Either I or II is strong.
D. Neither I nor II is strong.
E. Both I and II are strong.

Q.23 Direction: In the following question consists of a statement followed by two arguments I and II. You have to decide which of the arguments is a strong argument and which is a weak Argument.

Statement: Should all the infrastructural development projects in India be handed over to the private sector?

Arguments :

I. No. The private sector entities are not equipped to handle such projects.

II. Yes. Such projects are handled by the private sector in the developed countries.

A. Only argument I is strong.
B. Only argument II is strong.
C. Either I or II is strong.
D. Neither I nor II is strong.
E. Both I and II are strong.

Q.24 Direction: In the following question consists of a statement followed by two arguments I and II. You have to decide which of the arguments is a strong argument and which is a weak Argument.

Statement: Should all the colleges in India be allowed to devise their own curriculum and syllabus for the vocational courses promoting self-employment?

Arguments :

I. Yes. This is an important step to generate employment opportunities.

II. No. This will affect the quality of education due to a lack of uniformity in the syllabus.

A. Only argument I is strong.
B. Only argument II is strong.
C. Either I or II is strong.
D. Neither I nor II is strong.
E. Both I and II are strong.

Ques (25-30):Direction: The question given below is followed by two arguments numbered I and II. You have to decide which of the argument is a strong argument and which is a weak argument.

Q.25 Statement:

Should coal engines be replaced by electric engines in trains?

Arguments:

I. Yes, coal engines cause a lot of pollution.

II. No, India does not produce enough electricity to fulfill even the domestic needs.

A. Only I is strong
B. Only II is strong
C. Either I or II is strong
D. Both I and II are strong
E. Neither I nor II is strong

Q.26 Statement:

Should physical education be made compulsory in the Indian education system?

Arguments:

I. Yes, it helps in the fitness of students.

II. No, the students will be diverted from their studies.

A. Only I is strong
B. Only II is strong
C. Either I or II is strong
D. Both I and II are strong
E. Neither I or II is strong

Q.27 Statement:

Should non-vegetarian food be totally banned in our country?

Arguments:

I. Yes, it is expensive and therefore it is beyond the means of most people in our country.

II. No, any type of food should not be banned in a democratic country like ours.

A. Only I is strong
B. Only II is strong
C. Neither I nor II is strong
D. Both I and II are strong
E. Either I or II is strong

Q.28 Statement:

Should election expenses of the Central and State legislatures be met by the government?

Arguments:

I. Yes, it will put an end to political corruption.

II. No, it is not good for any country.

A. Only I is strong
B. Only II is strong
C. Either I or II is strong
D. Both I and II are strong
E. Neither I nor II is strong

Q.29 Statement:

Should Chinese products be banned in India?

Arguments:

I. Yes, nowadays we are totally dependent on Chinese products and it affects the market of Indian handmade products.

II. No, chinese products are cheaper and the middle-class and the poor people can afford them.

A. Only I is strong
B. Only II is strong
C. Either I or II is strong
D. Both I and II are strong
E. Neither I nor II is strong

Q.30 Statement:

Should India sign the Comprehensive Test Ban Treaty (CTBT)?

Arguments:

I. No, India will not be able to protect its border if it does so.

II. Yes, this is the only way to reduce tension in the Asian sub-continent.

A. Only I is strong
B. Only II is strong
C. Either I or II is strong
D. Both I and II are strong
E. Neither I nor II is strong

// Smart Answer Sheet //

| Correct | Indicates percentage of students who answered questions correctly. |

| Skipped | Indicates percentage of students who skipped questions. |

Q.	Ans.	Correct		Q.	Ans.	Correct		Q.	Ans.	Correct		Q.	Ans.	Correct		Q.	Ans.	Correct
		Skipped				Skipped				Skipped				Skipped				Skipped
1	E	64.72 % 33.69 %		7	A	55.8 % 43.54 %		13	B	65.28 % 31.16 %		19	E	68.68 % 30.69 %		25	A	52.78 % 40.32 %
2	B	48.41 % 31.86 %		8	B	55.02 % 34.61 %		14	A	46.83 % 38.68 %		20	A	56.16 % 31.53 %		26	A	50.75 % 36.56 %
3	A	66.7 % 32.06 %		9	E	64.47 % 32.3 %		15	B	47.07 % 43.31 %		21	B	65.73 % 31.81 %		27	B	83.3 % 12.87 %
4	E	47.1 % 48.6 %		10	E	52.53 % 43.14 %		16	C	41.5 % 49.23 %		22	A	65.72 % 32.46 %		28	A	46.95 % 48.04 %
5	A	59.8 % 37.2 %		11	B	47.33 % 48.56 %		17	A	59.91 % 39.54 %		23	D	66.87 % 30.26 %		29	D	83.96 % 13.87 %
6	A	64.41 % 34.34 %		12	B	59.53 % 30.36 %		18	D	48.74 % 30.76 %		24	A	51.91 % 42.68 %		30	A	64.86 % 32.39 %

Performance Analysis	
Avg. Score (%)	40.0%
Toppers Score (%)	63.33%
Your Score	

//Hints and Solutions//

1. Clearly, it is the advertisement which makes the customer aware of the qualities of the product and leads him to buy it. So, argument I is valid. But at the same time, advertising nowadays has become a costly affair and the expenses on it add to the price of the product. So, argument II also holds strong.

Hence, the correct option is (E).

2. Clearly, the luxury hotels are a mark of country's standard and a place for staying for the affluent foreign tourists. So, argument II holds. Argument I is not a strong reason because ban on hotels is not a way to do away with the activities of international criminals.

Hence, the correct option is (B).

3. Clearly, shifting agriculture is a practice in which a certain crop is grown on a land and when it becomes infertile it is left bare and another piece of land is chosen. Clearly, it is a wasteful practice. So, only argument I holds.

Hence, the correct option is (A).

4. Clearly, good behavior may at some point of time lead to mutual discussions and peaceful settlement of issues in the long run. So, the argument I hold strong. However, such behavior may be mistaken for our weakness and it would be difficult to continue with it if the other country doesn't stop its sinister activities. So, II also holds.

Hence, the correct option is (E).

5. Physical force can accomplish a task by compulsion, while the influential writings can mould the thinking of an individual and change his discretion into accomplishing the task wilfully. So, only argument I hold strong.

Hence, the correct option is (A).

6. Parents indulging in sex determination of their unborn child generally do so as they want to only a boy child and do away with a girl child. So, argument I holds. Also, people have a right to know only about the health, development and general well-being of the child before its birth, and not the sex. So, argument II does not hold strong.

Hence, the correct option is (A).

7. Clearly, persons with criminal backgrounds cannot stand to serve as the representatives of the common people. So, they should not be allowed to contest elections. Thus, only argument I holds, while II does not.

Hence, the correct option is (A).

8. Clearly, officers are paid duly for the jobs they do. So, they must do it honestly. Thus, argument II alone holds.

Hence, the correct option is (B).

9. Clearly, pesticides are meant to prevent the crops from harmful pests. But at the same time, they get washed away with water and contaminate the groundwater. Thus, both arguments hold strong.

Hence, the correct option is (E).

10. Clearly, trees play a vital role in maintaining ecological balance and so must be preserved. So, the argument I holds. Also, trees form the basic source of timber and a complete ban on cutting of trees would harm timber based industries. So, only a controlled cutting of trees should be allowed and the loss replenished by planting more trees. So, argument II is also valid.

Hence, the correct option is (E).

11. Clearly, refugees are people forced out of their homeland by some misery and need shelter desperately. So, argument II holds. Argument I against the statement is vague.

Hence, the correct option is (B).

12. Oil, being an essential commodity, our country must keep it in reserve. So, argument I is vague, while argument II holds as it provides a substantial reason for the same.

Hence, the correct option is (B).

13. Clearly, an increase in the number of High Courts will surely speed up the work and help to do away with the pending cases. So, argument II holds strong. In light of this, the expenditure incurred would be 'utilization', not 'wastage' of money. So, argument I does not hold.

Hence, the correct option is (B).

14. Clearly, independent judiciary is necessary for impartial judgement so that the Executive does not take wrong measures. So, only argument I holds.

Hence, the correct option is (A).

15. A doctor treating a patient individually can mislead the patient into wrong and unnecessary treatment for his personal gain. So, argument II holds strong. Also, a policy beneficial to common people cannot be termed 'undemocratic'. So, I is vague.

Hence, the correct option is (B).

16. Clearly, indulgence in politics trains the students for future leadership but It sways them from the studies. So, either of the arguments I or II can hold.

Hence, the correct option is (C).

17. The opinion polls may influence the thinking of an individual and thus divert his mind from his original choice. So, argument I holds strong. Further, blindly imitating a policy followed by other countries holds no relevance. So, argument II is vague.

Hence, the correct option is (A).

18. Clearly, with the ban on political parties, candidates can independently contest elections. So, it will not end democracy. Thus, argument II does not hold. Argument I does not give a strong reason.

Hence, the correct option is (D).

19. Merit, fair selection and equal opportunities for all - these three factors, if taken care of, can help government recruit competent officials and also fulfil the objectives of the Constitution. Thus, both arguments hold strong.

Hence, the correct option is (E).

20. Clearly, 15 year old vehicles are not Euro-compliant and hence cause much more pollution than the recent ones. So, argument I holds. Argument II is vague since owners of these vehicles need not shift themselves. They might sell off their vehicles and buy new ones - a small price which every citizen can afford for a healthy environment.

Hence, the correct option is (A).

21. A hike in fees is no means to make the students more serious in studies. So, argument I is vague. However, with the increase in fees, poor meritorious students would not be able to afford post-graduate studies. So, argument II holds.

Hence, the correct option is (B).

22. The armed forces must consist of physically strong and mentally mature individuals to take care of defence properly. So, argument I holds strong. Clearly, argument II holds no relevance.

Hence, the correct option is (A).

23. Clearly, such projects if handed over to the private sector shall be given to a competent authority. So, argument I is vague. Also, imitating a policy on the basis that it worked out successfully in other countries holds no relevance. Thus, argument II also does not hold strong.

Hence, the correct option is (D).

24. Clearly, colleges, if given a free hand, would through individual efforts come up with fresh, competent courses to draw in more students. This would open up new avenues for employment. So, argument I holds strong. In the light of this, argument II appears to be vague.

Hence, the correct option is (A).

25. I. Yes, coal engines cause a lot of pollution.

The argument states that coal engines cause a lot of pollution which is true and strong enough.

II. No, India does not produce enough electricity to fulfill even the domestic needs.

In India, we already have electric trains and government is working on this to increase electric trains. Thus, this argument is not strong.

Hence, the correct option is (A).

26. I. As we know that physical education is an important factor for students because it helps to keep the students healthy. So, the argument I is strong.

II. Physical education does not affect the studies of the students if their time is managed properly. So, argument II is weak here.

Hence, the correct option is (A).

27. I. As argument I this is true that non-vegetarian food is expensive and therefore it is beyond the means of most people in our country. But only for this reason, ban on non-vegetarian food is not desirable. So this argument is weak.

II. Argument II is strong here because in democratic countries any particular food should not be banned.

Hence, the correct option is (B).

28. If the election expenses are met by the government, then it will put an end to political corruption and because of this government can keep records of expenses.

But argument II is weak and ambiguous here. So, only argument I strong here.

Hence, the correct option is (A).

29. Argument I says that we are totally dependent on Chinese product and it affects the market of Indian handmade products.

Argument II says that the prices of Chinese product are cheaper as compared to Indian products, so poor people and middle-class people can easily afford them. A total ban is not the solution and we should try to increase the production and market of Indian products.

So, both arguments are strong here.

Hence, the correct option is (D).

30. India will be in danger of invasion by neighboring countries who possess atom bombs, long-range missiles, etc, if it signs the Comprehensive Test Ban Treaty (CTBT).

There is no tension in the Asian sub-continent due to CTBT.

So the argument I is strong and II is weak.

Hence, the correct option is (A).

Ques (1-4):Direction: Study the following information carefully and answer the given questions.

In a certain code language,

'Shagun knitted mat.' is written as 'Xa Zc Yb',

'Children sat on mat' is written as 'Ax Zc By Dw and

'Shagun taught children 'is written as 'Cx Xa Ax'.

Q.1 What is the code for 'children' in the given code language?
A. By   **B.** Zc   **C.** Ax   **D.** Yb
E. Dw

Q.2 If 'children on mat' is coded as 'Zc Ax Dw', then what does 'By' mean in the given code language?
A. sat   **B.** on   **C.** taught   **D.** mat
E. knitted

Q.3 Which of the following is the code for 'taught' in the given code language?
A. By   **B.** Zc   **C.** Ax   **D.** Cx
E. Dw

Q.4 What is the possible code for 'children knitted Shawl' in the given code language?
A. Ax Yb Cx   **B.** Ax Yb Sh
C. Zc Yb Cx   **D.** Zc Xa Cx
E. Dw By Cx

Ques (5-8):Direction: Study the following information carefully and answer the given questions.

In a certain code language, 'bank is open today' is written as 'sd cb vi zn', 'winter is coming' is written as 'ri dm zn', 'today is bank holiday' is written as 'zn vi cb pq', and 'they are coming today' is written as 'dm vi ki rt'.

Q.5 Code 'vi znsdri' is for which of the following sentence in given language?
A. Winter is bank holiday
B. Bank are close today
C. Winter is coming today
D. Today is open winter
E. Open holiday is coming

Q.6 Code 'pq' is for which word in the given language?
A. Are   **B.** Today   **C.** Open   **D.** Bank
E. Holiday

Q.7 What is a code of 'bank'?
A. cb   **B.** sd   **C.** vi   **D.** zn
E. ki

Q.8 'They' is coded by which of the following code?
A. ki or dm   **B.** an or ki   **C.** ki or rt   **D.** pq or rt
E. rt or vi

Ques (9-13):Direction: Study the information given carefully and answer the question given below.

In a certain code language,

"love france ban fresh" is written as N2G D2P H4J H4G.

"became risk chief put" is written as R2V T3M D3G E3H.

"how given team threat" is written as V2O I3P J2Y V4V.

"taken outfit too used" is written as V1Q Q3V V3P W2F.

Q.9 What is the code for "chief"?
A.   T3M
B.   R2V
C.   E3H
D.   Cannot be determined
E.   None of these

Q.10 What does the code J2Y" denote?
A.   How   **B.**   Given
C.   Team   **D.**   Threat
E.   None of these

Q.11 How will "X4C" be coded as?
A.   Varia
B.   Vellupura
C.   Vadodara
D.   Cannot be determined
E.   None of these

Q.12 What will be the code for "love is blind"?
A. N2G K1U D4F   **B.** K2G N1U F4D
C. F2D N4K K1U   **D.** F1U NIK D4F
E. None of these

Q.13 What will be the code for "fresh risk taken"?
A. T3M V2P J2Y   **B.** V2P T3M E3H
C. Q3V H4J E3H   **D.** H4J V3P T3M
E. None of these

Q.14 In a certain code language,

'New-Year party kept today' is 'ge va ng na',

'Today we kept Cheese pizza' is written as 'ri uvva si na',

'we will dress-up today' is written as 'na ya go uv'.

What does 'uv' stands for?
A. will   **B.** today
C. we   **D.** Either today or we
E. None of these

Ques (15-17):Direction: Study the information given to answer the question given below.

In a certain code language,

" Pharmacist is medicine" is coded as " J3R, N9D, Q11S"

" Medicine are treatment " is coded as " U10S, B4D, N9D"

" Doctor diagnose patient" is coded as " E9D, Q8S, E7Q

Q.15 What is the code used for "Patient taking Medicine"?
A. E9D, Q8S, E7Q
B. N9D, U7F, Q8S,
C. J3R, Q8S, U10S
D. Q7E, B5D, N9D
E. Q7A, M5D, N8D

Q.16 What will be coded for "Laboratory" in this coded language?
A. M11X
B. X11M
C. M15D
D. M11D
E. X11D

Q.17 "T8Q" may be the code for which of the following word?
A. Scissor
B. Sentence
C. Sudden
D. Spencer
E. Both (A) and (D)

Ques (18-21):Direction: Study the following information carefully and answer the given questions.

In a certain code language

'he si fi ka' means 'his health is affected',

'si wi ni he' means 'health is wealth indeed',

'pi si re fe' means 'he is super fit',

'ka li hi wi ' means 'his uncle has wealth'.

Q.18 Which of the following means 'wealth' in that code language?
A. si
B. wi
C. ni
D. he
E. li

Q.19 Code 'fi' is for which word in the given language?
A. wealth
B. health
C. is
D. affected
E. fit

Q.20 What would be the code for 'his wealth is affected indeed'?
A. ka wi si fi ni
B. hi wi fi si ni
C. ka he si fi ni
D. ka re fe ni wi
E. ka wi si pi re

Q.21 In a certain language, 'uncle has health and wealth' is coded as 'li hi he di wi', then what would be the code for 'and'?
A. di
B. wi
C. he
D. li
E. hi

Ques (22-26):Directions: In each question below is given a group of numbers/symbols followed by five combinations of letter codes numbered (A), (B), (C), (D) and (E). You have to find out which of the combinations correctly represents the group of numbers/symbols based on the following coding system and the conditions and mark the number of that combination as your answer:

Number	*	>	!	^	$	#	+	7	2	{	5	3	8	1	4	)	6	0	9

/ Symbols																				
Letter Code	Z	Q	D	L	H	A	P	f	U	O	Y	B	J	y	R	G	w	I	X

Conditions:

(1) If a number is immediately preceded by a number and immediately succeeded by a symbol, then all the symbols are to be coded as 'y'.

(2) If the second element is an even number and is immediately succeeded by a symbol then that even number is to be coded as the code for the symbol.

(3) If there are no odd numbers then the codes of the second and last element have to be interchanged.

If more than one conditions follow then the order of precedence will be in ascending order of the condition number.

Q.22 How *0{7+65^1 will be coded?
A. ZIOfPwYLy
B. ylyfywYyy
C. yFyyyyyyy
D. YfFWwHAYF
E. None of these

Q.23 What will be the code for {2!>42^?
A. DQOUUIDQ
B. yyyyRLD
C. OLDQRUD
D. DDDQRODI
E. None of these

Q.24 What will be the code for 8)646+2 ?
A. JGwRwpU
B. jUrwFPT
C. JGWRWPU
D. YRPjwRg
E. JUwRwyy

Q.25 How will you code 8>^$+26* ?
A. JyyyyUwy
B. fUOyYYwW
C. HAPPYyuy
D. JUUyyAHA
E. JYBDLyyy

Q.26 What will be the result after coding ^4{>#${5 ?
A. LrOQAHOY
B. LooQAHOY
C. LOOQAHOY
D. LROQAHOY
E. LOOQAOHY

Ques (27-30):Direction: Study the following information carefully and answer the given question:

In a certain code language:

'don't do that work' is written as 'fi di ti bi'

'this work is easy' is written as 'li ki si di'

'they should do that' is written as 'fi zi vi bi'

'should he do this' is written as 'fi vi si pi'

Q.27 What is the code for 'easy' in that language?

A. si

B. li

C. ki

D. di

E. Either li or ki

Q.28 Code 'vi' is for which word in that given code language?

A. Work   **B.** Don't   **C.** Should   **D.** They

E. This

Q.29 What would be the code for 'They don't work this' in that code language?

A. fi bi zi ti

B. bi zi ti di

C. pi ti di si

D. zi ti di si

E. vi di bi zi

Q.30 Code 'pi vi fi si' is for which of the following sentence in the following code language?

A. He should do that

B. He should do this

C. Don't do this work

D. They should do that

E. They should do this

// Smart Answer Sheet //

Correct — Indicates percentage of students who answered questions correctly.

Skipped — Indicates percentage of students who skipped questions.

Q.	Ans.	Correct / Skipped
1	C	40.83 % / 41.51 %
2	A	53.62 % / 42.74 %
3	D	45.42 % / 33.6 %
4	B	64.33 % / 31.34 %
5	D	84.06 % / 13.97 %
6	E	76.8 % / 12.15 %

Q.	Ans.	Correct / Skipped
7	A	77.93 % / 10.66 %
8	C	82.46 % / 12.7 %
9	C	89.68 % / 10.24 %
10	A	83.01 % / 15.88 %
11	C	88.26 % / 11.56 %
12	A	77.78 % / 14.02 %

Q.	Ans.	Correct / Skipped
13	D	80.46 % / 14.93 %
14	C	88.47 % / 11.42 %
15	B	48.05 % / 35.66 %
16	A	51.69 % / 36.2 %
17	E	48.48 % / 39.18 %
18	B	54.05 % / 41.09 %

Q.	Ans.	Correct / Skipped
19	D	44.26 % / 32.23 %
20	A	45.06 % / 38.47 %
21	A	66.55 % / 30.28 %
22	B	40.07 % / 47.29 %
23	B	50.24 % / 43.8 %
24	E	40.46 % / 31.85 %

Q.	Ans.	Correct / Skipped
25	A	46.18 % / 49.43 %
26	C	53.74 % / 32.59 %
27	E	60.21 % / 34.94 %
28	C	57.31 % / 30.72 %
29	D	69.45 % / 30.1 %
30	B	44.12 % / 48.73 %

Performance Analysis	
Avg. Score (%)	66.67%
Toppers Score (%)	70.0%
Your Score	

//Hints and Solutions//

Ques (1-4): First, let us decode the words,

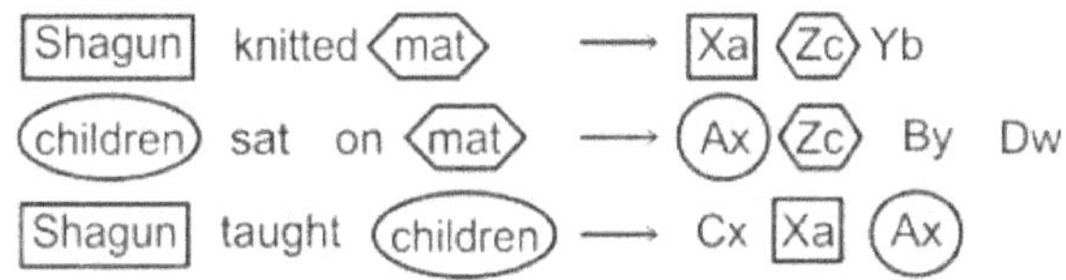

1. So, the code for 'children' in the given code language is Ax.

Hence, the correct option is (C).

2. So, if 'children on mat' is coded as 'Zc Ax Dw', then 'By' mean 'sat' in the given code language.

Hence, the correct option is (A).

3. So, the code for 'taught' in the given code language is Cx.

Hence, the correct option is (D).

4. So, the possible code for 'children knitted Shawl' in the given code language is Ax Yb Sh.

Hence, the correct option is (B).

Ques (5-8): First, let's decode the words,

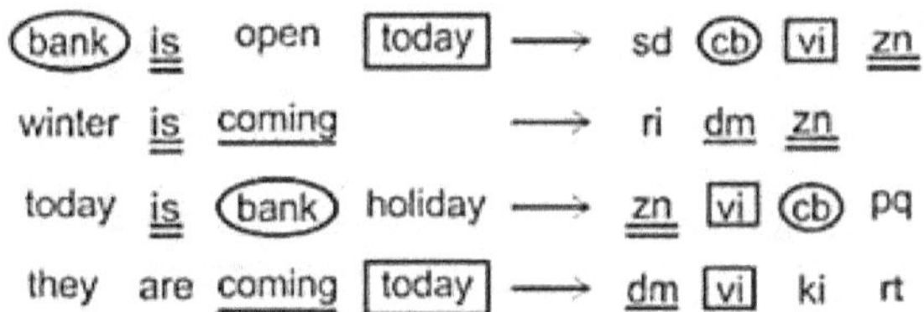

After decoding,

bank → cb

is → zn

open → sd

today → vi

winter → ri

coming → dm

holiday → pq

They → ki or rt

Are → ki or rt

5. So, code 'vi znsdri' is for 'today is open winter'

Hence, the correct option is (D).

6. So, "holiday" is the correct answer.

Hence, the correct option is (E).

7. So, "cb" is the correct answer.

Hence, the correct option is (A).

8. So, " ki or rt" is the correct answer.

Hence, the correct option is (C).

Ques (9-13): Logic:

1st element → First letter of the word + 2 (According to the alphabetical positions of the letters).

2nd element → Number of consonants.

3rd element → Last letter of the word + 2 (According to the alphabetical positions of the letters).

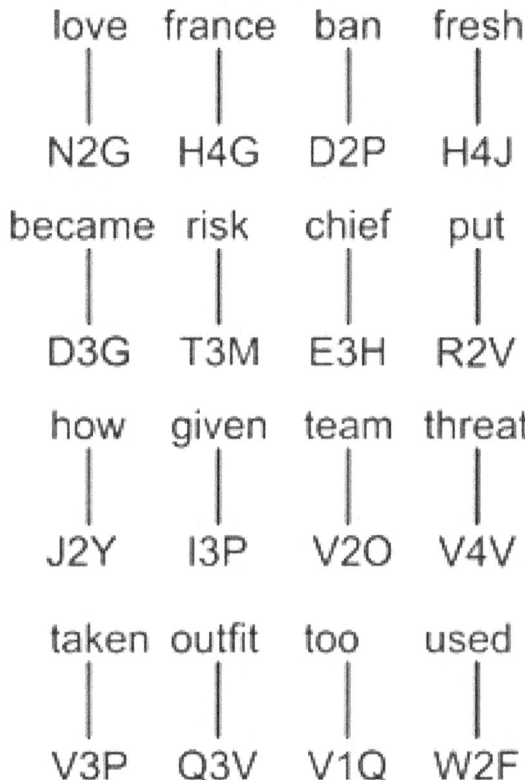

9. So, code for "chief" is "E3H".

Hence, the correct option is (C).

10. So, "J2Y" is the code for "How".

Hence, the correct option is (A).

11. According to the given coding language,

"X4C" will be coded as,

1st element is "X". So, the first letter of the word will be X - 2 = V

2nd element is "4". So, the word should consist of 4 consonants.

3rd element is "C". So, the last letter of the word will be C - 2 = A

So, the possible word from the given options is "Vadodara".

Hence, the correct option is (C).

12. According to the given coding language,

"love" can be coded as "N2G".

"is" can be coded as "K1U".

"blind" can be coded as "D4F".

So, "love is blind" can be coded as "N2G K1U D4F".

Hence, the correct option is (A).

13. According to the given coding language,

"fresh" can be coded as "H4J",

"risk" can be coded as "T3M",

"taken" can be coded as "V3P".

Hence, the correct option is (D).

14. Given code language:

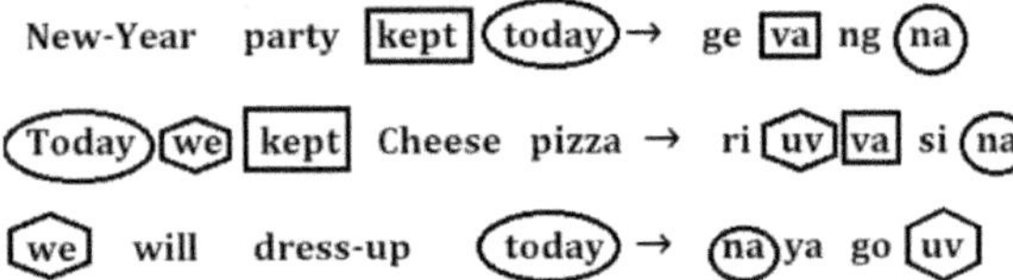

today → na

we → uv

kept → va

Here, 'uv' stands for 'we'.

Hence, the correct option is (C).

Ques (15-17): By looking at the common codes in the given question,

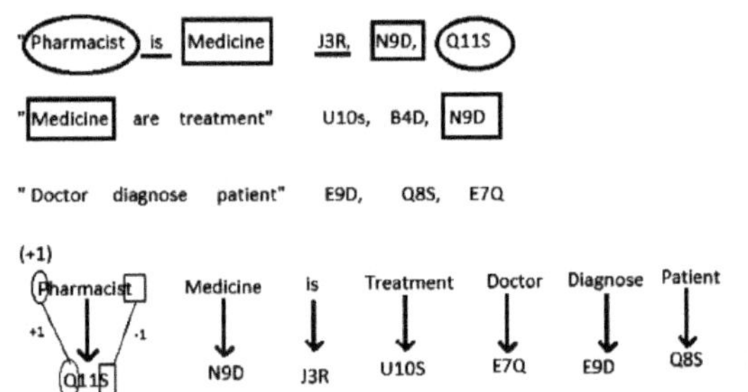

So,

Logic: All the codes are three - lettered capital words.

1) the First element of the code is a letter that represents the immediate next letter (in the capital form) of the first letter of the word.

2) The second element of the code is a number which represents the number of letter +1 in that word.

3) The third element of the code is the letter which represents the immediate previous letter of the last letter of the word.

15. Similarly

Patient → Q8S

Taking → U7F

Medicine → N9D

So, "Patient taking Medicine" is coded as "N9D, U7F, Q8S,".

Hence, the correct option is (B).

16. Similarly

Laboratory→ M11X

So, the correct M11X

Hence, the correct option is (A).

17. Similarly:

So, "T8Q: will be code for "Spencer" as well as " Scissor" as the no of letters, 1st letter & the 3rd letter in them are the same.

Hence, the correct option is (E).

Ques (18-21): In certain coding language,

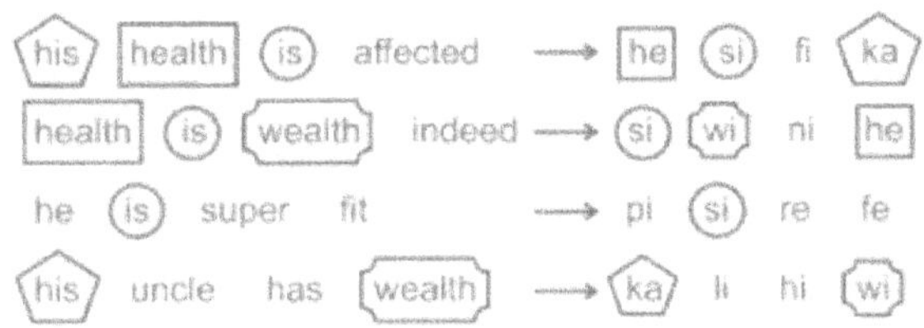

18. Thus, 'wealth' is coded as 'wi'.

Hence, the correct option is (B).

19. Thus, 'fi' is code for 'affected'.

Hence, the correct option is (D).

20. Code for 'his' is 'ka',

Code for 'wealth' is 'wi',

Code for 'is' is 'si',

Code for 'affected' is 'fi',

Code for 'indeed' is 'ni'.

Thus, the possible answer is 'ka wi si fi ni'.

Hence, the correct option is (A).

21. Code for 'uncle' is either 'li' or 'hi',

Code for 'has' is either 'li' or 'hi',

Code for 'health' is 'he',

Code for 'wealth' is 'wi',

Thus code for 'and' should be 'di'.

Hence, the correct option is (A).

Ques (22-26): Given table:

Number/Symbols	*	>	!	^	$	#	+	7	2	{	5	3	8	1	4	)	6	0	9
Le	Z	Q	D	L	H	A	P	f	U	O	Y	B	J	y	R	G	w	I	X

tte r Co de													

According to the given conditions,

Rule No.	Condition	Result
1	Number is immediately preceded by a number and immediately succeeded by a symbol	Symbols are to be coded as 'y'
2	Second element is an even number and is immediately succeeded by a symbol	Even number is to be coded as the code for the symbol
3	There are no odd numbers	The codes of the second and last element have to be interchanged

22. Here, only 1st rule applies. As per 1st rule, a number is immediately preceded by a number and immediately succeeded by a symbol. So, the symbols are to be coded as 'y'.

Therefore, *0{7+65^1 will be coded as ylyfywYyy.

Hence, the correct option is (B).

23. Here, the 1st, 2nd and 3rd rule applies. As per the 1st rule number is immediately preceded by a number and immediately succeeded by a symbol then all the symbols are to be coded as 'y' so yUyyRUL.As per the 2nd rule, the second element is an even number and is immediately succeeded by a symbol. So, even the number is to be coded as the code for the symbol i.e. yDyyRLy. Now as per 3rd rule, there are no odd numbers. So, the codes of the second and last element have to be interchanged i.e. yyyyRLD.

Therefore, {2!>42^ will be coded as yyyyRLD.

Hence, the correct option is (B).

24. 3rd rule also applies. As per 3rd rule, there are no odd numbers. So, the codes of the second and last element have to be interchanged.

Therefore, 8)646+2 will be coded as JUwRwyy.

Hence, the correct option is (E).

25. Here, 1st rule and 3rd rule applies. As per 1st rule, number is immediately preceded by a number and immediately succeeded by a symbol. So, symbols are to be coded as 'y' i.e. JyyyyUwy. As per 3rd rule, there are no odd numbers. So, the codes of the second and last element have to be interchanged i.e. JyyyyUwy.

Therefore, 8>^$+26* is coded as JyyyyUwy.

Hence, the correct option is (A).

26. Here, only 2nd rule applies. So as per the 2nd rule, the second element is an even number and is immediately succeeded by a symbol. So, even number is to be coded as the code for the symbol.

Therefore, ^4{>#${5 is coded as LOOQAHOY.

Hence, the correct option is (C).

Ques (27-30): From the above data:

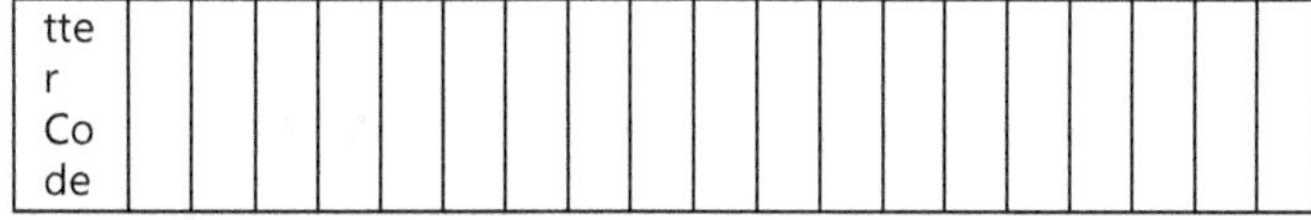
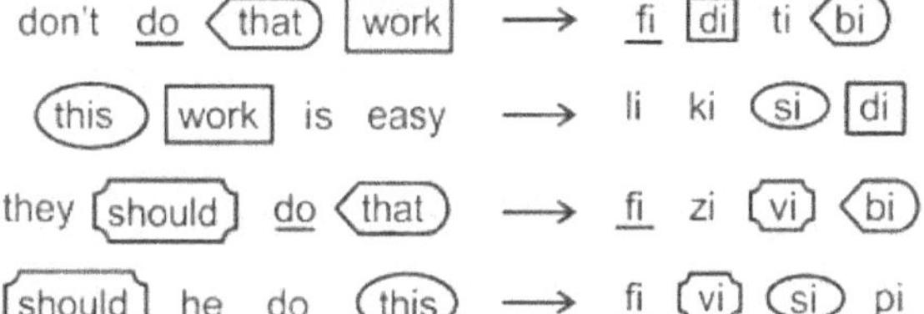

27. So, the code for 'easy' is either 'li or ki'.

Hence, the correct option is (E).

28. So, the code for 'VI' is for the word 'should'.

Hence, the correct option is (C).

29. Code for 'They' is 'zi'

Code for 'Don't' is 'ti'

Code for 'Work' is 'di'

Code for 'This' is 'si'

So, the code for 'They don't work this' is 'zi ti di si'.

Hence, the correct option is (D).

30. Code 'pi' represents 'he'

Code 'vi' represents 'should'

Code 'fi' represents 'do'

Code 'si' represents 'this'

So, the code 'pi vi fi si' is for the sentence 'he should do this'.

Hence, the correct option is (B).

Ques (1-5):Direction: Study the following series carefully and answer the question given below.

Q.1 A @ D 1 5 % K & 6 I 9 # V 8 E 3 ¥ 7 M L 2 U € F S © 9 1 X Z

How many such letters are there in the series each of which is immediately preceded by a symbol and followed by cube number?

A. One   **B.** Two   **C.** Three   **D.** Four
E. None

Q.2 A @ D 1 5 % K & 6 I 9 # V 8 E 3 ¥ 7 M L 2 U € F S © 9 1 X Z

If all the numbers in the above arrangement are deleted then which among the following element is ninth form the right end?

A. ¥   **B.** U   **C.** M   **D.** V
E. #

Q.3 A @ D 1 5 % K & 6 I 9 # V 8 E 3 ¥ 7 M L 2 U € F S © 9 1 X Z

If '@' is related to 'X', '5' is related to '©' in a certain way then 'K' is related to which of the following in the same way?

A. €   **B.** F   **C.** ¥   **D.** S
E. 8

Q.4 A @ D 1 5 % K & 6 I 9 # V 8 E 3 ¥ 7 M L 2 U € F S © 9 1 X Z

Which among the following element is second to the left of the tenth element from the left end?

A. 2   **B.** €   **C.** I   **D.** #
E. &

Q.5 A @ D 1 5 % K & 6 I 9 # V 8 E 3 ¥ 7 M L 2 U € F S © 9 1 X Z

Four of the five given in the options are same in a certain way. Choose the option which is different from others.

A. M7L   **B.** %5K   **C.** V#8   **D.** U2€
E. I96

Ques (6-10):Direction: Study the following arrangement carefully and answer the question:

H % 1 P ! F S ? * X 7 C T 4 $ 9 3 > @ / 6 N Q 5

Q.6 In the given arrangement, how many numbers are there which are immediately followed by a symbol?

A. None   **B.** One   **C.** Two   **D.** Three
E. Four

Q.7 What is the sum of the numbers between the element '*' and '>'?

A. 24   **B.** 17   **C.** 19   **D.** 23
E. 21

Q.8 If all the symbols are dropped from the arrangement then what would be the sixth element from the right end?

A. 9   **B.** T   **C.** 4   **D.** C
E. 7

Q.9 If all the numbers are dropped from the above arrangement, which of the following will be the fifth to the right of fourth from the left end?

A. ?   **B.** S   **C.** *   **D.** X
E. C

Q.10 How many letters are immediately preceded by consonants and immediately followed by a symbol?

A. None   **B.** One   **C.** Two   **D.** Three
E. Four

Ques (11-15):Direction: Study the following arrangement of numbers, letters, and symbols carefully and answer the question given below:

R @ 2 9 T V A Y 5 © # J 1 P 8 Q $ E 3 * H % 6 W 4 I 8 U Z

Q.11 Four of the following five are alike in a certain way based on their positions in the above arrangement and so form a group. Which is the one that does not belong to that group?

A. JP©   **B.** EQ*   **C.** WI%   **D.** 9V@
E. 1#$

Q.12 Which of the following is the fifth to the right of the nineteenth element from the right end?

A. P   **B.** V
C. W   **D.** 8
E. None of these

Q.13 How many such numbers are there in the above arrangement, each of which is immediately preceded by a consonant and immediately followed by a symbol?

A. Three   **B.** One
C. More than four   **D.** Four
E. Two

Q.14 If the positions of the last eighteen elements in the above arrangement are reversed, which of the following will be the seventeenth from the left end?

A. E   **B.** P
C. W   **D.** 6
E. None of these

Q.15 How many such vowels are there in the above arrangement, each of which is either immediately followed by a symbol or immediately preceded by a symbol?

A. One   **B.** Two   **C.** Three   **D.** Four
E. None

Ques (16-19):Direction: Study the following information carefully and answers the questions given below:

X 7 Z W Q P @ 7 6 G C 5 & D % K F O ^ T U # 2 3 H B 9 Y * M $ 1 4

Q.16 If all the numbers are dropped from the above arrangement, which of the following element will be twelfth from the right end?

A. U   B. H
C. B   D. F
E. None of these

Q.17 Which of the following element is fifth to the right of thirteenth to the left of 4 in the given arrangement?
A. B   B. 2
C. H   D. 3
E. None of these

Q.18 How many such symbols are there in the above arrangement, each of which is immediately preceded and immediately followed by a consonant?
A. 2   B. 3   C. 1   D. 4
E. None

Q.19 Which of the following element is 3rd to the right of 9th element from the right end?
A. B   B. *   C. 9   D. Y
E. M

Ques (20-22):Direction: These questions are based on the following arrangement. Study the arrangement carefully to answer these questions.

I 4 N 5 6 C 7 5 O 6 8 G 3 N 8 I 4 T O 8 M 5 O 3 D 3 4 6 E

Q.20 How many such numbers are there in the above series, each of which is immediately followed by a consonant as well as preceded by a vowel?
A. 5   B. 3   C. 8   D. 4
E. 7

Q.21 After dropping all the consonants, which element will be third to the left of the third vowel from the right end?
A. I   B. N   C. O   D. 3
E. 8

Q.22 After dropping all the numbers, which letter will be second to the right of the sixth letter from the left end?
A. I   B. N   C. O   D. T
E. C

Ques (23-26):Direction: Study the following information carefully to answer the given question.

M 1 E & D 2 G 9 $ F @ 4 N Z W © 8 C Y A * 6

Q.23 If all the numbers in the above arrangement are dropped, then which of the following will be the tenth from the right end?
A. $ B. D
C. F   D. Z
E. None of these

Q.24 Four of following five are alike in a certain way based on their positions in the above arrangement and so form a group. Which is the one that does not belong to that group?
A. ME2   B. G$4
C. NWC   D. YA6
E. None of these

Q.25 How many letters are there between the fourth element from the left and the eleventh element from the right end of the given arrangement?
A. None   B. One
C. Two   D. Three
E. More than three

Q.26 Which of the following is the fifth to the left of the eleventh element from the right end of the above arrangement?
A. H   B. G
C. %   D. D
E. None of these

Ques (27-30):Directions: Study the following arrangement carefully and answer the questions given below:

G 3 ? 2 D I 9 P K 4 8 2 L @ % J ! P $ K * 8 1 4 I M W 5 7 F 5 9 @ & H 5 ! # H

Q.27 If all the numbers are deleted from the arrangement, then which element will be 4th to the left of the 12th element from the left end?
A. *   B. @   C. K   D. P
E. $

Q.28 How many cases are there in the arrangement in which a letter is immediately preceded by a symbol?
A. One   B. Two
C. Three   D. Four
E. More than four

Q.29 Which of the following is eleventh to the left of the seventeenth element from the left end of the above arrangement?
A. I   B. L   C. 9   D. 4
E. D

Q.30 Which of the following is exactly in the middle of the tenth from the left end and the fourteen from the right end in the above arrangement?
A. P   B. K
C. $ D. @
E. None of these

// Smart Answer Sheet //

Correct   Indicates percentage of students who answered questions correctly.

Skipped   Indicates percentage of students who skipped questions.

Q.	Ans.	Correct / Skipped
1	B	57.83 % / 32.62 %
2	C	47.25 % / 35.52 %
3	B	48.76 % / 49.34 %
4	E	46.3 % / 39.67 %
5	E	67.15 % / 30.68 %
6	C	88.63 % / 10.86 %

Q.	Ans.	Correct / Skipped
7	D	87.93 % / 10.22 %
8	A	76.25 % / 14.3 %
9	D	85.82 % / 13.4 %
10	B	76.98 % / 12.27 %
11	E	60.85 % / 31.65 %
12	E	45.29 % / 39.81 %

Q.	Ans.	Correct / Skipped
13	B	41.61 % / 45.81 %
14	C	68.35 % / 30.16 %
15	A	43.75 % / 36.32 %
16	D	12.91 % / 86.86 %
17	C	46.25 % / 39.51 %
18	A	65.34 % / 32.2 %

Q.	Ans.	Correct / Skipped
19	D	81.33 % / 10.6 %
20	D	82.77 % / 10.82 %
21	E	85.86 % / 10.82 %
22	D	85.16 % / 10.68 %
23	C	83.07 % / 12.05 %
24	D	89.58 % / 10.29 %

Q.	Ans.	Correct / Skipped
25	D	84.25 % / 10.36 %
26	B	83.11 % / 11.79 %
27	B	49.92 % / 42.78 %
28	E	40.45 % / 46.63 %
29	A	58.45 % / 31.9 %
30	A	65.22 % / 31.06 %

Performance Analysis

Avg. Score (%)	26.67%
Toppers Score (%)	56.67%
Your Score	

//Hints and Solutions//

1. Given Series: Left side A @ D 1 5 % K & 6 I 9 # V 8 E 3 ¥ 7 M L 2 U € F S © 9 1 X Z Right side

1) Letters are there in the series each of which is immediately preceded by a symbol and followed by cube number.

A @ **D 1** 5 % K & 6 I 9 # **V 8** E 3 ¥ 7 M L 2 U € F S © 9 1 X Z

So, 'two' letters are there in the series each of which is immediately preceded by a symbol and followed by cube number.

Hence, the correct option is (B).

2. Given Series: Left side A @ D 1 5 % K & 6 I 9 # V 8 E 3 ¥ 7 M L 2 U € F S © 9 1 X Z Right side

1) If all the numbers in the above arrangement are deleted, an element which is ninth from the right end is:

A @ D % K & I # V E ¥ **M** L U € F S © X Z

So, if all the numbers in the above arrangement are deleted then 'M' is ninth from the right end.

Hence, the correct option is (C).

3. Given series-

Left side A @ D 1 5 % K & 6 I 9 # V 8 E 3 ¥ 7 M L 2 U € F S © 9 1 X Z Right side

'@' is related to 'X', '5' is related to '©' in a certain way.

The logic is-

1) '@' is second from the left side, 'X' is second from the right side.

2) '5' is fifth from the left side, '©' is fifth from the right side.

Similarly, 'K' is seventh from the left side, 'F' is seventh from the right side.

So, 'K' is related to 'F'.

Hence, the correct option is (B).

4. Given Series: Left side A @ D 1 5 % K & 6 I 9 # V 8 E 3 ¥ 7 M L 2 U € F S © 9 1 X Z Right side

1) Second to the left of the tenth element from the left end

Firstly, the tenth element from the left end

A @ D 1 5 % K & 6 **I** 9 # V 8 E 3 ¥ 7 M L 2 U € F S © 9 1 X Z

Now, second to the left of 'I'

A @ D 1 5 % K **&** 6 I 9 # V 8 E 3 ¥ 7 M L 2 U € F S © 9 1 X Z

So, '&' is second to the left of the tenth element from the left end.

Hence, the correct option is (E).

5. The given series is-

A @ D 1 5 % K & 6 I 9 # V 8 E 3 ¥ 7 M L 2 U € F S © 9 1 X Z

From option (A)- M7L

In the series, M lies between 7 (left) and L (right).

From option (B)- %5K

In the series, % lies between 5 (left) and K (right).

From option (C)- V#8

In the series, V lies between # (left) and 8 (right).

From option (D)- U2€

In the series, U lies between 2 (left) and € (right).

From option (E)- I96

In the series, I lies between 9 (right) and 6 (left).

The logic followed in the first four options is- The first element lies between the second element (left) and the third element (right).

The same logic is not followed in fifth option.

Therefore, I96 is different from others.

Hence, the correct option is (E).

6. Given Series: H % 1 P ! F S ? * X 7 C T 4 $ 9 3 > @ / 6 N Q 5

1) Numbers which are immediately followed by a symbol.

H % 1 P ! F S ? * X 7 C T **4 $** 9 **3 >** @ / 6 N Q 5

So, two numbers are there which are immediately followed by a symbol- 4$ and 3>.

Hence, the correct option is (C).

7. Given Series: H % 1 P ! F S ? * X 7 C T 4 $ 9 3 > @ / 6 N Q 5

1) Numbers between '*' and '>'

H % 1 P ! F S ? * X 7 C T 4 $ 9 3> @ / 6 N Q 5

So, the sum of the numbers between '*' and '>' = 7 + 4 + 9 + 3 = 23

Hence, the correct option is (D).

8. Given Series: H % 1 P ! F S ? * X 7 C T 4 $ 9 3 > @ / 6 N Q 5

1) On dropping all the symbols, the arrangement is.

Left Side H 1 P F S X 7 C T 49 3 6 N Q 5 Right Side

2) Element which is sixth from the right end.

Left Side H 1 P F S X 7 C T 4 9 3 6 N Q 5 Right Side

So, 9 is sixth from the right end.

Hence, the correct option is (A).

9. Given Series: H % 1 P ! F S ? * X 7 C T 4 $ 9 3 > @ / 6 N Q 5

1) On dropping all the numbers, the arrangement is.

Left Side H % P ! F S ? * X C T $ > @ / N Q Right Side

Right Side + Left Side = Left Side

5th to the Right + 4th to the Left = 9th from the Left

Left Side H % P ! F S ? * X C T $ > @ / N Q Right Side

So, X is fifth to the right of fourth to the left end.

Hence, the correct option is (D).

10. Given series: H % 1 P ! F S ? * X 7 C T 4 $ 9 3 > @ / 6 N Q 5

1) Letters which are immediately preceded by consonants and immediately followed by a symbol.

H % 1 P ! **F S ?** * X 7 C T 4 $ 9 3 > @ / 6 N Q 5

Hence, only one letter is there which is immediately preceded by consonants and immediately followed by a symbol i.e., FS?.

Hence, the correct option is (B).

11. Given series:

Left Side R @ 2 9 T V A Y 5 © # J 1 P 8 Q $ E 3 * H % 6 W 4 I 8 U Z Right Side

Pattern followed is: (First Term ± 2 = Second Term); (Second Term ± 4 = Third Term)

(E) 1#$ → 1 – 2 = #; # + 6 = $

(A) JP© → J + 2 = P; P – 4 = ©

(B) EQ* → E – 2 = Q; Q + 4 = *

(C) WI% → W + 2 = I; I – 4 = %

(D) 9V@ → 9 + 2 = V; V – 4 = @

Here, all except option (E) follow the pattern.

So, 1#$ does not belong to the given group.

Hence, the correct option is (E).

12. Given series:

Left Side R @ 2 9 T V A Y 5 © # J 1 P 8 Q $ E 3 * H % 6 W 4 I 8 U Z Right Side

1) The nineteenth element from the right is #.

2) The fifth element to the right of the nineteenth element from the right end; I.e. Fifth element to the right of #: **Q**

R @ 2 9 T V A Y 5 © # <u>J 1 P 8 **Q**</u> $ E 3 * H % 6 W 4 I 8 U Z

So, the answer is none of these.

Note: Right End– Right → 19th – 5[th] = 14th from right i.e., Q.

Hence, the correct option is (E).

13. Given series:

Left Side R @ 2 9 T V A Y 5 © # J 1 P 8 Q $ E 3 * H % 6 W 4 I 8 U Z Right Side

Numbers which are immediately preceded by a consonant and immediately followed by a symbol: **Consonant → Number → Symbol**

R @ 2 9 T V A **Y 5 ©** # J 1 P 8 Q $ E 3 * H % 6 W 4 I 8 U Z

E is a **vowel** hence 'E 3 * ' is not counted.

Clearly, only one number is there i.e., **Y 5 ©**

Hence, the correct option is (B).

14. Given series:

Left Side R @ 2 9 T V A Y 5 © # J 1 P 8 Q $ E 3 * H % 6 W 4 I 8 U Z Right Side

1) Positions of the last eighteen elements in the above arrangement are reversed:

R @ 2 9 T V A Y 5 © # Z U 8 I 4 W 6 % H * 3 E $ Q 8 P 1 J

2) The seventeenth element from the left end:

R @ 2 9 T V A Y 5 © # Z U 8 I 4 **W** 6 % H * 3 E $ Q 8 P 1 J

So, the seventeenth element from left in this arrangement can be easily seen as W.

Hence, the correct option is (C).

15. Given Series:

Left Side R @ 2 9 T V A Y 5 © # J 1 P 8 Q $ E 3 * H % 6 W 4 I 8 U Z Right Side

Vowels which are immediately followed by a symbol or immediately preceded by a symbol: Symbol → Vowel OR Vowel → Symbol

R @ 2 9 T V A Y 5 © # J 1 P 8 Q **$ E** 3 * H % 6 W 4 I 8 U Z

So, only one vowel is there which is immediately preceded by symbol.

Hence, the correct option is (A).

16. After dropping all the numbers from the arrangement, the element which is twelfth from the right end is: -

12th

X Z W Q P @ G C & D % K *F* O ^ T U # H B Y * M $

Hence, the correct option is (D).

17. H is fifth to the right of thirteenth to the left of 4 in the given arrangement.
Hence, the correct option is (C).

18. 2 symbols are there in the above arrangement, each of which is immediately preceded and immediately followed by a consonant i.e. (%) and (*).
Hence, the correct option is (A).

19. Y is 3rd to the right of 9th element from the right end.
Hence, the correct option is (D).

20. Given series: I 4 N 5 6 C 7 5 O 6 8 G 3 N 8 I 4 T O 8 M 5 O 3 D 3 4 6 E

We know, consonants are the letters other than vowels (A, E, I, O, U)

<u>I 4 N</u> 5 6 C 7 5 O 6 8 G 3 N 8 <u>I 4 T</u> O 8 M 5 <u>O 3 D</u> 3 4 6 E

Here we get four numbers which are immediately followed by a consonant and immediately preceded by a vowel.

Hence, the correct option is (D).

21. Given series: I 4 N 5 6 C 7 5 O 6 8 G 3 N 8 I 4 T O 8 M 5 O 3 D 3 4 6 E

New series: I 4 5 6 7 5 O 6 8 3 8 I 4 O 8 5 O 3 3 4 6 E

Here we have 3rd vowel is O and the third element to the left of it is 8.

Hence, the correct option is (E).

22. Given series: I 4 N 5 6 C 7 5 O 6 8 G 3 N 8 I 4 T O 8 M 5 O 3 D 3 4 6 E

New series: I N C O G N I **T** O M O D E

If we have a combination of different directions like Left and Right or Right and left then we do the addition of the number to find the final positions.

Therefore, 6 + 2 = 8

Here we get T as the eighth letter from the left end.

Hence, the correct option is (D).

23. Given series:

Left Side M 1 E & D 2 G 9 $ F @ 4 N Z W © 8 C Y A * 6 Right Side

If all the numbers are dropped:

M E & D G $ F @ N Z W © C Y A *

Then, the letter/symbol that is tenth from the right end is 'F'.

Hence, the correct option is (C).

24. Given series:

Left Side M 1 E & D 2 G 9 $ F @ 4 N Z W © 8 C Y A * 6 Right Side.

Here the group is formed in which second element is to the second next of the first element and the third element is third next to the second.

Therefore, YA6 does not belong to the group.

Hence, the correct option is (D).

25. Given series:

Left Side M 1 E & D 2 G 9 $ F @ 4 N Z W © 8 C Y A * 6 Right Side.

1) 4th element from the left end is '&'.

2) 11th element from the right end is '4'.

& **D** 2 **G** 9 $ **F** @ 4

Therefore, there are 3 letters between the fourth element from the left and the eleventh element from the right end D, G and F.

Hence, the correct option is (D).

26. Given series:

M 1 E & D 2 G 9 $ F @ 4 N Z W © 8 C Y A * 6

As, Right + Left = Right

11th from the Right + 5th from the left = 16th from the Right

Clearly, 16th from the Right is G.

Hence, the correct option is (B).

27. Given arrangement: (Left) G 3 ? 2 D I 9 P K 4 8 2 L @ % J ! P $ K * 8 1 4 I M W 5 7 F 5 9 @ & H 5 ! # H (Right)

After deleting all the numbers from the arrangement, we get

(Left) G ? D I P K L @ % J ! **P** $ K * I M W F @ & H ! # H (Right)

4th to the left of 12th element from the left end = 12 − 4 = 8th from the left end.

8th from the left end is @.

So, @ is 4th to the left of the 12th element from the left end.

Hence, the correct option is (B).

28. Given arrangement: G 3 ? 2 D I 9 P K 4 8 2 L @ % J ! P $ K * 8 1 4 I M W 5 7 F 5 9 @ & H 5 ! # H

Letters in the arrangement immediately preceded by a symbol: Symbol → Letter

G 3 ? 2 D I 9 P K 4 8 2 L @ <u>% J</u> ! <u>P $ K</u> * 8 1 4 I M W 5 7 F 5 9 @ <u>& H</u> 5 ! <u># H</u>

There are five such cases i.e. J, P, K, H and H - H is repeated twice in the arrangement.

So, more than four is the correct answer.

Hence, the correct option is (E).

29. Given arrangement: G 3 ? 2 D I 9 P K 4 8 2 L @ % J ! P $ K * 8 1 4 I M W 5 7 F 5 9 @ & H 5 ! # H

As, Left - left = left

17th from the left– 11th from the left = 6th from the left

Clearly, 6th from the left is I.

Therefore, 'I' is eleventh to the left of the seventeenth element from the left end of the above arrangement.

Hence, the correct option is (A).

30. Given arrangement: (left) G 3 ? 2 D I 9 P K 4 8 2 L @ % J ! P $ K * 8 1 4 I M W 5 7 F 5 9 @ & H 5 ! # H (right)

10th from the left is 4

14th from the right is M

(left) G 3 ? 2 D I 9 P K **4** 8 2 L @ % J ! <u>P</u> $ K * 8 1 4 I **M** W 5 7 F 5 9 @ & H 5 ! # H (right)

Terms between 4 and M are "8 2 L @ % J ! P $ K * 8 1 4 I" and P is exactly in the middle of them.

So, **P** is in the middle of the tenth from the left end and the fourteen from the right end in the above arrangement.

Hence, the correct option is (A).

Ques (1-5):Direction: The following questions are based on the three-digit numbers given below. Study the information carefully and answer the questions.

952   216   352   702   853

Q.1 If in each number first and third digits are interchanged, then how many odd numbers are there?

A. One   **B.** Two   **C.** Three   **D.** Four
E. Five

Q.2 If 157 is added in the smallest number and 175 is subtracted from the largest number, then what will be the number obtained by adding the first digit of the number obtained from the smallest number and the third digit of the number obtained from the largest number?

A. 10   **B.** 11   **C.** 14   **D.** 15
E. 20

Q.3 If 5 is added in each number and then all the three digits of each number are to be added, then the resulting number of which of the following will be a prime number?

A. 952   **B.** 216   **C.** 352   **D.** 853
E. 702

Q.4 If all the three digits of each number are arranged in ascending order, then which of the following will be the second highest?

A. 352   **B.** 853   **C.** 216   **D.** 952
E. 702

Q.5 If the first and third digits of each of the numbers are multiplied then the resulting number of which of the following numbers will not be exactly divisible by 6?

A. 216   **B.** 352   **C.** 702   **D.** 853
E. 952

Ques (6-10):Direction: The following questions are based on the three-digit numbers given below. Study the information carefully and answer the questions.

229   642   921   576   408

Q.6 If in each number, the digits are arranged in ascending order, how many numbers will remain unchanged?

A. One   **B.** Two   **C.** Three   **D.** Four
E. None

Q.7 If in each number, the digits are arranged in descending order, and then the middle digits of each of the numbers are added, what will be the resultant number thus obtained?

A. 18   **B.** 15   **C.** 19   **D.** 16
E. 14

Q.8 If in each number, the first and the second digits are interchanged, then which number in the given series will give the second-lowest number?

A. 229   **B.** 642   **C.** 921   **D.** 576
E. 408

Q.9 If in each number, the digits are arranged in descending order, then which number in the given series will give the lowest number?

A. 229   **B.** 642   **C.** 921   **D.** 576
E. 408

Q.10 If in each number, 2 is added to the second digit, then how many numbers thus formed will be divisible by 3?

A. One   **B.** Two   **C.** Three   **D.** Four
E. None

Ques (11-15):Direction: The following questions are based on the three-digit numbers given below. Study the information carefully and answer the questions.

315   584   926   427   154

Q.11 If in each number three digits are arranged in descending order, which of the following will be the lowest?

A. 926   **B.** 427   **C.** 315   **D.** 154
E. 584

Q.12 If in each number second and third digits are interchanged, then how many even numbers are there?

A. 4   **B.** 3   **C.** 5   **D.** 1
E. 2

Q.13 If the positions of the first and the second digit within each number are interchanged, which of the following will be the second-highest number?

A. 315   **B.** 154   **C.** 584   **D.** 427
E. 926

Q.14 If 2 is added to the last digit of each number and then the positions of the first and the third digits are interchanged, which of the following will be the highest number?

A. 584   **B.** 427   **C.** 154   **D.** 315
E. 926

Q.15 If the second and third digits of each of the numbers are added, the resulting sum of which of the following numbers will not be exactly divisible by 3?

A. 154   **B.** 926   **C.** 584   **D.** 427
E. 315

Ques (16-20):Direction: The following questions are based on the three-digit numbers given below. Study the information carefully and answer the questions.

947   384   718   673   952

Q.16 If 1 is subtracted from all the odd digits of the given number then what is the sum of the digits of the second lowest number?

A. 10   **B.** 15   **C.** 18   **D.** 12
E. 14

Q.17 If the first and second digits of the given numbers are interchanged and the resultant numbers are arranged in descending order then which of the following number is fourth from the left?

A. 673   **B.** 947   **C.** 718   **D.** 952
E. 384

Q.18 If all the even digits in the given numbers are added then what is the third-highest value obtained from the given numbers?

A. 6   **B.** 12   **C.** 10   **D.** 2
E. 8

Q.19 Each of the digits of the given numbers is arranged in ascending order from left to right then which among the following is the third lowest number?

A. 673   **B.** 952   **C.** 384   **D.** 718
E. 947

Q.20 Which among the following number obtains the highest number if the sum of the highest and the lowest digits in each of the given numbers is considered?

A. 718   **B.** 952   **C.** 384   **D.** 947
E. 673

Ques (21-25):Direction: The following questions are based on the three-digit numbers given below. Study the information carefully and answer the questions.

483   396   625   834   967

Q.21 What will be the number obtained if third digit of the smallest number is multiplied with second digit of the second largest number?

A. 20   **B.** 21   **C.** 14   **D.** 24
E. 18

Q.22 If in each number first and third digits are interchanged, then how many even numbers are there?

A. 3   **B.** 2   **C.** 4   **D.** 5
E. 1

Q.23 If each number is multiplied by 2, then what is the multiplication of the first digit of the lowest and last digit of the largest number?

A. 24   **B.** 30   **C.** 36   **D.** 28
E. 20

Q.24 If in the above set of numbers 1 is added to the last digit and 2 is subtracted from first digit, then which number will be third if arranged in descending order?

A. 396   **B.** 625   **C.** 967   **D.** 834
E. 483

Q.25 If 2 is added to the last digit of each number and then the positions of the first and the second digits are interchanged, which of the following will be the highest number?

A. 396   **B.** 625   **C.** 967   **D.** 834
E. 483

Ques (26-29):Direction: The following questions are based on the three-digit numbers given below. Study the information carefully and answer the questions.

712   843   648   257   423

Q.26 If 1 is subtracted from the middle digit of all the numbers and then the numbers are arranged in ascending order, which of the following numbers is the largest?

A. 712   **B.** 843   **C.** 648   **D.** 257
E. 423

Q.27 If the first and second digits are interchanged, which of the following becomes the second-largest number?

A. 712   **B.** 843   **C.** 648   **D.** 257
E. 423

Q.28 If we subtract 1 from the odd number and 2 from the even number, which of the following becomes the second smallest number?

A. 712   **B.** 843   **C.** 648   **D.** 257
E. 423

Q.29 If we arrange all the digits of each number in ascending order, which of the following becomes the largest number?

A. 712   **B.** 843   **C.** 648   **D.** 257
E. 423

Q.30 Direction: The following questions are based on the three-digit numbers given below. Study the information carefully and answer the questions.

245   854   457   652   129

If all the three digits of each of the numbers are added the resulting sum of which of the following numbers will be a perfect square?

A. 245   **B.** 854   **C.** 652   **D.** 129
E. 457

// Smart Answer Sheet //

Correct   Indicates percentage of students who answered questions correctly.

Skipped   Indicates percentage of students who skipped questions.

Q.	Ans.	Correct / Skipped
1	C	78.59 % / 18.97 %
2	A	82.08 % / 17.37 %
3	B	14.95 % / 70.87 %
4	D	88.85 % / 10.67 %
5	C	50.46 % / 44.31 %
6	A	87.44 % / 11.3 %

Q.	Ans.	Correct / Skipped
7	A	86.76 % / 13.09 %
8	A	80.06 % / 19.56 %
9	B	77.91 % / 19.16 %
10	A	40.56 % / 38.89 %
11	C	78.28 % / 15.86 %
12	B	40.39 % / 44.54 %

Q.	Ans.	Correct / Skipped
13	B	59.67 % / 37.83 %
14	B	12.64 % / 87.05 %
15	B	31.33 % / 68.01 %
16	E	54.07 % / 43.05 %
17	B	27.7 % / 68.68 %
18	A	58.29 % / 33.79 %

Q.	Ans.	Correct / Skipped
19	C	40.19 % / 38.06 %
20	D	57.96 % / 39.21 %
21	E	48.48 % / 48.35 %
22	A	78.62 % / 19.48 %
23	D	19.14 % / 70.18 %
24	B	29.37 % / 67.47 %

Q.	Ans.	Correct / Skipped
25	A	44.14 % / 46.34 %
26	B	77.25 % / 13.95 %
27	B	57.7 % / 35.83 %
28	E	44.23 % / 48.78 %
29	C	57.84 % / 40.99 %
30	E	19.06 % / 71.07 %

Performance Analysis	
Avg. Score (%)	30.0%
Toppers Score (%)	63.33%
Your Score	

//Hints and Solutions//

1. Given number series: 952   216   352   702   853

On interchanging the first and third digits, we get:

259   612   253   207   358

So, there are three (259, 253 and 207) odd numbers.

Hence, the correct option is (C).

2. Given number series: 952   216   352   702   853

Smallest number = 216

157 is added in the smallest number = 216 + 157 = 373

Largest number = 952

175 is subtracted from the largest number = 952 - 175 = 777

First digit of 373 = 3

Third digit of 777 = 7

So, the sum of the first digit of the number obtained from the smallest number and the third digit of the number obtained from the largest number = 3 + 7 = 10

Hence, the correct option is (A).

3. Given number series: 952   216   352   702   853

On adding 5 in each number, we get:

952 + 5 → 957 → 9 + 5 + 7 = 21

216 + 5 → 221 → 2 + 2 + 1 = 5

352 + 5 → 357 → 3 + 5 + 7 = 15

853 + 5 → 858 → 8 + 5 + 8 = 21

702 + 5 → 707 → 7 + 0 + 7 = 14

Here, only 5 is a prime number obtained from 216.

Hence, the correct option is (B).

4. Given number series: 952   216   352   702   853

On arranging all the three digits of each number in ascending order, we get:

027, 126, 235, 259, 358

Since 259 is the second-highest number obtained from 952.

Hence, the correct option is (B).

5. Given number series: 952   216   352   702   853

On multiplying the first and third digits, we get:

216 = 2 × 6 = 12

352 = 3 × 2 = 6

702 = 7 × 2 = 14

853 = 8 × 3 = 24

952 = 9 × 2 = 18

Here, only 14 is not divisible by 6 obtained from 702.

Hence, the correct option is (C).

6. Given number series: 229   642   921   576   408

If the digits in each of the numbers are arranged in ascending order, we get:

229   246   129   567   048

Thus, only 229 is the number which is unchanged.

Hence, the correct option is (A).

7. Given number series: 229   642   921   576   408

If the digits in each of the numbers are arranged in descending order, we get:

922   642   921   765   840

Therefore, the sum of the middle digits of each number = 2 + 4 + 2 + 6 + 4 = 18

Hence, the correct option is (A).

8. Given number series: 229   642   921   576   408

If the first and the second digit are interchanged, we get:

229   462   291   756   048

Thus, the second-lowest number is 229 which is obtained from 229.

Hence, the correct option is (A).

9. Given number series: 229   642   921   576   408

If the digits in each number are arranged in descending order, we get:

922   642   921   765   840

Therefore, the lowest number is 642 which is obtained from 642.

Hence, the correct option is (B).

10. Given number series: 229   642   921   576   408

If 2 is added to the second digit of each of the numbers, we get:

249   662   941   596   428

Thus, only 249 is divisible by 3.

Hence, the correct option is (A).

11. Given number series: 315   584   926   427   154

After arranging three-digit numbers in descending order, we get:

962   854   742   541   531

531 is the lowest number obtained from 315.

Hence, the correct option is (C).

12. Given number series: 315   584   926   427   154

On interchanging each number's second and third digits, we get:

351   548   962   472   145

So, there are three even numbers in the series.

Hence, the correct option is (B).

13. Given number series: 315   584   926   427   154

On interchanging first and second digits, we get:

135   854   296   247   514

Here, 514 is the second-highest number which is obtained from 154.

Hence, the correct option is (B).

14. Given number series: 315   584   926   427   154

On adding 2 to the last digit, we get:

317   586   928   429   156

On interchanging the first and the third digit, we get:

713   685   829   924   651

So, 924 is the highest number obtained from 427.

Hence, the correct option is (B).

15. Given number series: 315   584   926   427   154

On adding second and third digits, we get:

$315 \rightarrow 1 + 5 = 6$

$584 \rightarrow 8 + 4 = 12$

$926 \rightarrow 2 + 6 = 8$

$427 \rightarrow 2 + 4 = 9$

$154 \rightarrow 5 + 4 = 9$

Clearly, 8 is not divisible by 3 which is obtained from 926.

Hence, the correct option is (B).

16. Given number series: 947   384   718   673   952

On subtracting 1 from the odd digits, we get:

846   284   608   662   842

The second-lowest number is 608.

So, the sum of the second-lowest number = 6 + 0 + 8 = 14

Hence, the correct option is (E).

17. Given number series: 947   384   718   673   952

On interchanging the first and second digits of the numbers, we get:

$947 \rightarrow 497$

$384 \rightarrow 834$

$718 \rightarrow 178$

$673 \rightarrow 763$

$952 \rightarrow 592$

Arranging the numbers in descending order, we get:

834   763   592   497   178

So, 497 is fourth from the left which is obtained from 947.

Hence, the correct option is (B).

18. Given number series: 947   384   718   673   952

On adding the even digits of each number, we get:

947 = 4

384 = 8 + 4 = 12

718 = 8

673 = 6

952 = 2

So, 6 is the third-highest value obtained from 673.

Hence, the correct option is (A).

19. Given number series: 947   384   718   673   952

On arranging the digits in ascending order within the number, we get:

479   348   178   367   259

So, 348 is the third-lowest number which is obtained from 384.

Hence, the correct option is (C).

20. Given number series: 947   384   718   673   952

Sum of the highest and the lowest numbers,

947 = 9 + 4 = 13

384 = 8 + 3 = 11

718 = 8 + 1 = 9

673 + 7 + 3 = 10

952 = 9 + 2 = 11

So, 13 is the highest number obtained from 947.

Hence, the correct option is (D).

21. Given number series: 483   396   625   834   967

Smallest number = 396

Third digit of 396 (smallest number) = 6

Second Largest number = 834

Second digit of 834 (Second Largest number) = 3

On multiplying them we get, 6 × 3 = 18

So, the number obtained if the third digit of the smallest number is multiplied with the second digit of the second largest number is 18.

Hence, the correct option is (E).

22. Given number series: 483   396   625   834   967

On interchanging each number first and third digits, we get:

384   693   526   438   769

So, there are three even numbers in the series.

Hence, the correct option is (A).

23. Given number series: 483   396   625   834   967

After each number is multiplied by 2, we get:

966   792   1250   1668   1934

Lowest number = 792

First digit of the lowest number = 7

Largest number = 1934

Last digit of largest number = 4

So, the multiplication of the first digit of the lowest and last digit of the largest number = 7 × 4 = 28

Hence, the correct option is (D).

24. Given number series: 483   396   625   834   967

After adding 1 to the last digit and subtracting 2 from the first digit, we get:

284   197   426   635   768

On rearranging the series in descending order, we get:

768   635   426   284   197

So, the third number Is 426 made from 625.

Hence, the correct option is (B).

25. Given number series: 483   396   625   834   967

Adding 2 to the last digit, we get,

485   398   627   836   969

Interchanging the first and the second digit, we get:

845   938   267   386   699

So, 938 is the highest number which came from 396.

Hence, the correct option is (A).

26. Given number series: 712   843   648   257   423

On subtracting 1 from the middle digit of all the numbers, we get:

702 833 638 247 413

On arranging all the numbers in ascending order, we get:

247 413 638 702 833

Clearly, 833 is the largest number obtained from 843.

Hence, the correct option is (B).

27. Given number series: 712   843   648   257   423

On interchanging the first and second digits, we get:

172 483 468 527 243

Clearly, 483 is the second-largest number obtained from 843.

Hence, the correct option is (B).

28. Given number series: 712   843   648   257   423

On subtracting 1 from the odd number and 2 from the even number, we get:

710 842 646 256 422

We can clearly see that 422 is the second smallest number obtained from 423.

Hence, the correct option is (E).

29. Given number series: 712   843   648   257   423

On arranging all the digits of each number in ascending order, we get:

127 348 468 257 234

We can clearly see that 468 is the largest obtained from 648.

Hence, the correct option is (C).

30. Given number series: 245   854   457   652   129

On adding the digits, we get

245 → 2 + 4 + 5 = 11

854 → 8 + 5 + 4 = 17

652 → 6 + 5 + 2 = 13

129 → 1 + 2 + 9 = 12

457 → 4 + 5 + 7 = 16

So, 457 is the number whose sum is a perfect square.

Hence, the correct option is (E).

Q.1 In a row where all are facing north, Priya is 15th from the left end and Garima is 19th from the right end. They interchange their positions, and Ram who sits 24th from the left end sits at the 5th place to the left of Priya's new position. How many persons were there in the row?

A. 36 **B.** 42 **C.** 47 **D.** 56
E. 57

Q.2 During a prize distribution ceremony, Vikram was ninth from the left while Janhvi was eighth from the right in the front row. If Hariom was thirteenth from the left and was exactly in the middle of Vikram and Janhvi in the same row then what was the total number of people in the front row?

A. 18 **B.** 19 **C.** 21 **D.** 24
E. 25

Q.3 In a north-facing row of NCC Cadets, Trisha is 9th from the left end and Tina is 12th from the right end. There are 5 cadets between Trisha and Tanya which is equal to the number of cadets between Tanya and Tina. Find how many cadets are there in the row?

A. 34 **B.** 32
C. 31 **D.** 33
E. Can't be determined

Q.4 In a queue of students facing north, Ayesha and Anisha are standing at 10th and 8th position from the left and right end respectively. If another student Ariva who is 12th from the left end is exactly in between Ayesha and Anisha then find the position of Ayesha from right end?

A. 10th **B.** 12th
C. 15th **D.** 8th
E. Can't be determined

Q.5 In a class of 35 students, Ziya is placed 7th from the bottom where as Sofia is placed 9th from the top. Shahruk is placed in between the two. What is Ziya's position from Shahruk?

A. 10 **B.** 15 **C.** 19 **D.** 21
E. 25

Q.6 There are 25 students in a class and all of them are sitting in a row to do yoga. Meena is 11th from the top and Sneha is 6th from the bottom. Two students are sitting between Ananya and Reena. What is the position of Reena from the top?

A. 12th **B.** 13th
C. 16th **D.** 14th
E. Can't be determined

Q.7 In a state-level dance competition, a total of 75 people took part. Stuti's position was 13th from the top and Barkha stood 25th from the bottom. A total of how many participants stood between Stuti and Barkha?

A. 42 **B.** 30 **C.** 45 **D.** 37
E. 50

Q.8 On sports day in a school, 8 students took part in a race. They were all made to stand in a straight line. Sumit was standing 5th from the right end and there are 3 students standing in between Sumit and Ritesh. What is the rank of Ritesh from the left end of the line?

A. 6th **B.** 2nd **C.** 8th **D.** 9th
E. 5th

Q.9 In a row of girls, if Shilpa who is 8th from the left, and Reena who is 17th from the right. If they interchange their positions among themselves, Shilpa becomes 14th from the left. Find how many girls are there in this row?

A. 38 **B.** 28 **C.** 30 **D.** 25
E. 35

Q.10 In a row of children, Deepa is 9th from the left and Vijay is 13th from the right. When these two interchange their positions, Deepa becomes 17th from the left. Tell where will Vijay be from the right?

A. 9th **B.** 21st **C.** 20th **D.** 7th
E. 14th

Q.11 In a row of students, Ramesh is ninth from the left and Suman is sixth from the right. When Ramesh and Suman interchange their places, Ramesh becomes fifteenth from the left. Tell what will be the position of Suman from the right after the interchange?

A. 6th **B.** 13th **C.** 15th **D.** 12th
E. 14th

Q.12 Study the following information and answer the question based on it.

(A) 'Srikanth' is younger than Neelima.

(B) Pratima is taller than Srikant.

(C) Subhash is taller than Neelima but shorter than Hembrum.

(D) 'Nilima' is taller than Pratima.

If all of them are made to stand in a row in the order of their height, then who among them will be exactly in the middle of the row?

A. Shrikant **B.** Nilima
C. Pratima **D.** Hembram
E. Subhash

Q.13 Suresh is heavier than Anil but not as heavy as Raju. 'Anil' is heavier than Jayesh. 'Krishna' is heavier than Suresh but lighter than 'Raju'. Who is the lightest among them?

A. Krishna **B.** Suresh **C.** Jayesh **D.** Raju
E. Anil

Q.14 Sahil and Gaurav are standing in a row of persons. Sahil is 12th from the left side and Gaurav is 18th from the right side of the row. If they interchanged their positions Sahil becomes 25th from left. What is the total number of persons standing in the row?

A. 42 **B.** 52 **C.** 45 **D.** 46

E. 56

Q.15 In a School, there are 147 people, the ratio of girls : boys is 1:6. Soumya is a girl who stands 15th from the top of that row and 7 girls are in front of her. How many boys are behind her?

A. 100 **B.** 119 **C.** 110 **D.** 120
E. 125

Q.16 Height of five students A, K, L, M and T are compared. Height of K is more than only two students. Height of M is greater than T and Height of T is greater than K. How many students are smaller than T ?

A. 3 **B.** 4 **C.** 5 **D.** 1
E. 2

Q.17 Among A, B, C, D, and E, A is taller than B but shorter than C. B is taller than only E. If C is not the tallest, then who will be in the middle keeping them in order of height?

A. A **B.** B **C.** C **D.** D
E. E

Q.18 In a class of 60 students in which the number of girls is twice the number of boys, Kamal's rank is 17th from the top. If there are 9 girls ahead of Kamal then how many boys are behind him in the rank?

A. 3 **B.** 7 **C.** 12 **D.** 23
E. 20

Q.19 Kamal is 11th from the front in a row of girls. Leela is 3 places ahead of Sunita, who is 22nd from the lead. How many girls are there between Kamal and Leela in this row?

A. 6
B. 8
C. 7
D. 9
E. Cannot be determined

Q.20 In a row of children, Kailash is fifth from the left and Mona is sixth from the right. When they interchange their positions, then Kailash becomes thirteenth from the left. What will be the position of Mona from the right?

A. Fourth
B. Fourteenth
C. Eighth
D. Fifteenth
E. Cannot be determined

Q.21 Direction: Read the following information carefully and answer the question that follows.

In a row of 35 children, M is 15th from the right and there are 10 children between M and R. What is the position of R from the left end of the row?

A. 15th
B. 5th
C. 30th
D. 20th
E. Cannot be determined

Q.22 Direction: Read the following information carefully and answer the question that follows.

Of B, F, J, K and W each of different weights, F is heavier than just J. Heavier than B, F and W but not as much as K, who is the third heaviest?

A. B **B.** F **C.** K **D.** W
E. J

Q.23 A, B, C, D and E each having a different weight, D is heavier than A and E and B is lighter than C. Who is the heaviest among them?

A. D **B.** B
C. C **D.** E
E. Data insufficient

Q.24 40 girl students are in a row and they are facing north. Kailash is sixth to the left of Sonam. If Sonam is 30th from the left end of the row, then what is the position of Kailash from the right end of the row?

A. 17th **B.** 16th **C.** 15th **D.** 26th
E. 27th

Q.25 Madhu is 18th from the left and Sandhu is 11th from the right. If there are 40 boys in the class, then how many boys are there between Madhu and Sandhu?

A. 10 **B.** 9 **C.** 12 **D.** 11
E. 13

Q.26 Among five friends, Mahesh is taller than Karan but not as tall as Yash. Hrithik is taller than Yash but not as tall as Abhishek. If everyone is standing in a row in ascending order of height, then who will be the first person?

A. Abhishek **B.** Yash
C. Karan **D.** Hrithik
E. Data insufficient

Q.27 M is greater than R in age. Q, R and $N . N, M$. Who is the eldest among M, N, R and Q?

A. M **B.** R
C. M or R **D.** N
E. Data insufficient

Q.28 Mohan is older than Praveen, Suresh is younger than Praveen. Mihir is older than Suresh but younger than Praveen. Who is the youngest among the four?

A. Praveen **B.** Mihir
C. Mohan **D.** Suresh
E. Data insufficient

Q.29 In a row of children, Deepa is 5th from the left and Vijay is 6th from the right. When these two interchange their positions, Deepa becomes 13th from the left. Tell where will Vijay be from the right?

A. 4th **B.** 14th **C.** 8th **D.** 12th
E. 11th

Q.30 Kamal is 11th from the front in a row of girls. Leela is 3 places ahead of Sunita who is 22nd from the lead. How many girls are there between Kamal and Leela in this row?

A. 6

B. 8

C. 7

D. 9

E. Cannot be determined

// Smart Answer Sheet //

Correct   Indicates percentage of students who answered questions correctly.

Skipped   Indicates percentage of students who skipped questions.

Q.	Ans.	Correct / Skipped
1	C	57.96 % / 38.77 %
2	D	47.94 % / 32.93 %
3	B	41.97 % / 47.82 %
4	B	46.54 % / 42.78 %
5	A	69.59 % / 30.22 %
6	E	55.16 % / 37.3 %

Q.	Ans.	Correct / Skipped
7	D	46.8 % / 37.01 %
8	C	53.52 % / 34.9 %
9	C	45.05 % / 51.92 %
10	B	49.33 % / 32.75 %
11	A	32.54 % / 67.2 %
12	B	14.69 % / 68.6 %

Q.	Ans.	Correct / Skipped
13	C	62.09 % / 32.38 %
14	A	48.58 % / 36.68 %
15	B	45.76 % / 44.71 %
16	A	58.82 % / 40.23 %
17	A	68.11 % / 30.08 %
18	C	59.61 % / 37.39 %

Q.	Ans.	Correct / Skipped
19	B	59.1 % / 35.71 %
20	B	40.41 % / 59.38 %
21	E	54.35 % / 30.98 %
22	D	43.15 % / 46.05 %
23	E	50.55 % / 34.54 %
24	A	59.31 % / 33.1 %

Q.	Ans.	Correct / Skipped
25	D	41.57 % / 33.97 %
26	C	64.1 % / 32.88 %
27	A	50.51 % / 39.02 %
28	D	50.63 % / 34.96 %
29	B	51.2 % / 31.27 %
30	B	52.27 % / 40.19 %

Performance Analysis

Avg. Score (%)	**53.33%**
Toppers Score (%)	**60.0%**
Your Score	

//Hints and Solutions//

1. Using the given information we can create the following figure:

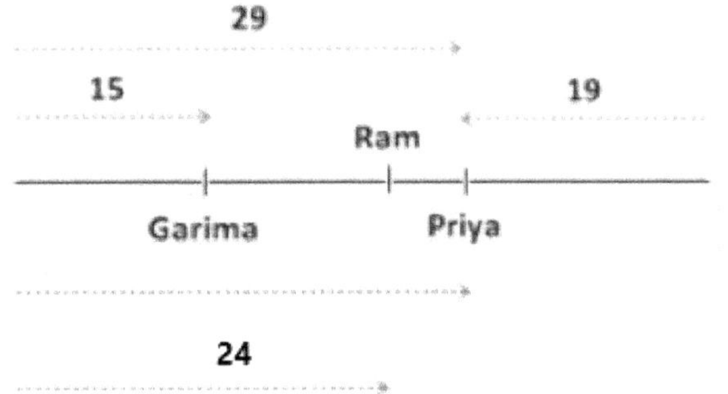

Ram's position from the left end = 24

Priya's position from Ram's position = 5

Priya's position from the left end = Ram's position from the left end + Priya's position from Ram's position

= 24 + 5 = 29

Total number of persons in the queue = [Position of Priya from right + Position of Priya from left] - 1

= (29 + 19 - 1) = 47

Hence, the correct option is (C).

2. Here, we know that Vikram was ninth from the left while Hariom was thirteenth from the left. So, we can say that there were 3 persons between Vikram and Hariom.

And, we also know that Hariom was exactly in the middle of Vikram and Janhvi so the number of persons between Hariom and Janhvi will also be 3.

At this point, using the given information we can create the following figure:

8 Persons	3 Persons	3 Persons	7 Persons
Vikram	Hariom	Janhvi	

Now, total number of people in the queue = (8 + Vikram + 3 + Hariom + 3 + Janhvi + 7)

= (8 + 1 + 3 + 1 + 3 + 1 + 7) = 24

Thus, the total number of people in the queue was 24.

Hence, the correct option is (D).

3. By the given information,

8 ← Trisha ← 5 → Tanya ← 5 → Tina → 11
    (9th)   (12th)

← Left end   Right end →

Adding all the persons in the above image, we get

8 + 1(Trisha) + 5 + 1(Tanya) + 5 + 1(Tina) + 11 = 32

Thus there are 32 cadets in the row.

Hence, the correct option is (B).

4. Given,

In a queue of students facing north, Ayesha and Anisha are standing at 10th and 8th position from the left and right end respectively.

From the given image it is clear that Ayesha is 12th from the right end.

9 — 10th Ayesha — 1 — 12th Ariva — 1 — 8th Anisha — 7

→ Left end   ← Right end

Position of Ayesha from right end = 7 + 1(Anisha) + 1 + 1(Ariva) + 1 + 1 = 12

Hence, the correct option is (B).

5. As seen in the figure, Shahruk is between Sofia and Ziya.

It's given that Ziya is 7th from the bottom and Sofia is 9th from the top.

Therefore, number of persons between Sofia and Ziya = 35 - (9 + 7) = 19

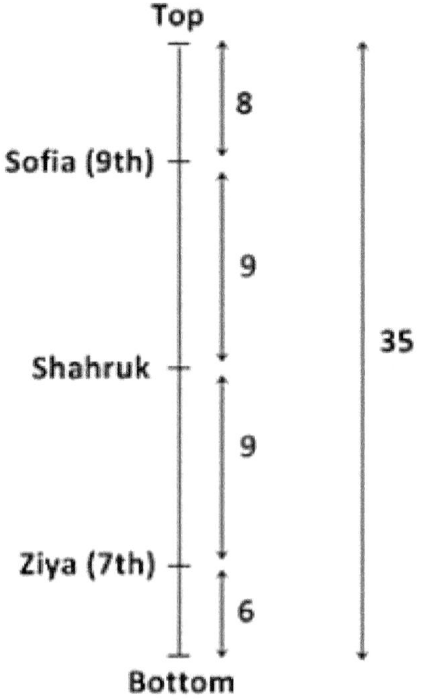

Sharuk's position between Sofia and Ziya = $\dfrac{19+1}{2} = 10$

Thus, Shahruk is at the middle i.e., at 10th position from both. Ziya, therefore, is at the 10th position from Shahruk.

Hence, the correct option is (A).

6. Given,

There are 25 students in a class and all of them are sitting in a row to do yoga. Meena is 11th from the top and Sneha is 6th from the bottom. Two students are sitting between Ananya and Reena.

From the above information, we cannot be sure about the position of Reena, as we don't have enough information about the position of Ananya and Reena.

Hence, the correct option is (E).

7. Given,

In a state-level dance competition, a total of 75 people took part.

Sonu's position = 13th from the top

Barkha's position = 25th from the bottom

So, the number of participants who were ranked after Stuti = 75-13 = 62

The number of participants who were ranked before Barkha = 75-25 = 50

Therefore, the number of participants who stood between both of them = 50-13 = 37

Hence, the correct option is (D).

8. Given,

On sports day in a school, 8 students took part in a race. They were all made to stand in a straight line. Sumit was standing 5th from the right end and there are 3 students standing in between Sumit and Ritesh.

As we can see,

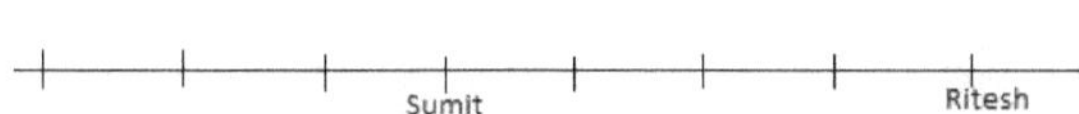

Thus, the rank of Ritesh from the left end of the line is 8th.

Hence, the correct option is (C).

9. Given,

In a row of girls, if Shilpa who is 8th from the left and Reena who is 17th from the right interchange their positions, then Shilpa is 14th from the left She goes.

After interchanging,

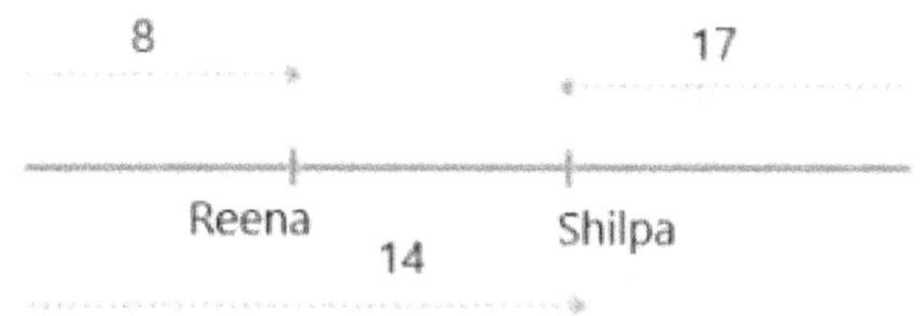

Then,

Shilpa's present position = 14

Reena's former position = 17

Total noumber of girls = (Shilpa's present position + Reena's former position) -1

$$= (14 + 17) - 1 = 30$$

Hence, the correct option is (C).

10. Given,

In a row of children, Deepa is 9th from the left and Vijay is 13th from the right. When these two interchange their positions, Deepa becomes 17th from the left.

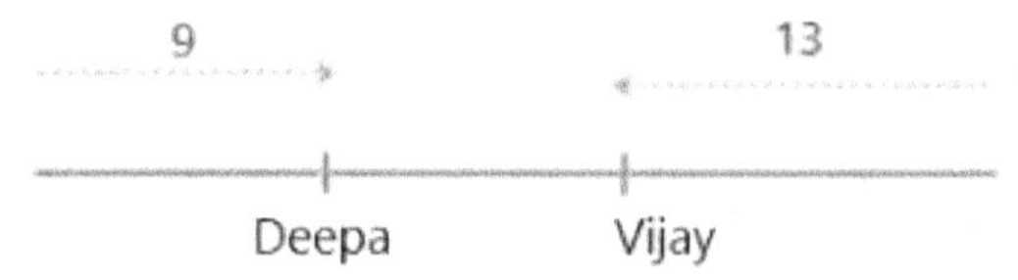

After interchanging,

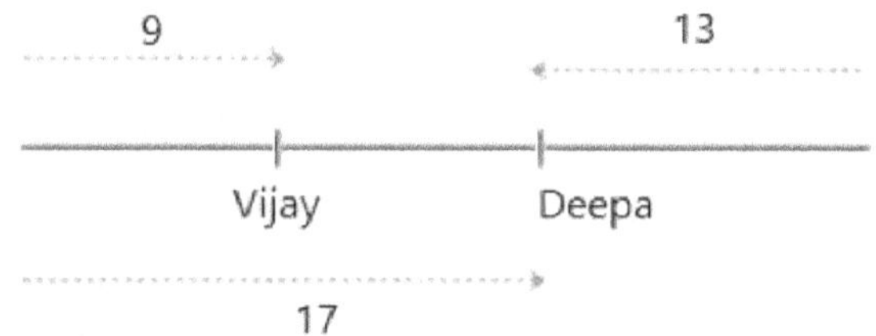

Then,

Present position of Deepa = 17

Former position of Deepa = 9

Difference of present and former position of Deepa = 17 - 9 = 8

Former position of Vijay = 13

Present position of Vijay = difference of present and previous position of Deepa + former position of Vijay

$$= (17 - 9) + 13 = 21\text{st}$$

Hence, the correct option is (B).

11. Given,

In a row of students, Ramesh is ninth from the left and Suman is sixth from the right. When Ramesh and Suman interchange their places, Ramesh becomes fifteenth from the left.

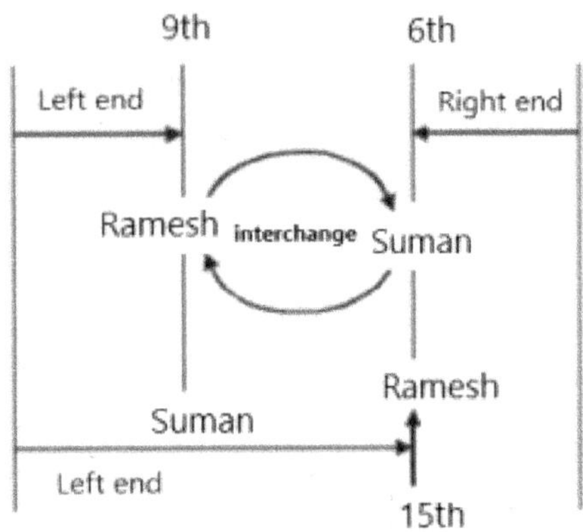

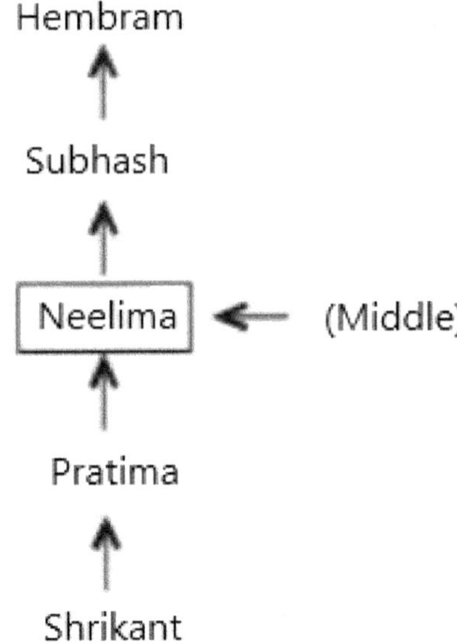

Thus the position of Suman changed from right to $= 6 + 5 +$ Suman

$$= 6 + 5 + 1 = 12$$

Thus Suman will be 12th from the right.

Hence, the correct option is (A).

12. According to the given information, their sequence in the order of height in the queue is as follows-

Shrikant < Neelima = Neelima $>$ Shrikant ...(i)

Pratima $>$ Shrikant ...(ii)

Hembram > Subhash > Neelima...(iii)

Neelima > Pratima ...(iv)

Here ' $>$ ' means 'longer than' and '<' means 'shorter than'.

On arranging their order from equations (i), (ii), (iii) and (iv),

Thus, Neelima will be right in the middle of the row.

Hence, the correct option is (B).

13. Given,

Suresh is heavier than Anil but not as heavy as Raju. 'Anil' is heavier than Jayesh. 'Krishna' is heavier than Suresh but lighter than 'Raju'.

The sequence is as follows,

Raju $>$ Krishna $>$ Suresh $>$ Anil $>$ Jayesh

Thus the lightest one is 'Jayesh'.

Hence, the correct option is (C).

14. Given,

Sahil and Gaurav are standing in a row of persons. Sahil is 12th from the left side and Gaurav is 18th from the right side of the row.

Position of Sahil from Left = 25 (after interchanging)

Total person = Position from Left + Position from right - 1

Position of Sahil from Right = 18 (position of Sahil from right end is same as Gaurav after interchanging) -1

Total person $= 25 + 18 - 1 = 42$

Thus, there are 42 persons in the row.

Hence, the correct option is (A).

15. Given,

In a School, there are 147 people, the ratio of girls: boys is 1:6. Soumya is a girl who stands 15th from the top of that row and 7 girls are in front of her.

Total number of students $= 147$

Girls : Boys $= 1:6$

Let the number of girls be x and the number of boys be $6x$.

Then,

$x + 6x = 147$

$\Rightarrow 7x = 147$

$\Rightarrow x = 21$

Then the number of girls = 21

The number of boys $= 6 \times 21 = 126$

Now Soumya is in 15th position from the top and 7 girls are in front of her.

Now boys are in front of him $= 7$ as total 14 students are in front of him.

So, the number of boys, behind him $= 126 - 7 = 119$

Hence, the correct option is (B).

16. Given,

Height of five students A, K, L, M and T are compared. Height of K is more than only two students. Height of M is greater than T and Height of T is greater than K.

Five students -A, K, L, M and T are compared.

1. Height of K is more than only two students.

_ > _ > K > _ > _

2. Height of M is greater than T and Height of T is greater than K.

M > T > K

From condition 1 and 2, we get

M > T > K > _ > _

So, 3 students are smaller than T.

Hence, the correct option is (A).

17. Given,

Of A, B, C, D and E A, B is longer than A, B but shorter than C. B is longer than E only. If C is not the longest.

According to the given information,

D > C > A > B > E

A will be in the middle if they stand in the order of height.

Hence, the correct option is (A).

18. Let the number of boys be x.

Then, the number of girls $= 2x$

According to the question,

$\therefore x + 2x = 60$

$\Rightarrow 3x = 60$

$\Rightarrow x = 20$

Hence, the number of boys $= 20$

And the number of girls $= 40$

Number of students behind Kamal in rank $= (60 - 17) = 43$

Number of girls ahead of Kamal in rank $= 9$

Number of girls behind Kamal in rank $= (40 - 9) = 31$

$\therefore$ Number of boys behind Kamal in rank $= (43 - 31) = 12$

Hence, the correct option is (C).

19. Kamal is 11th from the front in a row of girls. Leela is 3 places ahead of Sunita, who is 22nd from the lead.

According to the given information,

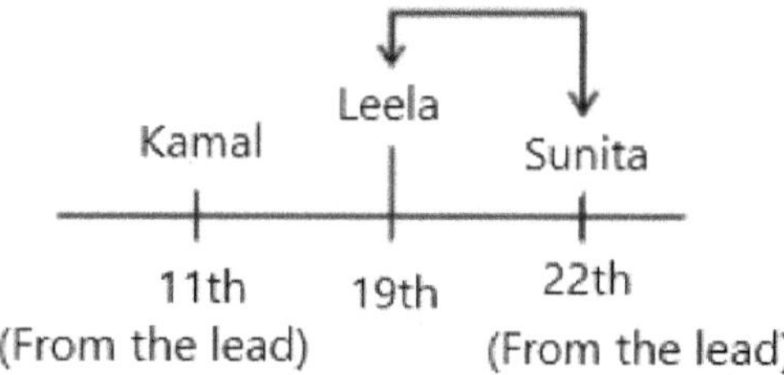

Girls in row between Kamal and Leela = 19 - 11 = 8

Hence, the correct option is (B).

20. Given,

In a row of children, Kailash is fifth from the left and Mona is sixth from the right. When they interchange their positions, then Kailash becomes thirteenth from the left.

According to the given information,

Kailash   Mona

1 2 3 4 (5) 6 7 8 9 10 11 12 (13) 14 15 16 17 18

After changing the position,

1 2 3 4 (5) 6 7 8 9 10 11 12 (13) 14 15 16 17 18

Mona   Kailash

We can say after looking at the diagram, Mona's position will be fourteenth from the right.

Present position of Kailash = 13

Former position of Kailash = 5

Difference of present and former position of Kailash = 13 - 5 = 8

Former position of Mona = 6

Mona's present position = Difference of Kailash's present and former position + Former position of Mona

= 8 + 6 = 14

Hence, the correct option is (B).

21. Given,

In a row of 35 children, M is 15th from the right and there are 10 children between M and R.

According to the given information,

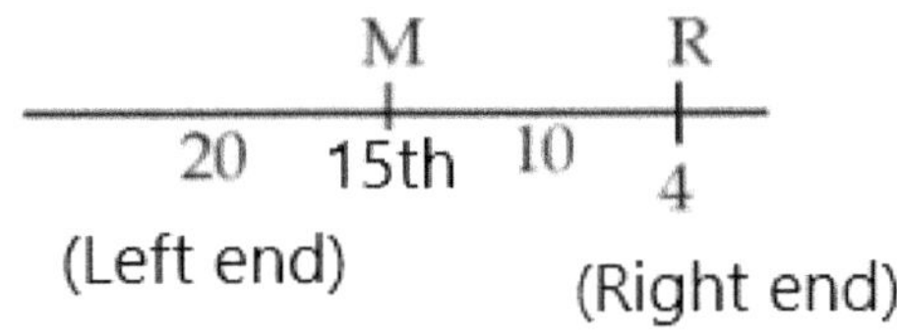

Or,

Thus the position of R cannot be determined.

Hence, the correct option is (E).

22. Given,

Of B, F, J, K and W each of different weights, F is heavier than just J. Heavier than B, F and W but not as much as K.

As per the given information, ascending order of weights:

$$J > F > W > B > K$$

Thus, W is the third heaviest.

Hence, the correct option is (D).

23. A, B, C, D and E each having a different weight, D is heavier than A and E and B is lighter than C.

According to the given information,

$$D > A, E$$

and $B < C$

The heaviest of these cannot be known.

Hence, the correct option is (E).

24. Given,

40 girl students are in a row and they are facing north. Kailash is sixth to the left of Sonam.

According to the given information,

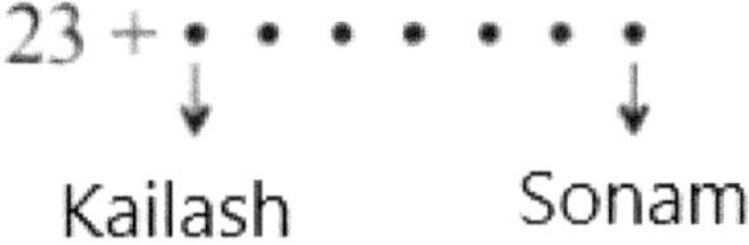

The position of Kailash from the right end $= 40 - 23 = 17$th

Hence, the correct option is (A).

25. Madhu is 18th from the left and Sandhu is 11th from the right. There are 40 boys in the class.

According to the given information,

$17 + \bullet$ Madhu $\bullet + 10$ Sandhu

∴ Number of boys between Madhu and Sandhu $= 40 - 18 - 11 = 11$

Hence, the correct option is (D).

26. Given,

Among five friends, Mahesh is taller than Karan but not as tall as Yash. Hrithik is taller than Yash but not as tall as Abhishek.

According to the given information,

Yash > Mahesh > Karan ....(i)

Abhishek > Hrithik > Yash ...(ii)

From equations (i) and (ii), we get

Karan < Mahesh < Yash < Hrithik < Abhishek

Hence, the correct option is (C).

27. Given,

M is greater than R in age. Q, R and N. N, M.

According to the given information,

$$R < M$$

$$Q < R, N$$

$$N < M$$

Then,

$$M > N/R > Q$$

Hence, the correct option is (A).

28. Given,

Mohan is older than Praveen, Suresh is younger than Praveen. Mihir is older than Suresh but younger than Praveen.

According to the given information,

Mohan $>$ Praveen $>$ Suresh

Praveen $>$ Mihir $>$ Suresh

Then we can say,

Mohan $>$ Praveen $>$ Mihir $>$ Suresh

Thus, among them the youngest is Suresh.

Hence, the correct option is (D).

29. Given,

In a row of children, Deepa is 5th from the left and Vijay is 6th from the right. When these two interchange their positions, Deepa becomes 13th from the left.

Present position of Deepa = 13

Former position of Deepa = 5

Difference of present and former position of Deepa = 13 - 5 = 8

Former position of Vijay = 6

Present position of Vijay = difference of present and previous position of Deepa $+$ former position of Vijay

$$= (13 - 5) + 6 = 14\text{th}$$

Hence, the correct option is (B).

30. Given,

Kamal is 11th from the front in a row of girls. Leela is 3 places ahead of Sunita who is 22nd from the lead.

According to the given information,

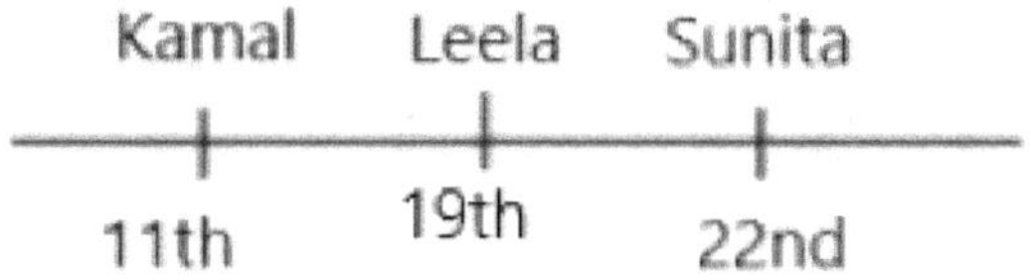

The number of girls are between Kamal and Sunita = 22 -11 = 11

The number of girls are between Kamal and Leela in this row = 11 - 3 = 8

Hence, the correct option is (B).

Ques (1-4):Direction: A family has seven members namely A, B, C, D, E, F, and G. they are related to each other in the following manner.

F is the only son of A who has three children. C is married to A. E is the maternal aunt of B who is married to D. A and G were of the same gender. Either both or none of the parents are alive.

Q.1 How is G related to E?

A. niece

B. nephew

C. sister

D. brother-in-law

E. brother

Q.2 How is D related to A?

A. Daughter

B. Son

C. Son-in-law

D. Daughter-in-law

E. Brother-in-law

Q.3 How is F related to D?

A. Sister-in-law

B. Brother-in-law

C. Nephew

D. Son

E. None of these

Q.4 Find the odd one out.

[LIC AAO (Generalist), 2021]

A. E   **B.** A   **C.** G   **D.** B

E. D

Ques (5-8):Direction: Study the information given below carefully and answer the questions that follow.

There are 7 members in the family. There are 2 married couples. R is son of H. S is mother of A. H is son of S. Y and H are married couples. A is aunt of I who is the daughter of Y. I is sister-in-law of J.

Q.5 What is relationship between A and R?

A. Aunt– Nephew

B. Father – Son

C. Mother – daughter

D. Aunt – Niece

E. Brother – Sister

Q.6 How is Y related to J?

A. Daughter – in – law

B. Uncle

C. Daughter

D. Mother– in – law

E. Son

Q.7 Who is daughter of H?

A. S   **B.** A   **C.** J   **D.** R

E. I

Q.8 How is S related to I?

A. Grandmother

B. Aunt

C. Sister

D. Grandfather

E. Brother

Ques (9-12):Directions: These questions are based on the following information.

P's mother is the sister of R who is Q's daughter. R's brother-in-law has only one son whose grandparents are Q and S, and they have only two daughters. A's husband B is Q's son-in-law.

Q.9 Who is R's sister?

A. P

B. Q

C. S

D. A

E. Cannot be determined

Q.10 Who is B's mother-in-law?

A. P

B. Q

C. S

D. B

E. Cannot be determined

Q.11 What is the relation between Q and A?

A. Father-in law and son-in-law

B. Father and daughter

C. Father/Mother and daughter

D. Mother and daughter

E. Cannot be determined

Q.12 How many grandsons do Q and S have?

A. 1

B. 2

C. 3

D. Either 1 or 2

E. Cannot be determined

Ques (13-17):Direction: Read the following information carefully to answer the question given below:

M, N, O, P, Q, R, S, T and U are members in a family. They are somehow related to one another. They have different blood groups such as A+, A-, B+, B-, AB+, AB-, O+ and O-.

Two members have blood group of the same type. There are more male members than female members.

The parents of S have positive blood groups. One married couple in the family is a positive donor and positive recipient. N has two off-springs and his off-springs are universal donors of both types. R is the maternal uncle of U. N and his maternal grandson, T has a negative blood group. P's son-in-law has an A- blood group. Q is married to a positive universal donor and has a positive blood group. U is the maternal grandson of P and has an A+ blood group. O's daughter is a negative universal recipient.

Q.13 How is R related to O?

A. Brother

B. Sister

C. Brother-in-law   **D.** Sister-in-law
E. None of these

Q.14 How is S related to T?
A. Brother   **B.** Sister
C. Cousin Brother   **D.** Cousin Sister
E. None of these

Q.15 The Blood Group of U's father is ________.
A. AB-   **B.** B+   **C.** A+   **D.** O+
E. AB+

Q.16 How is P related to S?
A. Maternal Grandfather
B. Maternal Grandmother
C. Paternal Grandfather
D. Paternal Grandmother
E. None of these

Q.17 The universal recipient blood groups in the family are ________.

A. Q and O   **B.** M and Q
C. Q and S   **D.** O and S
E. None of these

Q.18 Pointing to a photograph of a lady, Vishal says, "She is the sister–in–law of my grandfather's daughter". How is the lady in the photograph related to Vishal?
A. Cannot be determined
B. Paternal Aunt
C. Sister
D. Mother
E. None of above

Q.19 A family consisted of a man, his wife, his three sons, their wives and three children in each son's family. How many members are there in the family?
A. 12   **B.** 13
C. 15   **D.** 17
E. None of these

Q.20 Rajiv is the brother of Arun. Sonia is the sister of Sunil. Arun is the son of Sonia. How is Rajiv related to Sunil?
A. Son   **B.** Brother
C. Father   **D.** Nephew
E. None of these

Q.21 Maya said, "My mother is the sister of Ranjeet's brother". What is Ranjeet's relation with Maya?
Note: (Ranjeet is a male)
A. Cousin   **B.** Maternal uncle
C. Uncle   **D.** Brother-in-Law
E. None of these

Ques (22-25):Direction: Study the following information carefully and answer the given questions.

In a family of six members L, M, Q, R, S and G there are three generations. S is wife of R. Q is sister of R. G is son of Q. M is father of Q and married to L.

Q.22 How is L related to R?
A. Son   **B.** Mother
C. Father   **D.** Daughter
E. Aunt

Q.23 How is G related to M?
A. Grandfather   **B.** Grandmother
C. Father   **D.** Grandson
E. None of the above

Q.24 How is S related to G?
A. Grandmother   **B.** Mother
C. Aunt   **D.** Sister
E. None of the above

Q.25 How is S related to L?
A. Son-in-law   **B.** Daughter-in-law
C. Daughter   **D.** Son
E. None of the above

Ques (26-30):Direction: These questions are based on the information given below.

In a family, eight persons are there, of whom there are three couples. Ayub, Bhim, Chintu and Dada are the men and Elena, Fareeda, Gayatri and Hasini are the women in that family. It is also known that

(i) Hasini is the sister of Fareeda.

(ii) Gayatri is the daughter of Bhim.

(iii) Chintu is married to Elena.

(iv) Fareeda is the mother-in-law of Ayub.

(v) Gayatri's brother is one among the four men and he is married.

(vi) Hasini is a widow and she has only one child, who is unmarried.

Q.26 Who is the father-in-law of Elena?
A. Ayub   **B.** Bhim
C. Chintu   **D.** Dada
E. Data inadequate

Q.27 Who is the brother of Gayatri?
A. Ayub   **B.** Bhim
C. Chintu   **D.** Dada
E. Data inadequate

Q.28 Who is the brother of Gayatri?
A. Ayub   **B.** Bhim
C. Chintu   **D.** Dada
E. Data inadequate

Q.29 Dada is the son of ______.
A. Hasini   **B.** Bhim
C. Fareeda   **D.** Chintu
E. Data inadequate

Q.30 Which among the following is false?
A. Gayatri is the sister-in-law of Elena.

B. Bhim is the husband of Fareeda.

C. Ayub is the brother-in-law of Chintu.

D. Hasini is the aunt of Dada.

E. None of these

// Smart Answer Sheet //

Correct   Indicates percentage of students who answered questions correctly.

Skipped   Indicates percentage of students who skipped questions.

Q.	Ans.	Correct / Skipped	Q.	Ans.	Correct / Skipped	Q.	Ans.	Correct / Skipped	Q.	Ans.	Correct / Skipped	Q.	Ans.	Correct / Skipped
1	A	53.69 % / 43.09 %	7	E	49.8 % / 41.2 %	13	C	10.76 % / 82.85 %	19	D	30.83 % / 67.32 %	25	B	60.9 % / 35.62 %
2	C	62.96 % / 32.09 %	8	A	52.17 % / 38.02 %	14	D	41.54 % / 41.71 %	20	D	62.25 % / 32.63 %	26	B	78.06 % / 13.96 %
3	B	58.14 % / 37.94 %	9	D	20.24 % / 77.53 %	15	E	62.11 % / 30.48 %	21	B	77.14 % / 11.84 %	27	C	80.69 % / 19.04 %
4	E	54.82 % / 36.16 %	10	E	66.8 % / 31.78 %	16	B	68.67 % / 31.07 %	22	B	46.4 % / 40.19 %	28	A	43.22 % / 50.18 %
5	A	52.0 % / 44.43 %	11	C	64.82 % / 33.07 %	17	C	44.46 % / 39.11 %	23	D	49.44 % / 30.22 %	29	A	79.56 % / 19.86 %
6	D	58.32 % / 35.98 %	12	A	45.55 % / 34.48 %	18	A	43.75 % / 41.04 %	24	C	41.94 % / 38.76 %	30	D	47.3 % / 32.01 %

Performance Analysis

Avg. Score (%)	60.0%
Toppers Score (%)	70.0%
Your Score	

//Hints and Solutions//

Symbol in Diagram	Meaning
◯	Female
▢	Male
═══	Married Couple
───	Siblings
│	Difference of A Generation

Ques (1-4):

1. F is the only son of A who has three children. Hence other two children are daughters of A.

2. C is married to A.

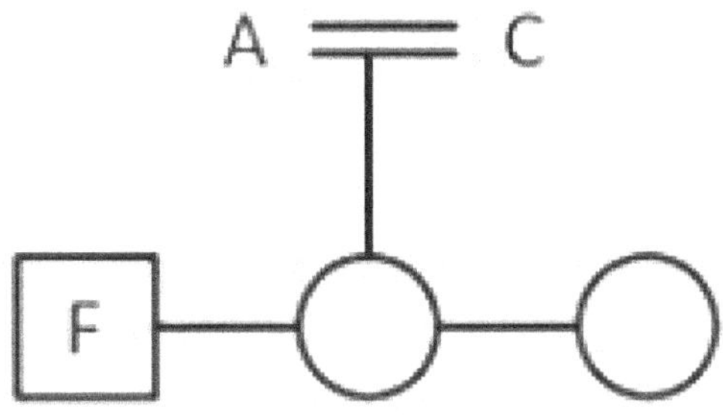

3. E is the maternal aunt of B who is married to D.

Three cases arise here,

Case I: Here, E is assumed to be one of the daughters of A

Since both parents have to be alive, so after making all arrangements we see that 8 members are arising which goes against the information provided.

Since there are 7 members in this family, this case will be eliminated.

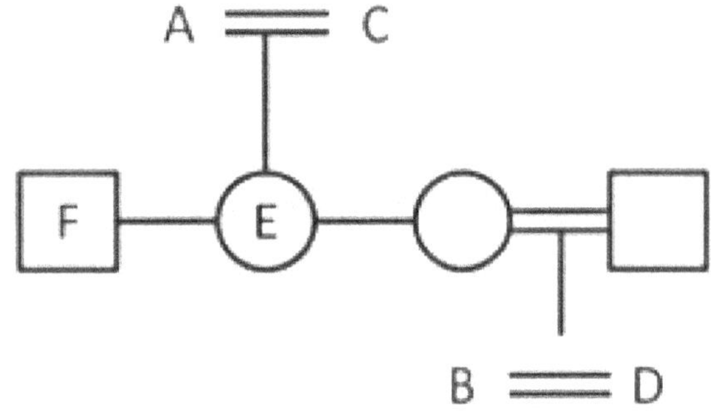

Case II: Here we consider that C is the mother of B and E is the sister of C

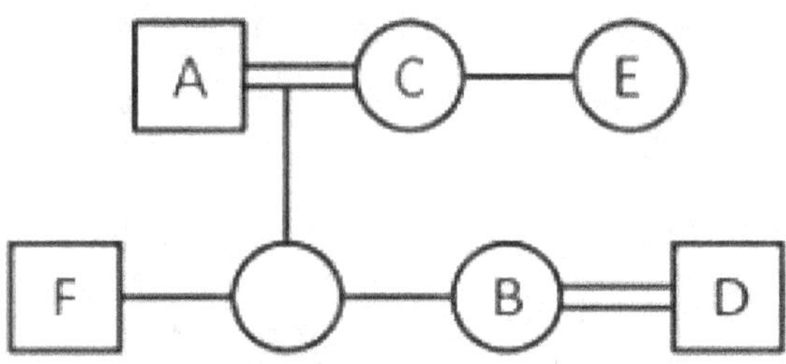

Case III: Here we consider that A is the mother of B and E is the sister of A

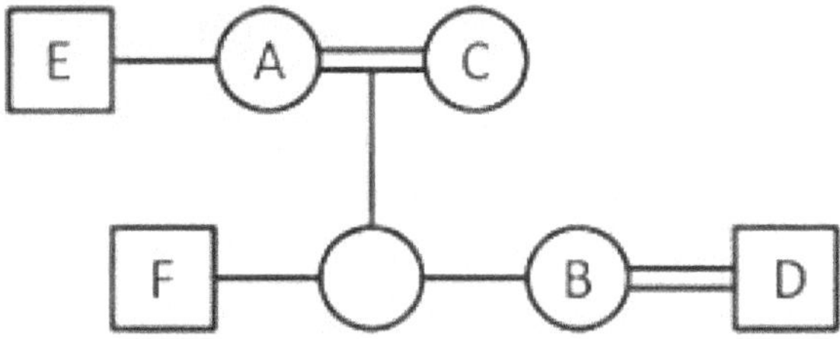

4. A and G were of the same gender.

So, in both cases 2 and 3 only one place is left for the daughter of A and C which will be filled by G

So, G is female and A will also be female according to the given information, Case II is also eliminated in this case.

Case III becomes our final solution here.

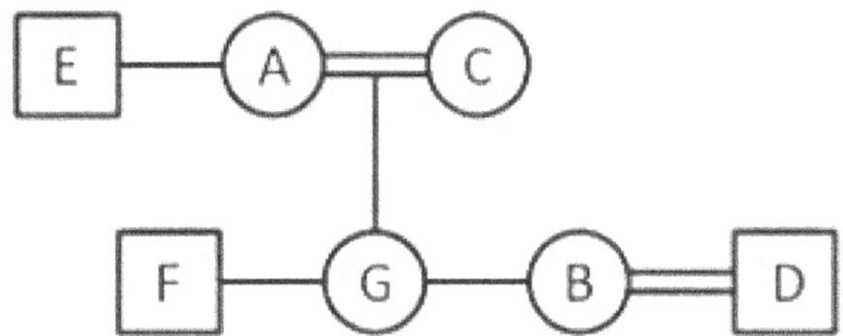

1. So, G is the niece of E.

Hence, the correct option is (A).

2. D being the husband of B who is the daughter of A will be the son-in-law of A.

Hence, the correct option is (C).

3. We can see that F is the brother-in-law of D.

Hence, the correct option is (B).

4. Among all the given options, D is the only male person while all others are female.

Hence, the correct option is (E).

Ques (5-8): Number of people: 7

There are two married couples.

Preparing the family tree using the following symbols:

Symbol in Diagram	Meaning
◯	Female
☐	Male
═══	Married Couple
───	Siblings
│	Difference of A Generation

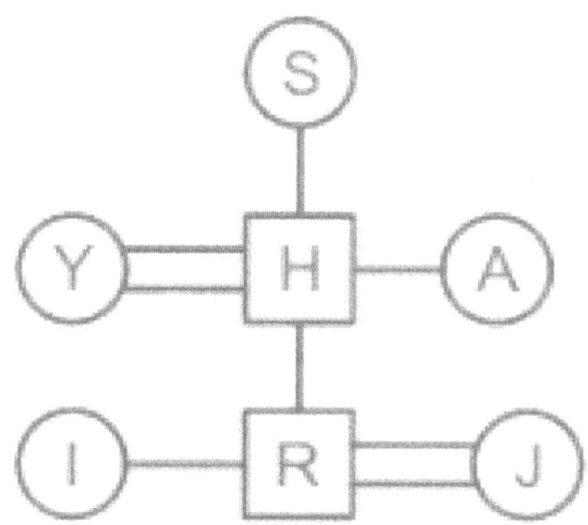

5. Thus, the relationship between A and R is Aunt – Nephew.

Hence, the correct option is (A).

6. Thus, Y is mother – in – law of J.

Hence, the correct option is (D).

7. Thus, I is daughter of H.

Hence, the correct option is (E).

8. Thus, S is grandmother of I.

Hence, the correct option is (A).

Ques (9-12): From the given information,

Symbol in Diagram	Meaning
◯	Female
☐	Male
═══	Married Couple
───	Siblings
│	Difference of A Generation

1) P's mother is R's sister.

2) R is Q's daughter.

3) R's brother-in-law has only one son whose grandparents are Q and S who have only two daughters.

4) A's husband is B.

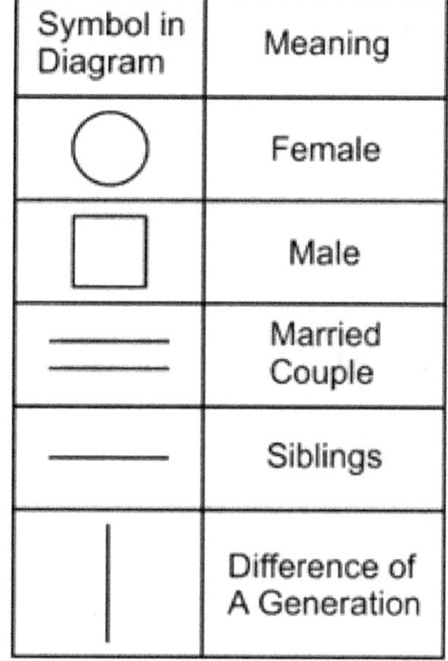

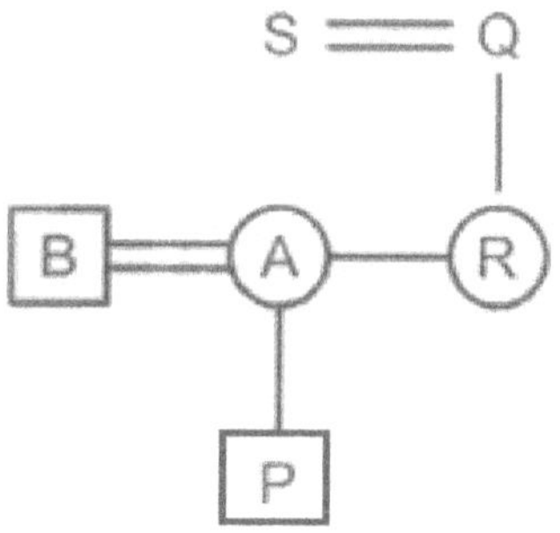

9. So, R's sister is A.

Hence, the correct option is (D).

10. As the gender of Q and S is not specified here, we cannot determine B's mother-in-law.

Hence, the correct option is (E).

11. Here, the gender of Q is not specified,

So, Q can be the mother or the father of A.

Therefore, the relation between Q and A will be 'Father/Mother and daughter.

Hence, the correct option is (C).

12. So, S and Q have only one Grandson.

Hence, the correct option is (A).

Symbol in Diagram	Meaning
◯	Female
▢	Male
═══	Married Couple
───	Siblings
│	Difference of A Generation

Ques (13-17):

Hint: Two members have blood group of the same type.

There are more male members than female members.

One married couple in the family is a positive donor and positive recipient.

Note: The Blood group O+ and O- are universal donors.

The Blood group AB+ and AB- are universal recipients.

Members: M, N, O, P, Q, R, S, T and U.

Blood Groups: A+, A-, B+, B-, AB+, AB-, O+ and O-.

1) N has two off-springs and his off-springs are universal donors of both types.

2) P's son-in-law has an A- blood group.

3) Q is married to a positive universal donor and has a positive blood group.

4) R is the maternal uncle of U.

5) U is the maternal grandson of P and has an A+ blood group.

6) The parents of S have positive blood groups.

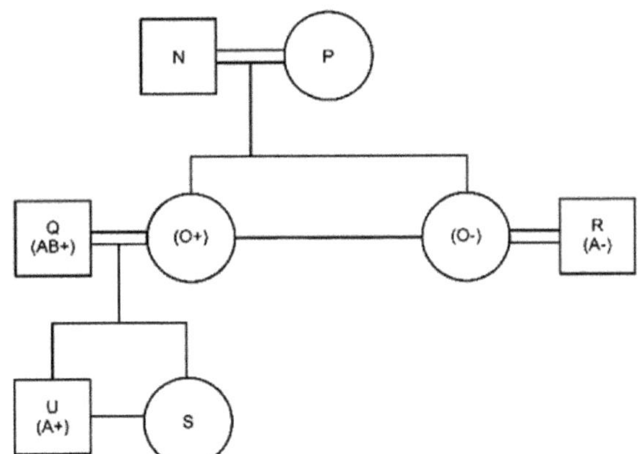

7) O's daughter is a negative universal recipient.

8) N and his maternal grandson, T has a negative blood group. (So the only group left is B-, and as already stated that two members have the same blood group.)

(Thus, P has a B+ blood group and M is a negative universal donor.)

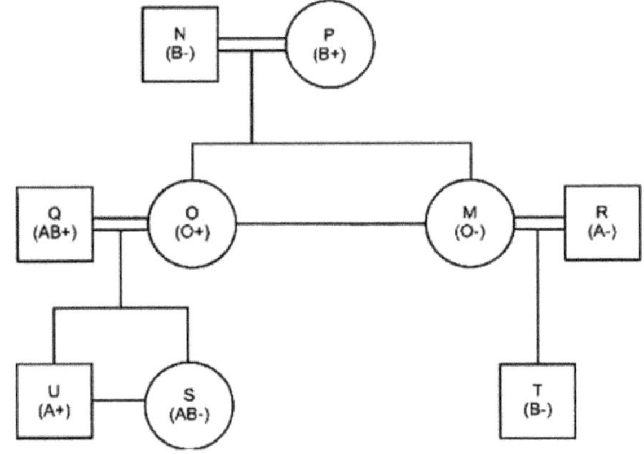

13. Thus, R is the Brother-in-law of O.

Hence, the correct option is (C).

14. Thus, S is the Cousin Sister of T.

Hence, the correct option is (D).

15. Thus, the Blood Group of U's father is AB+.

Hence, the correct option is (E).

16. Thus, P is the Maternal Grandmother of S.

Hence, the correct option is (B).

17. Thus, Q and S are the recipients in the family.

Hence, the correct option is (C).

18. Grandfather's daughter →Vishal's aunt.

Vishal's aunt sister-in-law →Aunt's spouse sister or Spouse brother's wife.

Nothing is clearly mentioned about Vishal's relation with the lady so, it can't be determined.
Hence, the correct option is (A).

19. The man and his wife = 2 members,

Three sons and their wives=6 members,

Three children each of the three sons = 3 × 3 = 9 members,

Total number of members = 2 + 6 + 9

= 17 members.
Hence, the correct option is (D).

20. Rajiv is the brother of Arun & Arun is the son of Sonia; therefore Rajiv is a son of Sonia too. Sonia is the sister of Sunil. Hence Sunil is an uncle of Rajiv or Rajiv is nephew of Sunil. Hence, the correct option is (D).

21. Maya said, "My mother is the sister of Ranjeet's brother".

Therefore Maya's mother is a sister of Ranjeet.

So, Ranjeet will be Maternal uncle of Maya.
Hence, the correct option is (B).

Ques (22-25):

Symbol in Diagram	Meaning
○	Female
□	Male
═	Married Couple
—	Siblings
│	Difference of A Generation

Possible tree diagram will be,

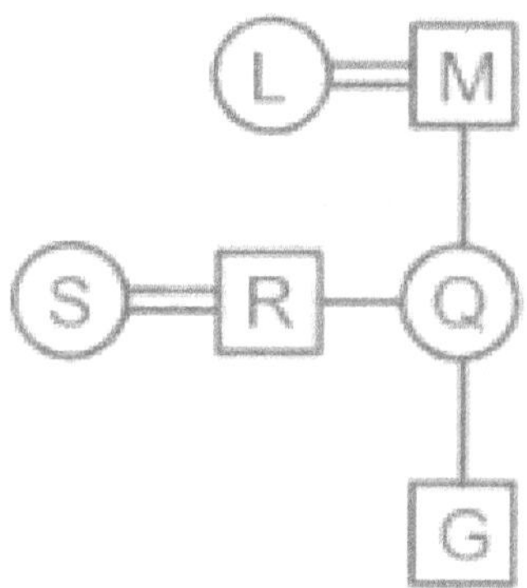

22. Thus, L is mother of R.

Hence, the correct option is (B).

23. Thus, G is grandson of M.

Hence, the correct option is (D).

24. Thus, S is Aunt of G.

Hence, the correct option is (C).

25. Thus, S is daughter-in-law of L.

Hence, the correct option is (B).

Ques (26-30): From (i), Fareeda is the sister of Hasini.

From (ii), Fareeda is the mother-in-law of Ayub.

So, Ayub should have a wife. Also children. So, Bhim cannot be the husband of Hasini as she has only one child.

Also Ayub's wife cannot be Fareeda, (She is his mother-in-law) cannot be Hasini (she is the sister of Fareeda) and cannot be Elena (she is the wife of Chetan)

So, Ayub's wife can be Gayatri and then Fareeda's husband will be Bhim and the married brother of Gayatri will be Chintu. So, the only child of Hasini will be Dada.

If each person is called with the first letter of his name, then the relationship will be as shown below.

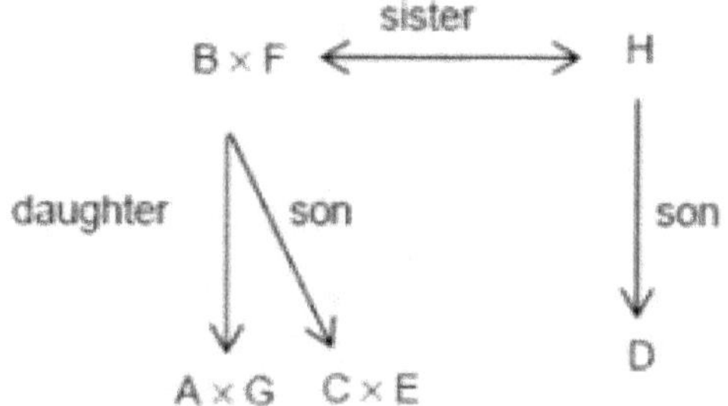

X- married couples.

26. Bhim is the father-in-law of Elena.

Hence, the correct option is (B).

27. Chintu is the brother of Gayatri

Hence, the correct option is (C).

28. Ayub is the husband of Gayatri

Hence, the correct option is (A).

29. Dada is son of Hasini.

Hence, the correct option is (A).

30. Hasini is the mother of Dada.

Hence, the correct option is (D).

Ques (1-4):Direction: Study the given information to answer the following question.

There are 10 cities A, B, Z, Y, K, T, R, J, M, and P in a state. City A is 10 km to the north of city K which is 10 km to the west of city M. City J is 5 km to the south of city M and city R is 5 km to the west of city J. City T is 5 km to the south of city K. City B is 15 km to the north of city M and city Y is 10 km to the south of city P which is 5 km to the south of city Z which is 10 km to the east of city B.

Q.1 What is the distance between city T and city R?

A. 10 km

B. 5 km

C. 15 km

D. 20 km

E. None of these

Q.2 What is the distance between city M and city Y?

A. 15 km

B. 20 km

C. 5 km

D. 10 km

E. None of these

Q.3 Find the direction of city M with respect to city Z.

A. South

B. South-east

C. South-west

D. North-east

E. West

Q.4 What is the distance between city A and city P?

A. 10 km

B. 20 km

C. 15 km

D. None of these

E. Cannot be determined

Q.5 Ratan walked 7 km from his home in north direction, then he took a left and walked 4 km. Then he took a right and walked 5 km. After taking another right he walked 4 km and reached at his friend's home.

Find how far and in which direction is his home from his friend's home?

A. 15 km, North

B. 8 km, South-east

C. 12 km, South

D. 6 km, North-west

E. 10 km, North-west

Q.6 Rahul moved 6 km in the east direction from his home to reach Taxi stand. From there he took a taxi and travelled a distance of 3 km in the north direction. Then he took a right turn and covered a distance of 4 km. Again he took a right turn and travelled a distance of 8 km. After taking another right he travelled 4 km to reach the Airport.

Find how far and in which direction is Airport from Taxi stand?

A. 5 km, North

B. 8 km, South-east

C. 5 km, South

D. 6 km, North-west

E. 10 km, North-west

Q.7 Bonny moves 30 meters towards south then turns to his right and starts moving straight till he completes another 30 meters. Then turning to his left he moves for 20 meters. He again then turns to his left and moves for 30 meters. How far is he from his initial position?

A. 30 meters

B. 50 meters

C. 10 meters

D. 60 meters

E. 70 meters

Ques (8-10):Direction: Read the following information carefully and answer the questions that follow:

A & B means A is 4 km to west of B,

A + B means A is 4 km to north of B,

A # B means A is 4 km to south of B,

A @ B means A is 4 km to east of B,

A % B means A is 1 km to east of B.

Q.8 If it is given that: U # T% Q; P & Q; U @ R % S. What is the distance between P and S?

A. 1 km   **B.** 2 km   **C.** 3 km   **D.** 4 km

E. 3.5 km

Q.9 If it is given that: A & F; C # F; C % E. What is the minimum distance between E and A?

A. 3 km   **B.** 4 km   **C.** 5 km   **D.** 6 km

E. 2 km

Q.10 If it is given that: A & B; F % B; C # D # F; E # C. What is the direction of A with respect to E?

A. North east

B. North west

C. South west

D. South east

E. None of these

Ques (11-13):Direction: Study the following information to answer the given question:

A girl started walking from point P and walks 7 km towards the east and stops at point Q. Now, she turns 60° to her left and walks 5 km to reach a point R. Now, she takes 60° right turn and walks 5 km to reach a point S. Then, she turns 120° to her right and walks 5 km to reach a point T. Finally, she turns 30° to her left and walks 5 km to reach a point U.

Q.11

What is the distance between Point P and Point U?

A. 10 km

B. 15 km

C. 13 km

D. 12 km

E. Insufficient data

Q.12 In which direction is point S with respect to point Q?

A. North-East

B. South-East

C. North-West

D. East

E. North

Q.13 What is the distance between Point Q and Point T?

A. 5 km   **B.** 4 km   **C.** 4.5 km   **D.** 6 km

E. 7 km

Ques (14-18):

Direction: Read the following information carefully and answer the questions that follow.

A & B means A is 5 km to the south of B.

A % B means A is 5 km to the east of B.

A + B means A is 1 km to the south of B.

A - B means A is 1 km to the east of B.

Q.14 If it is given that: C + B % A; D + E - B. What is the distance between C and D?

A. 1 km   **B.** 2 km   **C.** 3 km   **D.** 4 km
E. 5 km

Q.15 If it is given that: N % M; N - R - Q; O & Q; O + P. What is the distance between P and M?

A. 4 km   **B.** 5 km   **C.** 6 km   **D.** 8 km
E. 13 km

Q.16 If it is given that: X - Y & A; X + Z + W - V; W % U. What is the direction of X with respect to U?

A. East   **B.** West
C. North-East   **D.** South-West
E. South-East

Q.17 If it is given that: C + B % A; C % D. What is the distance between A and D?

A. 1 km   **B.** 2 km   **C.** 3 km   **D.** 4 km
E. 5 km

Q.18 If it is given that: S & T - U; S % R + Q + P. What is the distance between P and U?

A. 9 km   **B.** 4 km   **C.** 8 km   **D.** 12 km
E. 5 km

Ques (19-21):Direction: Read the following information carefully and answer the question which follow:

A boy starts walking from a point A, walks 4 km towards the south-east direction to reach a point B. He takes a 135° right turn and walks 6 km to reach point C. He takes 45° right turn and walks 4 km to reach point D. He takes 135° right turn and walks 8 km to reach point E and there he stops.

Q.19 What is the distance between the starting point and end point?

A. 3 km
B. 4 km
C. 6 km
D. 2 km
E. Cannot be determine

Q.20 In which direction is the boy facing when he is at point D before turning towards point E?

A. North-East   **B.** South-East
C. South-West   **D.** North-West
E. West

Q.21 What is the angle between AE and AB?

A. 180°   **B.** 135°   **C.** 120°   **D.** 90°
E. 45°

Ques (22-24):Direction: Read the following information carefully and answer the questions which follow:

Rahul walks 10 m towards the north. Turning to the left, he walks 20 m and then moves to his right. After moving a distance of 20 m, he turns to his left and walks 20 m and again he turns to his left and walks 20 m, from there he turns 10 m left. And finally, he turns to his right and moves 20 m to reach his house.

Q.22 What is the total distance covered by Rahul to reach his house?

A. 110   **B.** 120   **C.** 115   **D.** 105
E. 105

Q.23 In which direction Rahul house is from his starting point?

A. East   **B.** West
C. South-west   **D.** South-east
E. North-west

Q.24 What is the shortest distance between Rahul house and Rahul starting point?

A. $10\sqrt{10}$ m   **B.** 10 m
C. $10\sqrt{5}$ m   **D.** 30 m
E. None of these

Ques (25-27):Direction: Study the information given below carefully and answer the questions that follow.

From a common starting point, X and Y move 5 km towards east and west respectively, X moves 5 km towards north and similarly Y moves 5 km south. Then, X moves 10 km toward west and Y moves 10 km toward east.

Q.25 What is the shortest distance between the final positions of X and Y?

A. 5 km   **B.** 25 m
C. $10\sqrt{2}$ km   **D.** 20 m
E. $20\sqrt{2}$ km

Q.26 What is the shortest distance between the final position of X and the starting point?

A. $3\sqrt{2}$ km   **B.** $10\sqrt{2}$ km
C. $5\sqrt{2}$ km   **D.** 50 km
E. 25 km

Q.27 In which direction is the final position of point Y with respect to the final position of X?

A. North   **B.** East
C. South   **D.** North East
E. South East

Ques (28-30):Direction: Follow the given information to answer the questions:

X is 20 km to the west of B which is 10 km to the north of R. Z is 10 km to the south of T which is 10 km to the west of P. K is 30 km to the west of Z and R is 10 km to the west of T.

Q.28 Point K is in which direction of point P?

A. North-west   **B.** South-west
C. South   **D.** West
E. None of these

Q.29 What is the distance between point X and point K?

A. 10 km
B. 15 km
C. 20 km
D. None of these
E. Cannot be determined

Q.30 Point X is in which direction of point T?

A. North-west   **B.** South-west
C. West   **D.** North
E. None of these

// Smart Answer Sheet //

Correct	Indicates percentage of students who answered questions correctly.
Skipped	Indicates percentage of students who skipped questions.

Q.	Ans.	Correct / Skipped
1	B	40.42 % / 44.89 %
2	D	60.44 % / 36.44 %
3	C	63.66 % / 31.13 %
4	B	41.22 % / 46.06 %
5	C	87.23 % / 12.3 %
6	C	76.16 % / 14.17 %
7	B	82.67 % / 15.69 %
8	D	77.96 % / 19.74 %
9	C	84.7 % / 10.36 %
10	B	78.41 % / 10.12 %
11	C	18.83 % / 69.17 %
12	A	55.27 % / 44.4 %
13	A	45.49 % / 38.12 %
14	A	46.11 % / 30.34 %
15	B	60.41 % / 38.07 %
16	E	60.15 % / 31.62 %
17	A	88.66 % / 11.13 %
18	E	63.37 % / 32.98 %
19	D	12.08 % / 80.34 %
20	D	16.07 % / 79.98 %
21	E	26.47 % / 67.43 %
22	B	89.98 % / 10.01 %
23	C	58.62 % / 34.37 %
24	A	56.3 % / 36.25 %
25	C	65.4 % / 31.14 %
26	C	63.75 % / 34.35 %
27	D	67.33 % / 30.13 %
28	B	47.78 % / 40.53 %
29	C	62.06 % / 37.5 %
30	A	67.19 % / 30.25 %

Performance Analysis	
Avg. Score (%)	46.67%
Toppers Score (%)	60.0%
Your Score	

//Hints and Solutions//

Ques (1-4): City: A, B, Z, Y, K, T, R, J, M and P

1) City A is 10 km to the north of city K, which is 10 km to the west of city M.

2) City J is 5 km to the south of city M and city R is 5 km to the west of city J.

3) City B is 15 km to the north of city M and city Y is 10 km to the south of city P, which is 5 km to the south of city Z, which is 10 km to the east of city B.

4) City T is 5 km to the south of city K.

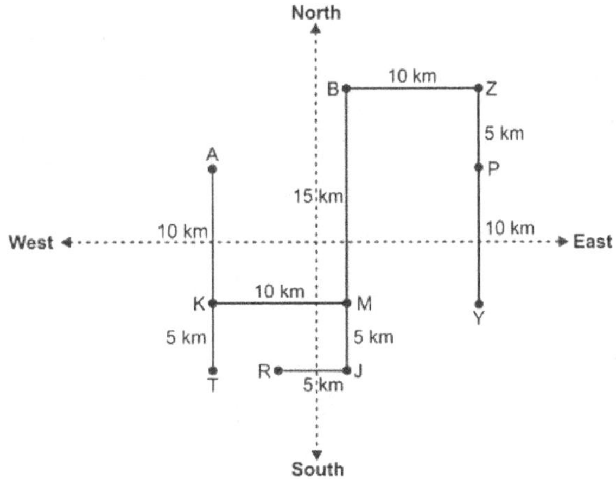

1. So, the distance between city T and city R is 5 km.

Hence, the correct option is (B).

2. So, the distance between city M and city Y is 10 km.

Hence, the correct option is (D).

3. So, city M is in the south-west direction from city Z.

Hence, the correct option is (C).

4. So, the distance between city A and city P is 20 km.

Hence, the correct option is (B).

5. From the following image it is clear that his home is 12 km south from his friend's home.

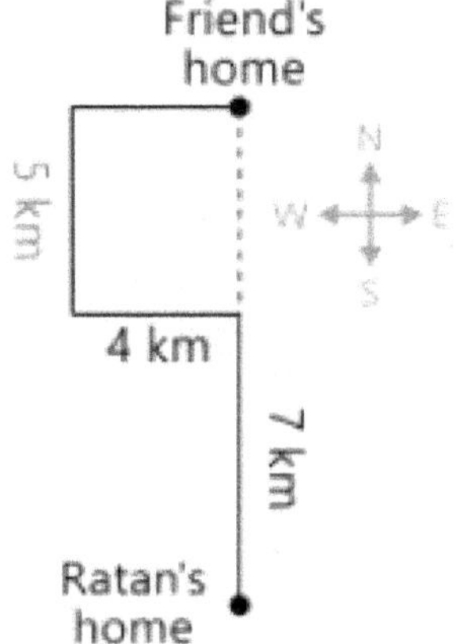

Hence, the correct option is (C).

6. From the following image it is clear that the Airport is 5 km south from the Taxi stand.

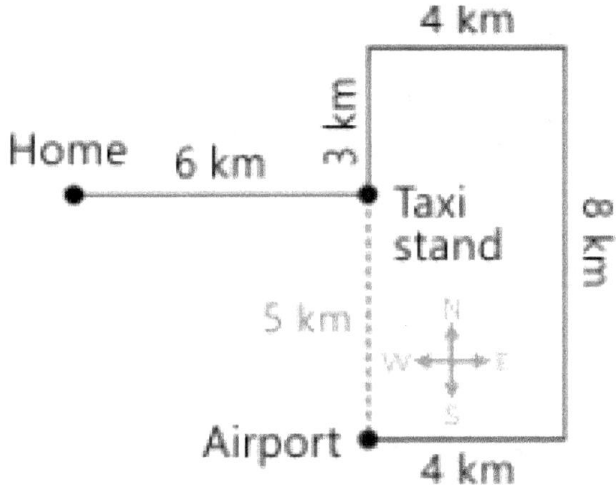

Hence, the correct option is (C).

7.

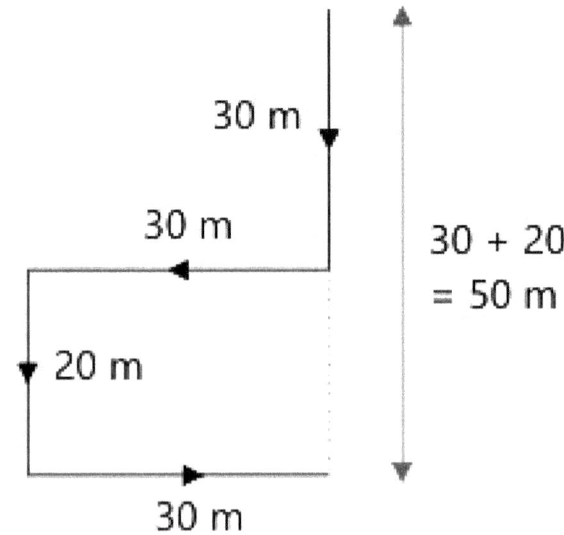

We can clearly observe from the above figure that, Bonny is 50 meters far from starting point.

Hence, the correct option is (B).

8. Following above instructions will lead to below diagram:

U # T% Q → U is 4 km to south of T which is 1 km to east of Q,

P & Q → P is 4 km to west of Q,

U @ R % S → U is 4 km to east of R is 1 km to east of S,

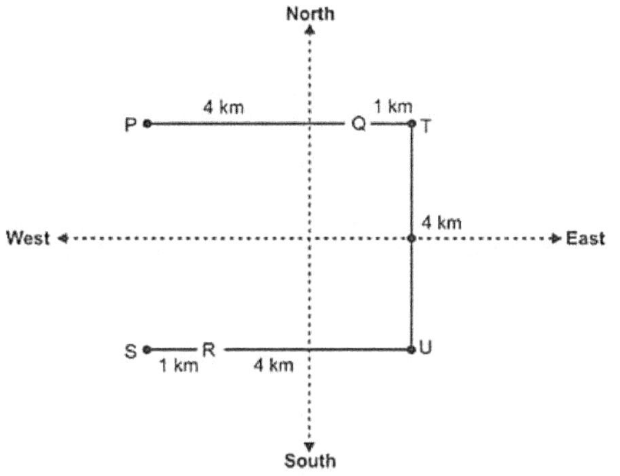

So, the distance between P and S is 4 km.

Hence, the correct option is (D).

9. Following above instructions will lead to below diagram:

A & F → A is 4 km to west of F

C # F → C is 4 km to south of F

C % E → C is 1 km east of E

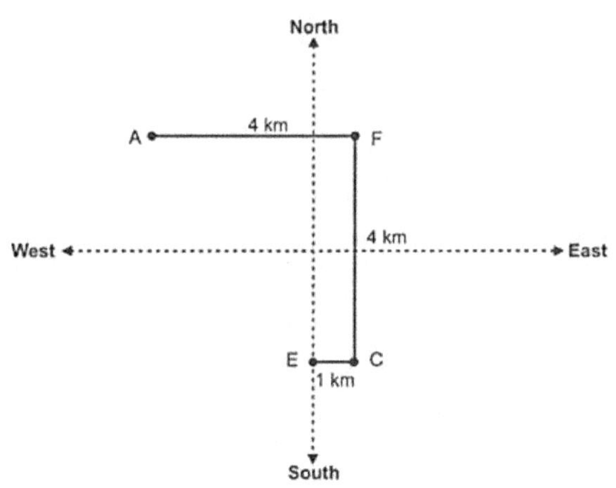

Using Pythagoras' theorem,

$$AE^2 = 4^2 + 3^2$$

$$AE^2 = 2^5$$

$$AE = 5$$

So, the minimum distance between E and A is 5 km.

Hence, the correct option is (C).

10. Following above instructions will lead to below diagram:

A & B → A is 4 km to west of B

F % B → F is 1 km east of B

C # D # F → C is 4 km to south of D which is 4 km to the south of F

E # C → E is 4 km to south of C

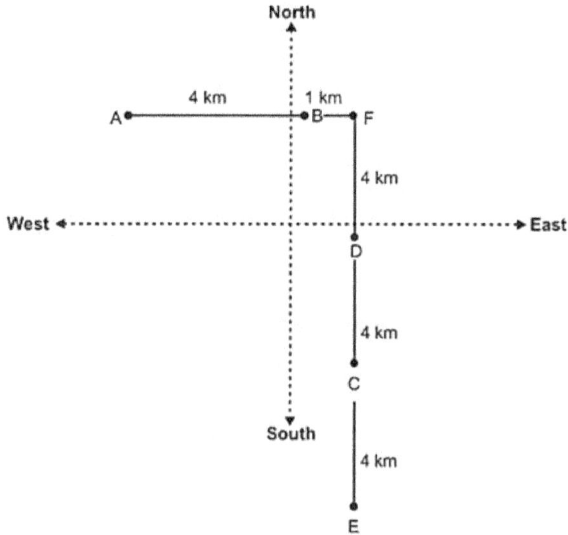

So, A is in North west direction with respect to E.

Hence, the correct option is (B).

11.

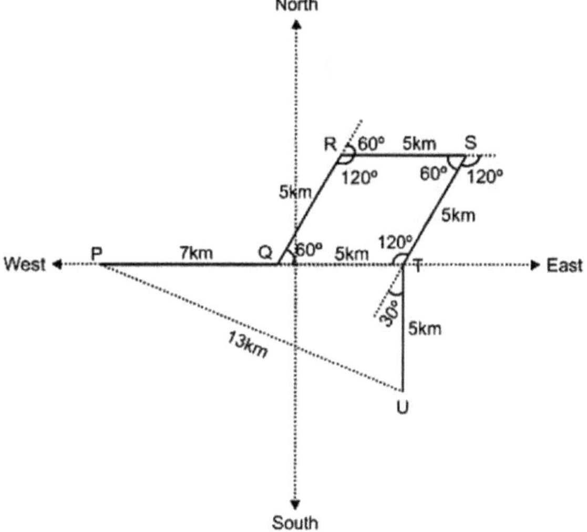

In ΔPTU

∠PTU = 90°

So, ΔPTU is right-angled triangle.

PT = PQ+QT = 7+5 = 12 km

and TU = 5 km

By Pythagoras theorem,

$PU^2 = PT^2 + TU^2$

$= 12^2 + 5^2$

$= 144 + 25$

$= 169$

$PU = \sqrt{169} = 13$ km

Therefore, the distance between point P and point U is 13 km.

Hence, the correct option is (C).

12.

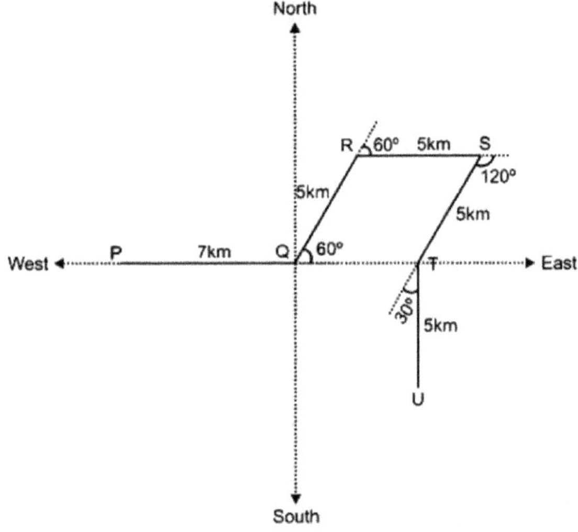

Thus, point S is in the North-East direction with respect to point Q.

Hence, the correct option is (A).

13.

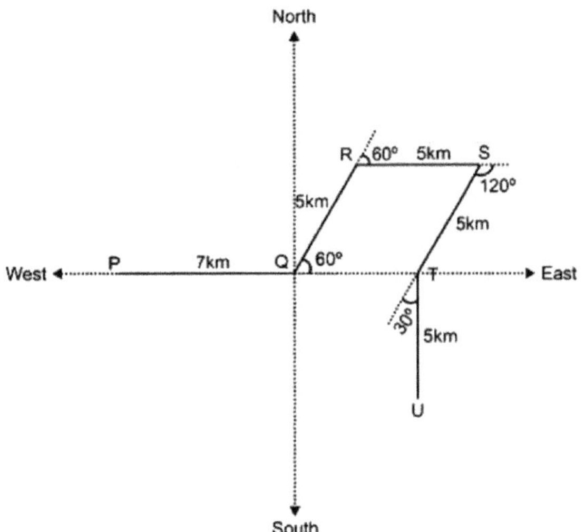

QRST is a rhombus so all sides are equal.

So, the distance between point Q and point T is 5 km.

Hence, the correct option is (A).

14. Following the above instructions will lead to the below diagram:

C + B % A= C is 1 km to the south of B which is 5 km to the east of A

D + E - B → D is 1 km to the south of E which is 1 km to the east of B

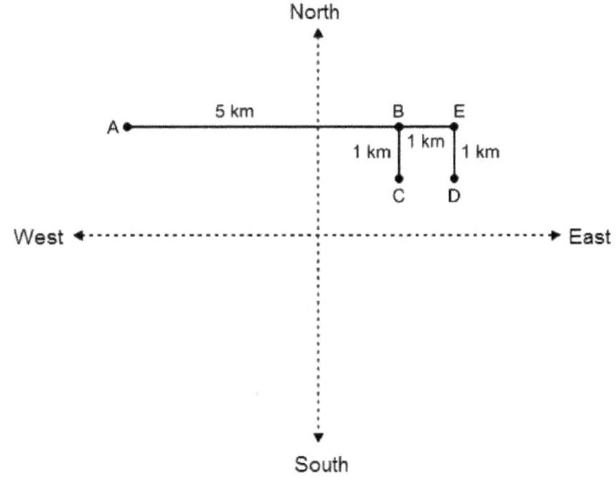

The distance between C and D is 1 km.

Hence, the correct option is (A).

15. Following the above instructions will lead to the below diagram:

N % M → N is 5 km to the east of M

N - R - Q → N is 1 km to the east of R which is 1 km to the east of Q

O & Q → O is 5 km to the south of Q

O + P → O is 1 km to the south of P

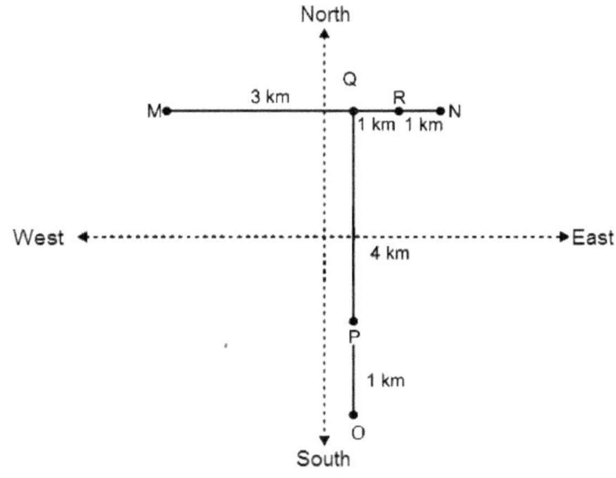

By, using Pythagoras theorem,

$PM^2 = 4^2 + 3^2$

$PM^2 = 25$

$PM = 5$

The distance between P and M is 5 km.

Hence, the correct option is (B).

16. Following the above instructions will lead to the below diagram:

X - Y & A → X is 1 km to the east of Y which is 5 km to the south of A

X + Z + W - V → X is 1 km to the south of Z which is 1 km to the south of V

W % U → W is 5 km to the east of U

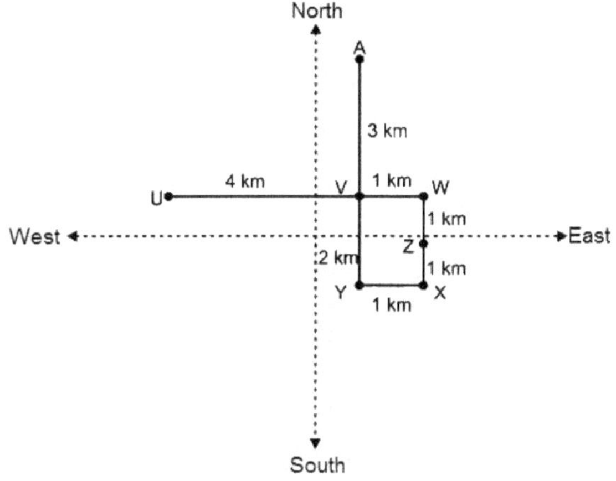

Therefore, X is in the South-East direction with respect to U.

Hence, the correct option is (E).

17. Following the above instructions will lead to the below diagram:

C + B % A → C is 1 km to the south of B which is 5 km to the east of A

C % D → C is 5 km to the east of D

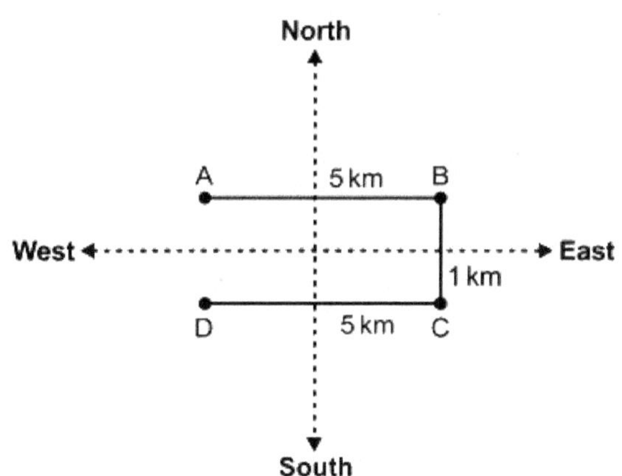

The distance between A and D is 1km.

Hence, the correct option is (A).

18. Following the above instructions will lead to the below diagram:

S & T - U → S is 5 km to the south of T which is 1 km to the east of U.

S % R + Q + P → S is 5 km to the east of R which is 1 km to the south of Q which is 1 km to the south of P.

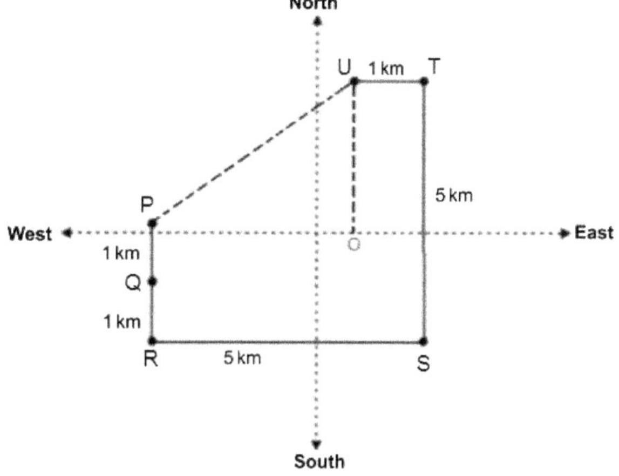

The distance between P and U is 5 km.

Given,

PQ + QR= PR

1 km+1 km= 2 Km

TS = 5 Km

So, TS - PR

= 5 - 2

= 3km

Also, RS -UT

= 5 - 1 = 4 km i.e., PO = 4 km

By using pythagoras theorem,

$PU^2=UO^2+PO^2$

$=3^2 + 4^2$

$= 9 + 16$

$PU^2 =25$

PU =5 km

Hence, the correct option is (E).

Ques (19-21): According to the information given,

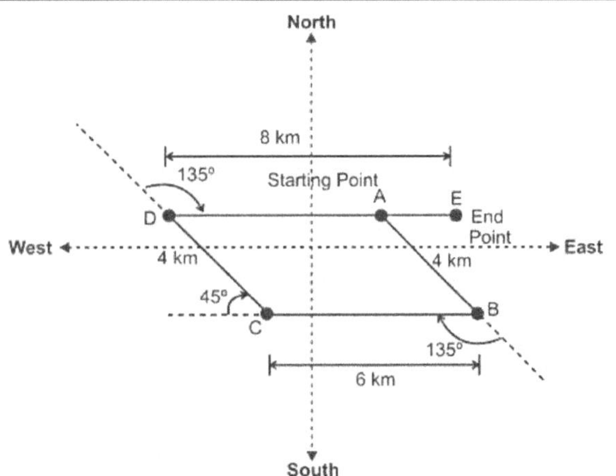

19. From the above diagram, the distance between DA and CB is equal.

Since the opposite or facing sides of a parallelogram are of equal length and the opposite angles of a parallelogram are of equal measure.

Therefore, distance between starting point A and ending point E = DE − DA = 8 − 6 = 2 km

Hence, the correct option is (D).

20. It is clear from the figure that the boy faces in the north-west direction at point D.

Hence, the correct option is (D).

21. It is clear from the figure that the angle between AE and AB is 45°.

Since the opposite or facing sides of a parallelogram are of equal length and the opposite angles of a parallelogram are of equal measure.

Hence, the correct option is (E).

Ques (22-24): According to the information given,

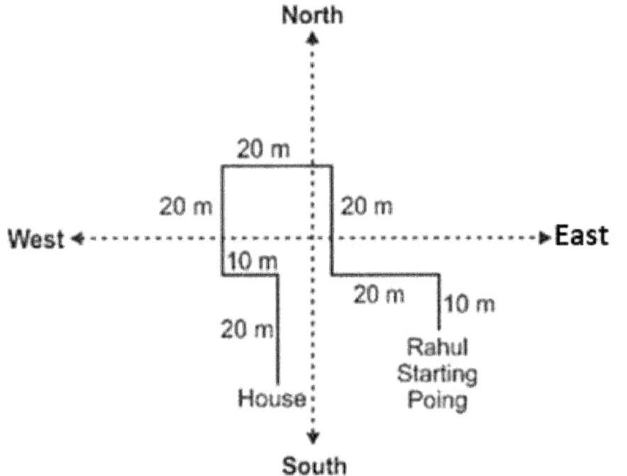

From the above diagram,

22. The total distance covered by Rahul = 10 + 20 + 20 + 20 + 20 + 10 + 20 = 120

Hence, the correct option is (B).

23. Rahul's house is in the South-west direction from his starting point.

Hence, the correct option is (C).

24. Distance between Rahul starting point and Rahul house;

(By applying Pythagoras theorem)

$$= \sqrt{(30^2 + 10^2)}$$

$$= \sqrt{1000}$$

$$= 10\sqrt{10} \text{ m}$$

Hence, the correct option is (A).

Ques (25-27): The figure according to the information given in the question will be as follows:

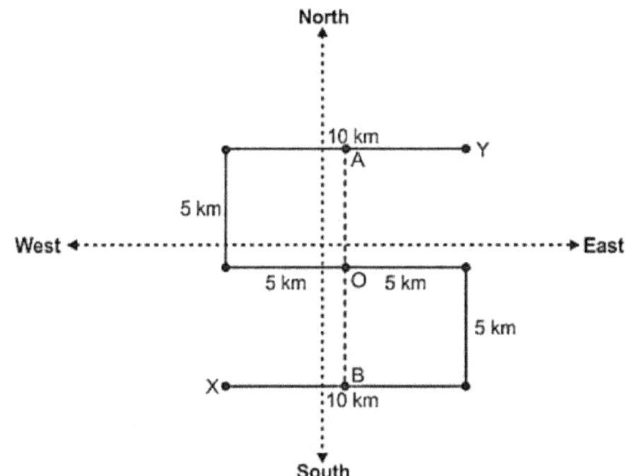

25. We know that, XY = XO + OY where O is the starting point.

By Pythagoras' theorem,

$OY^2 = AO^2 + OY^2$

$OY^2 = 5^2 + 5^2 = 50$

Similarly, $OX^2 = 50$

$\Rightarrow$ OX = OY = $5\sqrt{2}$

Therefore, XY = 2 × $5\sqrt{2}$ = $10\sqrt{2}$

So, the shortest distance between the final positions of X and Y is $10\sqrt{2}$ km.

Hence, the correct option is (C).

26. We know that, $XY = XO + OY$ where O is the starting point.

By Pythagoras' theorem,

$$OX^2 = BO^2 + BX^2$$

$$OX^2 = 5^2 + 5^2 = 50$$

$$\Rightarrow OX = 5\sqrt{2}$$

Hence, the shortest distance between the final position of X and the starting point is $5\sqrt{2}$ km.

Hence, the correct option is (C).

27. So, Y is in North-East direction with respect to X.

Hence, the correct option is (D).

Ques (28-30): X is 20 km to the west of B which is 10 km to the north of R. R is 10 km to the west of T

Z is 10 km to the south of T which is 10 km to the west of P. K is 40 km to the west of Z and R is 10 km to the west of T.

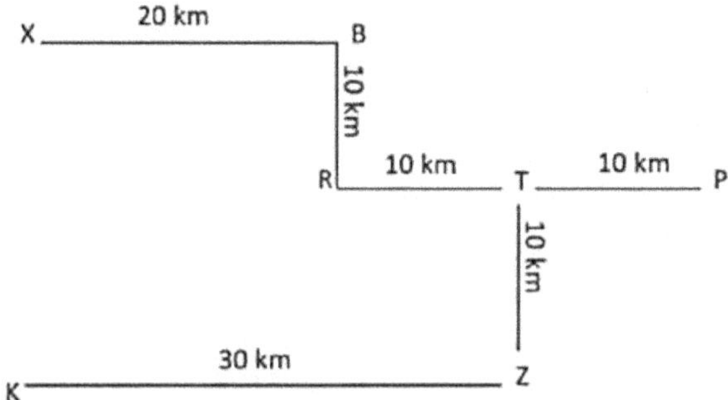

28. So, point K is in the south-west direction of point P.

Hence, the correct option is (B).

29. So, the distance between point X and point K is 20 km

Hence, the correct option is (C).

30. So, Point X is in the north-west direction of point T.

Hence, the correct option is (A).

Ques (1-5):Direction: In the question below are given three statements followed by three conclusions I, II and III. You have to take the given statements to be true even if they seem to be at variance from commonly known facts. Read all the conclusions and then decide which of the given conclusions logically follows from the given statements disregarding commonly known facts.

Q.1 Statements:

All schools are colleges.

Some universities are institutions.

No school is university.

Conclusions:

I. All colleges are universities is not a possibility.

II. No college is a university is not a possibility.

III. Some institutions are not schools is not a possibility.

[IDBI Bank Executive, 2021]

A. Only I follows

B. Only II follows

C. Only III follows

D. All follows

E. Only I and III follow

Q.2 Statements:

I. Some pillow are cushion.

II. All cushion are bed.

Conclusions:

I. All cushion are pillow.

II. Some cushion are pillow.

III. Some cushion are bed.

A. Either I or III follows

B. Only I and II follow

C. Only II and III follow

D. Only II follows

E. None follows

Q.3 Statements

No Chess is Board

Only few Board is Tennis

Every Board is carom

Only a few Board are Cricket

Conclusions

I. All Cricket is Carom is a possibility.

II. Some Carom is Board.

A. Only II follows

B. Only I follows

C. Either I or II follows

D. Both I and II follows

E. None follows

Q.4 Statements:

All dogs are hen

Some dogs are cat

Some cat are not birds

Only a few birds are sparrow

Conclusions:

I. All birds being cat is a possibility

II. Some Hen are Cat

A. Only I follows

B. Only II follows

C. Either I or II follows

D. Neither I nor II follows

E. Both I and II follow

Q.5 Statements:

Some cases are blur.

Only a few clear are captured.

All blur are captured.

Conclusions:

I. Some clear are not cases.

II. Some blur are not clear.

III. Some cases are captured.

A. If conclusion I follows

B. If conclusion II follows

C. If conclusion III follows

D. If conclusion II and III follow

E. If conclusion I and II follow

Ques (6-10):Directions: In the question, three statements are given, followed by three conclusions. You have to consider the statements to be true even if they seem to be at variance from commonly known facts. You have to decide which of the given conclusions, if any, follows from the given statements and select the appropriate option.

Q.6 Statements:

1. Some P are D.

2. All C are A.

3. No P is A.

Conclusions:

I. No C is P.

II. No C is D.

III. Some A are definitely D.

A. Only I follows

B. Only I, II, III follows

C. Only II, III follows

D. Only I, III follows

E. No conclusion follows

Q.7 Statements:

1. All C are X.

2. All X are P.

3. No Q is C.

Conclusions:

I. Some X are not Q.

II. Some Q may be both X and P.

III. Some P are not Q.

A. Only I follows

B. Only I, II, III follows

C. Only II, III follows

D. Only I, III follows

E. No conclusion follows

Q.8 Statements:

1. No F is E.

2. No E is C.

3. No Y is E.

Conclusions:

I. Some F are C.

II. Some Y are F.

III. Some C are Y.

A. Only I, II follows

B. Only I, II, III follows

C. Only II, III follows

D. Only III follows

E. No conclusion follows

Q.9 Statements:

1. All P are T.

2. Some T are J.

3. Some X are J.

Conclusions:

I. Some X may be P.

II. No J is p.

III. Some X may be both J and T.

A. Only I, III follows

B. Only I, II, III follows

C. Only II, III follows

D. Only I, II follows

E. No conclusion follows

Q.10 Statements:

1. All H are E.

2. All E are D.

3. All D are M.

Conclusions:

I. Some M are not H.

II. Some D are not H.

III. Some E are not M.

A. Only I, II follows

B. Only III follows

C. Only I, II, III follows

D. Only II, III follows

E. No conclusion follows

Ques (11-15):Direction: In each of the questions below are given four statements, followed by conclusions: I and II. You have to take the given statements to be true even if they seem to be at variance from commonly known facts. Read the conclusions and then decide which of the given conclusions logically follows from the given statements disregarding commonly known facts.

Q.11 Statements:

Only Indians are great.

Few legends are Indian.

Few winners are legends.

No Indians is loser.

Conclusions:

I. Many winners are losers.

II. Many Indians are winners is a possibility.

A. If conclusion I follows

B. If conclusion II follows

C. Either conclusion I or conclusion II follows

D. Neither conclusion I nor conclusion II follows

E. Both conclusions I and II follow

Q.12 Statements:

Only ice are fire.

Few ice are cloud.

No cloud is blue.

Few blues are white.

Conclusions:

I. Only ice are clouds.

II. few clouds are white is a possibility.

A. If conclusion I follows

B. If conclusion II follows

C. Either conclusion I or conclusion II follows

D. Neither conclusion I nor conclusion II follows

E. Both conclusions I and II follow

Q.13 Statements:

Only soldiers are heroes.

Some soldiers are great.

No actor is hero.

A few heroes are legends.

Conclusions:

I. No actor is legend.

II. Few actors are great.

A. If conclusion I follows

B. If conclusion II follows

C. Either conclusion I or conclusion II follows

D. Neither conclusion I nor conclusion II follows

E. Both conclusions I and II follow

Q.14 Statements:

Most wickets are bolds.

A few bolds are out.

No out is lbw.

Only LBW is DRS.

Conclusions:

I. Few wickets are LBW is a possibility.

II. Few Bolds are LBW is a possibility.

A. If conclusion I follows
B. If conclusion II follows
C. Either conclusion I or conclusion II follows
D. Neither conclusion I nor conclusion II follows
E. Both conclusions I and II follow

Q.15 Statements:

Few stricts are teacher.

A few brothers are stricts.

Only parents are teacher.

No teacher is brother.

Conclusions:

I. Few brothers are parents.

II. many parents are not strict.

A. If conclusion I follows
B. If conclusion II follows
C. Either conclusion I or conclusion II follows
D. Neither conclusion I nor conclusion II follows
E. Both conclusions I and II follow

Ques (16-20):Direction: In each of the questions below are given some statements followed by two conclusions. You have to take the given statements to be true even if they seem to be at variance with commonly known facts. Read all the conclusions and then decide which of the given conclusions logically follows from the given statements, disregarding commonly known facts. Give answer

Q.16 Statements:

Only a few seven are eight.

Only eight are nine.

Conclusions:

I. Some seven are nine.

II. All nine are eight.

A. Only I follows
B. Only II follows
C. Either I or II follows
D. Neither I nor II follows
E. Both I and II follows

Q.17 Statements:

Only a few Gmail are yahoo.

Some yahoo are windows.

Conclusions:

I. Some gmail are windows.

II. No gmail are windows.

A. Only I follows
B. Only II follows
C. Either I or II follows
D. Neither I nor II follows
E. Both I and II follows

Q.18 Statements:

Only a few female are aunty.

No aunty is children.

Conclusions:

I. Some childrenare female is a possibility.

II. Some female are not aunty.

A. Only I follows
B. Only II follows
C. Either I or II follows
D. Neither I nor II follows
E. Both I and II follows

Q.19 Statements:

All studious are student.

Some studious are teacher.

Conclusions:

I. Some teacher are student.

II. No student are teacher.

A. Only I follows
B. Only II follows
C. Either I or II follows
D. Neither I nor II follows
E. Both I and II follows

Q.20 Statements:

Only a few speaker are special.

Only speaker are spear.

Conclusions:

I. Some spear are special is a possibility.

II. only a few spear are special.

A. Only I follows
B. Only II follows
C. Either I or II follows
D. Neither I nor II follows
E. Both I and II follows

Q.21 Direction: In the question below are given two statements followed by two conclusions numbered I and II. You have to take the given statements to be true even if they seem to be at variance with commonly known facts. Read all the conclusions and then decide which of the given conclusions logically follows from the given statements disregarding commonly known facts.

Statements:

Some books are papers.

Some papers are tables.

Conclusions:

I. Some books are tables.

II. No books are tables.

A. Only I follows
B. Only II follows
C. Both I and II follow
D. Either I or II follows
E. None of these

Q.22 Direction: In the question below are given two statements followed by two conclusions numbered I and II. You have to take the given statements to be true even if they seem to be at variance from commonly known facts. Read both the

conclusions and then decide which of the given conclusions logically follows from the given statements disregarding commonly known facts.

Statements:

All mobiles are cameras.

All telephones are cameras.

Conclusions:

I. Some mobiles are telephones.

II. No mobile is a telephone.

A. Both follow

B. None follows

C. Either I or II follows

D. Only II follows

E. Only I follows

Q.23 Direction: In the question below are given two statements followed by two conclusions numbered I and II. You have to take the given statements to be true even if they seem to be at variance with commonly known facts. Read all the conclusions and then decide which of the given conclusions logically follows from the given statements disregarding commonly known facts.

Statements:

All B are S.

Some B are T.

Conclusions:

I. Some S are T.

II. All T are B.

A. Only I follows

B. Only II follows

C. Both I and II follow

D. Neither I nor II follows

E. None

Q.24 Direction: In the question below are given some statements followed by two conclusions numbered I and II. You have to take the given statements to be true even if they seem to be at variance with commonly known facts. Read all the conclusions and then decide which of the given conclusions logically follows from the given statements disregarding commonly known facts.

Statements:

All lions are bears.

All bears are cows.

Some cows are birds.

Conclusions:

I. Some lions are cows.

II. Some cows are bears.

A. Only conclusion I follow.

B. Only conclusion II follow.

C. Either conclusion I or II follows.

D. Neither conclusion I nor II follows.

E. Both conclusions I and II follow.

Q.25 Direction: In the question below are given two statements followed by two conclusions numbered I and II. You

have to take the given statements to be true even if they seem to be at variance with commonly known facts. Read all the conclusions and then decide which of the given conclusions logically follows from the given statements disregarding commonly known facts.

Statements:

Only a few dogs are cats.

All cats are tigers.

Conclusions:

I. All dogs are tigers.

II. Atleast some tigers are dogs.

A. Only II follows

B. Only I follows

C. Both I and II follow

D. Either I or II follows

E. Neither I nor II follows

Q.26 Direction: Two statements are given followed by three conclusions numbered I, II, and III. Assuming the statements to be true, even they seem to be at variance with commonly known facts decided which of the conclusions logically follow from the statement.

Statements:

Some cats are dogs.

All dogs are Deer.

Conclusions:

Some Deer are Cats.

All Deer are Cats.

No Deer is the dog.

A. Only conclusion I follow

B. Only conclusion III follow

C. Only conclusion I and III follow

D. Only conclusion II and II follow

E. None of these

Q.27 Direction: Two statements are given followed by three conclusions numbered I, II, and III. Assuming the statements to be true, even they seem to be at variance with commonly known facts decided which of the conclusions logically follow from the statement.

Statements:

Some vegetables are fruits.

No fruit is mango.

Conclusions:

I. some vegetables are Mangoes.

II. Some fruits are vegetables.

III. No vegetable is mango.

A. Only conclusion III follows

B. Only conclusion II follows

C. Only conclusion I and III follows

D. Only conclusion I follows

E. None of these

Q.28 Direction: In the following question, a relationship between different elements is shown in the statement(s). The statements are followed by Some conclusions.

Statements:

Some Poets are poems.

No poem is the song.

Conclusions:

I. Some Poems are not songs.

II. Some songs are poems.

A.   Only Conclusion I is true

B.   Only Conclusion II is true

C.   Either Conclusion I or II is true

D.   Neither Conclusion I nor II is true

E.   None of these

Q.29 Direction: Consider the following statements to be true even if they seem to be at variance from commonly known facts and decide which of the conclusions logically follows from the statements.

Statements:

Some song are movie.

Some movie are video.

Conclusions:

I. Some song are video.

II. All video are movie.

A.   Neither conclusion I nor II follows

B.   Only conclusion II follows

C.   Both conclusions I and II follow

D.   Only conclusion I follows

E.   Either conclusion I or conclusion II follows

Q.30 Direction: The statements given below are followed by two conclusions labeled I and II. Assuming that the information in the statement is true, even if it appears to be at variance with generally established facts, decide which conclusion(s) logically and definitely follow(s) from the information given in the statements.

Statements:

Some Files are Data.

All Documents are Data.

Conclusions:

I. Some Files are Document.

II. Some Data are Document.

A.   None of the conclusions follow

B.   Only conclusion I follows

C.   Only conclusion II follows

D.   Both the conclusions follow

E.   Either conclusion I or conclusion II follows

// Smart Answer Sheet //

Correct — Indicates percentage of students who answered questions correctly.

Skipped — Indicates percentage of students who skipped questions.

Q.	Ans.	Correct / Skipped
1	E	42.61 % / 37.51 %
2	C	57.22 % / 33.1 %
3	D	63.94 % / 30.27 %
4	E	50.94 % / 45.88 %
5	C	45.71 % / 49.54 %
6	A	44.64 % / 49.85 %
7	B	57.3 % / 37.33 %
8	E	40.55 % / 49.72 %
9	A	41.27 % / 47.23 %
10	E	56.85 % / 38.81 %
11	B	49.33 % / 36.17 %
12	B	57.11 % / 33.62 %
13	D	66.7 % / 30.16 %
14	E	57.64 % / 42.01 %
15	D	68.13 % / 31.23 %
16	B	64.42 % / 33.38 %
17	B	59.53 % / 32.82 %
18	E	43.84 % / 47.2 %
19	A	42.76 % / 31.78 %
20	D	65.67 % / 32.38 %
21	D	89.93 % / 10.04 %
22	C	80.43 % / 11.37 %
23	A	85.44 % / 11.72 %
24	E	77.09 % / 18.79 %
25	A	77.77 % / 12.84 %
26	A	50.69 % / 34.49 %
27	B	69.58 % / 30.06 %
28	B	63.97 % / 36.01 %
29	A	15.85 % / 70.33 %
30	C	59.32 % / 36.3 %

Performance Analysis

Avg. Score (%)	53.33%
Toppers Score (%)	63.33%
Your Score	

//Hints and Solutions//

1. The least possible Venn diagram for the given statements is drawn below. Now, we can verify the conclusions.

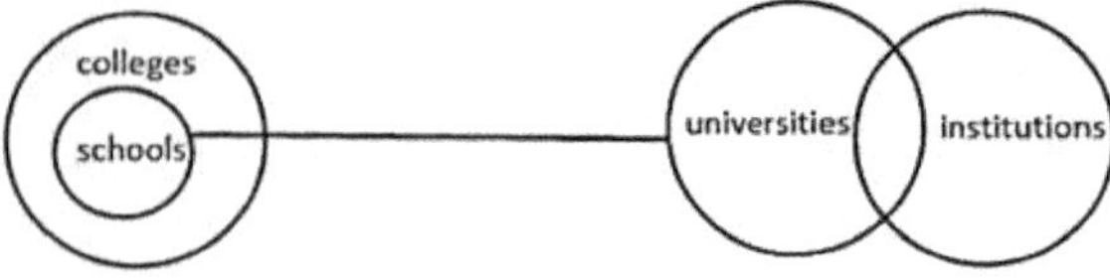

I. All colleges are universities is not a possibility → True

II. No college is a university is not a possibility → False

III. Some institutions are not schools is not a possibility → True (The institutions which are universities are not school. So, it is definite that some institutions are not schools. Therefore, the possibility of some institutions are not schools is false as a possibility under definite case is always false. Hence, the negative possibility of the same will be true)

So, only conclusion I and III follows.

Hence, the correct option is (E).

2. Least possible Venn diagram for the given statements is as follows,

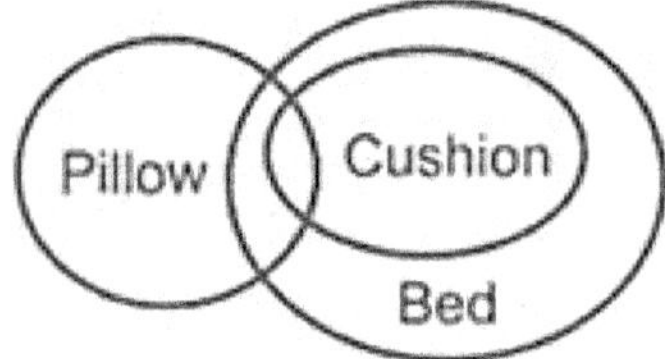

Conclusions:

I. All cushion are pillow → Not follows.

II. Some cushion are pillow → Follows.

III. Some cushion are bed → Follows.

Thus, only II and III follow.

Hence, the correct option is (C).

3. The least possible Venn diagram is shown below:

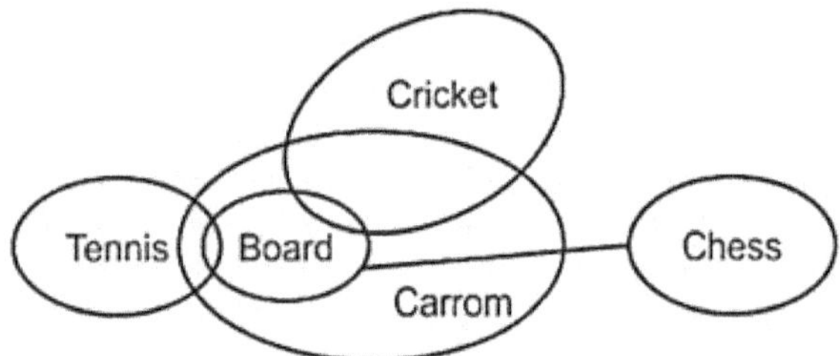

I. All Cricket is Carom is a possibility → true

II. Some Carom is Board → true

So, answer is Both I and II follows.

Hence, the correct option is (D).

4. The least possible Venn diagram is shown below:

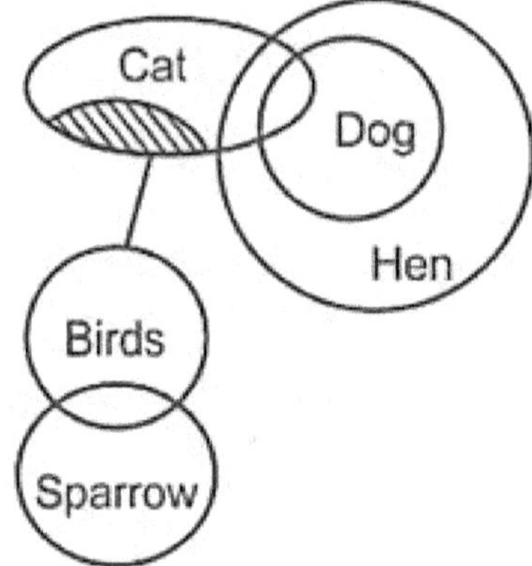

I. All birds being cat is possibility → true

II. Some Hen are Cat → true

So, both I and II follow.

Hence, the correct option is (E).

5. The only possible Venn diagram for the given statements is as follows:

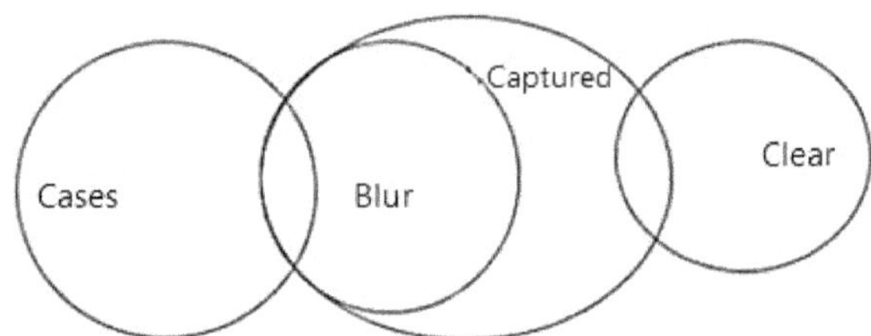

Conclusions:

I. Some clear are not cases → Does not follow as it is possible but not definite

II. Some blur are not clear → Does not follow as it is possible but not definite

III. Some cases are captured → Follows as some cases are blur and only captured are blur.

Hence, the correct option is (C).

6.

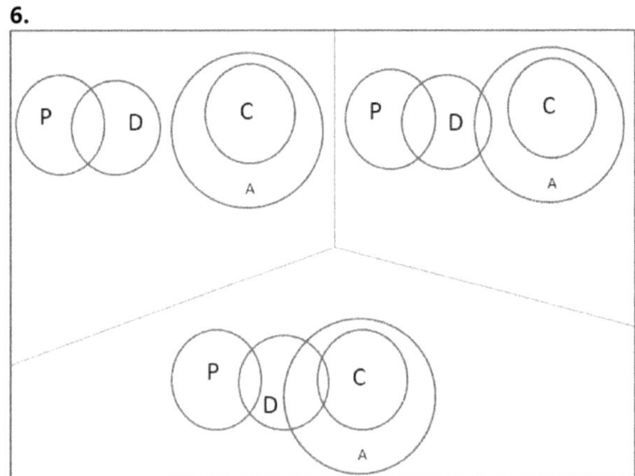

From all the diagrams we can see that all C are A and No P is A so no C is P.

From all the diagrams we can see that Some C may be D.

From all the diagrams we can see that Some A may/may not D.

So, we can say that only I conclusion follow.

Hence, the correct option is (A).

7.

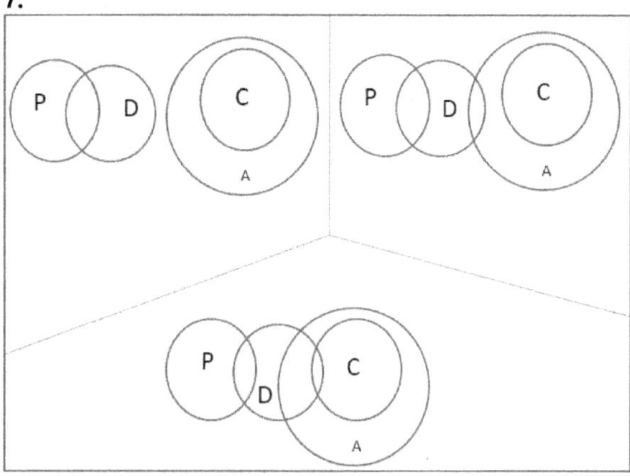

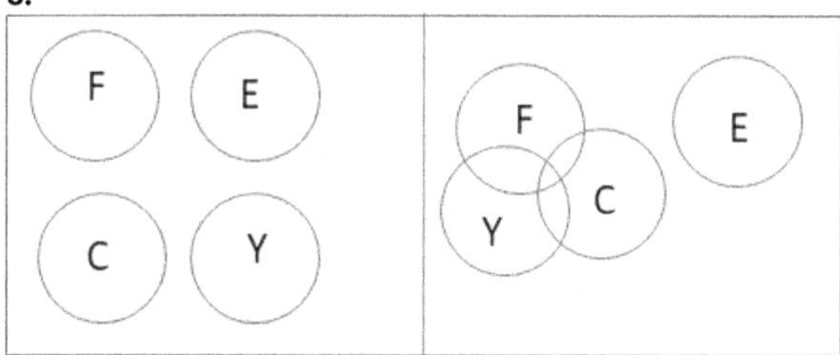

From all the diagrams we can see that all C those are part of X and P can't be Q so conclusions I, III follows.

From all the diagrams we can see that Some Q may be both X and P.

So, we can say that only all I, II, III conclusion follows.

Hence, the correct option is (B).

8.

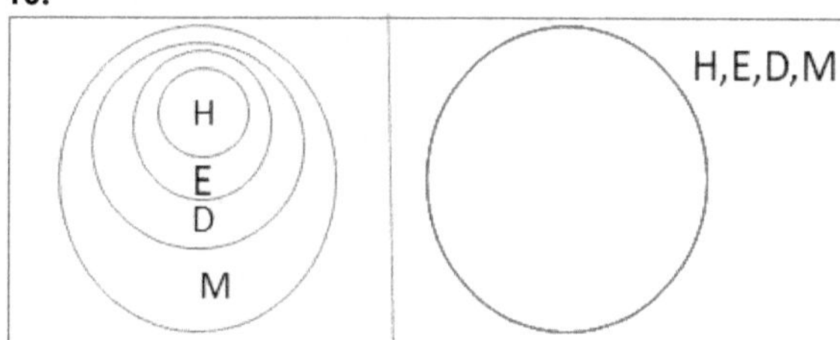

From both the diagrams, we can see that Some F may/may not be C.

From both the diagrams, we can see that Some Y may/may not be F.

From both the diagrams, we can see that Some C may/may not be Y.

So, we can say that no conclusion follows.

Hence, the correct option is (E).

9.

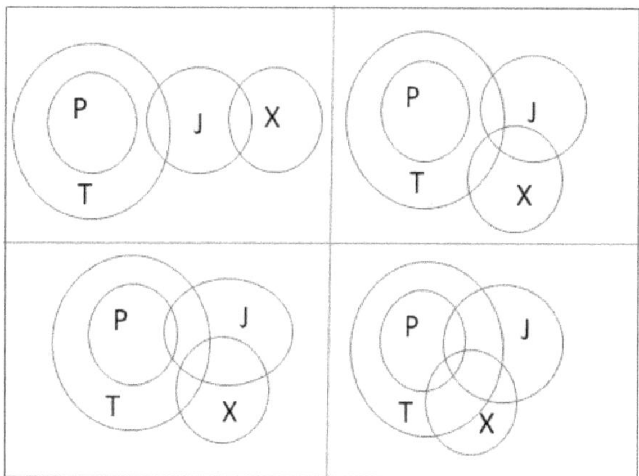

From all the diagrams we can see that Some X may be P.

From all the diagrams we can see that Some J may be P.

From all the diagrams we can see that Some X may be both J and T.

So, we can say that only I, III conclusion follows.

Hence, the correct option is (A).

10.

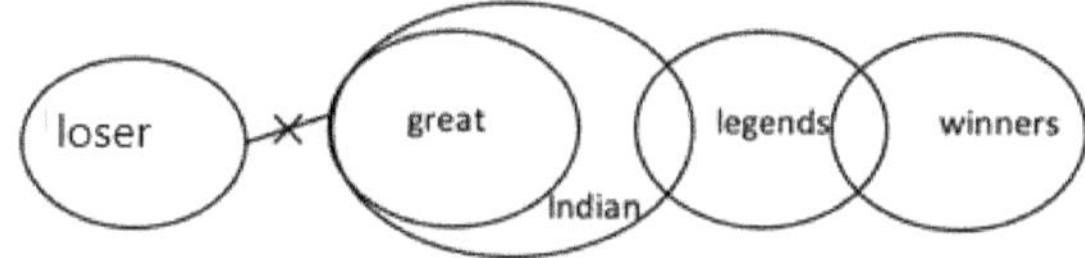

We can see from the diagram that when all H, E, D, M congruent then no conclusion follows.

Hence, the correct option is (E).

11. The only possible Venn diagram for the given statements is as follows:

Conclusions:

I. Many winners are losers → It's not sure, so it is false.

II. many Indians are winners is a possibility → It's sure, so it is true.

Hence, the correct option is (B).

12. The only possible Venn diagram for the given statements is as follows:

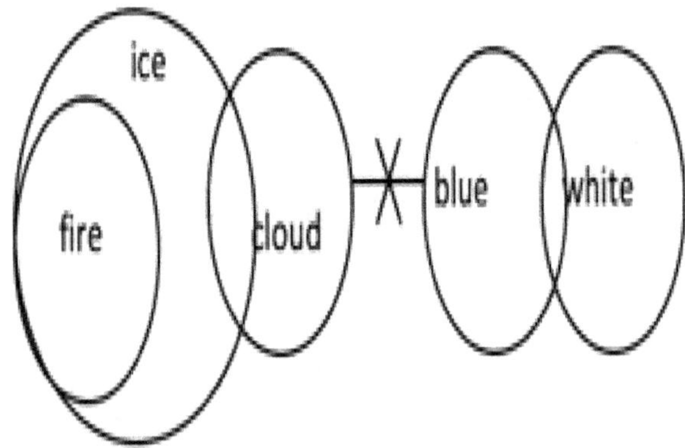

Conclusions:

I. Only ice are clouds → It's not possible, so it is false.

II. Few clouds are white is a possibility → It's sure, so it is true.

Hence, the correct option is (B).

13. The only possible Venn diagram for the given statements is as follows:

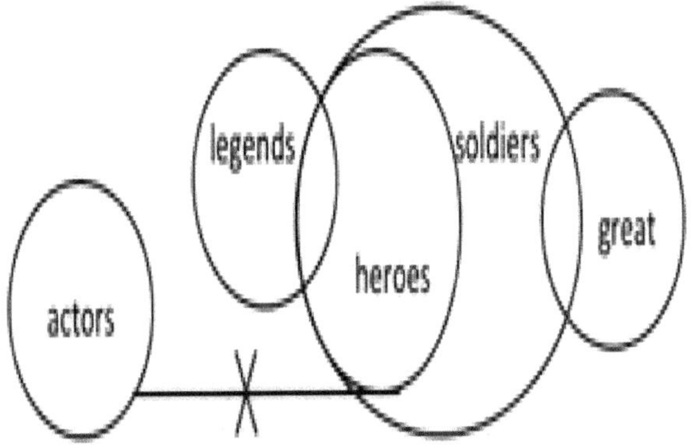

Conclusions:

I. No actor is a legend → It's not sure, so it is false.

II. Few actors are great → It's not sure, so it is false.

Hence, the correct option is (D).

14. The only possible Venn diagram for the given statements is as follows:

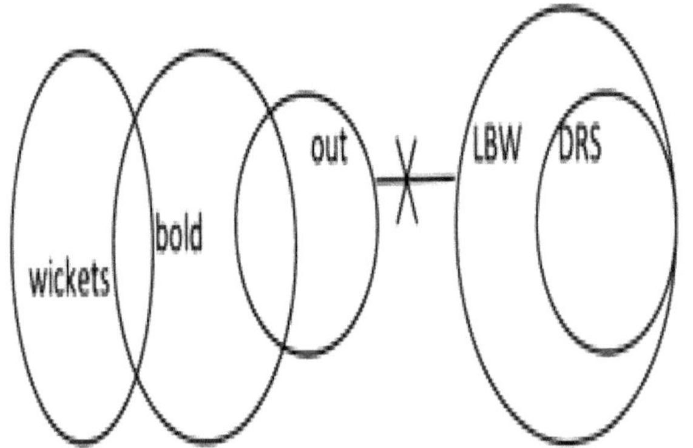

Conclusions:

I. Few wickets are LBW is a possibility → It's sure, so it is true.

II.Few Bolds are LBW is a possibility → It's sure, so it is true.

Hence, the correct option is (E).

15. The only possible Venn diagram for the given statements is as follows:

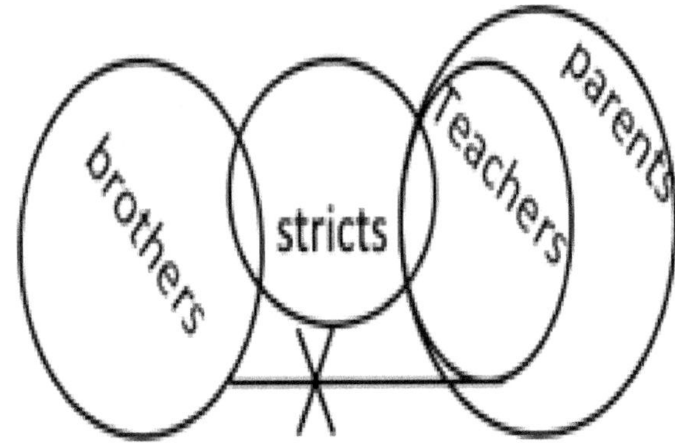

Conclusions:

I. Few brothers are parents → It's not sure, so it is false.

II. Many parents are not strict → It's not sure, so it is false.

Hence, the correct option is (D).

16. The least possible Venn diagram is as follows-

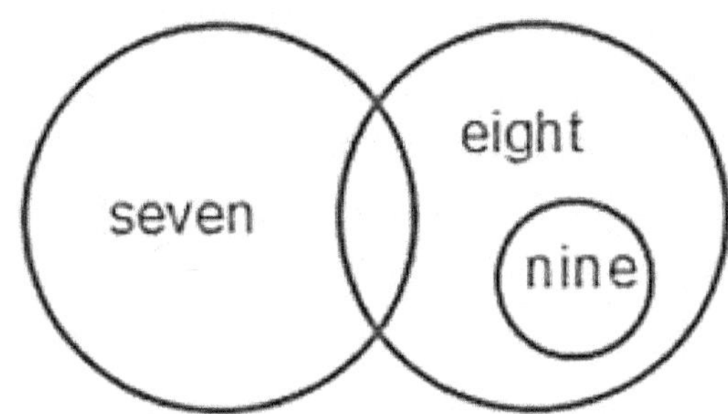

Conclusions – I some seven are nine – False (it is possible but not definite)

Conclusions – II All nine are eight – True (Only eight are nine)

So, only II follows.

Hence, the correct option is (B).

17. The least possible Venn diagram is as follows-

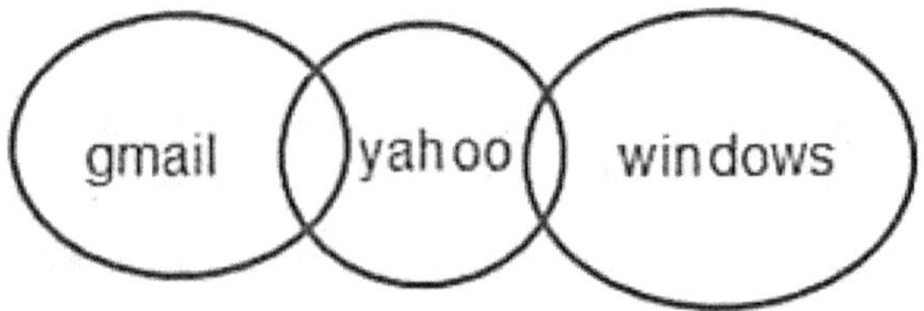

Conclusions – I Some gmail are windows – False

Conclusions – II No gmail are windows.– True

So, only II follows

Hence, the correct option is (B).

18. The least possible Venn diagram is as follows-

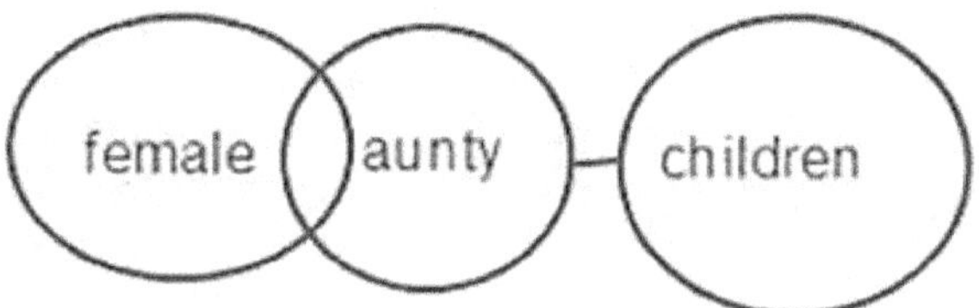

Conclusions – I some children are female is a possibility – True (It can be possible)

Conclusions – II Some female are not aunty – True (Only a few female are aunty)

So, both I and II follows

Hence, the correct option is (E).

19. The least possible Venn diagram is as follows-

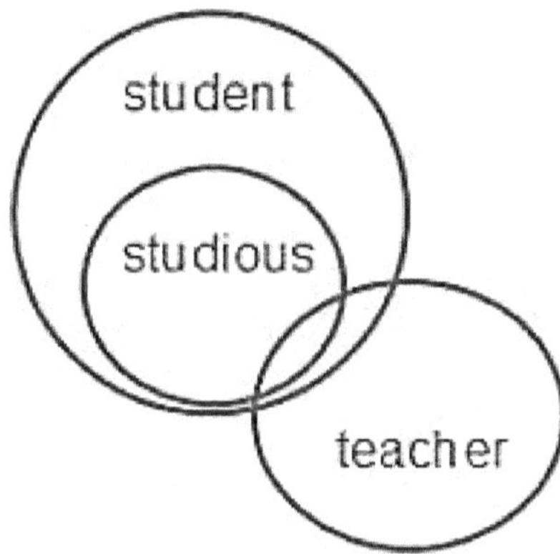

Conclusions – I Some teacher are student – True (All studious are student)

Conclusions – II No student are teacher – False (All studious are student)

So, only conclusions – I follows.

Hence, the correct option is (A).

20. The least possible Venn diagram is as follows-

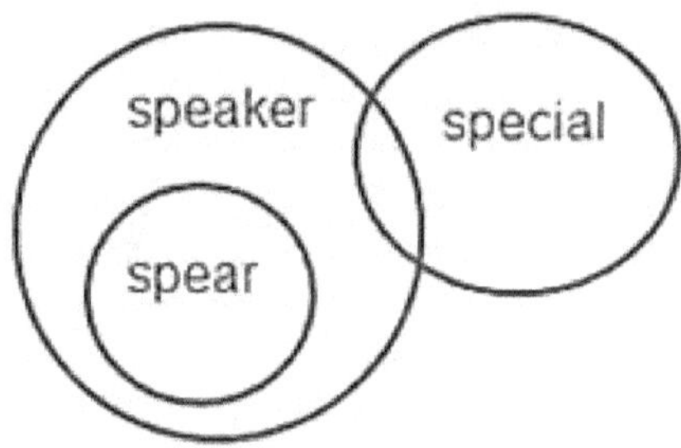

Conclusions – I some spear are special is a possibility – False (as only speaker is spear there is no relation possible between spear and any other except Speaker)

Conclusions – II only a few spear are special – False (Only a few speaker are special, Only speaker are spear)

So, neither I nor II follows.

Hence, the correct option is (D).

21. The least possible Venn diagram for the given statements is as follows:

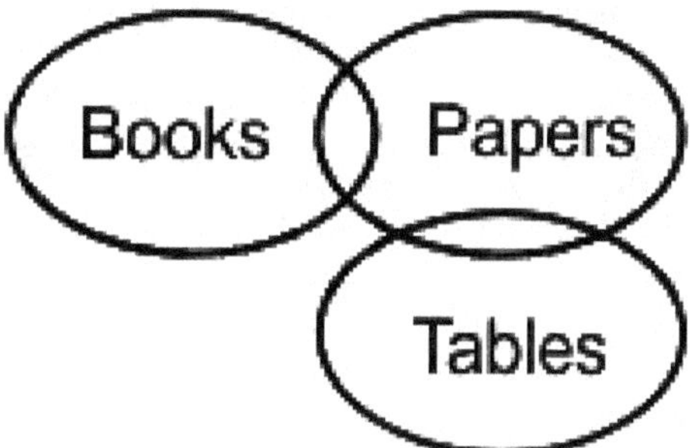

Conclusions:

I. Some books are tables → False (It is possible but not definite)

II. No books are tables → False (It is possible but not definite)

Conclusion I and II form a complementary pair.

Therefore, either I or II follows.

Hence, the correct option is (D).

22. The least possible Venn diagram for the given statements is as follows-

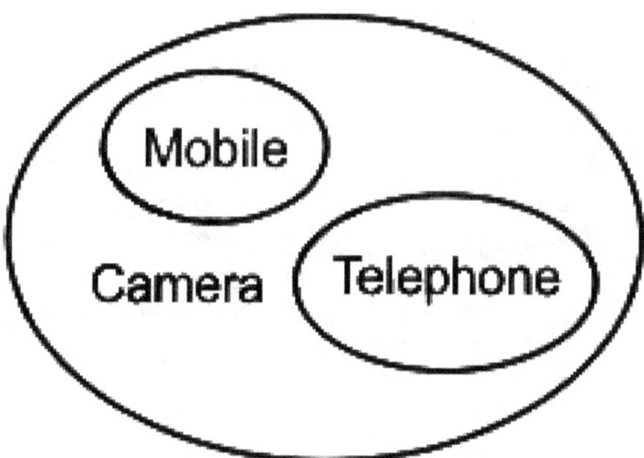

Conclusions:

I. Some mobiles are telephones. → False (It is possible but not definite.)

II. No mobile is telephone. → False (It is possible but not definite.)

Both the conclusions form a complimentary pair, hence either I or II follows.

A set of two conclusions is said to be a Complementary Pair and thus form a case of either or, when they follow the following conditions-

i) Both the objects must be same in both conclusions.

ii) Both the conclusions must be False individually.

Some of the cases of complementary pairs are-

Some + No & All + Some Not

Remember Some + Some not is never a complementary pair.

Hence, the correct option is (C).

23. The least possible Venn diagram for the given statements is as follows:

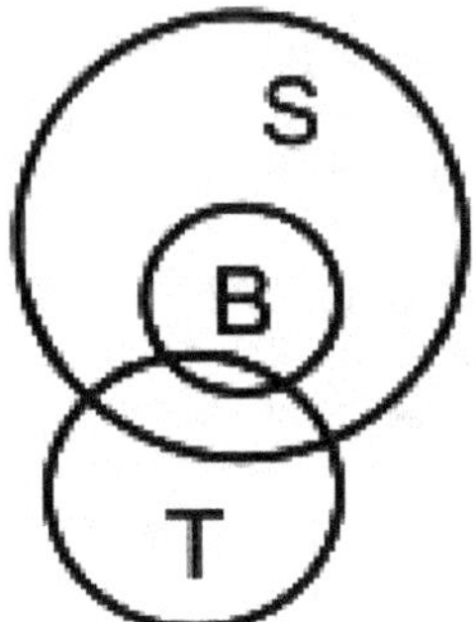

Conclusions:

I. Some S are T → True (It is definite as the diagram shows there is a definite relation between S and R)

II. All T are B → False (It is possible but not definite)

Therefore, Only I follows.

Hence, the correct option is (A).

24. The possible Venn diagram is:

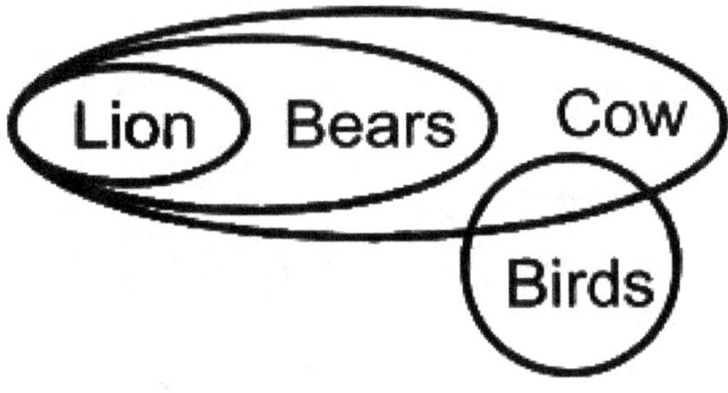

Explanation:

I. Some lions are cows → It is a definite case, therefore true.

II. Some cows are bears → It is a definite case, therefore true.

So, both conclusions I and II follow.

Hence, the correct option is (E).

25. The least possible Venn diagram for given statement is as follows,

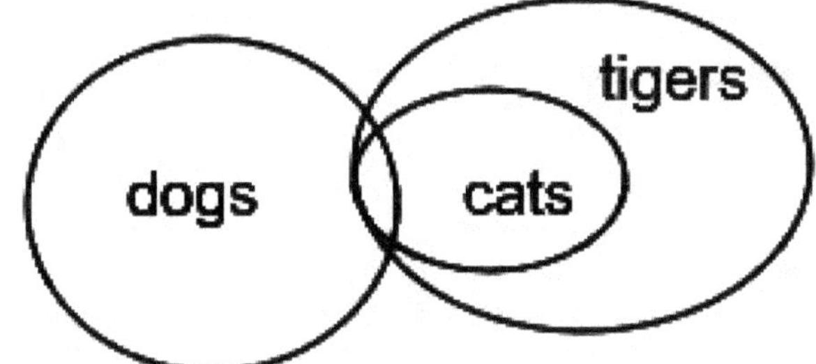

Conclusion:

I. All dogs are tigers → False (It is possible but not definite)

II. Atleast some tigers are dogs → True (Some part of tigers which is cat are dogs)

Thus, only conclusion II follows.

Hence, the correct option is (A).

26. The least possible Venn diagram from the given statement is as follows:

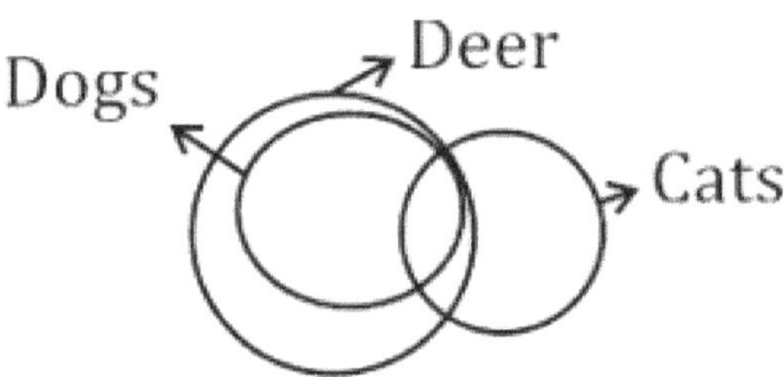

Conclusions:

Some Deer are Cats. (True) (It is possible because some deer are cats)

All Deer are Cats. (False) (It is not possible because all deers aren't cat)

No Deer is the dog. (False) (It is not possible because some deer are dogs)

So, the only conclusion I follow.

Hence, the correct option is (A).

27. The least possible Venn diagram from the given statement is as follows:

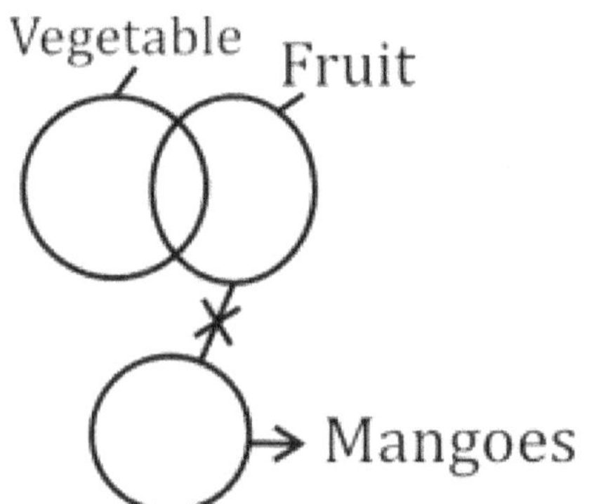

Conclusions:

I. some vegetables are Mangoes. (False) (It is not possible because no vegetable is mango)

II. Some fruits are vegetables. (True) (It is possible because some fruits are vegetables also)

III. No vegetable is mango. (False) (It is not possible because no vegetable is mango)

So, only conclusion II follows.

Hence, the correct option is (B).

28. From the following Statement we have these diagram:

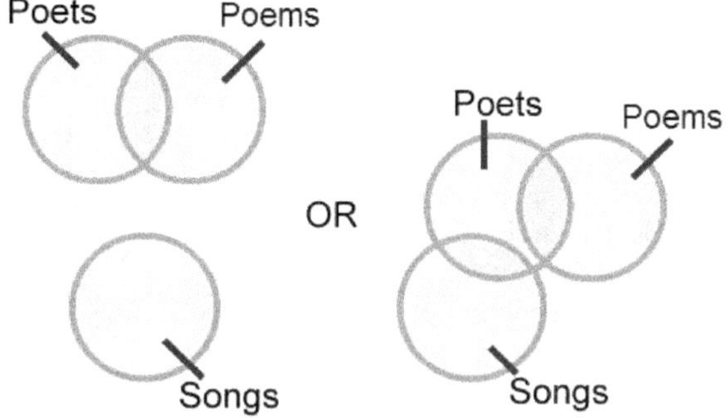

From the above diagram, we can have a conclusion that only I conclusion is true.

Hence, the correct option is (B).

29. The least possible Venn diagram is as follows,

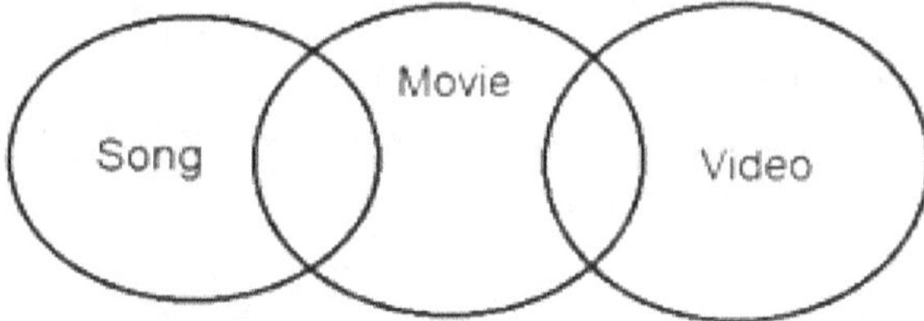

Conclusions:

I. Some song are video → It is possible but not definite, hence it is false.

II. All video are movie → It is possible but not definite, hence it is false.

Thus, neither conclusion I nor II follows.

Hence, the correct option is (A).

30. From the given information:

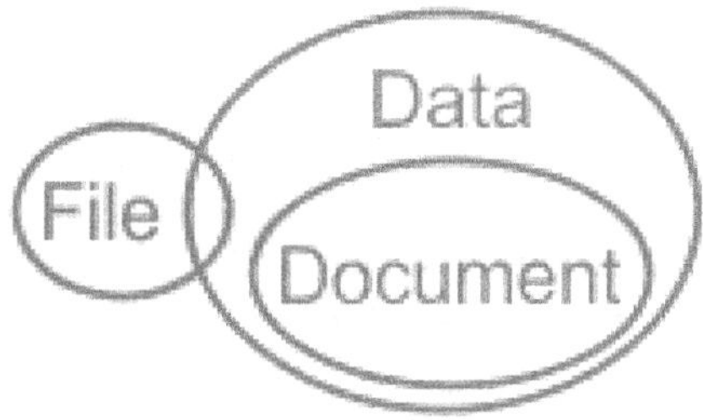

I. Some Files are Document → False (because it is possible but not definite)

II. Some Data are Document → True (all document are data imply that some data are definitely document)

Thus, only conclusion II follows.

Hence, the correct option is (C).

Ques (1-5):Direction: In the following question assuming the given statements to be True, find which of the conclusion among given conclusions is / are definitely true and then give your answers accordingly.

Q.1 Statements: P = Q < R > S = T; A < T < B; C > T < D

Conclusions:

I. C < A

II. D < A

A. None is true

B. Both I and II are true

C. Only II is true

D. Only I is true

E. Either I and II is true

Q.2 Statements: P = Q ≤ R ≤ S; S > A < B; C > D > A

Conclusions:

I. P > A

II. R < C

A. None is true

B. Both I and II are true

C. Only II is true

D. Only I is true

E. Either I and II is true

Q.3 Statements: A < B = C; C ≤ D ≤ E; E > F < G; G = H

Conclusions:

I. A < E

II. A < F

A. None is true

B. Both I and II are true

C. Only II is true

D. Only I is true

E. Either I and II is true

Q.4 Statements: P ≤ Q > R > S; S = T > U < V = W

Conclusions:

I. U < Q

II. V > T

A. None is true

B. Both I and II are true

C. Only II is true

D. Only I is true

E. Either I and II is true

Q.5 Statements: A > B < C; C > D > E; E < F > C

Conclusions:

I. C < F

II. C < E

A. None is true

B. Both I and II are true

C. Only II is true

D. Only I is true

E. Either I and II is true

Ques (6-10):Direction: In the following question assuming the given statement to be true. Find which of the following conclusion(s) among the given conclusions is/are definitely true and then give your answer accordingly.

Q.6 Statement:

F < D ≤ G, K > M > L ≥ G

Conclusion:

I. M > D

II. M = D

A. Only I is true

B. Only II is true

C. Both I and II are true

D. None is true

E. Either I or II is true

Q.7 Statement:

S > M ≥ O, O ≥ P ≥ N > K

Conclusion:

I. O > N

II. N ≤ M

A. None is true

B. Only II is true

C. Both I and II are true

D. Only I is true

E. Either I or II is true

Q.8 Statement: X > Y ≥ Z ≥ W, W > V ≥ U

Conclusion:

I. W < U

II. Y > W

A. Only I is true

B. Only II is true

C. Both I and II are true

D. None is true

E. Either I or II is true

Q.9 Statement: 1 < 2 ≤ 4, 3 > 5 ≥ 6 > 4

Conclusion:

I. 1 = 6

II. 6 > 1

A. Only I is true

B. Only II is true

C. Both I and II are true

D. None is true

E. Either I or II is true

Q.10 Statement: P > M > Q ≥ R, S < N ≤ O ≤ T = R

Conclusion:

I. M > N

II. Q ≤ T

A. None is true

B. Only II is true

C. Both I and II are true

D. Only I is true

E. Either I or II is true

Ques (11-15):Direction: In these questions, relationship between different elements is. shown in the statements. The statements are followed by conclusions. Study the conclusions based on the given statements and select the appropriate answer.

Q.11 Statement:

F > Y ≥ X < Z, C ≤ X < W

Conclusions:

I. Z > C

II. F > W

A. Only I follows

B. Only II follows

C. Either I or II follows

D. Neither I nor II follows

E. Both I and II follows

Q.12 Statement:

S > E ≥ F < N, F > R ≤ I > T

Conclusions-

I. N > R

II. E > T

A. Only I follows

B. Only II follows

C. Either I or II follows

D. Neither I nor II follows

E. Both I and II follows

Q.13 Statement:

H < A ≥ V, A ≤ N < C

Conclusions:

I. C > H

II. N ≥ V

A. Only I follows

B. Only II follows

C. Either I or II follows

D. Neither I nor II follows

E. Both I and II follows

Q.14 Statement:

C > O ≤ M > I > N, G ≤ N < P

Conclusions:

I. G > O

II. P > M

A. Only I follows

B. Only II follows

C. Either I or II follows

D. Neither I nor II follows

E. Both I and II follows

Q.15 Statement:

H = A ≥ N ≤ D > S, N ≥ O = R

Conclusions:

I. R > H

II.R = H

A. Only I follows

B. Only II follows

C. Either I or II follows

D. Neither I nor II follows

E. Both I and II follows

Ques (16-20):Direction: In these questions. relationship between different elements is shown in the statements. The statements are followed by two conclusions. Choose the correct answer for inequality given below:

Q.16 Statements: H ≥ M > Q; Z < K < Q

Conclusions:

I. H > K

II. Z ≥ M

A. Either conclusion I or II is true

B. Only conclusion II is true

C. Only conclusion I is true

D. Both conclusions I and II are true

E. None of the conclusions is true

Q.17 Statements: Z ≤ X < P; B < A ≤ Z < C

Conclusions:

I. C < P

II. A ≥ X

A. Either conclusion I or II is true

B. Only conclusion II is true

C. Only conclusion I is true

D. Both conclusions I and II are true

E. None of the conclusions is true

Q.18 Statements: R ≥ X > M; P ≤ N < M

Conclusions:

I. R ≤ M

II. X > P

A. Either conclusion I or II is true

B. Only conclusion II is true

C. Only conclusion I is true

D. Both conclusions I and II are true

E. None of the conclusions is true

Q.19 Statements: L ≤ Z < P; L ≥ T > M

Conclusions:

I. M < P

II. P > T

A. Either conclusion I or II is true

B. Only conclusion II is true

C. Only conclusion I is true

D. Both conclusions I and II are true

E. None of the conclusions is true

Q.20 Statements: K < O ≥ T; S = T > C > B

Conclusions:

I. O > S

II. K < C

A. Either conclusion I or II is true

B. Only conclusion II is true

C. Only conclusion I is true

D. Both conclusions I and II are true

E. None of the conclusions is true

Ques (21-25):Directions: In this question, the relationship between different elements is shown in the statements. These statements are followed by two conclusions.

Q.21 Statement: C ≥ M > F < A = B > S

Conclusions:

I. C > B

II. F < S

A. Only conclusion I follow

B. Only conclusion II follows

C. Either conclusion I or II follows

D. Neither conclusion I nor II follows

E. Both conclusions I and II follow

Q.22 Statements: H = M ≤ W; C ≥ W < S

Conclusions:

I. C = M

II. C > M

A. Only conclusion I is true

B. Only conclusion II is true

C. Either conclusion I or II is true

D. Neither conclusion I nor II is true

E. Both conclusions I and II are true

Q.23 Statement: H < Y, Y ≥ R, R > W

Conclusions:

I. W < Y

II. R ≤ Y

A. Only conclusion I is true

B. Only conclusion II is true

C. Either conclusion I or II is true

D. Neither conclusion I nor II is true

E. Both conclusion I and II are true

Q.24 Statement: A ≤ P > B; C > P; F ≤ B

Conclusions:

I. C > A

II. F < P

A. Only conclusions I is true

B. Only conclusions II is true

C. Either conclusions I or II is true

D. Neither conclusions I nor II is true

E. Both conclusions I and II are true

Q.25 Statements: A ≤ B < C; A ≥ E; C ≤ F

Conclusions:

I. E < C

II. F ≥ E

A. Only conclusion I is true

B. Only conclusion II is true

C. Only conclusion I or II is true

D. Neither conclusion I nor II is true

E. Both conclusions I and II are true

Ques (26-30):Direction: In the following question assuming the given statements to be true, find which of the conclusion(s) among given conclusions is/are definitely true and then give your answers accordingly.

Q.26 Statements: Z > Y ≥ X ≥ K; K = L ≥ M;

Which of the following are definitely true?

A. X > L   **B.** Z > L

C. K = Z   **D.** K < Y

E. None of the above

Q.27 Statement: M < N = O > P, Q > R < M, S ≤ P

Conclusion:

I. Q > P

II. N > S

III. R < O

IV. R ≥ O

A. None is true

B. Only IV is true

C. Both II and III are true

D. Either I or III and IV are true

E. Either I or III is true

Q.28 Statements: T ≥ C ≥ F; E = A < D; X > T; D < F = T

Conclusions:

I. F < E

II. C = F

III. A > T

A. Only I is True

B. Only II is True

C. Only III is True

D. Only I and III are True

E. None is True

Q.29 Statements: Y < Z > X; W > D < R; Y > T = R; X > W

Conclusions:

I. R < Z

II. X > D

III. T < W

A. Only I is True

B. Only II is True

C. Only I and II are True

D. Only II and III are True

E. Only III and I are True

Q.30 Statements: E ≥ U = D; R < A < F; W ≤ D; W > F

Conclusions:

I. U < R

II. E = W

III. E > W

A. Only II is True

B. Only III is True

C. Only I and II are True

D. Either I or II is True

E. Either II or III is True

// Smart Answer Sheet //

Correct — Indicates percentage of students who answered questions correctly.

Skipped — Indicates percentage of students who skipped questions.

Q.	Ans.	Correct / Skipped
1	A	46.96 % / 35.0 %
2	A	42.39 % / 33.96 %
3	D	41.34 % / 31.06 %
4	D	54.7 % / 33.12 %
5	D	49.0 % / 36.47 %
6	A	40.01 % / 44.69 %
7	B	55.11 % / 31.01 %
8	D	57.19 % / 38.14 %
9	B	44.71 % / 45.88 %
10	D	47.22 % / 48.32 %
11	A	40.42 % / 56.56 %
12	A	63.69 % / 33.26 %
13	E	47.35 % / 44.44 %
14	D	50.16 % / 46.14 %
15	D	56.05 % / 34.8 %
16	C	43.02 % / 47.58 %
17	E	63.11 % / 34.33 %
18	B	40.94 % / 53.38 %
19	D	47.14 % / 46.87 %
20	E	40.3 % / 50.58 %
21	D	65.66 % / 33.35 %
22	C	46.54 % / 39.16 %
23	E	65.75 % / 33.47 %
24	E	48.92 % / 49.11 %
25	A	48.53 % / 45.57 %
26	B	53.48 % / 42.71 %
27	C	69.95 % / 30.02 %
28	E	61.56 % / 34.15 %
29	C	54.47 % / 40.64 %
30	E	41.09 % / 31.77 %

Performance Analysis	
Avg. Score (%)	50.0%
Toppers Score (%)	66.67%
Your Score	

//Hints and Solutions//

1. Given statements: P = Q < R > S = T; A < T < B; C > T < D

On combining: P = Q < R > S = T < D, B; C > T > A

Conclusions:

I. C < A → False (as C > T > A)

II. D < A → False (as D > T > A)

Thus, none is true.

Hence, the correct option is (A).

2. Given statements: P = Q ≤ R ≤ S; S > A < B; C > D > A

On combining: P = Q ≤ R ≤ S > A < B; A < D < C

Conclusions:

I. P > A → False (as P = Q ≤ R ≤ S > A → therefore we cannot determine the relation between P and A)

II. R < C → False (as P = Q ≤ R ≤ S > A < B; A < D < C → therefore we cannot determine the relation between R and C)

Thus, none is true.

Hence, the correct option is (A).

3. Given statements: A < B = C; C ≤ D ≤ E; E > F < G; G = H

On combining: A < B = C ≤ D ≤ E > F < G = H

Conclusions:

I. A < E → True (as A < B = C ≤ D ≤ E)

II. A < F → False (as A < B = C ≤ D ≤ E > F)

Thus, only I is true.

Hence, the correct option is (D).

4. Given statements: P ≤ Q > R > S; S = T > U < V = W

On combining: P ≤ Q > R > S = T > U < V = W

Conclusions:

I. U < Q → True (as Q > R > S = T > U)

II. V > T → False (as T > U < V → therefore we cannot determine the relationship between V and T)

Thus, only I is true.

Hence, the correct option is (D).

5. Given statements: A > B < C; C > D > E; E < F > C

On combining: A > B < C > D > E; C < F > E

Conclusions:

I. C < F → True (as C < F > E)

II. C < E → False (as C < F > E)

Thus, only I is true.

Hence, the correct option is (D).

6. Given Statements: F < D ≤ G, K > M > L ≥ G

On combining: F < D ≤ G ≤ L < M < K

Conclusions:

I. M > D → True (as D ≤ G ≤ L < M → D < M)

II. M = D → False (as D ≤ G ≤ L < M → D < M)

Thus, only I is true.

Hence, the correct option is (A).

7. Given Statements: S > M ≥ O, O ≥ P ≥ N > K

On combining: S > M ≥ O ≥ P ≥ N > K

Conclusions:

I. O > N → False (as O ≥ P ≥ N → O ≥ N)

II. N ≤ M → True (as M ≥ O ≥ P ≥ N → M ≥ N)

Thus, only II is true.

Hence, the correct option is (B).

8. Given Statements: X > Y ≥ Z ≥ W, W > V ≥ U

On combining: X > Y ≥ Z ≥ W > V ≥ U

Conclusions:

I. W < U → False (as X > Y ≥ Z ≥ W > V ≥ U → W > U)

II. Y > W → False (as Y ≥ Z ≥ W → Y ≥ W, it is possible but not definite)

Thus, none is true.

Hence, the correct option is (D).

9. Given Statements: 1 < 2 ≤ 4, 3 > 5 ≥ 6 > 4

On combining: 1 < 2 ≤ 4 < 6 ≤ 5 < 3

Conclusions:

I. 1 = 6 → False (as 1 < 2 ≤ 4 < 6 → 1 < 6)

II. 6 > 1 → True (as 1 < 2 ≤ 4 < 6 → 1 < 6)

Thus, only II is true.

Hence, the correct option is (B).

10. Given Statements: P > M > Q ≥ R, S < N ≤ O ≤ T = R

On combining: P > M > Q ≥ R = T ≥ O ≥ N > S

Conclusions:

I. M > N → True (as M > Q ≥ R = T ≥ O ≥ N → M > N)

II. Q ≤ T → False(as Q ≥ R = T → Q ≥ T)

Thus, only I is true.

Hence, the correct option is (D).

11. Given statement F > Y ≥ X < Z, C ≤ X < W

On combining – we will get F > Y ≥ X ≥ C and F > Y ≥ X < W

Conclusions:

I. Z > C – True (Z > X ≥ C)

II. F > W – False (Relationship between F and W cannot be determine)

So, only conclusion I follow

Hence, the correct option is (A).

12. Given statement S > E ≥ F < N, F > R ≤ I > T

On combining – we will get S > E ≥ F > R ≤ I > T and N > F > R ≤ I > T

Conclusions:

I. N > R – True (N > F > R)

II. E > T False (Relationship between E and T cannot be determine)

So, only conclusion I follow

Hence, the correct option is (A).

13. Given statement H < A ≥ V, A ≤ N < C

On combining – we will get C > N ≥ A > H and C > N ≥ A ≥ V

Conclusions:

I. C > H – True (C > N ≥ A > H)

II. N ≥ V – True (C > N ≥ A ≥ V)

So, both conclusion I and II follow

Hence, the correct option is (E).

14. Given statement C > O ≤ M > I > N, G ≤ N < P

On combining – we will get P > N < I < M ≥ O < C and G ≤ N < I < M ≥ O < C

Conclusions:

I. N > O – False (Relationship between N and O cannot be determine)

II. P > M – False (Relationship between P and M cannot be determine)

So, neither conclusion I nor II follow

Hence, the correct option is (D).

15. Given statement H = A ≥ N ≤ D > S, N ≥ O = R

On combining – we will get H = A ≥ N ≥ O = R and S < D ≥ N ≥ O = R

Conclusions:

I. R > H – False (R ≤ H)

II.R = H – False (R ≤ H)

So, neither conclusion I nor II follow

Hence, the correct option is (D).

16. Given statements: H ≥ M > Q; Z < K < Q

On combining, we get,

H ≥ M > Q > K < Z

Conclusions:

I. H > K → True (As H ≥ M > Q > K, so, H > K)

II. Z ≥ M → False (As H ≥ M > Q > K < Z, the relation between Z and M cannot be determined)

So, only conclusion I is true.

Hence, the correct option is (C).

17. Given statements: Z ≤ X < P; B < A ≤ Z < C

On combining, we get,

P > X ≥ Z ≥ A > B; P > X ≥ Z < C

Conclusions:

I. C < P → False (As P > X ≥ Z < C, the relation between P and C cannot be determined)

II. A ≥ X False (As P > X ≥ Z ≥ A > B; so, X ≥ A)

So, none of the conclusions is true.

Hence, the correct option is (E).

18. Given statements: R ≥ X > M; P ≤ N < M;

On combining, we get

R ≥ X > M > N ≥ P

Conclusions:

I. R ≤ M → False (As R ≥ X > M > N ≥ P)

II. X > P → True (As R ≥ X > M > N ≥ P)

So, only conclusion II is true.

Hence, the correct option is (B).

19. Given statements: L ≤ Z < P; L ≥ T > M

On combining, we get

Z ≥ L ≥ T > M; P > Z ≥ L ≥ T > M

Conclusions:

I. M < P → True (As P > Z ≥ L ≥ T > M, P > M)

II. P > T → True (As P > Z ≥ L ≥ T > M)

So, both conclusions I and II are true.

Hence, the correct option is (D).

20. Given statements: K < O ≥ T; S = T > C > B

On combining, we get

O ≥ T > C > B; O ≥ T = S; K < O ≥ T > C

Conclusions:

I. O > S → False (As, O ≥ T = S, so, O ≥ S)

II. K < C → False (As, K < O ≥ T > C, the relation between K and C cannot be determined)

So, none of the conclusions is true

Hence, the correct option is (E).

21. Statement: C ≥ M > F < A = B > S

Conclusions:

I. C > B ⇒ It's not true as C > F and B > F so no direct relationship between C and B can be established.

II. F < S ⇒ It's not true as A > S and A > F so no direct relationship between S and F can be established.

So, neither conclusion I nor II follows.

Hence, the correct option is (D).

22. Given statements are: H = M ≤ W; C ≥ W < S

On rearranging: H = M ≤ W ≤ C; W < S

Conclusions:

I. C = M (False as C ≥ M)

II. C > M (False as C ≥ M)

But both the conclusions form a complementary pair; so either I or II follows.

Hence, the correct option is (C).

23. Given statements are: H < Y, Y ≥ R, R > W

On combining: H < Y ≥ R > W

Conclusions:

I. W < Y (True)

II. R ≤ Y (True)

So, both the conclusion follows.

Hence, the correct option is (E).

24. Statements: A ≤ P > B; C > P; F ≤ B

⇒ A ≤ P > B ≥ F; C > P

Conclusions:

I. C > A ⇒ true as C > P and A ≤ P ⇒ C > P ≥ A ⇒ C > A

II. F < P ⇒ true as P > B ≥ F ⇒ P > F

So, both conclusions I and II are true.

Hence, the correct option is (E).

25. Statements: A ≤ B < C; A ≥ E; C ≤ F

On combining: E ≤ A ≤ B < C ≤ F

Conclusions:

I. E < C ⇒ true as C > B and B ≥ E so C > E

II. F ≥ E ⇒ false as F > B and B ≥ E so F > E

So, only conclusion I is true.

Hence, the correct option is (A).

26. Given statements: Z > Y ≥ X ≥ K; K = L ≥ M;

On combining: Z > Y ≥ X ≥ K = L ≥ M;

Conclusions:

I. X > L → False (as X ≥ K and K = L implies X ≥ L, thus a clear relation cannot be determined)

II. Z > L → True (as Z > Y ≥ X ≥ K; K = L implies Z > L)

III. K = Z → False (as Z > Y ≥ X ≥ K implies K < Z)

IV. K < Y → False (as Z > Y ≥ X ≥ K implies Y ≥ K, thus a clear relation cannot be determined)

Hence, the correct option is (B).

27. Given Statements: M < N = O > P, Q > R < M, S ≤ P

On combining: M < N = O > P ≥ S, Q > R < M < N = O > P

Conclusions:

I. Q > P → False (as Q > R < M < N = O > P → Relation cannot be determined)

II. N > S → True (as N = O > P ≥ S→N>S)

III. R < O → True (as R < M < N = O → R < O)

IV. R ≥ O → False (as R < M < N = O → R < O)

Hence, the correct option is (C).

28. Given statements: T ≥ C ≥ F; E = A < D; X > T; D < F = T

On combining: E = A < D < F ≤ C ≤ T < X; F = T

Conclusions:

I. F < E → False (as E = A < D < F → E < F)

II. C = F → False (as per the given information F = T & T ≥ C ≥ F)

III. A > T → False (as A < D < F ≤ C ≤ T → A < F ≤ C ≤ T → A < C ≤ T → A < T)

Hence, the correct option is (E).

29. Given statements: Y < Z > X; W > D < R; Y > T = R; X > W

On combining: D < R = T < Y < Z > X > W > D

Conclusions:

I. R < Z → True (as R = T < Y < Z → R < Z)

II. X > D → True (as X > W > D → X > D)

III. T < W → False (as T < Y < Z > X > W → T < Z > W → thus clear relation between T and W cannot be determined)

Hence, the correct option is (C).

30. Given statements: E ≥ U = D; R < A < F; W ≤ D; W > F

On combining: E ≥ U = D ≥ W > F > A > R

Conclusions:

I. U < R → False (as U = D ≥ W > F > A > R → U ≥ W > R → U > R)

II. E = W → False (as E ≥ U = D ≥ W → E ≥ D ≥ W → E ≥ W)

III. E > W → False (as E ≥ U = D ≥ W → E ≥ D ≥ W → E ≥ W)

Since, conclusion II and III form complementary pair and E ≥ W.

Hence, the correct option is (E).

Ques (1-5):Direction: Study the following information carefully and answer the question given below.

In a cloth shop, eight stacks of yarn are kept above each other. The yarn is numbered in ascending order from 1 to 8 such that the topmost yarn is numbered as 8 while the bottom most yarn is numbered as 1. Each yarn is of a different fabric among – Cotton, Wool, Silk, Leather, Rayon, Satin, Velvet and Denim but not necessarily in the same order.

Three yarns are placed between Leather yarn and Satin yarn. Yarn of Rayon is kept second from the top. Number of yarns above Rayon is same as the number of yarns below Leather. Silk Yarn is not kept below Satin yarn or Rayon yarn. Yarn of Cotton is not kept at the bottom. Yarn of Wool is kept above Cotton yarn but below Denim yarn.

Q.1 If Yarn of Satin is exchanged with the Yarn of Cotton, then how many Yarns are placed between Yarn of Cotton and Yarn of Wool?

A. Three   **B.** One   **C.** Two   **D.** Five
E. Four

Q.2 Which if the following statement(s) is/are correct?
I. Yarn of Silk is kept below Yarn of Denim.
II. Yarn of Leather is kept immediately above Yarn of Velvet.
III. There are three Yarns between Yarn of Rayon and Yarn of Cotton.

A. I and II   **B.** II and III
C. I and III   **D.** All of these
E. Cannot determine

Q.3 Which fabric of yarn is kept at the bottom?
A. Denim   **B.** Velvet   **C.** Silk   **D.** Wool
E. Cotton

Q.4 Yarn of Denim is kept at what position?
A. Third from the top
B. Fourth from the bottom
C. Third from the bottom
D. Second from the bottom
E. Fourth from the top

Q.5 How many yarns are kept between yarn of velvet and wool?
A. 0   **B.** 3   **C.** 2   **D.** 1
E. 6

Ques (6-10):Direction: Study the following information carefully and answer the question given below.

Eight boxes A, B, C, D, E, F, G and H are placed one above another but not necessarily in the same order. Each box has a number written on it from 1 to 8 but not necessarily in that order. The boxes are arranged in ascending order such that the lowest numbered box is at the top and the highest numbered one at the bottom.

C is placed just above G. G is the bottom most box. There are four boxes placed between D and G. Two boxes are placed between B and G. Number of boxes between A and G is same as between H and B. H is placed above B. Two boxes are placed between F and D. There are at least 2 boxes between E and B.

Q.6 Which box is the topmost?
A. A   **B.** H   **C.** E   **D.** B
E. F

Q.7 How many boxes are placed between E and F?
A. 1   **B.** 2   **C.** 3   **D.** 4
E. 5

Q.8 Which box is placed between H and D?
A. A   **B.** E   **C.** C   **D.** B
E. F

Q.9 Which box is placed immediately above A?
A. D   **B.** E   **C.** C   **D.** B
E. F

Q.10 Which box is placed immediately below F?
A. D   **B.** E   **C.** C   **D.** B
E. G

Ques (11-15):Direction: Study the following information carefully and answer the question given below.

Eight different boxes are kept one above the other, but not necessarily kept in the same order. Each box contains different books History, Geography, Physics, Chemistry, Botany, Zoology, Mathematics, and Computer. The boxes are numbered as 1 to 8. The bottom-most box is numbered as 1 and the box above 1 is numbered as 2 and so on and the topmost box is numbered as 8. Mathematics is kept in the topmost box. Only three boxes are kept below Geography. Physics is kept immediately above History and immediately below Computer. Only two boxes are kept between Geography and History. Botany is kept above Zoology and kept below Chemistry.

Q.11 What is the box number in which Zoology is kept?
A. 7th   **B.** 6th   **C.** 5th   **D.** 3rd
E. 4th

Q.12 Four among the five are the same in a certain way which among the following does not belong to that group?
A. Computer   **B.** Chemistry
C. History   **D.** Physics
E. Zoology

Q.13 The number of boxes above the box on which Botany is kept is the same as the number of boxes below the box on which __________ is kept.

A. physics   **B.** geography
C. zoology   **D.** computer
E. history

Q.14 How many boxes are there between the box on which Chemistry is kept and the box on which Geography is kept?

A. Two   **B.** Three   **C.** Four   **D.** Five
E. None

Q.15 Which of the following book is kept at the bottommost box?

A. Botany   **B.** History
C. Physics   **D.** Zoology
E. Computer

Ques (16-20):Direction: Study the following information carefully and answer the question given below.

In a store seven boxes of different names are kept. They are: P, Q, R, S, T, U and V. Each box has a number written on it from 1 to 7 but not necessarily in the same order. The boxes are arranged in a stack in ascending order with the lowest number on the top.

Box Q is immediately above the box T. T is place on an odd number. Two boxes are kept between Q and S. Not more than one box is placed between S and P, in which S is placed above P. Two boxes are kept between T and R. The box V is placed immediately below box T but not immediately above the box U.

Q.16 Which of the following condition is true?

A. R - 8th   **B.** U - 1st
C. V - 6th   **D.** P - 3rd
E. None of these

Q.17 How many boxes are there between box Q and R?

A. 2   **B.** 5
C. 4   **D.** 3
E. None of these

Q.18 Which box is at the bottom?

A. P   **B.** S
C. U   **D.** T
E. None of these

Q.19 Box V is which number box?

A. 3rd   **B.** 6th
C. 4th   **D.** 5th
E. None of these

Q.20 Which box is kept between box S and P?

A. V   **B.** R
C. Q   **D.** T
E. None of these

Ques (21-25):Direction: Study the following information carefully and answer the question given below.

Eight chocolate boxes namely Fivestar, Dairy Milk, KitKat, Snicker, Twix, Bournville, Cadbury and Candy are placed one above the other but not necessarily in the same order. Three chocolate boxes are placed between Dairy Milk and Snicker. Two boxes are placed between Twix and Dairy Milk. Twix is placed below Dairy Milk. Four boxes are placed between Twix and Cadbury. The number of boxes above Cadbury is the same as the number of boxes below Candy. Bournville is placed above Kitkat but below Fivestar. Bournville is not placed just above KitKat.

Q.21 Which of the following chocolate box is placed between Bournville and Fivestar?

A. Cadbury   **B.** Dairy Milk
C. Candy   **D.** KitKat
E. Twix

Q.22 Which of the following box is placed at the top?

A. Fivestar   **B.** Cadbury   **C.** KitKat   **D.** Twix
E. Snicker

Q.23 How many boxes are placed between Twix and Snicker?

A. None   **B.** Two
C. Three   **D.** Four
E. More than four

Q.24 Which of the following box is placed immediately below the box of Candy?

A. KitKat   **B.** Dairy Milk
C. Bournville   **D.** Snicker
E. None of these

Q.25 How many boxes are placed above Cadbury?

A. None   **B.** One   **C.** Two   **D.** Three
E. Four

Ques (26-30):Direction: Study the following information carefully and answer the question given below.

Eight boxes are kept one above another to make up a stack. The topmost box is numbered as 8 while the bottommost box is numbered as 1. Each box is filled with different colours: Blue, Yellow, Black, Pink, Green, Red and Purple, But not necessarily in the same order. One of the boxes in the arrangement is empty.

Green colour box is immediately above Red colour box. Red colour box is an even number box below box number 5. Three boxes are kept between Red colour box and Yellow colour box. Two boxes are kept between Pink colour box and Purple colour box. Purple Coloured box is not kept at the top. Blue colour box is immediately below Pink colour box. One of the boxes above box number 5 is empty. Black colour box is an odd number box.

Q.26 Which of the following condition is true?

A. Red - 2nd   **B.** Yellow - 8th
C. Black - 4th   **D.** Purple - 5th
E. None of these

Q.27 How many boxes are there between Yellow colour box and Pink colour box?

A. 6   **B.** 3
C. 5   **D.** 4
E. None of these

Q.28 Which colour box is at the bottom?

A. Black   **B.** Red
C. Blue   **D.** Pink
E. None of these

Q.29 Which colour is filled in box number 5?

A. Purple   B. Pink
C. Green   D. Blue
E. None of these

Q.30 Which number box is empty?

A. 8   B. 7
C. 6   D. 5
E. None of these

// Smart Answer Sheet //

| Correct | Indicates percentage of students who answered questions correctly. |
| Skipped | Indicates percentage of students who skipped questions. |

Q.	Ans.	Correct / Skipped
1	B	11.45 % / 88.5 %
2	B	57.87 % / 39.02 %
3	B	86.95 % / 11.48 %
4	E	49.7 % / 30.98 %
5	C	64.93 % / 33.32 %
6	B	83.18 % / 13.56 %

Q.	Ans.	Correct / Skipped
7	C	43.68 % / 51.73 %
8	B	64.78 % / 33.63 %
9	A	46.59 % / 44.0 %
10	C	51.42 % / 44.77 %
11	C	28.36 % / 68.93 %
12	D	46.99 % / 45.03 %

Q.	Ans.	Correct / Skipped
13	D	57.21 % / 38.29 %
14	A	51.05 % / 34.89 %
15	B	83.51 % / 10.26 %
16	B	54.91 % / 40.09 %
17	D	67.65 % / 30.81 %
18	A	85.75 % / 11.75 %

Q.	Ans.	Correct / Skipped
19	C	53.12 % / 35.36 %
20	B	64.17 % / 34.37 %
21	A	16.62 % / 71.76 %
22	E	40.36 % / 49.84 %
23	E	51.46 % / 30.66 %
24	A	52.72 % / 38.05 %

Q.	Ans.	Correct / Skipped
25	C	48.07 % / 48.67 %
26	B	45.6 % / 30.02 %
27	D	62.71 % / 36.53 %
28	A	84.92 % / 14.93 %
29	C	86.74 % / 13.16 %
30	B	85.51 % / 10.38 %

Performance Analysis	
Avg. Score (%)	60.0%
Toppers Score (%)	60.0%
Your Score	

//Hints and Solutions//

Ques (1-5): Yarn of Fabrics: Cotton, Wool, Silk, Leather, Rayon, Satin, Velvet and Denim

1) Yarn of Rayon is kept second from the top. The number of yarns above Rayon is the same as the number of yarns below Leather. Thus, the number of yarns below Leather yarn is one.

Therefore, Yarn of Leather is placed at the second position.

Number	Fabric Yarn
8	
7	Rayon
6	
5	
4	
3	
2	Leather
1	

2) Three yarns are placed between Leather yarn and Satin yarn.

Number	Fabric Yarn
8	
7	Rayon
6	Satin
5	
4	
3	
2	Leather
1	

3) Silk Yarn is not kept below Satin yarn or Rayon yarn. Thus, it is kept at the top.

Number	Fabric Yarn
8	Silk
7	Rayon
6	Satin
5	
4	
3	
2	Leather
1	

4) Yarn of Cotton is not kept at the bottom. Yarn of Wool is kept above Cotton yarn but below Denim yarn. Thus, Yarn of Velvet will be placed at the bottom.
The final arrangement will be:

Number	Fabric Yarn
8	Silk
7	Rayon
6	Satin
5	Denim
4	Wool
3	Cotton
2	Leather
1	Velvet

1. The new arrangement will be as follows:

Number	Fabric Yarn
8	Silk
7	Rayon
6	Cotton
5	Denim
4	Wool
3	Satin
2	Leather
1	Velvet

So, If Yarn of Satin is exchanged with the Yarn of Cotton, then 'One' yarn will be placed between Yarn of Cotton and Yarn of Wool.

Hence, the correct option is (B).

2. I. Yarn of Silk is kept below Yarn of Denim → False (Yarn of Silk is kept at the top)

II. Yarn of Leather is kept immediately above Yarn of Velvet → True

III. There are three Yarns between Yarn of Rayon and Yarn of Cotton → True

Hence, the correct option is (B).

3. So, Yarn of 'Velvet' is kept at the bottom.

Hence, the correct option is (B).

4. So, Yarn of Denim is kept fourth from the top.

Hence, the correct option is (E).

5. So, there are two yarns between yarn of velvet and wool.

Hence, the correct option is (C).

Ques (6-10):8 boxes: A, B, C, D, E, F, G, and H

1) C is placed just above G. G is the bottommost box. There are four boxes placed between D and G.

Number	Box
1	
2	
3	D
4	
5	
6	
7	C
8	G

2) Two boxes are placed between B and G. Number of boxes between A and G is same as between H and B. H is placed above B.

Number	Box
1	H
2	
3	D
4	A
5	B
6	

7	C
8	G

3) Two boxes are placed between F and D. There are at least 2 boxes between E and B.

Number	Box
1	H
2	E
3	D
4	A
5	B
6	F
7	C
8	G

6. So, Box H is the topmost.

Hence, the correct option is (B).

7. So, 3 boxes are placed between E and F.

Hence, the correct option is (C).

8. So, box E is placed between H and D.

Hence, the correct option is (B).

9. So, box D is placed immediately above A.

Hence, the correct option is (A).

10. So, box C is placed immediately below F.

Hence, the correct option is (C).

Ques (11-15): Eight boxes: 1 to 8

Eight books: History, Geography, Physics, Chemistry, Botany, Zoology, Mathematics, and Computer

1) Mathematics is kept in the topmost box.

2) Only three boxes are kept below Geography.

Case 1	
Box	Items
8	Mathematics
7	
6	
5	
4	Geography
3	
2	
1	

3) Physics is kept immediately above History and immediately below Computer.

Case 1	
Box	Items
8	Mathematics
7	
6	
5	
4	Geography

3	Computer
2	Physics
1	History

Case 2	
Box	Items
8	Mathematics
7	Computer
6	Physics
5	History
4	Geography
3	
2	
1	

4) Only two boxes are kept between Geography and History. (This eliminates Case 2)

5) Botany is kept above Zoology and kept below Chemistry.

Case 1	
Box	Items
8	Mathematics
7	Chemistry
6	Botany
5	Zoology
4	Geography
3	Computer
2	Physics
1	History

11. So, Zoology is kept in box number 5.

Hence, the correct option is (C).

12. All the boxes are kept in the odd number box except Physics, while Physics is kept in the even number box.

So, 'Physics' does not belong to that group.

Hence, the correct option is (D).

13. The number of boxes above the box on which Botany is kept is 2 and the same as the number of boxes below the box on which Computer is kept is also 2.

Hence, the correct option is (D).

14. So, 'two' boxes are there between the box on which Chemistry is kept and the box on which Geography is kept.

Hence, the correct option is (A).

15. So, History is kept at the bottommost box.

Hence, the correct option is (B).

Ques (16-20): Boxes: 1 to 7 in ascending order

Boxes names: P, Q, R, S, T, U and V

1) Box Q is immediately above the box T.

2) T is place on an odd number.

3) Two boxes are kept between Q and S.

Box	Case 1	Case 2	Case 3	Case 4
1			S	
2	Q			
3	T			S
4		Q	Q	
5	S	T	T	
6				Q
7		S		T

4) Not more than one box is placed between S and P, in which S is placed above P.

Box	Case 1	Case 2	Case 3	Case 4	Case 5
1			S		P
2	Q				
3	T		P	S	S
4		Q	Q		
5	S	T	T	P	
6				Q	Q
7	P	S		T	T

As case 2 and 5 does not fulfil the above condition, it is thus eliminated.
5) Two boxes are kept between T and R.
6) The box V is placed immediately below box T but not immediately above the box U.

Box	Case 1	Case 3	Case 4
1	U	S	
2	Q	R	
3	T	P	S
4	V	Q	R
5	S	T	P
6	R	V	Q
7	P	U	T

As case 3 and 4 does not fulfil the above condition, it is thus eliminated.
The final arrangement will be:

Box	Names
1	U
2	Q
3	T
4	V
5	S
6	R
7	P

16. As U is the 1st number box.

So, the condition U - 1st is true and the other conditions are false.

Hence, the correct option is (B).

17. So, 3 boxes are there between box Q and R.

Hence, the correct option is (D).

18. So, box P is at the bottom.

Hence, the correct option is (A).

19. So, box V is 4th number box.

Hence, the correct option is (C).

20. So, Box R is kept between box S and Box P.

Hence, the correct option is (B).

Ques (21-25): Eight chocolate boxes namely Fivestar, Dairy Milk, KitKat, Snicker, Twix, Bournville, Cadbury and Candy.

1) Three chocolate boxes are placed between Dairy Milk and Snicker.

2) Two boxes are placed between Twix and Dairy Milk.

3) Twix is placed below Dairy Milk.

Case 1	Case 2
Snicker	Dairy Milk
	Twix
Dairy Milk	Snicker
Twix	

4) Four boxes are placed between Twix and Cadbury.5) The number of boxes above Cadbury is the same as the number of boxes below Candy.

Case 1	Case 2
Snicker	Cadbury
Cadbury	Dairy Milk
Dairy Milk	
Candy	Twix
	Snicker
Twix	Candy

6)Bournville is placed above Kitkat but below Fivestar.7) Bournville is not placed just above KitKat. (This eliminates case 2)

Case 1	Case 2
Snicker	Cadbury
Fivestar	Fivestar
Cadbury	Dairy Milk
Bournville	Bournville
Dairy Milk	Kitkat
Candy	Twix
Kitkat	Snicker
Twix	Candy

Final arrangement:

Case 1
Snicker
Fivestar
Cadbury

Bournville
Dairy Milk
Candy
Kitkat
Twix

21. Therefore, Cadbury is placed between Bournville and Fivestar.

Hence, the correct option is (A).

22. Therefore, Snicker is placed at the top.

Hence, the correct option is (E).

23. Six boxes are placed between Twix and Snicker.

Therefore, more than four boxes are placed between Twix and Snicker.

Hence, the correct option is (E).

24. Therefore, Kitkat is placed just below the Candy.

Hence, the correct option is (A).

25. Therefore, 'two' boxes are placed above Cadbury.

Hence, the correct option is (C).

Ques (26-30): Boxes: 1 to 8 in descending order

Colours: Blue, Yellow, Black, Pink, Green, Red and Purple

1) Green colour box is above Red colour box.

2) Red colour box is an even number box below box number 5.

3) Three boxes are kept between Red colour box and Yellow colour box.

Box	Case 1	Case 2
8	Yellow	
7		
6		Yellow
5	Green	
4	Red	
3		Green
2		Red
1		

4) Two boxes are kept between Pink colour box and Purple colour box.

5) Blue colour box is immediately below Pink colour box.

Box	Case 1	Case 2
8	Yellow	Pink
7		Blue
6	Purple	Yellow
5	Green	Purple
4	Red	
3	Pink	Green
2	Blue	Red
1		

6) One of the boxes above box number 5 is empty.

7) Black colour box is an odd number box.

Box	Case 1	Case 2

8	Yellow	Pink
7		Blue
6	Purple	Yellow
5	Green	Purple
4	Red	
3	Pink	Green
2	Blue	Red
1	Black	Black

As case 2 does not fulfil the above condition, it is thus eliminated. The final arrangement will be:

Box	Colour
8	Yellow
7	
6	Purple
5	Green
4	Red
3	Pink
2	Blue
1	Black

26. As Yellow colour is filled in 8th number box.

So, the condition Yellow - 8th is true and the other conditions are false.

Hence, the correct option is (B).

27. So, 4 boxes are there between Yellow colour box and Pink colour box.

Hence, the correct option is (D).

28. So, Black colour box is at the bottom.

Hence, the correct option is (A).

29. So, Green colour is filled in box number 5.

Hence, the correct option is (C).

30. So, 7 number box is an empty box.

Hence, the correct option is (B).

Ques (1-5):Direction: Read the following information carefully and answer the questions given below:

10 different people – P, Q, R, S, T, U, V, W, X and Y live in a 12-floor building. Each person lives on a different floor but not necessarily in the same order. Two floors are vacant. Each floor is numbered as 1 to 12 from bottom to top respectively. Each of them likes different movies – Hum, Raaz, Krish, Airlift, Baby, Baahubali, Drishyam, PK, Kick and Holiday. The person who likes Baahubali lives on one of the floors which is below the 4th floor. Number of floors between T and the person who likes Baahubali is same as the number of floors below the person who likes Baahubali. One of the five floors is vacant which are between the T's floor and the floor of the person who likes PK. P lives two floors above the person who likes PK. The person who likes Baby lives on a perfect square numbered floor. W lives eight floors below the person who likes Airlift. W doesn't live immediately below the person who likes Baby. The person who likes Airlift doesn't live on the 12th floor. There are four floors between the X's floor and the floor of the person who likes Airlift. Y lives seven floors above the floor of Q. Q doesn't like Baahubali. The person who likes Hum lives immediately below Y's floor. R lives on an even numbered floor. The person who likes Drishyam lives immediately below R's floor. There is only one floor between S's floor and the floor of the person who likes Drishyam. U lives three floors above the floor of the person who likes Kick. The person who likes Raaz lives below the floor of the person who likes Holiday but not immediate. W doesn't like Krish.

Q.1 Who among the following likes Baahubali?

A. Q

B. U

C. V

D. W

E. The person who lives immediately below W

Q.2 Which of the following two floors are vacant?

A. 1st and 7th   **B.** 1st and 5th

C. 5th and 12th   **D.** 5th and 11th

E. 6th and 12th

Q.3 Who lives on the 9th floor?

A. The person who lives immediately below the floor of the person who likes Hum

B. The person who lives immediately below the floor of the person who likes PK

C. The person who lives immediately above the floor of the person who likes Baby

D. The person who likes PK

E. The person who likes Airlift

Q.4 Which movie does Q like?

A. Krish   **B.** Kick

C. Holiday   **D.** Raaz

E. Drishyam

Q.5 Which of the following combination is not correct?

A. 2nd floor – T – Krish

B. 4th floor – W – Raaz

C. 8th floor – R – PK

D. 10th floor – P – Hum

E. 11th floor – Y - Airlift

Ques (6-10):Direction: Read the following information carefully and answer the questions given below:

In a six floor building the ground floor is numbered one, the floor above it is numbered two and so on such that the topmost floor is numbered six. One out of six people viz. Aditi, Reema, Mayank, Trisha, David and Gaurav lives on each floor. No one lives between Mayank and Gaurav. There are two floors between the floors on which Aditi and Trisha live. Aditi lives on floor above the floor on which Trisha lives. David lives on odd numbered floor. Trisha does not live on ground floor. Reema does not live on a floor immediately above or below Trisha's floor.

Q.6 Who lives on the floor immediately above on which David lives?

A. Aditi   **B.** Trisha

C. Mayank   **D.** Gaurav

E. None of these

Q.7 How many people live between the floors on which Aditi and Reema lives?

A. Four   **B.** Three   **C.** One   **D.** Two

E. None

Q.8 Which of the following is true with respect to the given information?

A. Trisha lives on ground floor.

B. Reema lives immediately above the floor on which Aditi lives.

C. Aditi lives on the topmost floor.

D. Two people live between Mayank and Gaurav.

E. None of these

Q.9 Who among the following lives on floor number 3?

A. Either Mayank or Gaurav

B. Mayank

C. David

D. Gaurav

E. Can't determine

Q.10 Which pair of persons lives on an odd numbered floor?

A. Reema, Gaurav   **B.** Mayank, Reema

C. David, Trisha   **D.** Aditi, David

E. None of the above

Ques (11-15):Direction: Read the following information carefully and answer the questions given below:

There are eight persons Ahmed, Sameer, Parvez, Nargis, Nadeem, Shairazi, Usman and Meena live on four different floors among floor 1, floor 2, floor 3, and floor 4. Each floor has two different flats flat 1 and flat 2 from left to right in such a way that flat 1 of the fourth floor is exactly above flat 1 of the third floor and flat 1 of the third floor is exactly above the flat 1 of the second floor and others are situated in the same way.

Sameer lives one floor above on which Parvez lives. Shirazi lives with Parvez who lives two floors below Nargis. Parvez lives on second floor. Nadeem lives in flat 2 of first floor. Usman lives on third floor but not in flat 1. Meena does not live on the fourth floor but lives in flat 1. Parvez lives in even numbered flat. Ahmed and Sameer live in flat 1 but on different floors.

Q.11 Who live on the fourth floor of flat 2?

A. Meena   **B.** Sameer   **C.** Ahmad   **D.** Nadeem
E. Nargis

Q.12 Which of the following given pair is different from other?

A.   Meena and Sameer
B.   Usman and Nadeem
C.   Sameer and Shairazi
D.   Ahmed and Shairazi
E.   Parvez and Nargis

Q.13 Who live on the same floors?

A. Meena and Usman   **B.** Shairazi and Parvez
C. Sameer and Parvez   **D.** Nadeem and Nargis
E. None of these

Q.14 Who lives two floors below the floor on which Usman lives in the same flat number?

A. Ahmed   **B.** Shairazi
C. Sameer   **D.** Nadeem
E. None of these

Q.15 Who live in the flat 1 of floor 2?

A. Parvez   **B.** Sameer   **C.** Shairazi   **D.** Ahmed
E. Usman

Ques (16-20):Direction: Read the following information carefully and answer the questions given below:

Seven friends A, B, C, D, E, F, and G live on the separate floors of a building but not necessarily in the same order. The ground floor is numbered 1, the first floor is numbered 2, and so on until the topmost floor which is numbered 7. Only two people live above A. The same number of people live above the floor on which C lives as below the floor on which D lives. Not more than one person lives between A and C. F lives three floors above E. F does not live on the topmost floor. B does not live immediately above either C or D.

Q.16 Who lives immediately above G?

A. F   **B.** E   **C.** A   **D.** C
E. None

Q.17 On which of the following floors does E live?

A. 3rd   **B.** 5th   **C.** 2nd   **D.** 4th
E. 6th

Q.18 Who amongst the following lives on the floor between the floors on which C and B live?

A. A   **B.** G
C. F   **D.** Both (A) and (C)
E. Both (A) and (B)

Q.19 If all the persons live in alphabetical order starting from bottom to top, then the position of how many persons will remain unchanged?

A. Two   **B.** Four   **C.** Three   **D.** One
E. None

Q.20 Who among the following lives three floors below A?

A. C   **B.** D   **C.** G   **D.** E
E. B

Ques (21-25):Direction: Read the following information carefully and answer the questions given below:

Eight friends Suruchi, Surbhi, Suman, Sachita, Sakshi, Sangeeta, Sabita and Shristi live in an eight-floor building. Each of them likes a different flavor ice-creams strawberry, vanilla, chocolate almond, butterscotch, vanilla almond, chocolate mint, banana and chocolate, but not necessarily in the same order. The lowermost floor is numbered 1 and the topmost floor is numbered 8.

Surbhi lives above Suman. Sakshi lives on an odd number floor but not at the bottom. More than 3 person lives between Sakshi and one who likes vanilla almond. Sachita likes butterscotch. Suruchi who likes chocolate mint lives above Sakshi on an even number floor. 3 person lives between Suruchi and one who likes vanilla. 2 person lives between person liking chocolate mint and chocolate almond. Sabita likes bananas. Person liking vanilla and banana lives on the adjacent floor. Sachita lives above the floor where the person liking vanilla lives. Shristi likes chocolate and lives below Suruchi but not immediately below. Sachita does not lives adjacent to Shristi, neither sits on the topmost floor. Suman neither likes vanilla nor vanilla almonds. Only 2 person lives between Sangeeta and the one who likes strawberry. Surbhi lives above person liking chocolate.

Q.21 Choose the odd one out.

A. Surbhi   **B.** Suman   **C.** Sangeeta   **D.** Sachita
E. Shristi

Q.22 Which of the following statement is correct?

A.   Sachita likes chocolate.
B.   Sangeeta lives on floor 4.
C.   The one who likes strawberry lives below Suruchi.
D.   The persons liking chocolate and vanilla lives adjacent to each other.
E.   Suman likes banana.

Q.23 What is the floor number of Sangeeta?

A. 5   **B.** 4   **C.** 7   **D.** 3
E. 2

Q.24 Who likes chocolate almond?

A. Sachita   **B.** Shristi   **C.** Suman   **D.** Suruchi
E. Sakshi

Q.25 Who lives on floor 4?

A. Suman　　**B.** Surbhi　　**C.** Sabita　　**D.** Shristi
E. Sangeeta

Ques (26-30):Direction: Read the following information carefully and answer the questions given below:

A certain number of persons are living in a building having six Floors. Each Floor has two Flats such as Flat 2 is in the east of Flat 1. The ground Floor is numbered Floor 1 and the top Floor is Floor 6. Flat 1 of Floor 2 is just above Flat 1 of Floor 1 and just below Flat 1 of Floor 3 and so on. Only the persons who are mentioned below are considered to be living in the building. On each Floor maximum of 3 people resides.

There are 5 Flats gap between the Flats in which E and U live. U and F live in an adjacent Flat. Two people live between M and P. There is a 2-Floor gap where T and D live and both live on the same Flat number. E and O are not neighbors. No one lives above the Floor where D lives. K lives in a Flat which is west of D's Flat on the same Floor. C lives on a Floor above R but below Q on the same Flat number. R does not live on the ground Floor. B does not share his Flat with anyone. S lives in Flat number 2 just above B who lives on an even number Floor. F lives on an odd-numbered Floor and Flat alone in his Flat. There is 2 Flats gap between R and M. O lives on an odd-numbered Floor. L and X share his Flat but do not live on Floor number 2. E and K are neighbors.

Q.26 Where does Q live?

A. Flat 2, Floor 5　　　　**B.** Flat 1, Floor 3
C. Flat 1, Floor 2　　　　**D.** Flat 1, Floor 5
E. Flat 2, Floor 4

Q.27 How many people live between Q and R?

A. 5　　　　**B.** 6　　　　**C.** 7　　　　**D.** 4
E. 8

Q.28 Choose the odd one.

A. T, P, M　　**B.** S, B, T　　**C.** K, Q, C　　**D.** C, F, L
E. D, O, B

Q.29 Who live on Floor just above U?

A. Both C and B　　　　**B.** C
C. B　　　　　　　　　**D.** Q
E. Both B and Q

Q.30 Total how many person lives in the building?

A. 15　　　　**B.** 18　　　　**C.** 16　　　　**D.** 27
E. 19

// Smart Answer Sheet //

Correct — Indicates percentage of students who answered questions correctly.

Skipped — Indicates percentage of students who skipped questions.

Q.	Ans.	Correct / Skipped
1	C	24.94 % / 71.83 %
2	C	57.33 % / 37.47 %
3	A	15.6 % / 68.41 %
4	B	67.02 % / 30.91 %
5	B	83.05 % / 10.54 %
6	B	21.85 % / 75.0 %

Q.	Ans.	Correct / Skipped
7	E	31.94 % / 67.49 %
8	B	41.42 % / 47.95 %
9	A	82.0 % / 10.63 %
10	D	57.47 % / 30.27 %
11	E	21.81 % / 77.55 %
12	C	28.71 % / 68.59 %

Q.	Ans.	Correct / Skipped
13	B	64.28 % / 34.05 %
14	D	81.14 % / 14.47 %
15	C	44.68 % / 47.97 %
16	B	13.01 % / 77.57 %
17	A	62.03 % / 31.45 %
18	D	44.65 % / 38.89 %

Q.	Ans.	Correct / Skipped
19	D	82.1 % / 15.88 %
20	C	65.9 % / 31.56 %
21	A	47.23 % / 31.02 %
22	C	79.4 % / 18.99 %
23	E	44.81 % / 38.1 %
24	E	55.85 % / 43.76 %

Q.	Ans.	Correct / Skipped
25	D	56.08 % / 37.97 %
26	D	69.2 % / 30.49 %
27	C	24.38 % / 70.03 %
28	D	30.12 % / 69.37 %
29	A	40.53 % / 41.95 %
30	C	65.69 % / 33.65 %

Performance Analysis

Avg. Score (%)	46.67%
Toppers Score (%)	56.67%
Your Score	

//Hints and Solutions//

Ques (1-5):10 people: P, Q, R, S, T, U, V, W, X and Y

10 movies: Hum, Raaz, Krish, Airlift, Baby, Baahubali, Drishyam, PK, Kick and Holiday

Floors: 1 to 12

(1) The person who likes Baahubali lives on one of the floors which is below the 4th floor.

Possible options are 1st, 2nd and 3rd floor.

(2) Number of floors between T and the person who likes Baahubali is same as the number of floors below the person who likes Baahubali.

Possible options are 2, 1, 0 (means there is no floor between them).

(3) One of the five floors is vacant which are between the T's floor and the floor of the person who likes PK.

Case 1:

Floor (from top to bottom)	People	Movie
12		PK
11		
10		
9		
8		
7		
6	T	
5		
4		
3		Baahubali
2		
1		

Case 2:

Floor (from top to bottom)	People	Movie
12		
11		
10		PK
9		
8		
7		
6		
5		
4	T	
3		
2		Baahubali
1		

Case 3:

Floor (from top to bottom)	People	Movie
12		
11		
10		
9		
8		PK
7		
6		
5		
4		
3		
2	T	
1		Baahubali

(4) P lives two floors above the person who likes PK.

Thus, case 1 gets eliminated.

Case 2:

Floor (from top to bottom)	People	Movie
12	P	
11		
10		PK
9		
8		
7		
6		
5		
4	T	
3		
2		Baahubali
1		

Case 3:

Floor (from top to bottom)	People	Movie
12		
11		
10	P	
9		
8		PK
7		
6		
5		
4		
3		
2	T	
1		Baahubali

(5) The person who likes Baby lives on a perfect square numbered floor.

Possible options are 4th and 9th floor.

Case 2(a):

Floor (from top to bottom)	People	Movie
12	P	
11		
10		PK
9		Baby
8		
7		

Floor (from top to bottom)	People	Movie
6		
5		
4	T	
3		
2		Baahubali
1		

Case 2(b):

Floor (from top to bottom)	People	Movie
12	P	
11		
10		PK
9		
8		
7		
6		
5		
4	T	Baby
3		
2		Baahubali
1		

Case 3(a):

Floor (from top to bottom)	People	Movie
12		
11		
10	P	
9		Baby
8		PK
7		
6		
5		
4		
3		
2	T	
1		Baahubali

Case 3(b):

Floor (from top to bottom)	People	Movie
12		
11		
10	P	
9		
8		PK
7		
6		
5		
4		Baby
3		
2	T	
1		Baahubali

(6) W lives eight floors below the person who likes Airlift.

(7) W doesn't live immediately below the person who likes Baby.

(8) The person who likes Airlift doesn't live on the 12th floor.

Case 2(a):

Floor (from top to bottom)	People	Movie
12	P	
11		Airlift
10		PK
9		Baby
8		
7		
6		
5		
4	T	
3	W	
2		Baahubali
1		

Case 2(b):

Floor (from top to bottom)	People	Movie
12	P	
11		
10		PK
9		Airlift
8		
7		
6		
5		
4	T	Baby
3		
2		Baahubali
1	W	

Case 3(a):

Floor (from top to bottom)	People	Movie
12		
11		Airlift
10	P	
9		Baby
8		PK
7		
6		
5		
4		
3	W	
2	T	
1		Baahubali

Case 3(b):

Floor (from top to bottom)	People	Movie
12		
11		
10	P	
9		Airlift
8		PK
7		
6		

Floor	People	Movie
5		
4		Baby
3		
2	T	
1	W	Baahubali

(9) There are four floors between the X's floor and the floor of the person who likes Airlift.

Thus, case 2(b) gets eliminated.

Case 2(a):

Floor (from top to bottom)	People	Movie
12	P	
11		Airlift
10		PK
9		Baby
8		
7		
6	X	
5		
4	T	
3	W	
2		Baahubali
1		

Case 3(a):

Floor (from top to bottom)	People	Movie
12		
11		Airlift
10	P	
9		Baby
8		PK
7		
6	X	
5		
4		
3	W	
2	T	
1		Baahubali

Case 3(b):

Floor (from top to bottom)	People	Movie
12		
11		
10	P	
9		Airlift
8		PK
7		
6		
5		
4	X	Baby
3		
2	T	
1	W	Baahubali

(10) Y lives seven floors above the floor of Q.

(11) Q doesn't like Baahubali.

(12) The person who likes Hum lives immediately below Y's floor.

Case 2(a):

Floor (from top to bottom)	People	Movie
12	P	
11		Airlift
10		PK
9		Baby
8	Y	
7		Hum
6	X	
5		
4	T	
3	W	
2		Baahubali
1	Q	

Case 3(a):

Floor (from top to bottom)	People	Movie
12		
11	Y	Airlift
10	P	Hum
9		Baby
8		PK
7		
6	X	
5		
4	Q	
3	W	
2	T	
1		Baahubali

Case 3(b):

Floor (from top to bottom)	People	Movie
12	Y	
11		Hum
10	P	
9		Airlift
8		PK
7		
6		
5	Q	
4	X	Baby
3		
2	T	
1	W	Baahubali

In case 2(a), we have only one vacant floor which is wrong so this case will be eliminated.

In case 3(b), we will have two vacant floors between T's floor and the floor of the person who likes PK which is also wrong as per point no. 3, so this case will also be eliminated.

Now, we have left only with Case 3(a).

(13) R lives on an even numbered floor.

Possible option for R is 8th and 12th floor.

(14) The person who likes Drishyam lives immediately below R's floor.

So, R lives on 8th floor.

(15) There is only one floor between S's floor and the floor of the person who likes Drishyam.

S can't be on 5th floor as there is one floor vacant as per point no. 3.

So, S lives on 9th floor.

Case 3(a):

Floor (from top to bottom)	People	Movie
12		
11	Y	Airlift
10	P	Hum
9	S	Baby
8	R	PK
7		Drishyam
6	X	
5	Vacant	
4	Q	
3	W	
2	T	
1		Baahubali

So, we get that 12th floor is also vacant.

(16) U lives three floors above the floor of the person who likes Kick.

So, U lives on the 7th floor and V lives on the 1st floor.

(17) The person who likes Raaz lives below the floor of the person who likes Holiday but not immediate.

(18) W doesn't like Krish.

Thus, the final table is as follows:

Floor (from top to bottom)	People	Movie
12	Vacant	
11	Y	Airlift
10	P	Hum
9	S	Baby
8	R	PK
7	U	Drishyam
6	X	Holiday
5	Vacant	
4	Q	Kick
3	W	Raaz
2	T	Krish
1	V	Baahubali

1. Thus, V likes Baahubali.

Hence, the correct option is (C).

2. Thus, 5th and 12th floors are vacant.

Hence, the correct option is (C).

3. Thus, the person who lives immediately below the floor of the person who likes Hum lives on the 9th floor.

Hence, the correct option is (A).

4. Thus, Q likes Kick.

Hence, the correct option is (B).

5. Thus, the combination '4th floor – W – Raaz' is not correct.

Hence, the correct option is (B).

Ques (6-10): Number of floors: 1, 2, 3, 4, 5 and 6

Name of persons: Aditi, Reema, Mayank, Trisha, David and Gaurav

(1) David lives on odd numbered floor, thus we have to consider three cases as Case-1, Case-2 and Case-3.

Floor	Case-1	Case-2	Case-3
6			
5	David		
4			
3		David	
2			
1			David

(2) There are two floors between the floors on which Aditi and Trisha live.

(3) Trisha does not live on ground floor.

(4) Aditi lives on floor above the floor on which Trisha lives.

(5) Reema does not live on a floor immediately above or below Trisha's floor.

Floor	Case-1	Case-2	Case-3
6	Reema	Aditi	Reema
5	David		Aditi
4	Aditi	Trisha	
3		David	
2			Trisha
1	Trisha (x)	Reema	David

(6) Here in Case-1, Trisha lives on ground floor which does not satisfied the given conditions thus Case-1 is eliminated.

(7) No one lives between Mayank and Gaurav.

Floor	Case-2	Case-3
6	Aditi	Reema
5		Aditi
4	Trisha	Mayank/Gaurav
3	David	Gaurav/Mayank
2		Trisha
1	Reema	David

(8) Here, only Case-3 satisfied the given condition in which no one lives between Mayank and Gaurav. Thus, Case-2 will also be eliminated.

(9) So, the final arrangement of floors will be satisfied by Case-3 as shown below:

Floor	Case-3
6	Reema
5	Aditi
4	Mayank/Gaurav
3	Gaurav/Mayank
2	Trisha
1	David

6. Clearly, Trisha lives on the floor immediately above on which David lives.

Hence, the correct option is (B).

7. Clearly, no one live between the floors on which Aditi and Reema lives.

Hence, the correct option is (E).

8. Clearly, Reema lives immediately above the floor on which Aditi lives.

Hence, the correct option is (B).

9. Clearly, either Mayank or Gaurav lives on floor number 3.

Hence, the correct option is (A).

10. Clearly, Aditi lives on floor 5 and David live on floor 1, both lives on an odd numbered floor.

Hence, the correct option is (D).

Ques (11-15): People: Ahmed, Sameer, Parvez, Nargis, Nadeem, Shairazi, Usman and Meena

Floor: 1 to 4, 2 flat each

(1) Parvez lives on second floor.

(2) Sameer lives one floor above on which Parvez lives.

So, there are four cases for that.

Floor	Case - 1		Case - 2		Case - 3		Case - 4	
	Flat 1	Flat 2	Flat 1	Flat 2	Flat 1	Flat 2	Flat 1	Flat 2
4								
3	Sameer			Sameer	Sameer			Sameer
2	Parvez		Parvez			Parvez		Parvez
1								

(3) Shairazi lives with Parvez who lives two floors below Nargis.

(4) Nadeem lives in flat 2 of first floor.

Floor	Case - 1		Case - 2		Case - 3		Case - 4	
	Flat 1	Flat 2	Flat 1	Flat 2	Flat 1	Flat 2	Flat 1	Flat 2
4								
3	Sameer			Sameer	Sameer			Sameer
2	Parvez	Shairazi	Parvez	Shairazi	Shairazi	Parvez	Shairazi	Parvez

1		Nadeem		Nadeem		Nadeem		Nadeem

(5) Usman lives on third floor but not in flat 1.

(6) Parvez lives in even numbered flat.

So, case - 1, case - 2 and case - 4 are eliminated.

Floor	Flat 1	Flat 2
4		
3	Sameer	Usman
2	Shairazi	Parvez
1		Nadeem

(7) Meena does not live on the fourth floor but lives in flat 1.

(8) Ahmed and Sameer live in flat 1 but on different floors.

Floor	Flat 1	Flat 2
4	Ahmed	Nargis
3	Sameer	Usman
2	Shairazi	Parvez
1	Meena	Nadeem

11. Thus, Nargis lives on the fourth floor of flat 2.

Hence, the correct option is (E).

12. Only Sameer and Shairazi pair of odd and even floors.

Therefore, Sameer and shairazi is different from others.

Hence, the correct option is (C).

13. Therefore, Shairazi and Parvez lives on same floor.

Hence, the correct option is (B).

14. Therefore, Nadeem lives two floors below the floor on which Usman lives in the same flat number.

Hence, the correct option is (D).

15. Therefore, Shairazi lives in the flat 1 of floor 2.

Hence, the correct option is (C).

Ques (16-20):7 Person: A, B, C, D, E, F, and G

Floor: 7 (Ground floor numbered 1 and Topmost floor numbered 7)

(1) Only two people live above A.

(2) The same number of people lives above the floor on which C lives as below the floor on which D lives.

(3) Not more than one person lives between A and C.

	Case I	Case II
Floor	Person	Person
7	C	
6		C
5	A	A
4		
3		
2		D
1	D	

(4) F lives three floors above E.

(5) F does not live on the topmost floor.

	Case I	Case II
Floor	Person	Person
7	C	
6	F	C
5	A	A
4		F
3	E	
2		D
1	D	E

(6) B does not live immediately above either C or D. Therefore, case II eliminates here.

Thus, the final arrangement is as follows:

	Case I
Floor	Person
7	C
6	F
5	A
4	B
3	E
2	G
1	D

16. Therefore, E lives immediately above G.

Hence, the correct option is (B).

17. Therefore, E lives on the 3rd floor.

Hence, the correct option is (A).

18. We can see that both F and A live on the floor between the floors on which C and B live.

Hence, the correct option is (D).

19. Thus, the position of only F remains unchanged.

Hence, the correct option is (D).

20. Thus, G lives three floors below A.

Hence, the correct option is (C).

Ques (21-25):(1) Sakshi lives on an odd floor but not at the bottom. So, Sakshi has 3 probable floors available i.e., floor 3, 5 and 7.

(2) More than 3 person lives between Sakshi and one who likes vanilla almond i.e., minimum 4 persons must be living between Sakshi and person liking vanilla almond.(3) Floor 5 cannot be assigned to Sakshi because the person liking vanilla almond will not get its position either upward or downward. Now we have 3 cases for arranging Sakshi and person liking vanilla almond.

Case I:

8		vanilla almond
7		
6		
5		
4		
3	Sakshi	
2		
1		

Case II:

8		
7	Sakshi	
6		
5		
4		
3		
2		vanilla almond
1		

Case III:

8		
7	Sakshi	
6		
5		
4		
3		
2		
1		vanilla almond

(4) Suruchi who likes chocolate mint lives above Sakshi on an even floor.(5) 3 person lives between Suruchi and one who likes vanilla.(6) 2 person lives between person liking chocolate mint and chocolate almond.

(7) Person liking vanilla and banana lives on the adjacent floor.
(8) Sabita likes bananas.

Case I:

Suruchi can live on floor 4 or 6. If she lives on number 4 person liking vanilla will not get its place as after 3 places upward person liking vanilla almond is already living and after 3 places downward there is no floor available. So, Suruchi must live on number 6 and person liking vanilla on floor 2.

8		vanilla almond
7		
6	Suruchi	chocolate mint
5		
4		
3	Sakshi	
2		vanilla
1		

Case II:

Suruchi lives on floor 8.

8	Suruchi	chocolate mint
7	Sakshi	
6		
5		
4		vanilla
3		
2		vanilla almond
1		

Case III:

8	Suruchi	chocolate mint

7	Sakshi	
6		
5		
4		vanilla
3		
2		
1		vanilla almond

(9) 2 person lives between person liking chocolate mint and chocolate almond.
(10) Person liking vanilla and banana lives on the adjacent floor.
(11) Sabita likes bananas.
Case I:

8		vanilla almond
7		
6	Suruchi	chocolate mint
5		
4		
3	Sakshi	chocolate almond
2		vanilla
1	Sabita	banana

Case II:

8	Suruchi	chocolate mint
7	Sakshi	
6		
5		chocolate almond
4		vanilla
3	Sabita	banana
2		vanilla almond
1		

Case III:

8	Suruchi	chocolate mint
7	Sakshi	
6		
5		chocolate almond
4		vanilla
3	Sabita	banana
2		
1		vanilla almond

(12) Shristi likes chocolate and lives below Suruchi but not immediately below.
(13) Sachita likes butterscotch.
(14) Sachita does not lives adjacent to Shristi, neither live the topmost floor.
Case I:
Shristi lives on floor 4 and Sachita must live on floor 7 because only floor 7 is vacant for the person having taste different than vanilla almond.

8		vanilla almond
7	Sachita	butterscotch
6	Suruchi	chocolate mint
5		
4	Shristi	chocolate
3	Sakshi	chocolate almond

2		vanilla
1	Sabita	banana

Case II:

8	Suruchi	chocolate mint
7	Sakshi	
6		
5		chocolate almond
4		vanilla
3	Sabita	banana
2		vanilla almond
1		

Case III:

8	Suruchi	chocolate mint
7	Sakshi	
6		
5		chocolate almond
4		vanilla
3	Sabita	banana
2		
1		vanilla almond

(15) Only 2 person lives between Sangeeta and the one who likes strawberry.
(16) Suman neither likes vanilla nor vanilla almonds.
(17) Surbhi lives above Suman.
(18) Surbhi lives above person liking chocolate.
(19) Shristi likes chocolate and lives below Suruchi but not immediately below.
(20) Sachita does not lives adjacent to Shristi, neither lives at the topmost floor.
(21) Sakshi lives on an odd floor but not at the bottom.
Case I:
In this case, we can say person liking strawberry lives on floor 5. Suman does not like vanilla and Surbhi lives above Suman, so, Surbhi lives on floor 8 and Suman on floor 5. Sangeeta lives on floor 2.

8	Surbhi	vanilla almond
7	Sachita	butterscotch
6	Suruchi	chocolate mint
5	Suman	Strawberry
4	Shristi	chocolate
3	Sakshi	chocolate almond
2	Sangeeta	vanilla
1	Sabita	banana

Case II:
Shristi likes chocolate. Surbhi lives above person liking chocolate. Shristi must live on floor 1.
Sachita likes butterscotch.
Only 2 person lives between Sangeeta and the one who likes strawberry.
So, Person liking strawberry must live on floor 7 and Sangeeta on floor 4.
Surbhi lives above Suman.

8	Suruchi	chocolate mint
7	Sakshi	Strawberry

6	Sachita	butterscotch
5	Surbhi	chocolate almond
4	Sangeeta	vanilla
3	Sabita	banana
2	Suman	vanilla almond
1	Shristi	chocolate

Suman neither likes vanilla nor vanilla almonds but here on floor 2 Suman is liking vanilla almond.

Therefore, case II got cancelled.

Case III:

Shristi likes chocolate. Surbhi lives above person liking chocolate. Shristi must live on floor 2.

Sachita likes butterscotch. So, Sachita lives on floor 6.

Only 2 person lives between Sangeeta and the one who likes strawberry.

So, Person liking strawberry must live on floor 7 and Sangeeta on floor 4.

Surbhi lives above Suman. So, Surbhi goes to floor 5 and Suman to floor 1.

8	Suruchi	chocolate mint
7	Sakshi	strawberry
6	Sachita	butterscotch
5	Surbhi	chocolate almond
4	Sangeeta	vanilla
3	Sabita	banana
2	Shristi	chocolate
1	Suman	vanilla almond

Suman neither likes vanilla nor vanilla almonds but here on floor 1 Suman is liking vanilla almond.

Therefore, case III got cancelled.

The final arrangement is:

8	Surbhi	vanilla almond
7	Sachita	butterscotch
6	Suruchi	chocolate mint
5	Suman	Strawberry
4	Shristi	chocolate
3	Sakshi	chocolate almond
2	Sangeeta	vanilla
1	Sabita	banana

21. Therefore, all except Surbhi lives on one of the middle floors.

Hence, the correct option is (A).

22. Therefore, person who likes strawberry lives below Suruchi.

Hence, the correct option is (C).

23. Therefore, Sangeeta lives on floor 2.

Hence, the correct option is (E).

24. Therefore, Sakshi likes chocolate almond.

Hence, the correct option is (E).

25. Therefore, Shristi lives on floor 4.

Hence, the correct option is (D).

Ques (26-30):(1) No one lives above the Floor where D lives. This implies that D lives on Floor 6.

(2) K lives in a Flat which is west of D's Flat on the same Floor. This implies that K lives on Flat 1 of Floor 6 which is the topmost Floor and D lives on Flat 2 on the same Floor.

Note, now only 1 more person can live on Floor 6.

(3) There is a 2-Floor gap where T and D live and both live on the same Flat number. Here T lives on Flat 2 of Floor 3.

(4) E and K are neighbors. So, E must live in Flat 2 on Floor 6.

Now, the arrangement on Floor 6 is complete.

(5) There are 5 Flats gap in between where E and U live. So, U shares his Flat with T in Flat 2 on Floor 3.

(6) F lives on an odd number Floor and Flat alone in his Flat.

(7) U and F live in the adjacent Flat. This implies F lives in Flat 1 on Floor 3.

Now our arrangement on Floor 3 and 6 is complete.

Floors	Flat 1	Flat 2
Floor 6	K	D, E
Floor 5		
Floor 4		
Floor 3	F	T, U
Floor 2		
Floor 1		

(8) C lives on a Floor above R but below Q on the same Flat number. This implies C can live on either Flat of Floor 2 or Floor 4.

(9) R does not live on the ground Floor. So, R lives on Floor 2, C on Floor 4 and Q on Floor 5. Flat of these people not decided yet.

(10) S lives in Flat 2 just above B who lives on an even numbered Floor.

So, the only place for B on an even numbered Floor with one above Floor vacant is Floor 4.

Therefore, B lives in Flat 2 on Floor 4 and S lives in Flat 2 on Floor 5.

(11) B does not share his Flat with anyone.

Since C also lives on Floor 4. Therefore, C lives in Flat 1 of Floor 4. R and Q also live in Flat 1 of their respective Floors 2 and 5.

Floors	Flat 1	Flat 2
Floor 6	K	D, E
Floor 5	Q	S
Floor 4	C	B
Floor 3	F	T, U
Floor 2	R	
Floor 1		

(12) There are 2 Flats gap between R and M.

So, M lives in Flat 2 on Floor 1 as B lives alone in Flat 2 on Floor 4.

(13) L and X share his Flat but do not live on Floor 2. This implies L and X live in Flat 1 on Floor 1.

Since only Floor except Floor 2 which can accommodate 2 people, L and X is Floor 1. As the maximum number of people on one Floor is 3 people.

(14) Two people live between M and P. This implies P live in Flat 2 on Floor 1.

(15) O lives on an odd-numbered Floor.

(16) E and O are not neighbors.

Therefore, O lives in Flat 2 of Floor 5.

Floors	Flat 1	Flat 2
Floor 6	K	D, E
Floor 5	Q	S, O
Floor 4	C	B
Floor 3	F	T, U
Floor 2	R	P
Floor 1	L, X	M

26. Therefore, Q lives in Flat 1 on Floor 5.

Hence, the correct option is (D).

27. Therefore, total 7 people live between Q and R.

Hence, the correct option is (C).

28. So, a total of 16 persons live in the building.

Thus, all except C, F, L live on adjacent Floors.

Hence, the correct option is (D).

29. Therefore, Both C and B lives on Floor just above U.

Hence, the correct option is (A).

30. Therefore, total 16 person lives in the building.

Hence, the correct option is (C).

Ques (1-5):Direction: Read the given information carefully and answer the question given follows:

Ten persons namely Pravin, Rani, Raman, Seetha, Tushar, Umesh, Vinoth, Wahab, Ximon and Yousuf are sitting in two parallel rows containing five people each in such a way that there is an equal distance between adjacent persons. People sitting in Row-1 facing north direction while people sitting in Row-2 facing south direction. Therefore people sitting in Row-1 face the people sitting in Row-2. They were born in the following months among January, March, April, May, June, July and August. Exactly two persons were born in each of the months of April, May and June. All the above information is not necessarily in the same order.

Seetha sits exactly in the middle of the north-facing row. Tushar sits with Ximon and Wahab and opposite Umesh. Pravin sits at the extreme right end of the south-facing row. Only one person sits between the two persons who were born in April. Rani sits opposite Raman and to the immediate right of the person, who was born in May month. Raman doesn't face south direction. Wahab was born in August month. The person who was born in March sits to the immediate right of Yousuf and opposite to the person who is born in April. The person born in January sits to the right of the person born in July but they don't sit at any of the ends. Only one person sits between the two persons who were born in May.

Q.1 Who sits to the immediate right of Umesh?

A.   The One who was born in June

B.   The one who was born in July

C.   The one who was born in March

D.   The one who was born in May

E.   None of the above

Q.2 Which of the following in pairs are born in same month?

A. Yousuf and Vinoth   **B.** Pravin and Rani

C. Raman and Tushar   **D.** Both A and B

E. Both A and C

Q.3 In which month was the person born who sits opposite to Ximon?

A. January   **B.** July

C. May   **D.** June

E. None of these

Q.4 Four of the following five are alike in a certain way and hence form a group. Which of the following does not belong to the group?

A. Raman-March   **B.** Tushar-April

C. Umesh-January   **D.** Vinoth-June

E. Yousuf-July

Q.5 Which of the following statements is definitely true?

A.   Only two persons are sitting between Pravin and Ximon.

B.   The persons were born in June month sitting in different rows.

C.   The one who was born in March sits third to the left of Umesh.

D.   The one who was born in August month and the one who was born in March month are sitting diagonally opposite to each other.

E.   None of the above

Ques (6-10):Direction: Study the following information carefully and answer the question given beside:

Twelve persons A, B, C, D, E, F, U, V, W, X, Y and Z are sitting in two parallel rows. A, B, C, D, E and F are sitting in row-1 facing south direction and U, V, W, X, Y and Z are sitting in row-2 facing north direction in such a way that each person sitting in row-1 faces the person sitting in row-2.

Only one person sits between U and W who is sitting at the extreme left end of the row. B, who is sitting at the extreme left end, sits second to the left of A. C faces the one who is an immediate neighbour of U. V faces D. E, who sits at one of the extreme ends of the row sits third to the right of the one who faces Z. X faces the one who sits second to the left A.

Q.6 Who among the following faces C?

A. W   **B.** X

C. Y   **D.** Z

E. None of these

Q.7 Who among the following faces Z?

A. A   **B.** B

C. E   **D.** F

E. None of these

Q.8 If the names of all the persons sitting in the second row are to be arranged in alphabetical order (starting from the right end of second row) then who among the following will face F?

A. W   **B.** U

C. Y   **D.** X

E. None of these

Q.9 Who among the following sits third to the right of the one, who is facing the one, who is second to the left of E?

A. U   **B.** V

C. X   **D.** Z

E. None of these

Q.10 Who among the following faces the immediate neighbour of W?

A. A   **B.** D

C. F   **D.** C

E. None of these

Ques (11-15):Direction: Study the following information carefully to answer the given question:

Eight persons from different bank viz. UCO bank, Syndicate bank, Canara bank, PNB, Dena Bank, Oriental Bank of

Commerce, Indian bank and Bank of Maharashtra are sitting in two parallel rows containing four people each, in such a way that there is an equal distance between adjacent persons. In row 1: A, B, C and D are seated and all of them are facing south. In row 2: P, Q, R and S are seated and all of them are facing north. Therefore, in the given seating arrangements each member seated in a row faces another member of the other row. (All the information given above does not necessarily represent the order of seating as in the final arrangement).

- C sits second to right of the person from Bank of Maharashtra. R is an immediate neighbor of the person who faces the person from Bank of Maharashtra.

- Only one person sits between R and the person for PNB. Immediate neighbour of the person from PNB faces the person from Canara Bank.

- The person from UCO bank faces the person from Oriental Bank of Commerce. R is not from Oriental Bank of Commerce. P is not from PNB. P does not face the person form Bank of Maharashtra

- Q faces the person from Dena Bank. The one who faces S sits to the immediate left of A.

- B does not sit at any of the extreme ends of the line. The person from Bank of Maharashtra does not face the person from Syndicate Bank.

Q.11 Four of the following five are alike in a certain way based on the given seating arrangement and thus from a group, which is the one that does not belong to that group?

A. Canara bank

B. R

C. Syndicate bank

D. Q

E. Oriental Bank of Commerce

Q.12 P is related to Dena Bank in the same way as B is related to PNB based on the given arrangement. To who amongst the following is D related to following the same pattern?

A. Syndicate bank

B. Canara bank

C. Bank of Maharashtra

D. Indian Bank

E. Oriental Bank of Commerce

Q.13 Who amongst the following sit at extreme ends of the rows?

A. D and the person from PNB

B. The person from Indian bank and UCO bank

C. The person from Dena bank and P

D. The person form Syndicate bank and D

E. C, Q

Q.14 Who is seated between R and the person from PNB?

A. The person from Oriental Bank of Commerce

B. P

C. Q

D. The person from Syndicate bank

E. S

Q.15 Which of the following is true regarding A?

A. The person from UCO bank faces A

B. The person from Bank of Maharashtra is an immediate neighbor of A

C. A faces the Person who sits second to right of R

D. A is from Oriental Bank of Commerce

E. A sits at one of the extreme ends of the line

Ques (16-20):Direction: Study the following information to answer the given question:

Eight people are sitting in two parallel rows containing four people each, in such a way that there is an equal distance between adjacent persons. In row-1, Asha, Bheem, Chelsi and Deep are seated (but not necessarily in the same order) and all of them are facing South. In row-2, Preet, Qureshi, Raunit and Sana are seated (but not necessarily in the same order) and all of them are facing North. Therefore, in the given seating arrangement each member seated in a row faces another member of the other row. Raunit sits second to left of the person who faces Asha. Sana is an immediate neighbour of Raunit. Only one person sits between Asha and Deep. One of the immediate neighbours of Chelsi faces Qureshi. Bheem does not sit at any of the extreme ends of the line.

Q.16 Who amongst the following faces Bheem?

A. Preet

B. Qureshi

C. Raunit

D. Sana

E. Cannot be determined

Q.17 Who amongst the following faces Raunit?

A. Asha

B. Bheem

C. Chelsi

D. Deep

E. Cannot be determined

Q.18 Which of the following is true regarding Chelsi?

A. Chelsi sits second to right of Deep

B. Asha sits to immediate right of Chelsi

C. Sana faces Chelsi

D. Deep is an immediate neighbour of chelsi

E. The person who faces Chelsi is an immediate neighbor of Raunit

Q.19 Four of the following five are alike in certain way based on the given seating arrangement and thus form a group. Which is the one that does not belong to the group?

A. Chelsi   **B.** Raunit   **C.** Qureshi   **D.** Preet

E. Deep

Q.20 Who amongst the following sits second to the right of the person who faces Preet?

A. Asha

B. Bheem

C. Chelsi

D. Deep

E. Cannot be determined

Ques (21-25):Direction: There are exactly ten stores and no other store on a straight in Bistupur Market. On the northern side of the street, from West to East, are stores 1, 3, 5, 7 and 9; on the southern side of the street, also from West to East, are stores 2, 4, 6, 8 and 10 The stores on the northern side are located directly across the street from those on the southern side, facing each other in pairs, as follows: 1 and 2; 3 and 4; 5 and 6; 7 and 8; 9 and 10. Each store is decorated with lights in exactly one of the following colours: green, red, and yellow. The stores have been decorated with lights according to the following conditions:

1. No store is decorated with lights of the same colour as those of any store adjacent to it.

2. No store is decorated with lights of the same colour as those of the store directly across the street from it.

3. Yellow lights decorate exactly one store on each side of the street.

4. Red lights decorate store 4.

5. Yellow lights decorate store 5.

Q.21 How many store/s are decorated by red colored light?

A. 1
B. 2
C. 3
D. 4
E. Cannot be determined

Q.22 Suppose that yellow lights decorate exactly two stores on the south side of the street and exactly one store on the north side. If all other conditions remain the same, then which one of the following statements must be true?

A. Green lights decorate store 1
B. Red lights decorate store 7
C. Red lights decorate store 10
D. Yellow lights decorate store 2
E. Yellow light decorate store 8

Q.23 Which one of the following statements must be true?

A. Red lights decorate store 1
B. Green lights decorate store 10
C. Red lights decorate store 8
D. Yellow lights decorate store 10
E. Yellow lights decorate store 8

Q.24 If green lights decorate store 7, then each of the following statements could be false Except:

A. Green lights decorate store 2
B. Green lights decorate store 10
C. Red lights decorate store 8
D. Yellow lights decorate store 2
E. Red lights decorate store 9

Q.25 Which one of the following could be an accurate list of the colors of the lights that decorate stores 2, 4, 6, 8 and 10, respectively?

A. Green, red, green, red, green
B. Green, red, green, yellow, red
C. Green, red, yellow, red, green
D. Yellow, green, red, green, red
E. Yellow, red, green, red, yellow

Ques (26-30):Direction: Study the following information carefully and answer the given question.

Eight persons are sitting in two parallel rows in which four persons are sitting in each row A, B, C and D are sitting in row-1 and all of them are facing south. While in row- 2 P, Q, R and S are sitting and all of them are facing north.

Hence, in the given seating arrangement each member sitting in a row faces another member of the other row. They all like different colours.

B sits second to the right of the one who likes the yellow colour. C sits opposite to the one who likes the Orange colour, who sits second to the left of S. Q sits immediately the left of the one who likes black colour. A sits immediate right of the one who likes gray colour. The one who likes white color sits opposite to B. P sits opposite to the one who likes green color but does not sit at the end. C likes neither Olive color nor Blue colour. The one who likes Blue color faces south.

Q.26 Who sits between A and the one who likes the Blue colour?

A. B
B. C
C. D
D. The one who likes black
E. The one who likes gray

Q.27 Who among the following sits at the extreme ends of the rows?

A. Q and the one who likes white
B. R and the one who likes Olive
C. S and the one who likes Orange color
D. D and the one who likes Blue
E. A and the one who likes Green

Q.28 Who among the following faces the one who likes Olive?

A. The one who likes green color
B. The one who likes Blue color
C. The one who likes gray color
D. The one who likes yellow color
E. D

Q.29 Who among the following likes the Blue colour?

A. B
B. C
C. D
D. A
E. Cannot be determined

Q.30 Who among the following likes white colour?

A. R
B. C
C. D
D. A
E. Cannot be determined

// Smart Answer Sheet //

Correct   Indicates percentage of students who answered questions correctly.

Skipped   Indicates percentage of students who skipped questions.

Q.	Ans.	Correct / Skipped
1	A	31.41 % / 67.82 %
2	A	11.43 % / 76.06 %
3	B	31.69 % / 67.59 %
4	E	29.16 % / 70.06 %
5	E	16.75 % / 76.53 %
6	C	23.96 % / 70.28 %

Q.	Ans.	Correct / Skipped
7	A	64.4 % / 31.43 %
8	D	63.96 % / 35.64 %
9	C	56.13 % / 32.12 %
10	D	19.9 % / 69.89 %
11	D	58.13 % / 38.58 %
12	D	63.71 % / 36.05 %

Q.	Ans.	Correct / Skipped
13	D	59.17 % / 38.17 %
14	E	63.55 % / 32.59 %
15	B	47.65 % / 47.86 %
16	D	58.98 % / 31.27 %
17	D	49.38 % / 33.86 %
18	B	62.48 % / 34.58 %

Q.	Ans.	Correct / Skipped
19	C	48.05 % / 44.04 %
20	B	56.5 % / 31.52 %
21	E	29.52 % / 68.31 %
22	D	26.27 % / 69.06 %
23	A	46.14 % / 30.55 %
24	E	44.31 % / 54.26 %

Q.	Ans.	Correct / Skipped
25	B	17.74 % / 74.9 %
26	B	26.19 % / 72.57 %
27	D	19.29 % / 76.68 %
28	D	51.22 % / 40.58 %
29	A	53.09 % / 35.46 %
30	A	65.43 % / 32.44 %

Performance Analysis

Avg. Score (%)	26.67%
Toppers Score (%)	56.67%
Your Score	

//Hints and Solutions//

Ques (1-5): According to the given information from the question:

Seetha sits exactly in the middle of Row-1 and faces north direction. Seetha sits exactly in the middle of the north-facing row. Pravin sits at the extreme right end of the south-facing row. Wahab was born in August month. Tushar sits with Ximon and Wahab and opposite Umesh. Only one person sits between the two persons who were born in May. Raman faces the north direction and sits opposite to Rani. Rani faces the south direction and sits to the immediate right of the person, who was born in May month. Exactly two persons were born in each of the month of April, May and June.

There is only one possible arrangement that follows all these conditions:

Month (South)	May	April	May	April	August
Person (Row-2)	Pravin	Rani	Ximon	Tushar	Wahab
Person (Row-1)	Yousuf	Raman	Seetha	Umesh	Vinoth
Month (North)	June	March	July	January	June

1. According to the seating arrangement of the above ten persons, Vinoth was born in June month and sits to the immediate right of Umesh.

Hence, the correct option is (A).

2. According to the seating arrangement of the above ten persons, we get "Yousuf and Vinoth were born in June month".

Hence, the correct option is (A).

3. According to the seating arrangement of the above ten persons, Ximon sits opposite Seetha and Seetha was born in July month.

Hence, the correct option is (B).

4. According to the seating arrangement of the above ten persons, "Yousuf-July, wrongly paired i.e. Yousuf was born in June month". The remaining options are correctly paired.

Hence, the correct option is (E).

5. According to the seating arrangement of the above ten persons, all the statements are false.

Hence, the correct option is (E)

Ques (6-10): According to the given information,

- Only one person sits between U and W, who is sitting at the extreme left end of the row.
- B, who is sitting at the extreme left end with respect to his row, sits second to the left of A.
- X faces the one who sits second to the left A.

Using the given hints we can fix the positions of A, B, W, U and X in their respective rows.

Row-1 Facing South			A		B

←Right End   Left end→

Row-2 Facing North	W		U			X

← Left End   Right End→

- C faces the one who is an immediate neighbour of U.
- V faces D.
- E, who sits at one of the extreme ends of the row sits third to the right of the one who faces Z.

Row-1 Facing South	E	C		A	D	B

←Right End   Left end→

Row-2 Facing North	W		U	Z	V	X

← Left End   Right End→

At this point, we can easily fix the positions of Y and F in their respective rows as well.

Row-1 Facing South	E	C	F	A	D	B

←Right End   Left end→

Row-2 Facing North	W	Y	U	Z	V	X

← Left End   Right End→

6. Following the final arrangement, we can say that Y faces C.

Hence, the correct option is (C).

7. Following the final arrangement, we can say that A faces Z.

Hence, the correct option is (A).

8. Following the final solution, we can say that if the names of all the persons sitting in the second row are to be arranged in alphabetical order (starting from right end of the second row) then X will face F.

Hence, the correct option is (D).

9. Following the final solution, we can say that X is sitting third to the right of one, who is facing the one, who is second to the left of E.

Hence, the correct option is (C).

10. Following the final sitting arrangement, we can say that C faces the immediate neighbour of W.

Hence, the correct option is (D).

Ques (11-15): In row 1: A, B, C and D are seated and all of them are facing South.

In row 2: P, Q, R and S are seated and all of them are facing North.

1) C sits second to right of the person from Bank of Maharashtra.

2) R is an immediate neighbor of the person who faces the person from Bank of Maharashtra.

CASE 1

CASE 2

CASE 3

3) Only one person sits between R and the person for PNB.

4) Immediate neighbour of the person from PNB faces the person from Canara Bank.

So, CASE 1 is not possible.

CASE 2

CASE 3

5) The person from UCO bank faces the person from Oriental Bank of Commerce.

6) R is not from Oriental Bank of Commerce.

CASE 2

CASE 3

7) P is not from PNB.

8) P does not face the person form Bank of Maharashtra.

CASE 2

CASE 3

9) Q faces the person from Dena Bank.

CASE 2

CASE 3

10) The one who faces S sits to the immediate left of A.

11) B does not sit at any of the extreme ends of the line.

So, CASE 2 is not possible.

CASE 3

12) The person from Bank of Maharashtra does not face the person from Syndicate Bank.

Thus S is from Indian bank.

So we get the final arrangement.

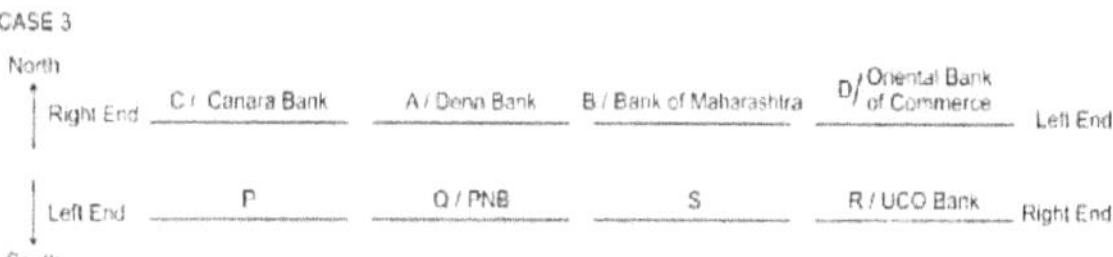

CASE 3

11. According to the above sitting arrangement All the person are sitting at the extreme ends of the rows and their Banks, belong to this group. Q doesn't belong to this group.

Hence, the correct option is (D).

12. According to the above sitting arrangement P is sitting to the left of person facing the person from Dena Bank. Same is the case of person from PNB.

So, using same pattern, we get person from Indian Bank is sitting to the left of person facing D.

Hence, the correct option is (D).

13. According to the above sitting arrangement C from Canara Bank, D from Oriental Bank of Commerce, P from Syndicate Bank and R from UCO bank are sitting at the extreme ends.

Hence, the correct option is (D).

14. According to the above sitting arrangement S is sitting between R and Q, the person from PNB.

Hence, the correct option is (E).

15. According to the above sitting arrangement:

(A) The person from UCO bank faces A → False

(B) The person from Bank of Maharashtra is an immediate neighbor of A → True

(C) A faces the person who sits second to right of R → False

(D) A is from Oriental Bank of Commerce → False

(E) A sits at one of the extreme ends of the line → False

So, 'The person from Bank of Maharashtra is an immediate neighbor of A' is the only correct option.

Hence, the correct option is (B).

Ques (16-20): According to the given information in the question, we conclude Sana is an immediate neighbour of Raunit and Raunit sits second to the left of the person who faces Asha. Sana can also sit to the right of Raunit Only one person sits between Asha and Deep. One of the immediate neighbours of Chelsi faces Qureshi.

So three cases are possible:

Case I:

Case II:

Case III:

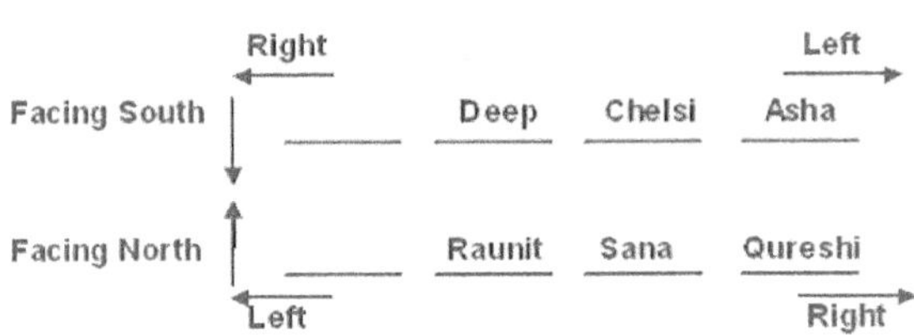

In case I, Chelsi can also sit to the left of Asha so there is again a case:

Case IV:

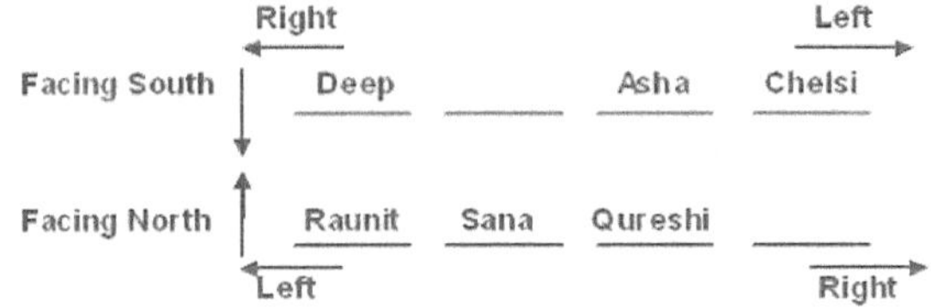

Bheem does not sit at any of the extreme ends of the line.

Discarding Cases I, II, III as in all these three cases the only position left is an extreme one. So taking Case IV,

It is the final arrangement.

16. Clearly, Sana faces Bheem.

Hence, the correct option is (D).

17. So, Deep Faces Raunit.

Hence, the correct option is (D).

18. We can see that from the options, Asha is an immediate neighbor of Chelsi is true.

Hence, the correct option is (B).

19. Chelsi, Raunit, Preet, Deep sit at the extreme ends while Qureshi doesn't.

So, he doesn't belong to the group.

Hence, the correct option is (C).

20. So, Bheem sits second to the right of the person who faces Preet.

Hence, the correct option is (B).

Ques (21-25): According to the given information in the question, we conclude:

1. No two adjacent and opposite stores have same light.
2. Yellow lights decorate exactly one store on each side of the street.
3. Red lights decorate store 4.
4. Yellow lights decorate store 5.

So, store 6 and store 3 are decorated with green as per given conditions. And so, store 1 must be decorated with Red.

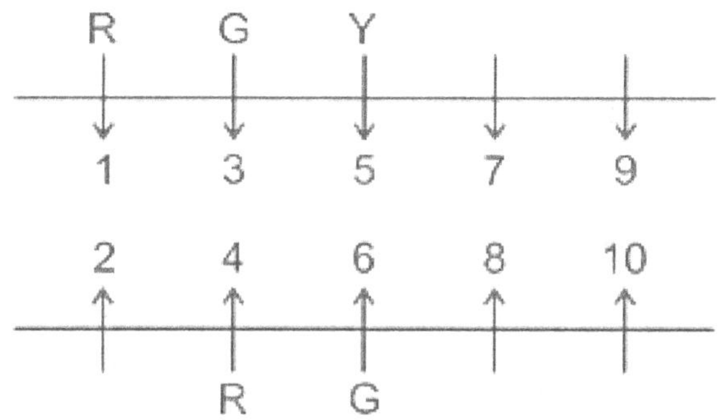

Now, there must be exactly one store in South row that's decorates with yellow lights. Yellow light can decorate either of store 2, 4 or 6.

Case 1:

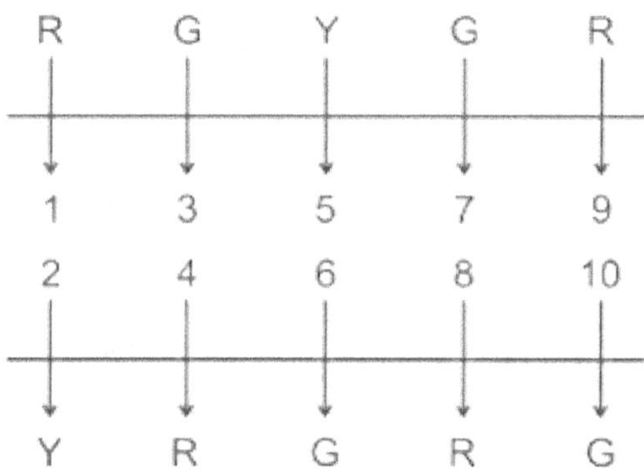

In case 1, 4 store are decorated with red lights.

Case 2:

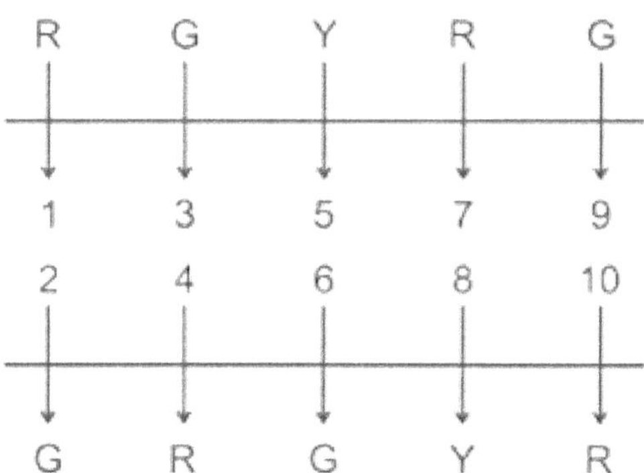

In case 2, 4 store are decorated with red lights.

Case 3:

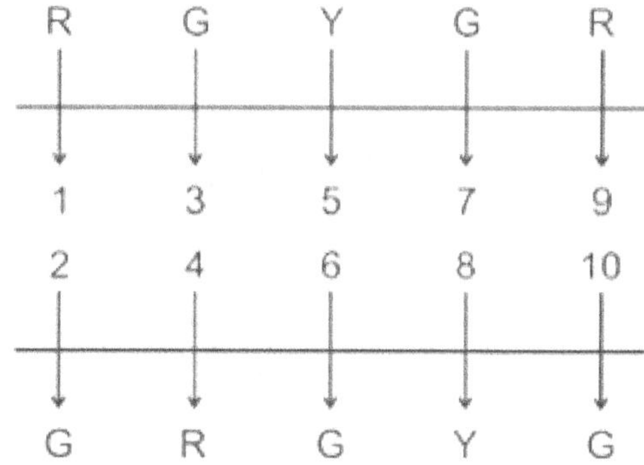

In case 3, 3 store are decorated with red lights.

Case 4:

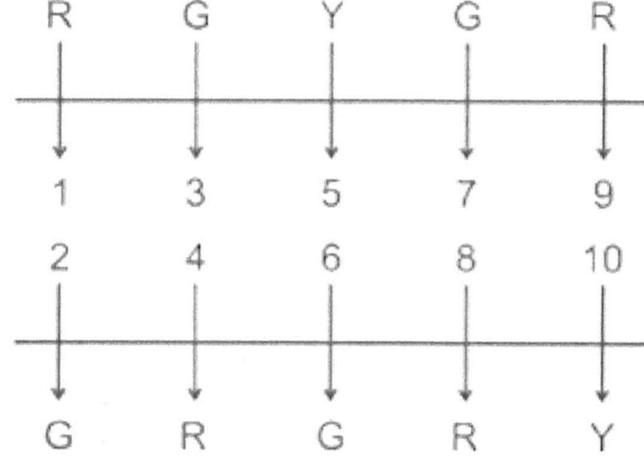

In case 4, again 4 store are decorated with red lights.

21. Clearly, the number of store decorated with red lights is different in different cases.

Hence, the correct option is (E).

22. From the above cases, lets evaluate the given options:

(A). Green lights decorate store 1 $\Rightarrow$ False

(B). Red lights decorate store 7 $\Rightarrow$ False

(C). Red lights decorate store 10 $\Rightarrow$ This is possible but not definite

(D). Yellow lights decorate store 2 $\Rightarrow$ True

(E). Yellow light decorate store 8 $\Rightarrow$ This is possible but not definite

Hence, the correct option is (D).

23. From the above cases, lets evaluate the given options:

(A). Red lights decorate store 1 $\Rightarrow$ This is possible definitely.

(B). Green lights decorate store 10 $\Rightarrow$ This is possible but not definite

(C). Red lights decorate store 8 ⇒ This is possible but not definite

(D). Yellow lights decorate store 10 ⇒ This is possible but not definite

(E). Yellow lights decorate store 8 ⇒ This is possible but not definite

Hence, the correct option is (A).

24. From the above cases, lets evaluate the given options:

(A). Green lights decorate store 2 ⇒ This is possible but not definite

(B). Green lights decorate store 10 ⇒ This is possible but not definite

(C). Red lights decorate store 8 ⇒ This is possible but not definite

(D). Yellow lights decorate store 2 ⇒ This is possible but not definite

(E). Red lights decorate store 9 ⇒ This is possible definitely.

Hence, the correct option is (E).

25. So, green, red, green, yellow, red list is correct.

Hence, the correct option is (B).

Ques (26-30): According to the given information,

First of all, we will decide the position of the B, person who likes yellow colour, C and the one who likes orange colour. The one who sits second to the left of S. Here the word 'who' is used for the person who likes orange color-

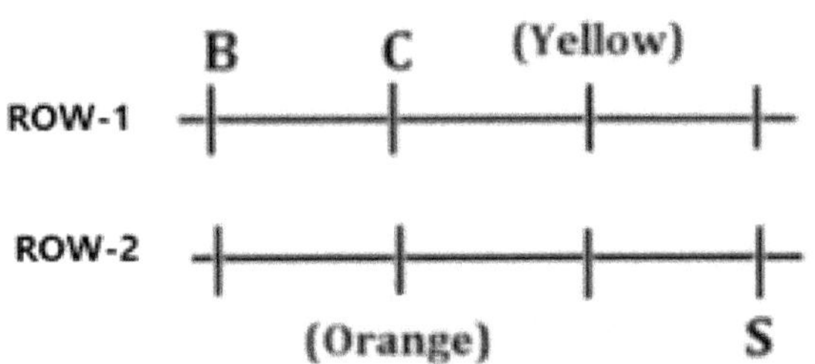

P is opposite to the one who likes Green, and he does not sit at the end also, similarly, C does not like Olive color and he is also not at the end, so on these clues, we can determine the final seating arrangement as follows-

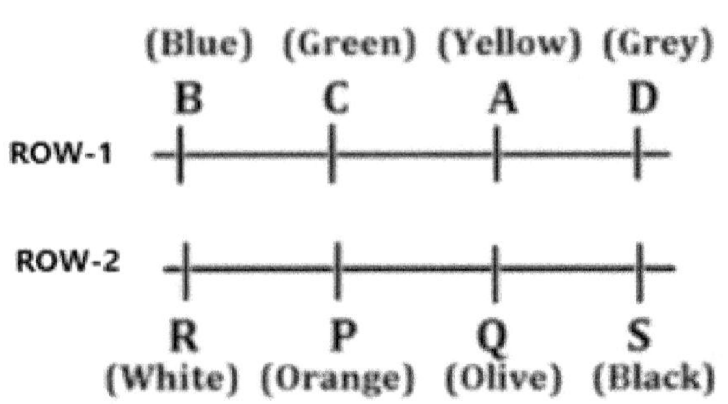

26. As per above seating arrangement C sits between A and the one who likes the Blue colour.

Hence, the correct option is (B).

27. As per the above seating arrangement D and the one who likes Blue sits at extreme ends.

Hence, the correct option is (D).

28. As per above seating arrangement the one who likes the Yellow color faces the one who likes Olive.

Hence, the correct option is (D).

29. According to the above seating arrangement, among the following B likes Blue colour.

Hence, the correct option is (A).

30. R likes white color as per above seating arrangement.

Hence, the correct option is (A).

Ques (1-5):Direction: Read the following information carefully and answer the given questions:

There are ten persons M, N, O, P, Q, R, S, T, U and V are sitting in two parallel lines facing each other but not necessarily in the same order. Each row consist of five persons each. The persons sitting in row 1 are facing towards south direction and the persons sitting in row 2 are facing towards north direction. Each one of them like different movies viz. ZNMD, Welcome, Jai ho, Pirates, Ironman, Spiderman, Race, Avengers, Cindrella, and Golmaal, but not necessarily in the same order.

The person who likes Race sit second to the right of U facing south. N is sitting on the immediate left of S who likes Avenger. T is sitting on an extreme end of the line facing south and does not like Race. Number of persons sitting to the left of R is equal to the number of persons sitting on the right of the person who likes ZNMD. Q likes Spiderman and sit on the immediate left of the person who faces the person who like Race. Only one person is sitting between Q and N. P is sitting on the immediate right of the person who is facing the person who likes Avengers. O is sitting third left of V. The persons who like Ironman and Golmaal does not face north. N faces the person who likes Golmaal and does not like ZNMD and Welcome. The person who likes Pirates sit diagonally opposite to Welcome. The person who face Cindrella does not like Pirates and Golmaal. M sit diagonally opposite to the person who likes Welcome.

Q.1 Four of the five are alike in a certain way so form a group. Which of the following does not belong to the group?

A. Race **B.** Avengers

C. Golmaal **D.** ZNMD

E. Ironman

Q.2 If, O and T interchanges their position, then who is sitting third to the right of T?

A. S **B.** N **C.** V **D.** U

E. R

Q.3 Choose the correct pair:

A. T, ZNMD **B.** P, Avengers

C. Q, Welcome **D.** U, Spiderman

E. N, Jai ho

Q.4 Which of the following movie is liked by the person who is facing R?

A. Welcome **B.** Spiderman

C. Jai ho **D.** ZNMD

E. Cindrella

Q.5 Which of the following movie is liked by N?

A. Welcome **B.** Ironman

C. ZNMD **D.** Jai ho

E. Cindrella

Ques (6-10):Direction: Read the following information carefully and answer the given questions:

Ten students are sitting in a straight line. Some of them are facing north while some of them are facing south. They all likes different subjects viz. Hindi, English, Maths, Physics, Biology, History, Geography, Computer, Commerce and Account but necessarily in the same order.

A likes Computer sits third from one of the extreme ends. A faces the same direction as C. Three students sit between A and H, who likes Math. G sits second to the right of H, who is not facing south direction. G sits third to the left of J and both are facing the same direction. The one who likes History is neither an immediate neighbor of the one who likes Math's nor A. B likes History and sits third to the right of F, who likes Commerce. Neither B nor F sits at extreme ends. The one who likes Biology and the one who likes Account are the immediate neighbors of each other. The students sit at extreme ends are facing the opposite direction.

There are as many students sit between C and the one who likes English as between D and one who likes English. C does not like Account. B and F are facing the same direction (Same direction means if B faces north then F also faces north and vice-versa). The one who likes Geography is not an immediate neighbor of E. E and I face the same direction as D, who faces the opposite direction of B. The one who likes Physics sits third to the left of the one who likes Hindi.

Q.6 Four among the following are the same in a certain way and thus form a group. Who among the following does not belong to that group?

A. A **B.** I **C.** H **D.** D

E. E

Q.7 Which among the following statement is not true about J?

A. J likes English

B. J is facing south direction

C. J sits immediate right of B

D. Only one student sits between J and F

E. All statements are true

Q.8 E likes which of the following Subject?

A. Geography **B.** Physics

C. Hindi **D.** Account

E. Biology

Q.9 Who among the following student likes Physics?

A. D **B.** I **C.** E **D.** C

E. G

Q.10 How many students are facing in the south direction?

A. Two **B.** Three **C.** Four **D.** Five

E. Six

Ques (11-15):Direction: Read the following information carefully and answer the given questions:

Six persons P, Q, R, S, T and U are sitting in a row. R sits one of the extreme ends of the row. S sits third from the right end. Only one person sits between P and U, where U is to the right of P. Neither P nor U is a neighbour of R. T does not sit at an extreme ends. Number of persons to the left of Q is same the number of persons to the right of R.

Q.11 How many person(s) does not change their positions when they arranged in English alphabetical order from the left side?
A. One   **B.** Two   **C.** None   **D.** Three
E. Four

Q.12 Who among the following sit at an extreme end?
A. S   **B.** T   **C.** P   **D.** U
E. Q

Q.13 How many persons sit between T and U?
A. None   **B.** One   **C.** Two   **D.** Three
E. Four

Q.14 Who is an immediate neighbour of Q?
A. P   **B.** S   **C.** R   **D.** U
E. T

Q.15 Who sits second from the left end?
A. R   **B.** T   **C.** P   **D.** S
E. U

Ques (16-20):Direction: Read the following information carefully and answer the given questions:

Nine people A, B, C, D, E, F, G, H, and I are seated in a straight line facing south direction but not necessarily in the same order.

D and C are sitting at the extreme ends. A sits second to the right of C. E sits third to the right of G. two people are sitting between F and C but none of them are E and G. C and I are not neighbors. D sits third to the right of H.

Q.16 Which of the following statements are true with respect to the given arrangement?
A. E is sitting at one of the ends.
B. F is the immediate neighbor of A and G.
C. C sits exactly in the middle of the line.
D. Two people are sitting to the left of I.
E. None of these.

Q.17 How many persons are seated between H and B?
A. 5   **B.** 4   **C.** 3   **D.** 2
E. 1

Q.18 Which of the following is immediate neighbor of each other?
A. G, F   **B.** D, I   **C.** A, C   **D.** B, H
E. E, C

Q.19 What is the position of I with respect to F?
A. Third to the left.   **B.** Fourth to the right.
C. Second to the right   **D.** Second to the left
E. Third to the right

Q.20 Who among the following sits between G and A?
A. B   **B.** H   **C.** I   **D.** E
E. F

Ques (21-25):Direction: Read the following information carefully and answer the given questions:

There are eight people B, C, M, N, P, V, X and Z. They all are sitting in a row but not necessarily in the same order. Some of them are facing North and some of them are facing South. People sitting near to each other are facing opposite direction (It means that if a person is facing the North then neighbor of this person will face South direction). Z is sitting one of the corner and third to the right of X, who is facing south direction. V is sitting third to the left of N, who is facing North direction. V is the only neighbor of Z. C is sitting second to the right of B. P is not near to B.

Q.21 How many people are sitting between V and M?
A. One   **B.** Two   **C.** Three   **D.** Four
E. Five

Q.22 Who is the neighbor of P?
A. Z and V   **B.** X and N   **C.** N and V   **D.** C and N
E. V and X

Q.23 Who is sitting second to the right of C?
A. N   **B.** X   **C.** P   **D.** V
E. Z

Q.24 From the given who is sitting at one of the corner?
A. V   **B.** P   **C.** C   **D.** B
E. M

Q.25 Who is sitting third to the right of P?
A. X   **B.** N   **C.** C   **D.** M
E. B

Ques (26-30):Direction: Read the following information carefully and answer the given questions:

A certain number of people are sitting in a row equidistant to each other facing both north and south directions. Some of them like different fruits.

The person who likes banana sits second to the left of the person who likes apples and face the same direction as K. M sits exactly between L and K but not on the left side of K. No person sits on the right of P who likes mango and he is an immediate neighbor of L. Only one person sits between N and the person who likes orange. L is an immediate neighbor of the person who likes orange. The person who likes apple faces the opposite direction to the person who likes mango. Only two people sit between M and the person who likes apple. S faces the same direction as M and sits fourth to the left of the person who likes orange. Z faces the south direction and only two people sit to his left. The person who likes apple sits immediate right of Z. K sits fourth to the right of L.

Q.26 Who sits exactly between L and Z?
A. P
B. The person who likes apple
C. M

D. K

E. The person who likes banana

Q.27 Who sits third to the left of S?

A. M   **B.** L   **C.** K   **D.** P

E. Z

Q.28 Who likes banana?

A. P   **B.** L   **C.** M   **D.** N

E. K

Q.29 How many people are sitting to the left of K?

A. 3

B. 4

C. 5

D. 6

E. Cannot be determined

Q.30 How many people are sitting in the row?

A. 6   **B.** 7   **C.** 10   **D.** 8

E. 9

// Smart Answer Sheet //

Correct — Indicates percentage of students who answered questions correctly.

Skipped — Indicates percentage of students who skipped questions.

Q.	Ans.	Correct / Skipped
1	C	12.95 % / 81.74 %
2	C	55.25 % / 42.79 %
3	E	87.66 % / 12.28 %
4	D	32.81 % / 67.09 %
5	D	51.72 % / 32.12 %
6	A	20.38 % / 79.05 %

Q.	Ans.	Correct / Skipped
7	C	60.33 % / 36.48 %
8	C	80.69 % / 11.14 %
9	B	45.29 % / 36.01 %
10	E	69.08 % / 30.03 %
11	A	19.58 % / 79.92 %
12	E	41.56 % / 35.91 %

Q.	Ans.	Correct / Skipped
13	C	19.55 % / 70.36 %
14	D	49.1 % / 46.76 %
15	B	78.11 % / 13.34 %
16	B	24.41 % / 68.31 %
17	C	21.98 % / 77.98 %
18	A	49.16 % / 41.93 %

Q.	Ans.	Correct / Skipped
19	E	86.16 % / 13.08 %
20	E	45.61 % / 33.09 %
21	D	30.47 % / 67.67 %
22	D	45.16 % / 35.9 %
23	B	20.09 % / 73.71 %
24	D	84.29 % / 12.4 %

Q.	Ans.	Correct / Skipped
25	C	64.38 % / 33.74 %
26	E	21.9 % / 67.57 %
27	A	47.07 % / 41.56 %
28	D	85.25 % / 11.04 %
29	B	64.57 % / 32.52 %
30	C	76.77 % / 11.97 %

Performance Analysis	
Avg. Score (%)	53.33%
Toppers Score (%)	60.0%
Your Score	

//Hints and Solutions//

Ques (1-5): Eight persons: M, N, O, P, Q, R, S, T, U and V

Eight movies: ZNMD, Welcome, Jai ho, Pirates, Ironman, Spiderman, Race, Avengers, Cindrella, and Golmaal

1. T is sitting on an extreme end of the line facing south and does not like Race.

2. The person who likes Race sit second to the right of U facing south.

3. Q likes Spiderman and sit on the immediate left of the person who faces the person who like Race.

On combining these three sentences we get, three possible cases:

Case 1a: When T is sitting on the extreme end of the line from the right side.

U is is sitting on the extreme end of the line from the left end.

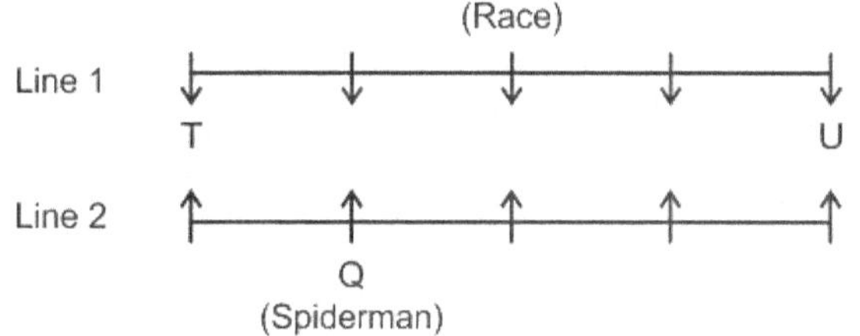

Case 1b: When T is is sitting on the extreme end of the line from the right side.

U is sitting second from the left end.

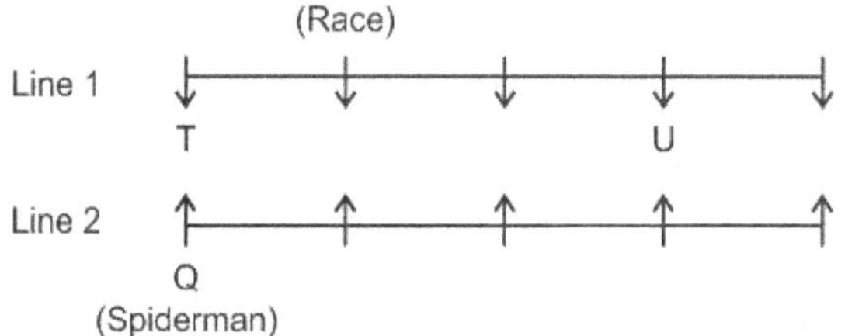

Case 2: When T is sitting on the extreme end of the line from the left end.

U is sitting second from the left end.

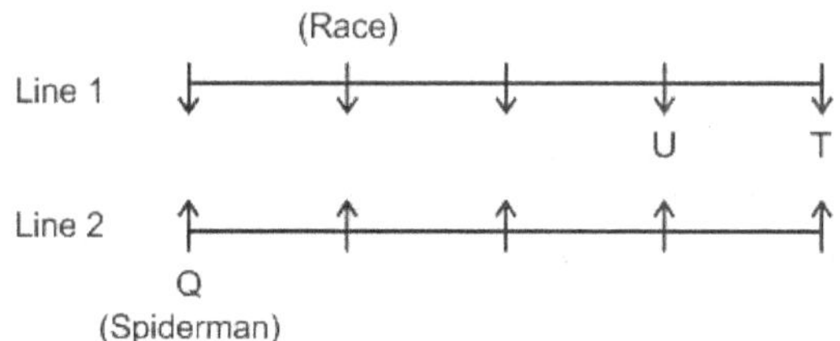

4. Only one person is sitting between Q and N.

5. N is sitting on the immediate left of S who likes Avenger.

Case 1a:

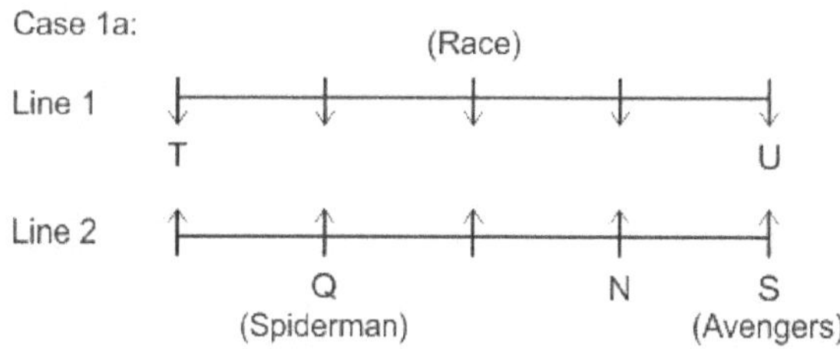

Case 1b:

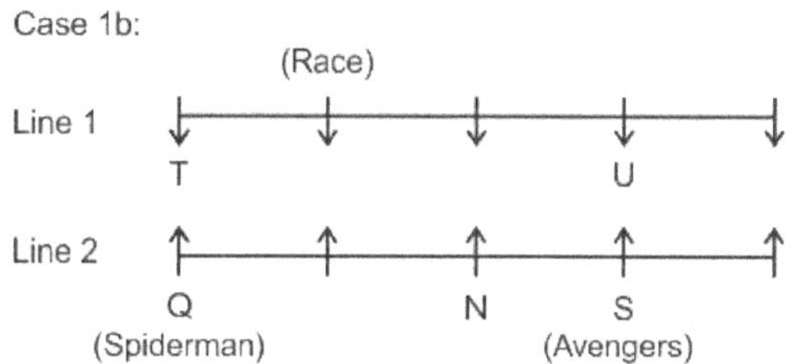

Case 2:

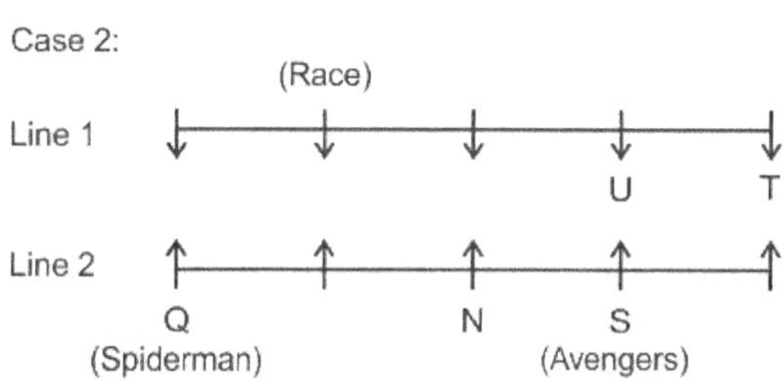

6. P is sitting on the immediate right of the person who is facing the person who likes Avengers.

7. N faces the person who likes Golmaal and does not like ZNMD and Welcome.

8. The person who likes Pirates sit diagonally opposite to Welcome.

On combining these three sentences we get,

Case 1a: In this case P will like Golmaal, as he is sitting on the immediate right of the person who faces the person who likes Avengers, i.e. S.

The person who likes Pirates and Welcome will sit on the extreme ends of the line from the left end of the line.

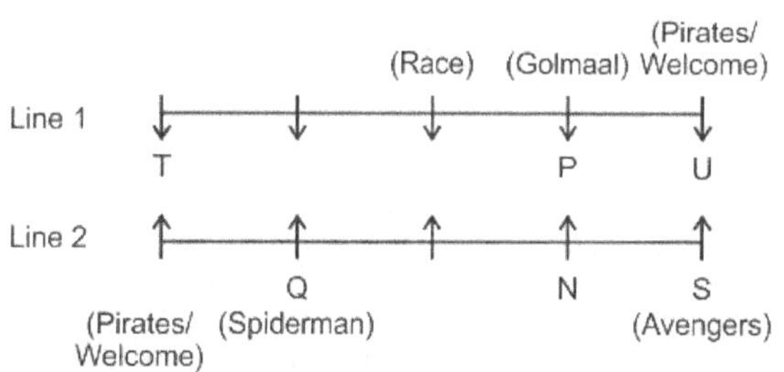

Case 1b: In this case P will like Golmaal, as he is sitting on the immediate right of the person who faces the person who likes Avengers, i.e. S.

The person who likes Pirates and Welcome will sit on the extreme ends of the line from the right end of the line.

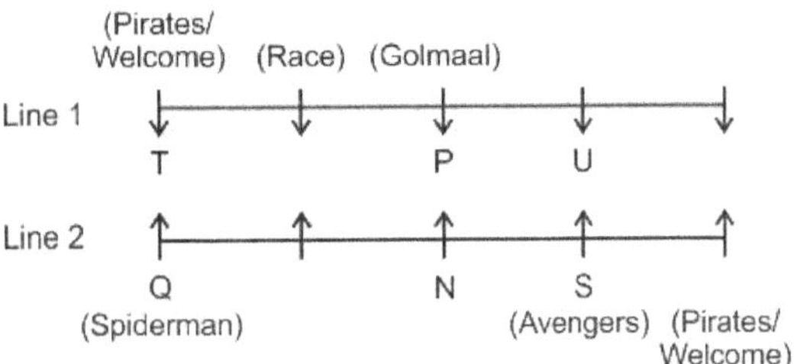

Case 2: In this case P will like Golmaal, as he is sitting on the immediate right of the person who faces the person who likes Avengers, i.e. S.

The person who likes Pirates and Welcome will sit on the extreme ends of the line from the right end of the line.

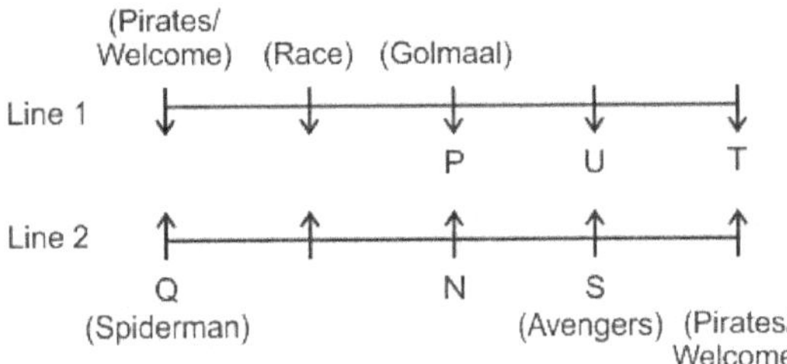

9. O is sitting third left of V.

10. Number of persons sitting to the left of R is equal to the number of persons sitting on the right of the person who likes ZNMD.

On combining these two sentences we get,

Case 1a is eliminated, as there is no space left for O and V to sit according to the question.

And from the 9. statement we have again three cases for the position of O and V.

Case 1b (1): When V sit second from the right side facing south.

In this case only when R sit on the extreme end of the line from the right end facing north, and O likes ZNMD, this condition is possible, as no other place is available to satisfied this condition.

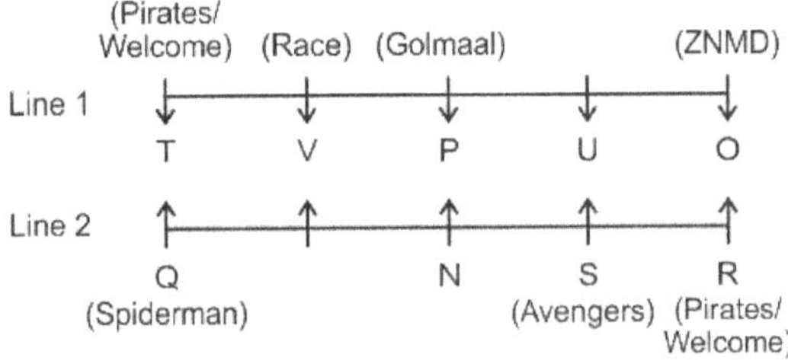

Case 1b (2): When V sit on the extreme end from right end of the line facing North.

In this case R likes Race movie and O likes ZNMD, and they will face each other, only then there will be equal number of persons

to the left of R and equal number of persons to the right of the person who likes ZNMD i.e. O is possible.

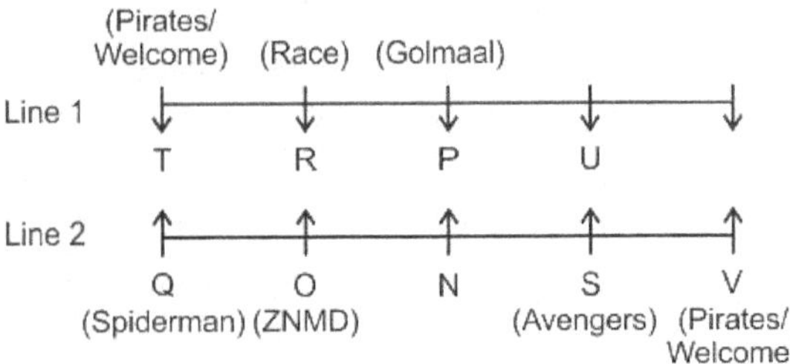

Case 2: When V sit on the extreme end from the right end of the line facing North.

In this case R likes Race movie and O likes ZNMD, and they will face each other, only then there will be equal number of persons to the left of R and equal number of persons to the right of the person who likes ZNMD i.e. O is possible.

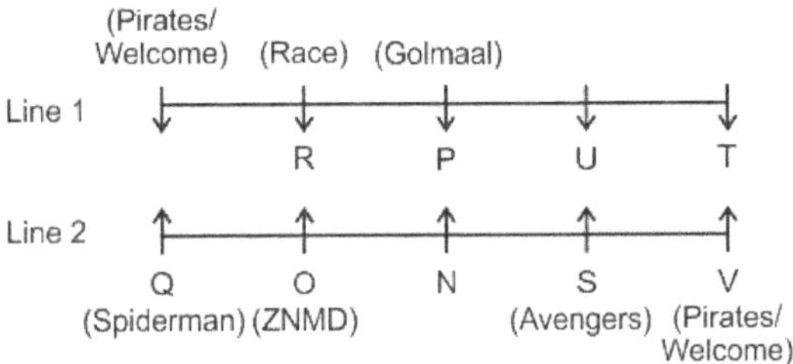

11. M sit diagonally opposite to the person who likes Welcome.

12. The person who face Cindrella does not like Pirates and Golmaal.

13. The persons who like Ironmen and Golmaal does not face north.

On combining these three sentences,

Case 1b (1) is eliminated, as there is no place left for M to sit in this case, and it is mentioned in the question that M sit diagonally opposite.

Case 1b (2) is eliminated, as in this case M sit diagonally opposite to the person who likes Spiderman which is not possible.

Now, In Case 2, M will sit on the extreme end of the line from the right side facing south, from this V likes Welcome movie, and T likes Pirates movie.

T will like Cindrella as, it is facing the person who likes Welcome movie which is V.

U will like Ironman as, it is mentioned that the person who likes Ironman does not face north, so automatically U likes Ironman.

Now, only N is left and only one movie is left i.e. Jai ho, so N likes Jai ho.

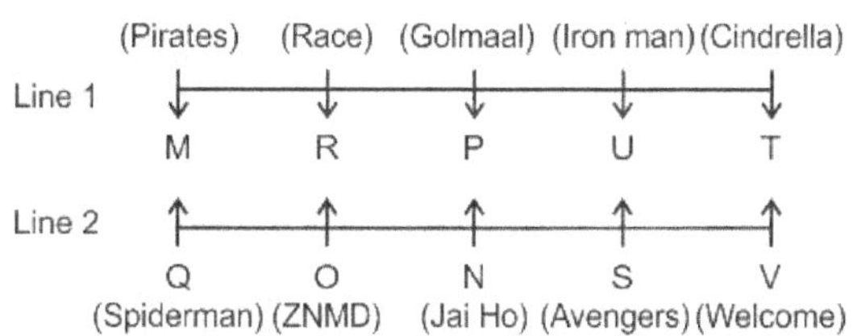

The final arrangement:

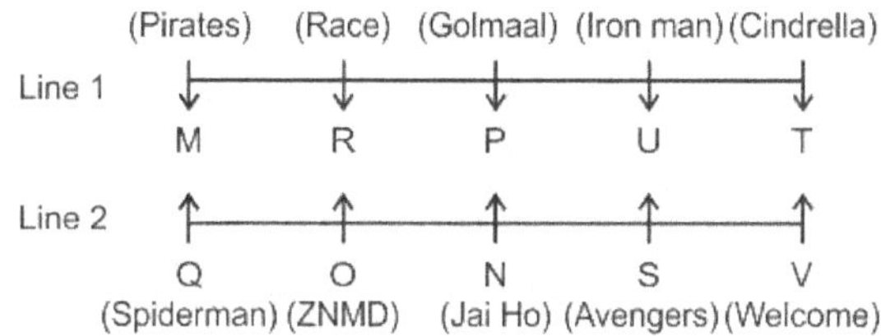

1. Except, Golmaal all the four movies are liked by the persons who is sitting on the extreme end of the line.

So, Golmaal does not belong to the group.

Hence, the correct option is (C).

2. So, V sit third to the right of T, if O and T interchanges their position.

Hence, the correct option is (C).

3. So, N-Jai ho is correct.

Hence, the correct option is (E).

4. O is facing R.

O likes ZNMD movie.

So, ZNMD is the movie which is liked by the person who is facing R.

Hence, the correct option is (D).

5. So, N likes Jai ho movie.

Hence, the correct option is (D).

Ques (6-10):(1) A likes Computer sits third from one of the extreme ends.

(2) Three students sit between A and H who like Maths.

(3) G sits second to the right of H, who is not facing south direction.

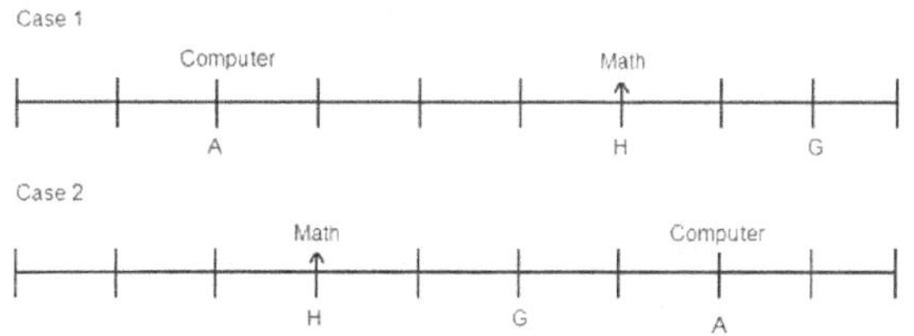

(4) G sits third to the left of J and both are facing the same direction. (This creates one more case in case 2 so here we say case 3)

(5) The one who likes History is neither an immediate neighbor of the one who likes Maths nor A.

(6) B likes History and sits third to the right of F, who likes Commerce. Neither B nor F sits at extreme ends. (Here again, one more case with case 1 because in case 1 F can be either side of B. we name that condition Case 4)

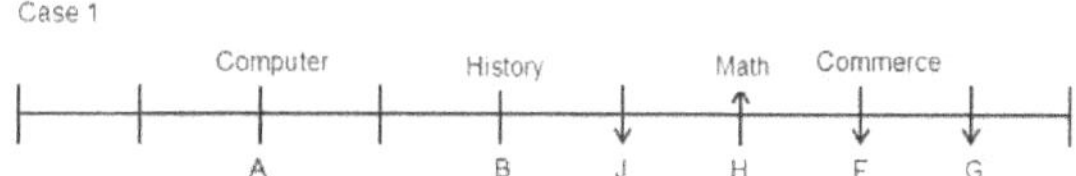

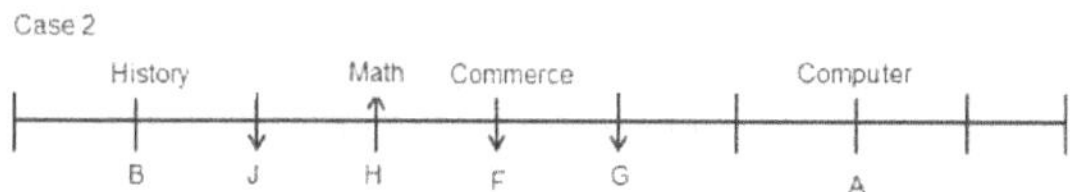

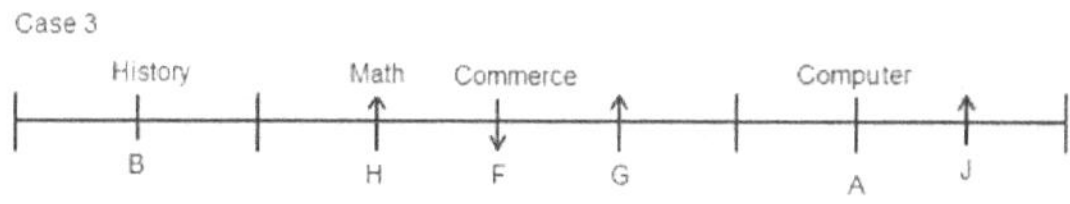

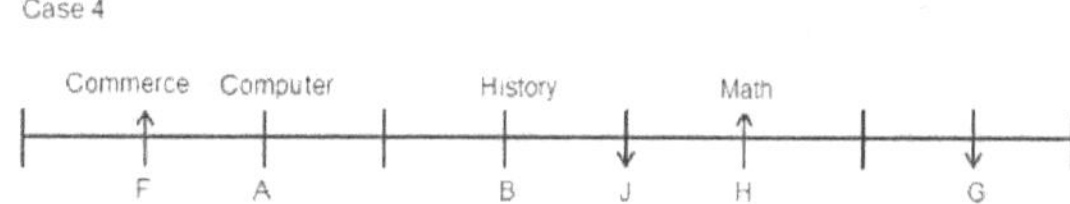

(7) There are as many students sits between C and the one who likes English as between D and one who likes English. (This eliminates case 2 and case 3)

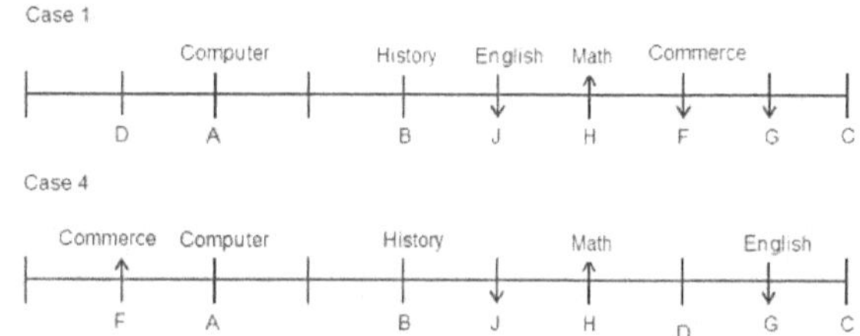

(8) The one who likes Biology and the one who likes Account are the immediate neighbors of each other. (This eliminates case 4)

(9) C does not like Account.

(10) B and F are facing the same direction

(11) E and I face the same direction as D, who faces the opposite direction of B.

(12) The one who likes Physics sits third to the left of the one who likes Hindi.

(13) The one who likes Geography is not an immediate neighbor of E.

(14) The students sit at extreme ends are facing the opposite directions.

(15) A faces the same direction as C.

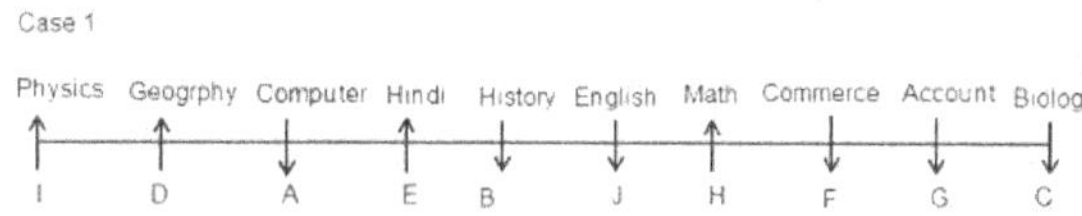

6. All are facing north except A.

So, A does not belong to that group.

Hence, the correct option is (A).

7. So, Clearly, J sits immediate left of B.

Hence, the correct option is (C).

8. So, E likes Hindi.

Hence, the correct option is (C).

9. So, I likes Physics

Hence, the correct option is (B).

10. Clearly, Six students are facing south direction.

Hence, the correct option is (E).

Ques (11-15): Six persons: P, Q, R, S, T and U

1.R sits one of the extreme ends of the row.

2.S sits third from the right end.

Following are the possibilities we get,

Case -1

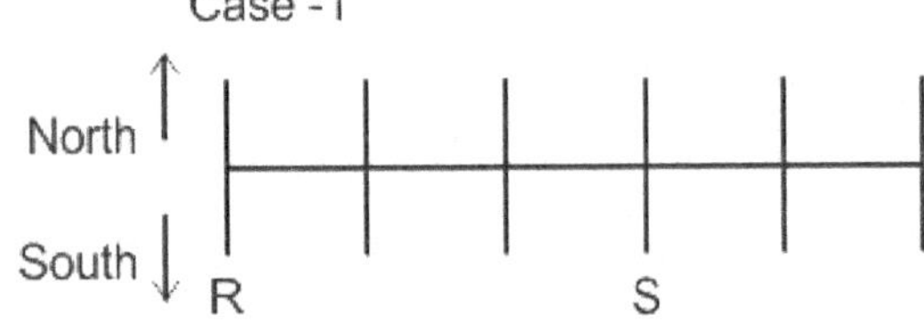

Case -2

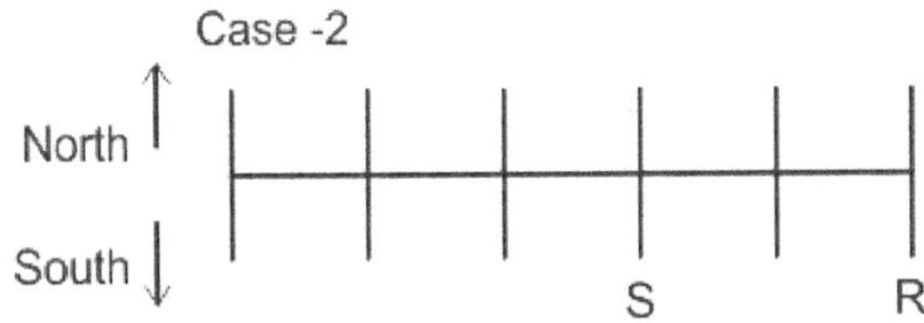

3. Only one person sits between P and U.

4. Neither P nor U is a neighbor of R, where U is to the right of P.

5. Number of persons to the left of Q is same the number of persons to the right of R.

6. T does not sit at an extreme end.

Here, this statement is violated in case II. so it is eliminated and the final arrangement is:

Final arrangement is:

11. So, one person does not change its position.

Hence, the correct option is (A).

12. So, Q sits at an extreme end.

Hence, the correct option is (E).

13. So, two persons sit between T and U.

Hence, the correct option is (C).

14. So, U is an immediate neighbour of Q.

Hence, the correct option is (D).

15. So,T sits second from the left.

Hence, the correct option is (B).

Ques (16-20): Persons: A, B, C, D, E, F, G, H, and I

I. D and C are sitting at the extreme ends.

II. A sits second to the right of C.

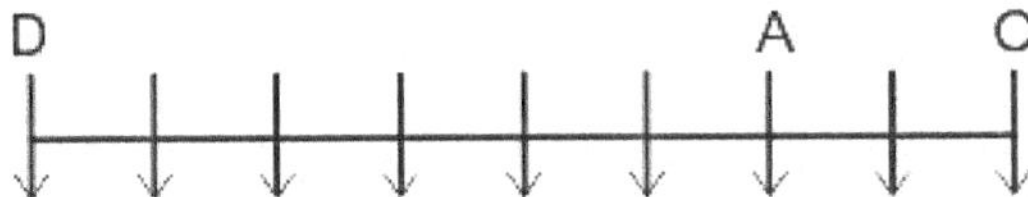

III. Two people are sitting between F and C but none of them are E and G.

IV. E sits third to the right of G.

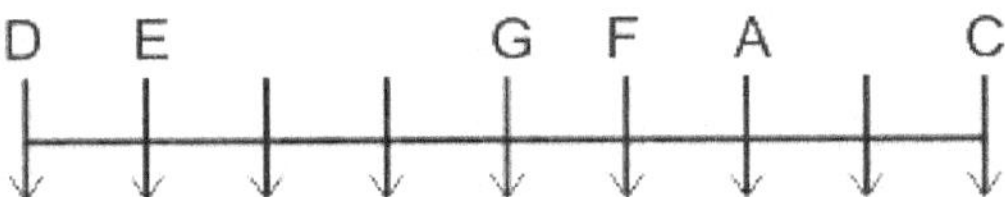

V. C and I are not neighbors.

VI. D sits third to the right of H.

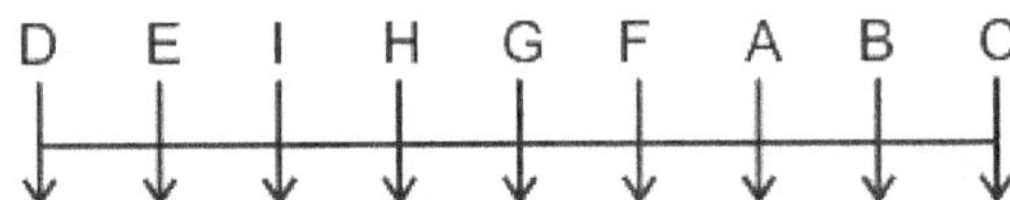

16. So, F is the immediate neighbor of A and G is the true statement.

Hence, the correct option is (B).

17. So, 3 persons are seated between H and B.

Hence, the correct option is (C).

18. So, G, F are immediate neighbor of each other.

Hence, the correct option is (A).

19. So, I sit third to the right F.

Hence, the correct option is (E).

20. So, F sits between A and G.

Hence, the correct option is (E).

Ques (21-25): From the given information,

(I) Z is sitting one of the corner and he is sitting third to the right of X, who is facing south direction, there will be only condition by which we can place both X and Z.

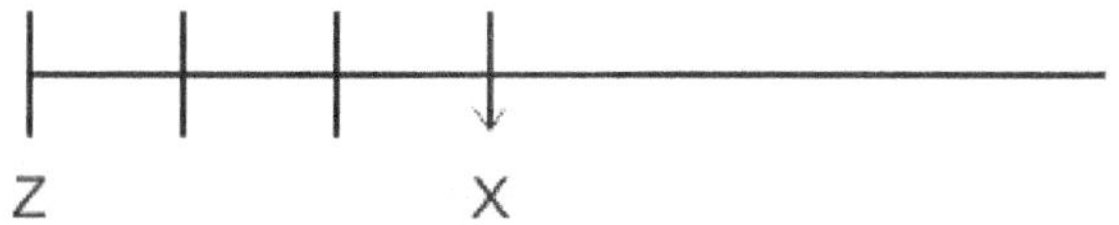

(II) V is the neighbor of Z and V is sitting third to the left of N who is facing North direction. So according to the given condition N will sit just left of X, because from there only V will be third to left of N.

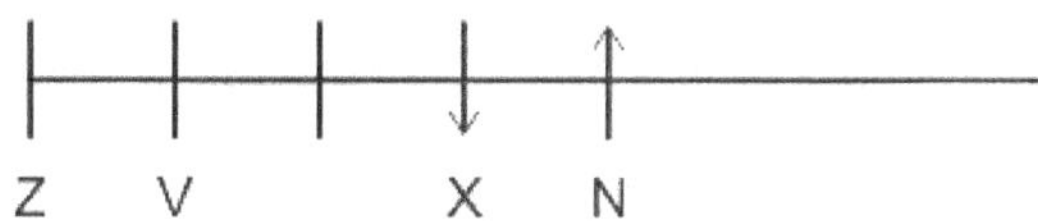

(III) C is sitting second to the right of B. So in the row there is only place for B and C because no other place satisfy the condition of B and C. Here B will face South direction because if B is facing North then it will not satisfy the condition of C is second right to B because in this condition B will be near to N who is already facing North. This will contradict the given condition of neighbor facing opposite direction.

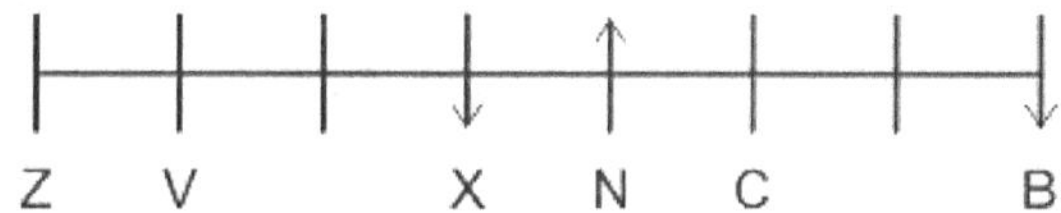

(IV) P is not near to B so P will sit between V and X. Remaining one person M will sit between C and B.

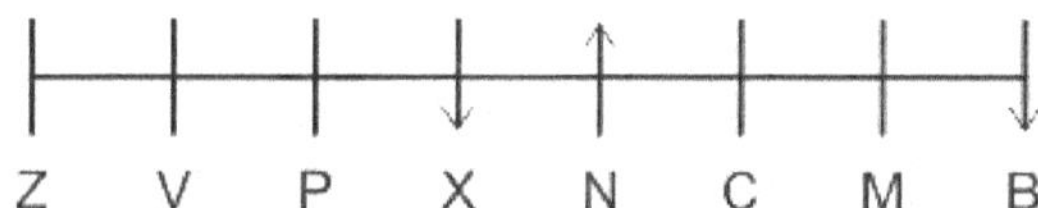

(V) All the people are placed in the row now we have decide their direction according to the given condition which is People sitting near to each other are facing opposite.

(VI) Here M will face opposite to B so M will be in North then C will face opposite to M so C will be in South direction.

(VII) P will face opposite of X so P will be in North direction same as V will opposite to P then V will face South direction and in final Z will face opposite to V so Z will be facing in North direction.

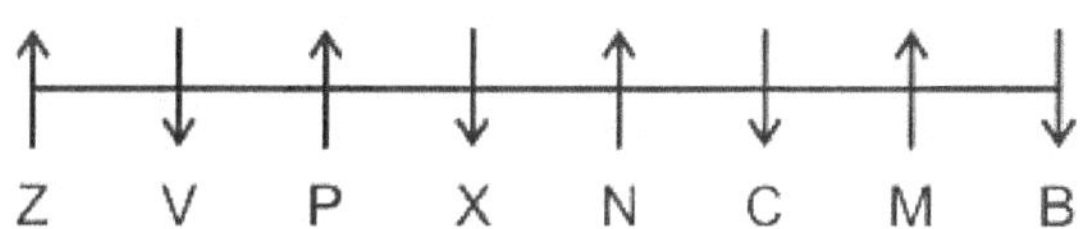

This is the final arrangement.

21. So,There are four people sitting between V and M.

Hence, the correct option is (D).

22. So, V and X are the neighbor of P.

Hence, the correct option is (D).

23. So, X is sitting second to right of C.

Hence, the correct option is (B).

24. So, From the given B is sitting at one corner.

Hence, the correct option is (D).

25. So, C is sitting third to the right of P.

Hence, the correct option is (C).

Ques (26-30):(1) Z faces the south direction and only two people sit to his left.

(2) The person who likes apple sits immediate right of Z.

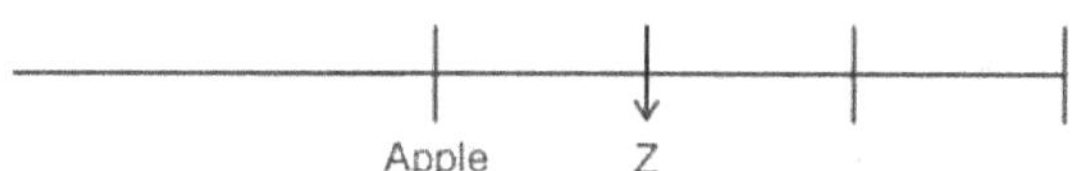

(3) No person sits on the right of P who likes mango and he is an immediate neighbor of L.

There are two cases are possible.

(4) The person who likes apple faces the opposite direction to the person who likes mango.

(5) L is an immediate neighbor of the person who likes orange.

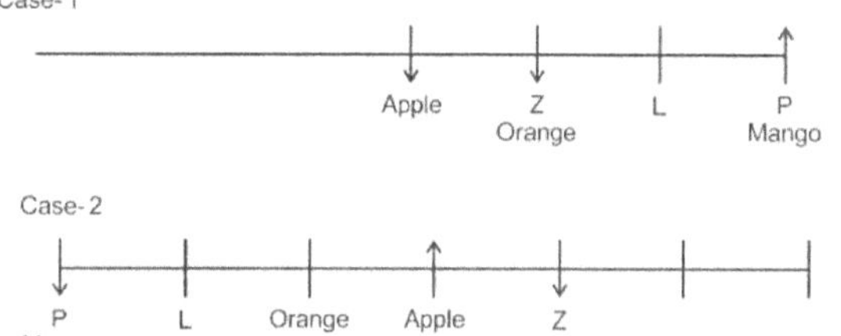

(6) K sits fourth to the right of L.

(7) M faces north sits exactly between L and K but not on the left side of K.

(8) Only two people sit between M and the person who likes apple.

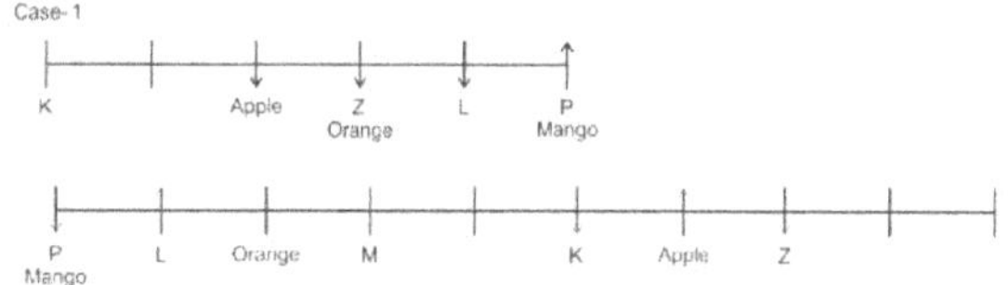

Here case 1 gets eliminated as there is no sit for M.

(9) Only one person sits between N and the person who likes orange.

(10) The person who likes banana sits second to the left of the person who likes apples and faces the same direction as K.

(11) S faces the same direction as M and sits fourth to the left of the person who likes orange.

The final arrangement is-

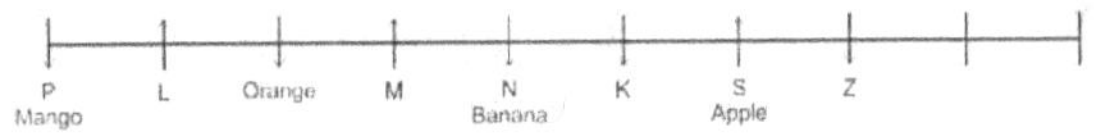

26. So, the person who likes banana sits exactly between L and Z.

Hence, the correct option is (E).

27. So, M sits third to the left of S.

Hence, the correct option is (A).

28. So, N likes banana.

Hence, the correct option is (D).

29. So, 4 people are sitting to the left of K.

Hence, the correct option is (B).

30. So, 10 people are sitting in a row.

Hence, the correct option is (C).

Ques (1-5):Direction: Read the information carefully and answer the questions given below.

Eight people E, F, G, H, I, J, K and M having different professions are sitting around a circular table. Some of them are facing the centre and some are facing away from the centre. F is sitting second to the left of K who is facing the centre. The Musician is an immediate neighbour of K and F. There are only three people between the Musician and E. Only one person sits between the Architect and E. The Doctor sits to the immediate right of the Architect, who is facing the centre. M is second to the right of K. H is the Musician. G and J are immediate neighbours of each other. The Pilot sits to the immediate right of F. The Lawyer is second to the left of the Doctor. The Scientist is an immediate neighbour of the Architect. G is second to the left of E, who is a Professor. One of them is Engineer.

Q.1 Who is third to the right of the Musician?

A. E

B. Pilot

C. J

D. Lawyer

E. Cannot be determined

Q.2 Who is the Scientist?

A. J   **B.** K   **C.** F   **D.** G

E. E

Q.3 Four of the following five are alike in a certain way and so form a group. Which is the one that does not belong to the group?

A. Doctor-M   **B.** Pilot-G

C. Architect-H   **D.** Lawyer-J

E. Scientist-K

Q.4 Which of these statements is definitely false?

A. The Engineer is second to the left of the Lawyer

B. Five people face the centre

C. H sits between the Engineer and the Scientist

D. There are three people between the Pilot and the Architect

E. The Scientist and the Doctor are to the immediate left of each other

Q.5 Who is the Architect?

A. J   **B.** G   **C.** E   **D.** M

E. I

Ques (6-10):Direction: Read the information carefully and answer the questions given below.

Eight students M, N, O, P, Q, R, S and T are sitting around a circular table such that 3 persons are facing towards the centre and rest are facing away from the centre but not necessarily in the same order.

There are two persons gap between O and T and both are facing opposite direction. P sits third to the right of O. Q sits opposite to T and facing the same direction as T. M is neither the neighbour of T nor P. There are three persons gap between M and P and both are facing opposite direction to each other. M is facing opposite direction as Q is facing. There are three persons gap between N and S and both are facing away from the centre. R is sitting second to the right of N and both the neighbours of R facing opposite to the R. R is facing towards the centre.

Q.6 Who is sitting third to the right of N?

A. R   **B.** P

C. T   **D.** Q

E. None of these

Q.7 Q is sitting in which direction from T?

A. Fourth to the right   **B.** Fourth to the left

C. Third to the right   **D.** Third to the left

E. Both (A) and (B)

Q.8 If N is related to R in the same way T is related to P then Q is related to which person?

A. P   **B.** N

C. M   **D.** S

E. None of these

Q.9 Who is sitting second to the left of M?

A. Q   **B.** O

C. R   **D.** T

E. None of these

Q.10 Who is sitting opposite to O?

A. R   **B.** S

C. T   **D.** Q

E. None of these

Ques (11-15):Direction: Read the information carefully and answer the questions given below.

Eight people Amar, Brijesh, Pinky, Deep, Eshwar, Nancy, Gurkamal and Harsh are sitting around a circular table. All are facing towards the center but not necessarily in the same order.

Nancy is third to the right of Pinky and second to the left of Harsh. Deep is not an immediate neighbour of Pinky or Harsh. Eshwar is to the immediate right of Amar, who is second to the right of Gurkamal.

Q.11 Who is second to the left of Pinky?

A. Amar

B. Eshwar

C. Brijesh

D. Deep

E. Either Amar or Deep

Q.12 Who is to the immediate right of Pinky?

A. Amar   **B.** Brijesh
C. Brijesh or Deep   **D.** Deep
E. Eshwar

Q.13 Which of the following pair of persons has the first person sitting to the right of the second person?

A. Pinky and Brijesh
B. Amar and Eshwar
C. Nancy and Gurkamal
D. Harsh and Amar
E. Deep and Brijesh

Q.14 Who sits between Gurkamal and Deep?

A. Harsh   **B.** Deep
C. Nancy   **D.** Brijesh
E. None of these

Q.15 Which of the following is the correct position of Brijesh with respect to Harsh?

I. Second to the right
II. Fourth to the right
III. Fourth to the left
IV. Second to the left

A. Only I   **B.** Only II
C. Only III   **D.** Both II and III
E. None of these

Ques (16-20):Direction: Read the information carefully and answer the questions given below.

At a reunion party, eight friends named A, B, C, D, E, F, G and H sit together on a round table facing the centre. Interestingly all eight friends are pursuing bachelor's degree in different subjects namely Mathematics, Economics, English, History, Physics, Chemistry, Sociology and Hindi. They are not necessarily seated in the mentioned order. A sits adjacent to D who is studying Economics. B is studying History and does not sit adjacent to C or D. F is sitting fifth to the left of A and is studying Physics. One who is studying Chemistry sits immediate left to F. G sits opposite to A. Neither H nor E is immediate neighbour of G. One who is studying Hindi sits fifth to the left of G, who is learning Sociology. C does not study chemistry. E is studying English and sits next to the one who is studying Hindi.

Q.16 What does the person study who is sitting third to the left of C?

A. Mathematics   **B.** Physics
C. Sociology   **D.** History
E. None of these

Q.17 Who is diagonally opposite to B?

A. D   **B.** A   **C.** H   **D.** F
E. G

Q.18 Who sits between A and E?

A. D   **B.** H   **C.** C   **D.** B
E. F

Q.19 Which subject is A studying?

A. Sociology   **B.** English

C. Chemistry   **D.** History
E. Mathematics

Q.20 Who is studying Chemistry?

A. A   **B.** B
C. F   **D.** H
E. None of these

Ques (21-25):Direction: Read the information carefully and answer the questions given below.

Eight people, A, B, C, D, E, F, G, and H are sitting around a circular table. Four of these eight people are facing towards the center (inward direction) while four of them are facing away from the center (outward direction). No three consecutive people are facing the same direction.

D is sitting second to the right of G. C is sitting second to the right of B. Both H and E are facing the same direction. F is sitting second to the right of D and they are facing different directions. B is not an immediate neighbour of E. G is facing the inward direction. H is sitting third to the right of E. F is an immediate neighbour of H. Only one person is sitting between G and E.

Q.21 Who is sitting third to the right of A?

A. F   **B.** C   **C.** G   **D.** H
E. D

Q.22 Who is sitting third to the left of C?

A. G   **B.** A   **C.** E   **D.** F
E. D

Q.23 What is the position of H with respect to the position of D?

A. Second to the left   **B.** Immediate right
C. Immediate left   **D.** Third to the left
E. Third to the right

Q.24 Four of the following five are alike in some way and thus form a group. Which of the following does not belong to the group?

A. A   **B.** G   **C.** F   **D.** D
E. C

Q.25 Who are the immediate neighbours of B?

A. D, H   **B.** D, A   **C.** C, G   **D.** G, D
E. A, F

Ques (26-30):Direction: Read the information carefully and answer the questions given below.

Eight people A, B, C, D, E, F, G, and H are sitting around a circular table facing towards the table and not in the same order. Each of them likes a different color i.e., Purple, pink, red, green, blue, black, yellow, and orange but not necessarily in the same order.

The one who likes red sits to the immediate left of the one who likes black. D does not like the yellow color. F sits third to the left of A, who likes purple and the person who likes purple sits to the immediate left of G. C sits to the immediate right of E and neither of them likes blue. The one who likes green and B has two people sitting in between them. C, F, and G, neither of them like green color. F and the person who likes blue has one person in between them. D sits second to the right of H. E sits opposite the person who likes yellow and the person who likes yellow sits immediately next to the one who likes orange.

Q.26 Which color does the person who sits third to the right of D likes?

A. Blue   **B.** Red   **C.** Pink   **D.** Orange
E. Purple

Q.27 Who among the following likes black color?

A. D   **B.** H   **C.** C   **D.** F
E. G

Q.28 Four of the following five are alike in a certain way and hence form a group. Which is the one that does not belong to that group?

A. Blue, D   **B.** Yellow, B
C. Pink, A   **D.** Black, C
E. Orange, H

Q.29 How many people sit between the one who likes orange and C, when counted from right of C?

A. One   **B.** Two
C. Three   **D.** Four
E. More than four

Q.30 Who among the following is an immediate neighbor of the one who likes Red color?

A. D   **B.** C   **C.** E   **D.** F
E. H

// Smart Answer Sheet //

Correct   Indicates percentage of students who answered questions correctly.

Skipped   Indicates percentage of students who skipped questions.

Q.	Ans.	Correct / Skipped
1	E	29.79 % / 67.22 %
2	B	86.77 % / 10.88 %
3	C	47.8 % / 30.6 %
4	E	18.39 % / 79.93 %
5	E	80.33 % / 16.76 %
6	B	49.77 % / 45.25 %
7	E	44.19 % / 37.14 %
8	C	52.93 % / 46.23 %
9	D	55.2 % / 31.21 %
10	A	45.45 % / 48.97 %
11	A	63.7 % / 35.88 %
12	B	79.94 % / 10.17 %
13	E	69.96 % / 30.02 %
14	C	79.26 % / 20.33 %
15	D	69.47 % / 30.27 %
16	C	14.58 % / 76.37 %
17	A	57.8 % / 34.87 %
18	C	79.87 % / 16.25 %
19	E	68.5 % / 30.65 %
20	D	84.85 % / 13.85 %
21	C	57.42 % / 42.34 %
22	D	59.59 % / 39.44 %
23	B	68.44 % / 30.23 %
24	C	85.24 % / 12.22 %
25	D	50.98 % / 44.93 %
26	C	50.74 % / 32.0 %
27	D	64.55 % / 35.42 %
28	D	48.1 % / 46.19 %
29	A	81.26 % / 15.83 %
30	D	50.44 % / 46.26 %

Performance Analysis

Avg. Score (%)	33.33%
Toppers Score (%)	60.0%
Your Score	

//Hints and Solutions//

Ques (1-5): Eight people: E, F, G, H, I, J, K and M

1) F is sitting second to the left of K, who is facing the centre.

2) The Musician is an immediate neighbour of F and K

Therefore, the Musician will sit between F and K.

3) There are three people between the Musician and E i.e., the Musician is opposite to E.

4) H is the Musician.

5) M is second to the right of K.

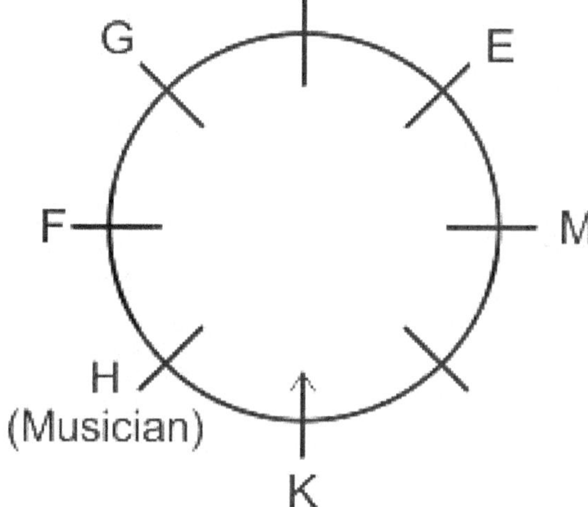

6) G and J are immediate neighbours of each other.

7) G is second to the left of E, who is a Professor.

Therefore, E will face outside and I sits at only seat left seat i.e., between M and K.

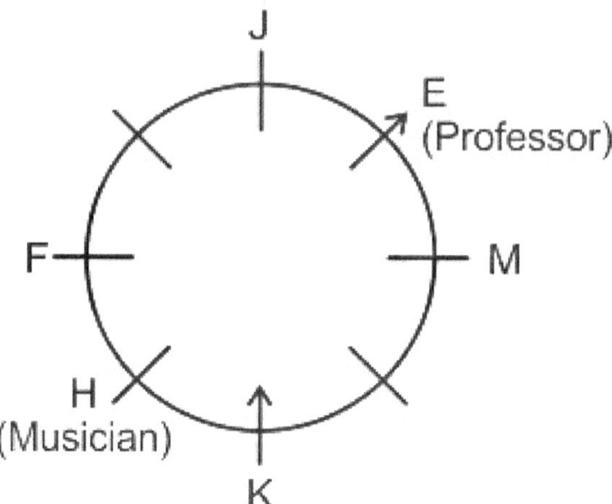

8) The pilot is to the immediate right of F.

Therefore, F faces outside, and G is a Pilot.

9) Only one person sits between the Architect and E.

Therefore, I is Architect.

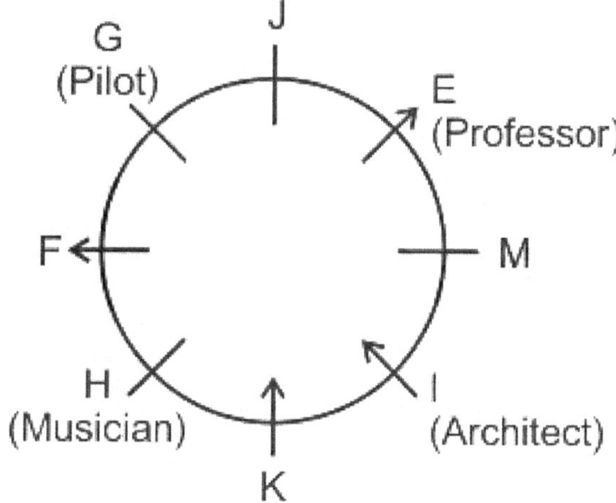

Since the Architect faces the centre and the Doctor is at the immediate right of the Architect, M should be Doctor.

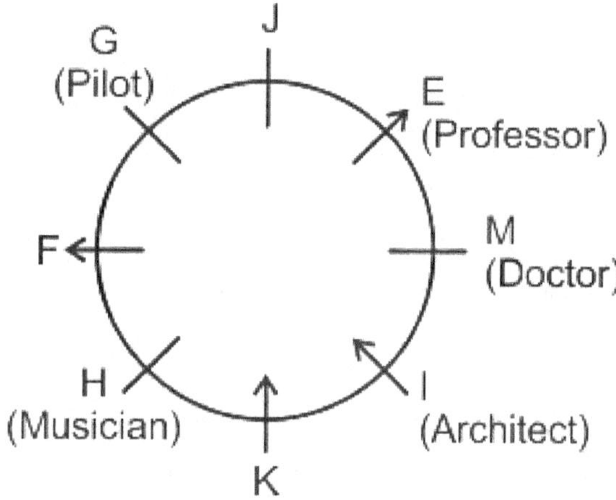

10) The Scientist is an immediate neighbour of the Architect.

Therefore, K should be the Scientist.

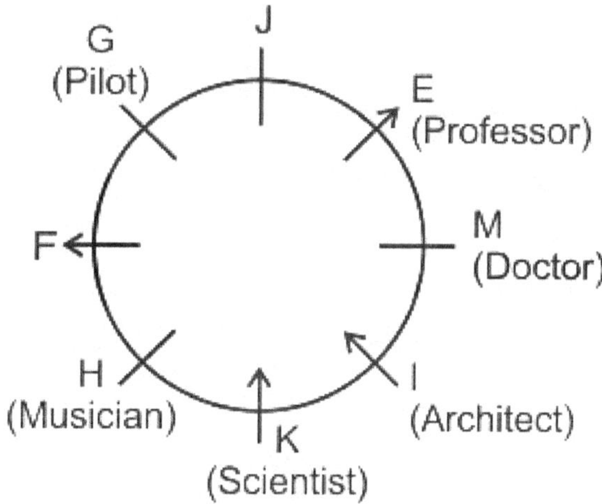

11) The Lawyer is second to the left of the Doctor.

Therefore, M faces outside and J is Lawyer.

12) One of them is Engineer.

Thus, the final arrangement is:

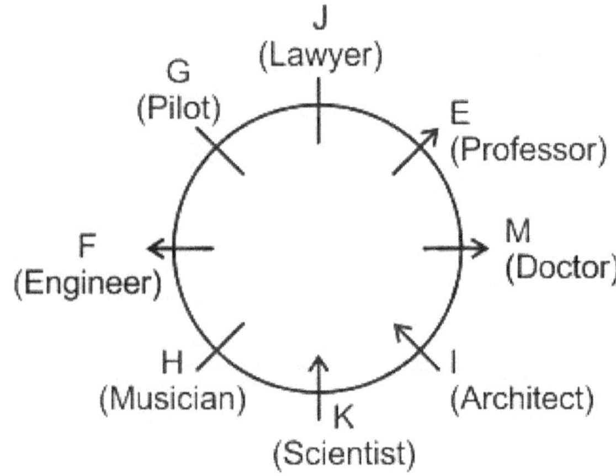

1. The directions of H, G and J cannot be found. Therefore, M or J can be third to the right of the Musician (H).

Hence, the correct option is (E).

2. Thus, K is the Scientist.

Hence, the correct option is (B).

3. Therefore, H – Architect is incorrect as H is the Musician.

Hence, the correct option is (C).

4. 1) The Engineer is second to the left of the Lawyer → False (Possibility is true)

2) Five people face the centre → False (Possibility is true)

3) H sits between the Engineer and the Scientist → True

4) There are three people between the Pilot and the Architect → True

5) The Scientist and the Doctor are to the immediate left of each other → Definitely False (as the Scientist and Doctor are second to the right of each other)

Hence, the correct option is (E).

5. Thus, I is the Architect.

Hence, the correct option is (E).

Ques (6-10): Persons: M, N, O, P, Q, R, S and T

5: Facing Out

3: Facing In

1) There are two persons gap between O and T and both are facing the opposite direction.

2) P sits third to the right of O.

3) Q sits opposite to T and facing the same direction as T.

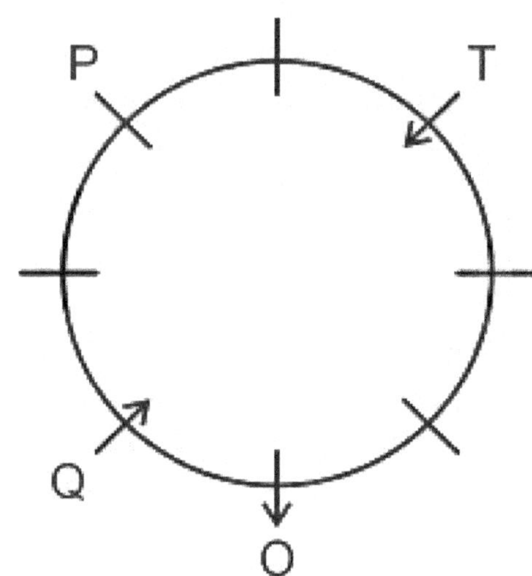

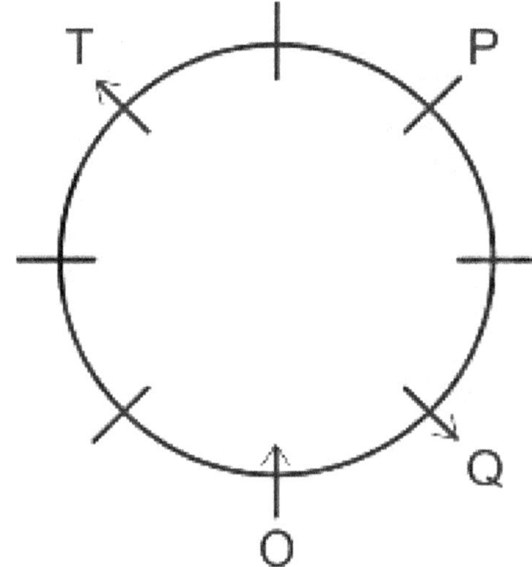

In Case-1 P sits third to right of O if O facing inside then we can't make P to the third right of O. Same in Case-2 if O facing outside then we can't make P to the third right of O.

4) M is neither the neighbour of T nor P.

5) There are three persons gap between M and P and both are facing opposite direction to each other.

6) M is facing opposite direction as Q is facing.

Case- 1

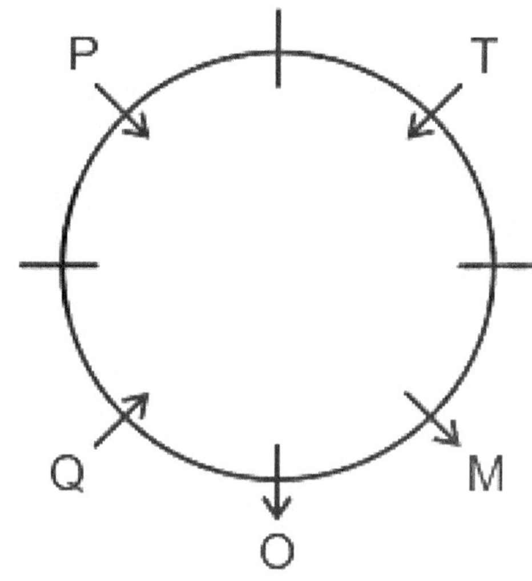

Case- 1

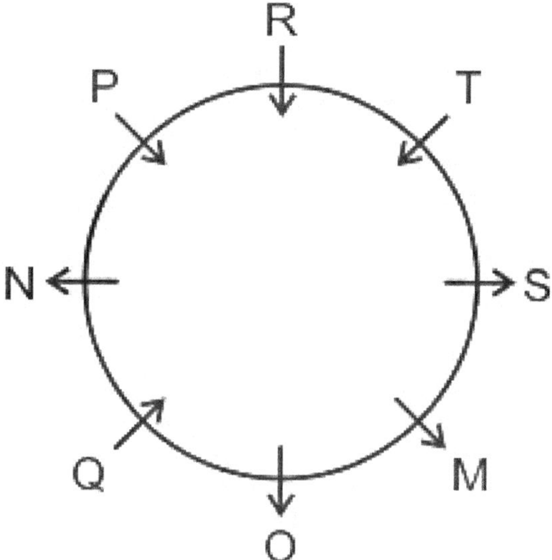

Case- 2

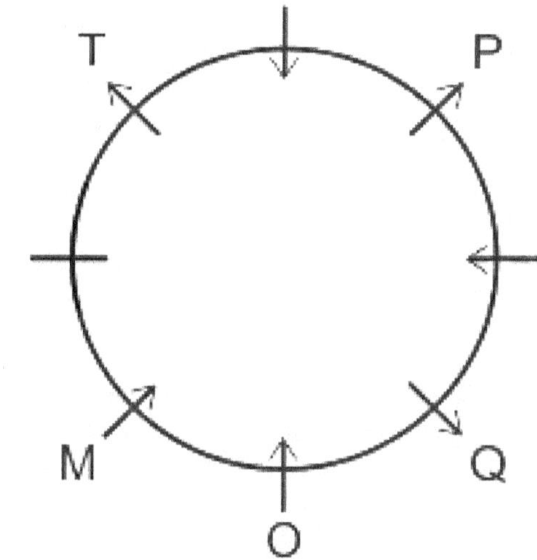

Case- 2

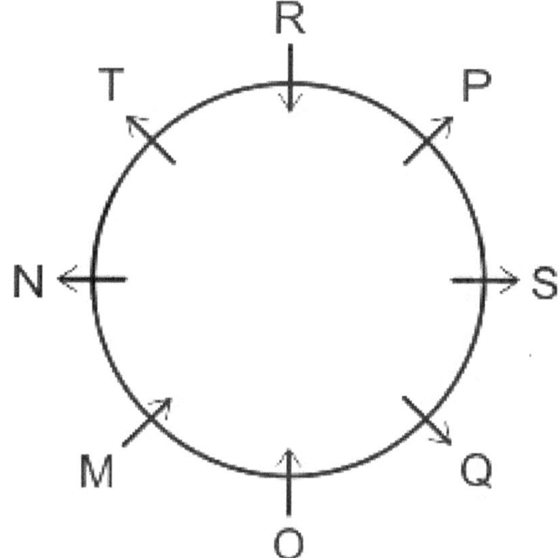

7) There are three persons gap between N and S and both are facing away from the centre.

8) R is sitting second to the right of N and both the neighbours of R facing opposite to the R.

9) R is facing towards the centre.

Here Case-1 gets cancelled because It is clearly given that 3 persons are facing the centre and 5 facing outside the centre, but in Case-1 if R is facing the centre then 4 persons are facing the centre that is not possible.

So, the final diagram is given below:

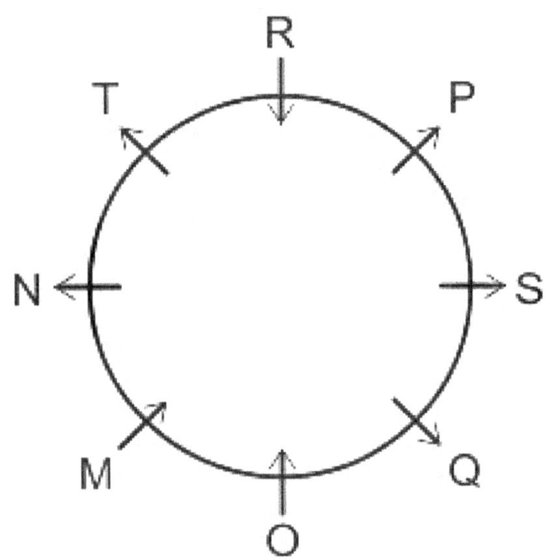

6. Therefore, P is sitting third to the right of N.

Hence, the correct option is (B).

7. Therefore, Q is sitting fourth to the left of T and also fourth to the right of T.

Hence, the correct option is (E).

8. N is second to the right of R.

P is second to the right of T.

Similarly,

M is second to the right of Q.

Hence, the correct option is (C).

9. Therefore, T is sitting second to the left of M.

Hence, the correct option is (D).

10. Therefore, O is sitting opposite to R.

Hence, the correct option is (A).

Ques (11-15): Eight people: Amar, Brijesh, Pinky, Deep, Eshwar, Nancy, Gurkamal and Harsh

1) Nancy is third to the right of Pinky and second to the left of Harsh.

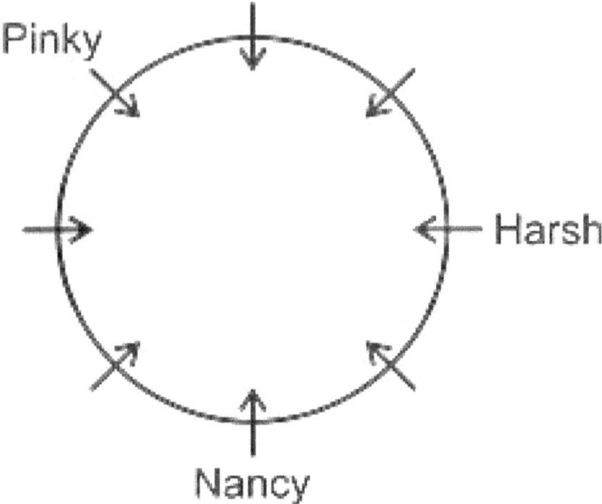

2) Deep is not an immediate neighbour of Pinky or Harsh.

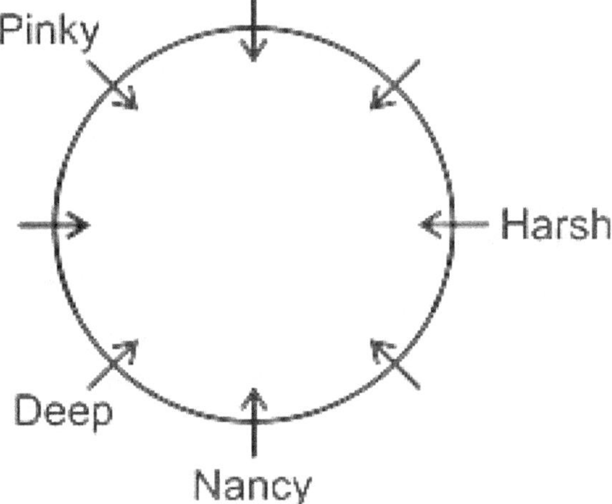

3) Eshwar is to the immediate right of Amar, who is second to the right of Gurkamal.

Here the only position possible for Aman is to the immediate right of Harsh.

Thus, the vacant place is occupied by Brijesh.

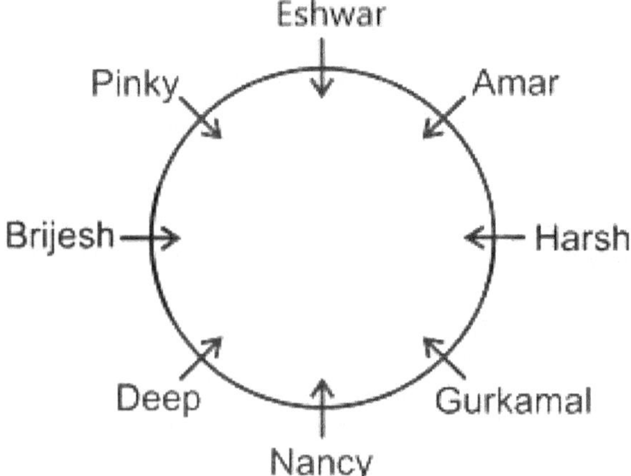

11. Thus, Amar is second to the left of Pinky.

Hence, the correct option is (A).

12. Thus, Brijesh is to the immediate right of Pinky.

Hence, the correct option is (B).

13. Here Deep is sitting to the right of Brijesh. Thus, the correct pair is Deep and Brijesh.

Hence, the correct option is (E).

14. Thus, Nancy sits between Gurkamal and Deep.

Hence, the correct option is (C).

15. Brijesh is sitting in front of Harsh, so Brijesh is both fourth to the right and fourth to the left of Harsh.

Hence, the correct option is (D).

Ques (16-20): Eight friends: A, B, C, D, E, F, G and H

Subjects: Mathematics, Economics, English, History, Physics, Chemistry, Sociology and Hindi

1) A sits adjacent D who is studying Economics.

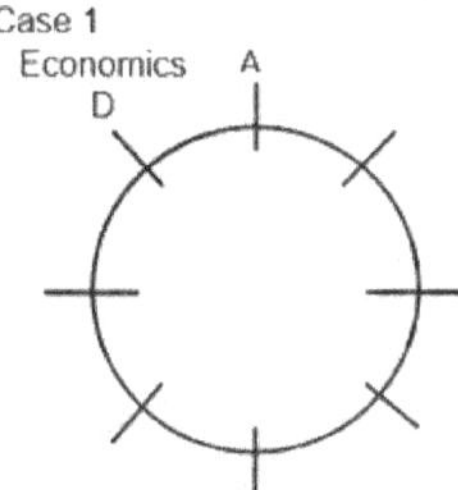
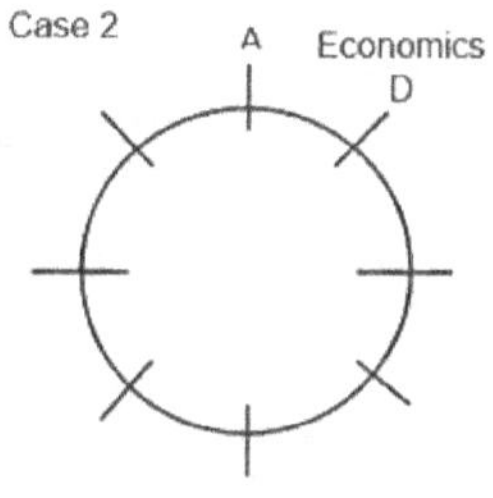

2) F is sitting fifth to the left of A and is studying Physics.

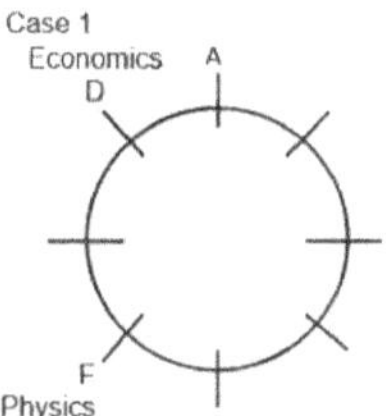
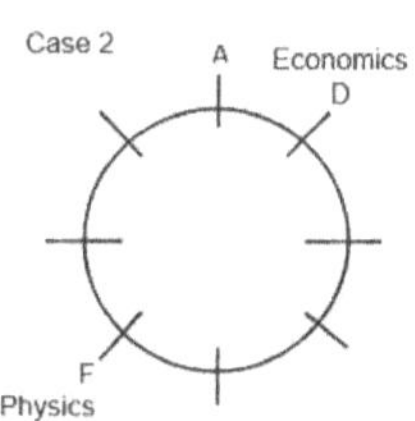

3) One who is studying Chemistry sits left to F.

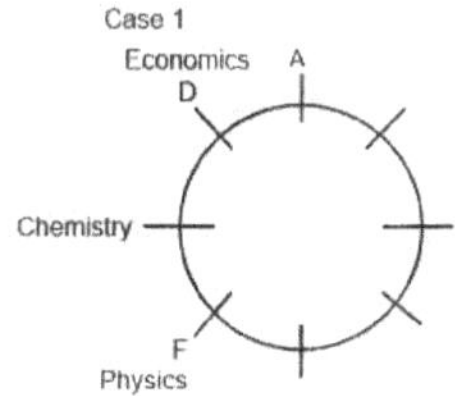
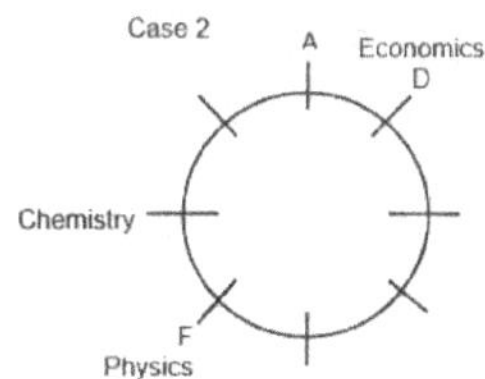

4) G sits opposite to A.

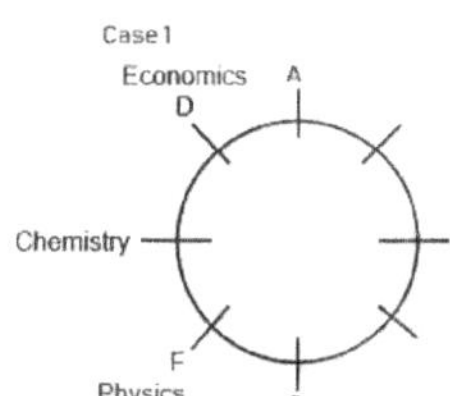
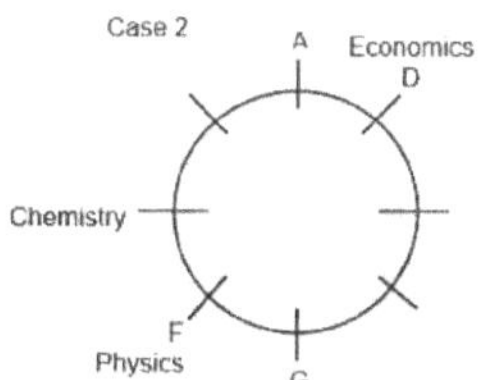

5) One who is studying Hindi sits fifth to the left of G, who is learning Sociology.

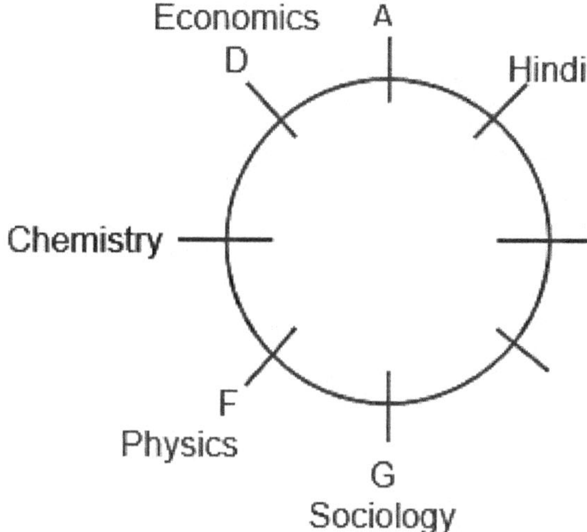

Thus, case 2 has been ruled out.

6) E is studying English and sits next to the one who is studying Hindi.

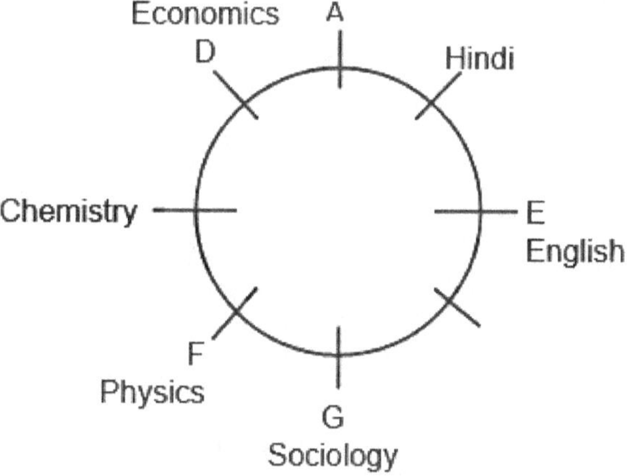

7) B is studying History and does not sit adjacent to C or D. Neither H nor E is immediate neighbour of G.

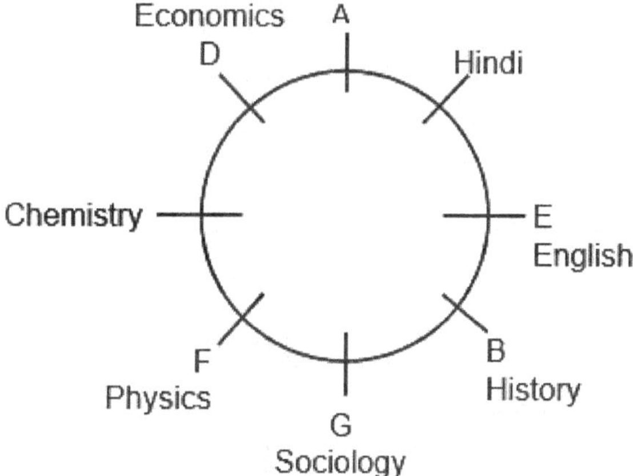

8) C does not study chemistry.

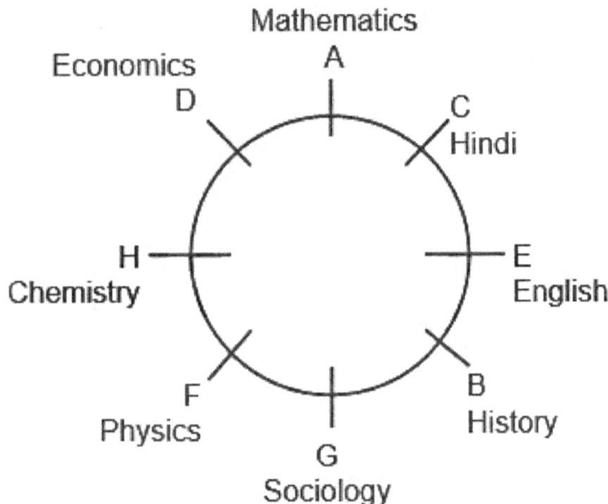

3) G is facing the inward direction.

4) Only one person is sitting between G and E.

5) D is sitting second to the right of G.

(It is only possible if we place E second to the left of G then only we can place D second to the right of G.)

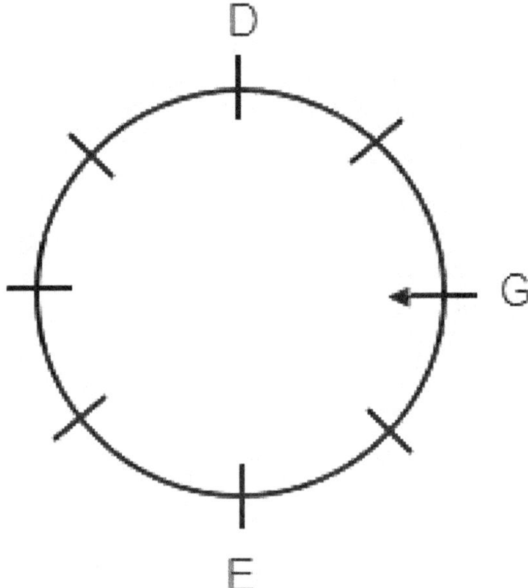

16. Thus, G is sitting third to the left of C and studies Sociology.

Hence, the correct option is (C).

17. Thus, D is sitting diagonally opposite to B.

Hence, the correct option is (A).

18. Thus, C sits between A and E.

Hence, the correct option is (C).

19. Thus, A is studying Mathematics.

Hence, the correct option is (E).

20. Thus, H is studying Chemistry.

Hence, the correct option is (D).

Ques (21-25): Eight person: A, B, C, D, E, F, G and H

1) H is sitting third to the right of E.

2) Both H and E are facing the same direction.

(As it is a circular arrangement, we can randomly pick a seat for E and then we can place H according to the direction that E is facing.)

6) If we place H between D and G then that would mean that E is facing inward direction but, in that case, F would not be an immediate neighbour of H. Therefore, both E and H are facing outward direction.

7) H is sitting third to the right of E and immediate neighbour of F. (It further implies that F is sitting to the immediate left of H as it is the only possibility.)

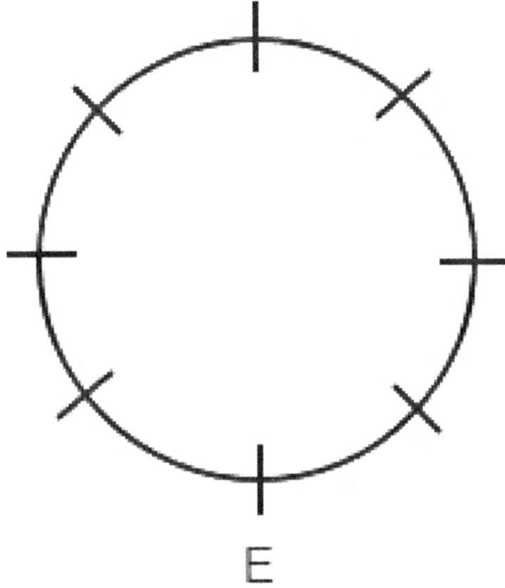

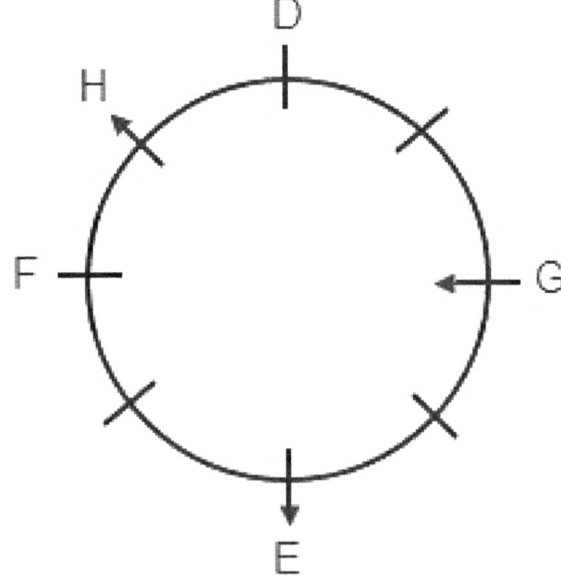

8) F is sitting second to the right of D and they are facing different directions.

(It is only possible if D is facing inward direction and F is facing outward direction. Also, as no three consecutive people are facing the same direction implies that the person sitting to the immediate left of F is facing inward direction.)

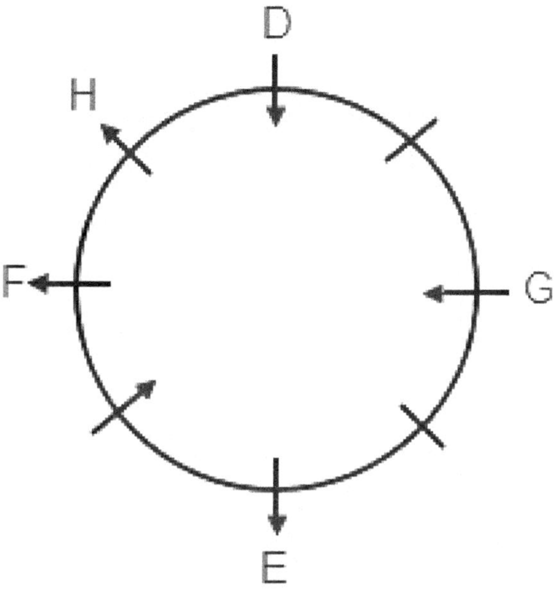

9) B is not an immediate neighbour of E.

(Implies, B is sitting between D and G. It is the only possibility.)

10) C is sitting second to the right of B.

(It is only possible if B is facing outward direction. Also, now that we have identified four people who are facing outward, we can say that the other four are facing inward direction. Therefore, C is facing the inward direction. Also, now only A is left to be placed implies that A is sitting to the immediate left of F.)

Thus, the final arrangement is:

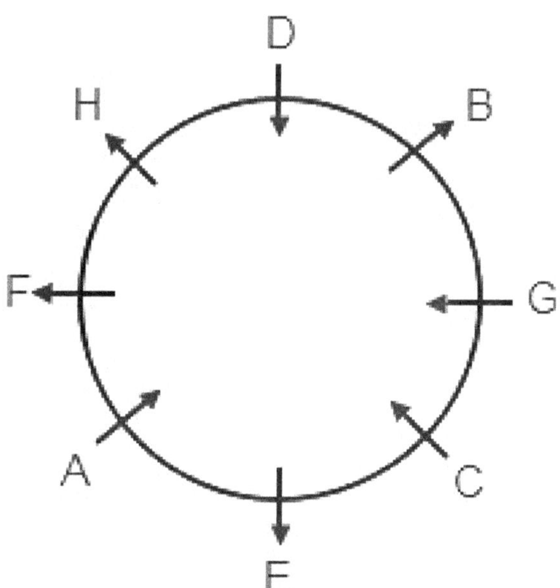

21. Clearly, G is sitting third to the right of A.

Hence, the correct option is (C).

22. Clearly, F is sitting third to the left of C.

Hence, the correct option is (D).

23. Clearly, H is sitting to the immediate right of D.

Hence, the correct option is (B).

24. Except F, all are facing inward direction.

Therefore, F does not belong to the group.

Hence, the correct option is (C).

25. Clearly, G and D, are the immediate neighbours of B.

Hence, the correct option is (D).

Ques (26-30): Eight people: A, B, C, D, E, F, G, and H

Eight Colors: Purple, pink, red, green, blue, black, yellow, and orange

1) F sits third to the left of A, who likes purple, and the person who likes purple sits to the immediate left of G.

2) F and the person who likes blue has one person in between them.

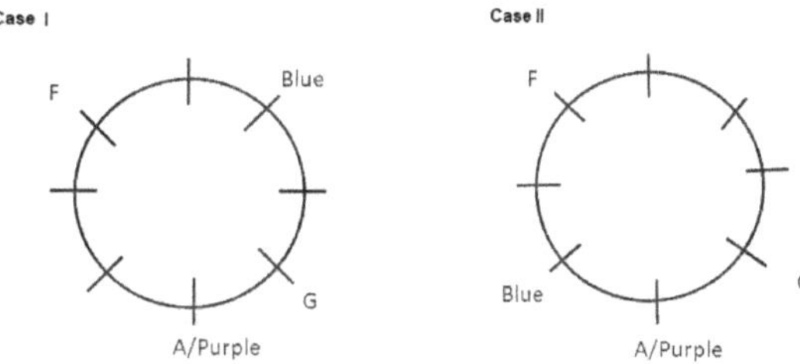

3) C sits to the immediate right of E and neither of them likes blue.

4) E sits opposite the person who likes yellow and the person who likes yellow sits immediately next to the one who likes orange.

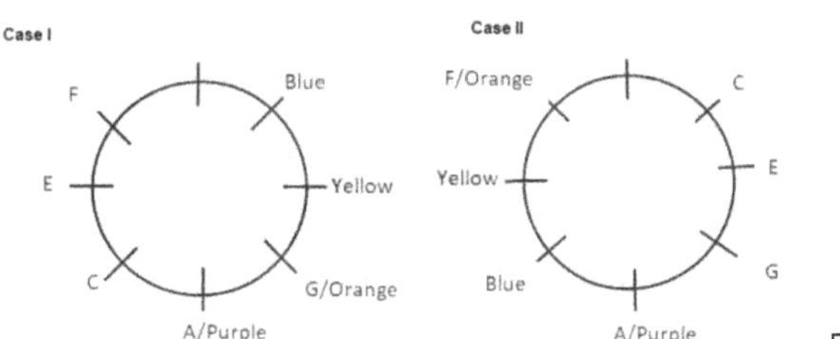

5) The one who likes green and B has two people sitting in between them.

6) C, F and G, neither of them like green color.

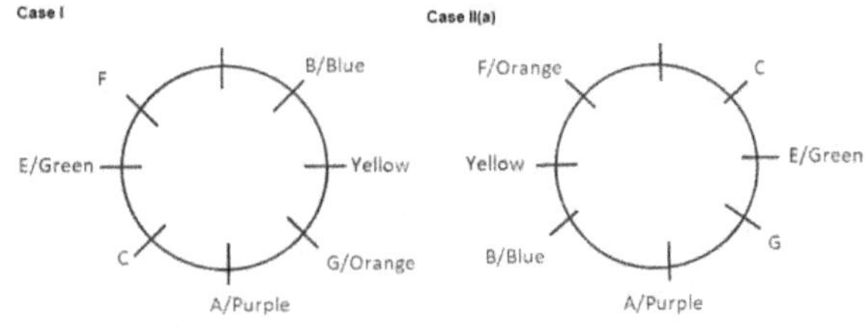

Case II(b)

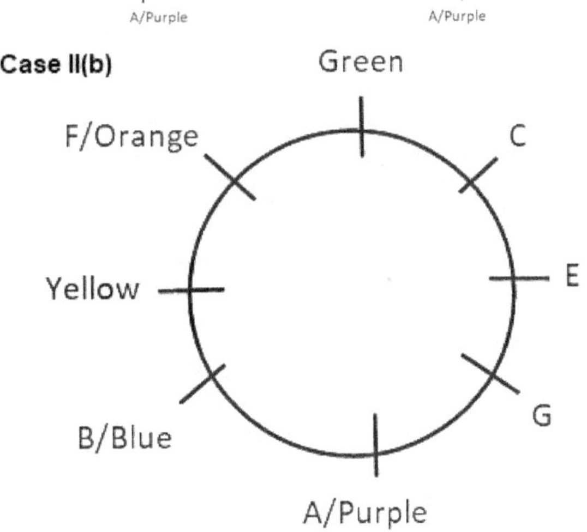

sits second to the right of H.

8) D does not like the yellow color.

This is not possible in cases II(a) and II(b), therefore both the cases get eliminated.

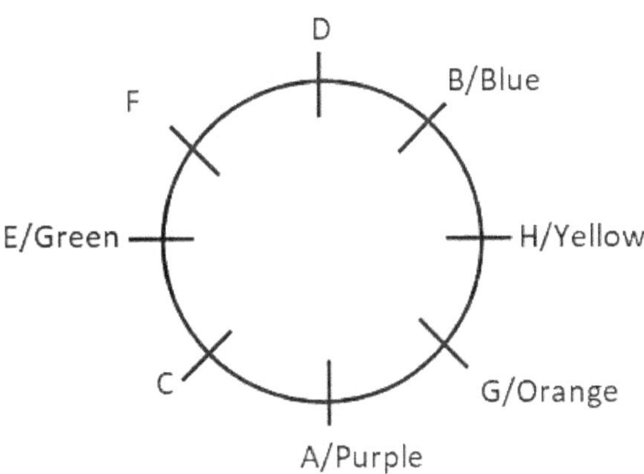

9) The one who likes red sits to the immediate left of the one who likes black.

Thus, the final arrangement is:

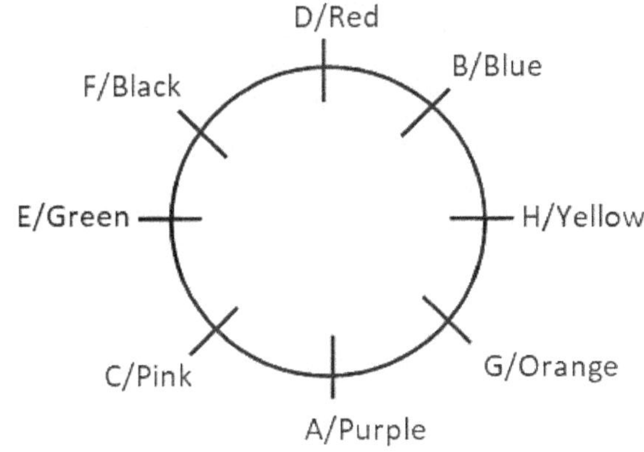

7) D

26. Clearly, the person sitting third to the right of D likes pink color.

Hence, the correct option is (C).

27. Clearly, F likes the black color.

Hence, the correct option is (D).

28. Clearly, "Black and C" does not belong to the group as all the other pairs sit adjacent to each other.

Hence, the correct option is (D).

29. Clearly, only one person sits between the one who likes orange and C, when counted from C's right.

Hence, the correct option is (A).

30. Clearly, F is an immediate neighbor of the one who likes red color.

Hence, the correct option is (D).

Ques (1-5):Direction: Study the following information carefully and answer the question given below.

A number arrangement machine, when given a particular input, rearranges it following a particular rule. The following is the illustration of the input and the steps of arrangement.

Input: 39 121 49 19 66 102 10 52 54 98

Step I: 10 39 121 49 19 66 102 52 54 98

Step II: 10 39 49 19 66 102 52 54 98 121

Step III: 10 19 39 49 66 102 52 54 98 121

Step IV: 10 19 39 49 66 52 54 98 102 121

Step V: 10 19 39 49 52 66 54 98 102 121

Step VI: 10 19 39 49 52 54 66 98 102 121

And Step VI is the last step for this input. As per rules followed in the above steps, find out the question in the appropriate step for the given input.

Q.1 What will be step III for the following input?
Input: 55 176 29 82 119 36 11 49
A.   11 29 55 119 82 36 49 176
B.   11 29 55 82 119 36 49 176
C.   11 55 29 82 119 36 49 176
D.   There will be no such step
E.   None of these

Q.2 What will be step III for the following input?
Input: 55 176 29 82 119 36 11 49
A.   11 29 55 119 82 36 49 176
B.   11 29 55 82 119 36 49 176
C.   11 55 29 82 119 36 49 176
D.   There will be no such step
E.   None of these

Q.3 What will be the last step for the following input?
Input: 132 53 39 83 79 112 22 66
A.   22 39 53 66 79 83 112 132
B.   22 39 66 53 79 83 112 132
C.   22 39 53 56 83 79 112 13
D.   Cannot be determined
E.   None of these

Q.4 How many steps will be required for getting the final output for the following input?
Input 116 85 66 50 73 39 146 25 112 79
A. Five   B. Six
C. Seven   D. Eight
E. None of the above

Q.5 In the penultimate step which of the following would be at 6th position from the right?

Input: 17 32 43 82 69 93 49 56 99 106
A. 69   B. 93
C. 17   D. 56
E. None of the above

Ques (6-10):Direction: Study the following information carefully and answer the given question.

A word and number arrangement machine when given an input line of words and numbers rearranges them following a particular hide in each step. The following is an illustration of input and rearrangement. (All the numbers are two digit numbers).

Input: 76 toy high 12 wish 98 10 flag link dig 54 87 58

Step I: dig 76 toy high 12 wish 98 flag link 54 87 58 10

Step II: flag dig 76 toy high wish 98 link 54 87 58 12 10

Step III: high flag dig 76 toy wish 98 link 87 58 54 12 10

Step IV: link high flag dig toy wish 98 87 76 58 54 12 10

Step V: toy link high flag dig wish 98 87 76 58 54 12 10

Step VI: wish toy link high flag dig 98 87 76 58 54 12 10

And Step VI is the last step of the above input, as the desired arrangement is obtained.

As per the hides followed in the above steps, find out in the question, the appropriate step for the given input. (All the numbers are two-digit numbers).

Input: height math 23 98 11 ugly and 54 owl 20 67 queen fish 32

Q.6 What is the position of "height" in step V?
A.   Fourth from the right
B.   Third from the right
C.   Twelfth from right
D.   Tenth from right
E.   None of above

Q.7 Which is the last step after all arrangements?
A. V   B. VII   C. IX   D. VIII
E. IV

Q.8 What will be position of 98 in third step?
A.   Fifth from the left
B.   Fifth from the right
C.   Seventh from the right
D.   Eighth from left
E.   None of above

Q.9 Which would be IV step?
A.   math height fish and 98 ugly owl 67 queen 54 32 23 20 11
B.   queen owl math height fish and ugly 98 67 54 32 23 20 11
C.   ugly queen owl math height fish and 98 67 54 32 23 20 11

D. height fish and math 98 ugly 54 owl 67 queen 32 23 20 11

E. owl math height fish and 98 ugly queen 67 54 32 23 20 11

Q.10 What is the position of "fish" in last step?

A. Eighth from right **B.** Fifth from left

C. Sixth from left **D.** Seventh from right

E. None of above

Ques (11-15):Direction: Study the given information carefully and answer the following question.

A word arrangement machine when given an input of words, rearranges them following a particular rule in each step. The following is an illustration of input and steps rearrangement.

Input: Bowl Tongs Whisks Couch Lamp Rags

Step I: Whisks Bowl Tongs Couch Lamp Rags

Step II: Whisks Tongs Bowl Couch Lamp Rags

Step III: Whisks Tongs Rags Bowl Couch Lamp

Step IV: Whisks Tongs Rags Lamp Bowl Couch

Step V: Whisks Tongs Rags Lamp Couch Bowl

This is the final arrangement and step 5 is the last step.

As per the rules followed in the given steps, answer the question given below for the following input.

Input: Broom Windex Detergent Towel Napkin Curd.

Q.11 What would be the second step of the following input?

A. Windex Broom Detergent Towel Napkin Curd

B. Windex Towel Broom Detergent Napkin Curd

C. Windex Towel Napkin Broom Detergent Curd

D. Windex Towel Napkin Detergent Broom Curd

E. Windex Towel Napkin Broom Curd Detergent

Q.12 How many words are there between "Towel" and "Detergent" in the penultimate step?

A. 1 **B.** 2

C. 3 **D.** 4

E. Either 2or 4

Q.13 Which word comes exactly between "Napkin" and "Broom" in the second last step?

A. Curd

B. Windex

C. Detergent

D. Either Curd or Towel

E. None of these

Q.14 Which element is 5th from the right in the final step?

A. Windex **B.** Curd **C.** Broom **D.** Towel

E. Napkin

Q.15

What would be the final output of the given input?

A. Windex Broom Detergent Towel Napkin Curd

B. Windex Towel Napkin Detergent Curd Broom

C. Windex Towel Napkin Broom Detergent Curd

D. Windex Towel Napkin Detergent Broom Curd

E. Windex Towel Napkin Broom Curd Detergent

Ques (16-20):

Direction: Study the following information carefully and answer the given question.

A word and number arrangement device when given an input line of words and numbers rearranges them following a particular pattern in each step. The following is an illustration of input and rearrangement.

INPUT: Harsha made kannauj his Capital

Step I: Capital Harsha his kannauj made

Step II: 14A3   12A8   6I8   14A11   8A13

Step III: 17C   20C   14K   25C   21C

Step IV: QC   TC   NK   YC   UC

Step V: N   Q   C   V   R

And Step V is the last step of the above input, as the desired arrangement is obtained.

As per the logic followed in the above steps, find out the following question in the appropriate step for the given input.

INPUT: Clean clams crammed in clean cans.

Q.16 Among the terms given in the alternatives, which term is present in step III?

A. 13L **B.** 17R **C.** 14N **D.** 17T

E. 11A

Q.17 In which of the following options QT and MN comes together?

A. Step II **B.** Step III

C. Step V **D.** Step I

E. None of the above

Q.18 Which of the given option is the last term in step IV?

A. KA **B.** 4N9 **C.** 13N **D.** QR

E. MP

Q.19 Which of the given option is the last step of the given input?

A. H I A B I A **B.** A H A H H H

C. H A A A C C **D.** A A A A H A

E. H A H H A H

Q.20 Which of the given option is second from the right end in step III?

A. 10L3 **B.** 14R3 **C.** 11A **D.** 13L

E. 17T

Ques (21-25):Direction: Study the following information carefully and answer the given question.

A word and number arrangement device when given an input line of words and numbers rearranges them following a particular pattern in each step. The following is an illustration of input and rearrangement.

Input: 23 Quality Tractor Popular 57 38 93 Handle

Step 1: Handl Qualit Tracto Popula 57 38 93 23

Step 2: Handl 23 Qualit Tracto Popula 57 38 93

Step 3: Hand 23 Popul 38 Quali Tract 57 93

Step 4: Han 23 Popu 38 Trac 57 Qual 93

Step 5: Ha 23 Pop 38 Tra 57 Qua 93

Step 6: H 23 Po 38 Tr 57 Qu 93

And Step 6 is the last step of the above input.

As per the pattern followed in the above steps, find out the following question in the appropriate step for the given input.

Input: 20 Rational Trader Particle 41 29 87 Helmet

Q.21 What will be the position of 'He' in Step 5?

A. Fifth from the right end
B. Ninth from the right end
C. Sixth from the left end
D. Sixth from the right end
E. None of these

Q.22 Which of the following is second to the right of the one that is 4th from the right end in Step 4?

A. Part
B. Ratio
C. Hel
D. Tra
E. None of these

Q.23 In Step 4, if in a certain way, 'Hel' is related to 'Parti' and 'Ratio' is related to 'Tar', then which of the following would '41' be related to, following the same pattern.

A. 87
B. Part
C. Rati
D. Cannot be determined
E. None of these

Q.24 Which of the following will be the last step of the rearrangement?

A. 4
B. 6
C. 7
D. 5
E. None of these

Q.25 Which of the following will be Step 3 of the rearrangement?

A. Helm 20 Part 41 Ration 29 Trade 87
B. Helm 20 Ratio 29 Trad Partic 41 87
C. Helm 20 Partic 29 Ration Trad 41 87
D. Helm 29 Partic 20 Ration Trad 41 87
E. Helm 20 Ration 29 Trade Partic 41 87

Ques (26-30):Direction: Study the following information carefully and answer the given question.

When a word arrangement machine is given an input of line number and word, it arranges them by following a certain rule and certain conditions. Following is an illustration of input and rearrangement.

Read the following information and answer the question that follow.

INPUT: Eye Cover Hen An Back Lenovo Package Quantity

Step 1: Quantity Eye Cover Hen An Back Lenovo Package

Step 2: Quantity An Eye Cover Hen Back Lenovo Package

Step 3: Quantity An Package Eye Cover Hen Back Lenovo

Step 4: Quantity An Package Back Eye Cover Hen Lenovo

Step 5: Quantity An Package Back Lenovo Eye Cover Hen

Step 6: Quantity An Package Back Lenovo Cover Eye Hen

Step 7: Quantity An Package Back Lenovo Cover Hen Eye

Step 7 is the last step. As per rule followed in the given step, find out the appropriate step for the given input.

INPUT: Jack Mango Cat All Nose Base Use Zoo

Q.26 Which element come exactly between the 'Jack' and 'Cat' in the step 3 of the given input?

A. Mango **B.** Zoo **C.** Use **D.** All
E. Nose

Q.27 What is the last step of the given input?

A. Zoo Jack Mango Cat All Nose Base Use
B. Zoo All Use Base Nose Jack Mango Cat
C. Zoo All Use Base Nose Cat Mango Jack
D. Zoo All Jack Mango Cat Nose Base Jack
E. None of these

Q.28 Which of the following is the fourth element from the right end of the step 4?

A. All **B.** Zoo
C. Jack **D.** Nose
E. None of these

Q.29 Which step number would be the following output?
Zoo All Use Base Nose Cat Jack Mango

A. Step 3 **B.** Step 6 **C.** Step 7 **D.** Step 4
E. Step 1

Q.30 Which of the following statement is correct?

A. 'Mango' is second from right in step 6.
B. There are only 9 steps for given input.
C. 'Base' is exactly between the 'use' and 'nose' in step 5.
D. 'Jack' is fourth from left end in step 4.
E. None of these

// Smart Answer Sheet //

Correct Indicates percentage of students who answered questions correctly.

Skipped Indicates percentage of students who skipped questions.

Q.	Ans.	Correct / Skipped
1	B	22.9 % / 68.18 %
2	B	26.79 % / 68.72 %
3	A	21.72 % / 67.19 %
4	D	15.22 % / 77.82 %
5	D	10.96 % / 78.15 %
6	C	15.48 % / 79.39 %

Q.	Ans.	Correct / Skipped
7	B	59.83 % / 32.4 %
8	A	62.2 % / 32.23 %
9	A	32.94 % / 67.0 %
10	C	56.01 % / 40.1 %
11	B	46.63 % / 32.94 %
12	A	60.06 % / 33.24 %

Q.	Ans.	Correct / Skipped
13	C	66.6 % / 32.6 %
14	D	40.09 % / 55.07 %
15	B	49.2 % / 30.37 %
16	D	22.86 % / 69.38 %
17	E	27.89 % / 71.53 %
18	E	21.22 % / 75.11 %

Q.	Ans.	Correct / Skipped
19	C	13.46 % / 85.79 %
20	E	27.35 % / 71.95 %
21	E	12.36 % / 79.58 %
22	D	57.62 % / 41.86 %
23	A	58.86 % / 38.83 %
24	B	69.29 % / 30.37 %

Q.	Ans.	Correct / Skipped
25	C	68.91 % / 30.34 %
26	A	62.63 % / 30.04 %
27	C	57.22 % / 40.5 %
28	C	52.72 % / 38.53 %
29	B	40.18 % / 30.31 %
30	C	65.62 % / 31.96 %

Performance Analysis

Avg. Score (%)	46.67%
Toppers Score (%)	63.33%
Your Score	

//Hints and Solutions//

Ques (1-5): Logic:

In the given problem the following pattern is followed:

Step I: The smallest number is arranged in the first position from the leftmost side in the sequence.

Step II: The highest number is pushed to the last position from the rightmost side in the sequence.

Similarly, the lowest numbers are arranged from the left side and the highest to the right side.

In the final position, all the numbers are arranged in ascending order.

1. In the final position, all the numbers are arranged in ascending order.

Now the given input is 55 176 29 82 119 36 11 49

Step I: 11 55 176 29 82 119 36 49

Step II: 11 55 29 82 119 36 49 176

Step III: 11 29 55 82 119 36 49 176

Thus, '11 29 55 82 119 36 49 176' is the correct sequence.

Hence, the correct option is (B).

2. Final position is all the numbers are arranged in ascending order.

Now the given input is 55 176 29 82 119 36 11 49

Step I: 11 55 176 29 82 119 36 49

Step II: 11 55 29 82 119 36 49 176

Step III: 11 29 55 82 119 36 49 176

Thus, '11 29 55 82 119 36 49 176' is the correct sequence.

Hence, the correct option is (B).

3. Final position is all the numbers are arranged in ascending order.

Hence, the correct option is (A).

4. Final position is all the numbers are arranged in ascending order.

Now the given input is 116 85 66 50 73 39 146 25 112 79

Step 1: 25 116 85 66 50 73 39 146 112 79

Step 2: 25 116 85 66 50 73 39 112 79 146

Step 3: 25 39 116 85 66 50 73 112 79 146

Step 4: 25 39 85 66 50 73 112 79 116 146

Step 5: 25 39 50 85 66 73 112 79 116 146

Step 6: 25 39 50 85 66 73 79 112 116 146

Step 7: 25 39 50 66 85 73 79 112 116 146

Step 8: 25 39 50 66 73 79 85 112 116 146

So, eight steps are required for the final arrangement.

Hence, the correct option is (D).

5. Final position is all the numbers are arranged in ascending order.

Now the given input is 17 32 43 82 69 93 49 56 99 106

Step 1: 17 32 43 49 82 69 93 56 99 106

Step 2: 17 32 43 49 82 69 56 93 99 106

Step 3: 17 32 43 49 56 82 69 93 99 106

Step 4: 17 32 43 49 56 69 82 93 99 106

So the number 56 is 6th from the right-hand side.

Hence, the correct option is (D).

Ques (6-10): In the given illustration-

A word and number is arranged simultaneously.

All the words are arranged on the left side i.e. beginning and numbers are arranged on the right side i.e. ending.

i. In first step first word according to the dictionary is arranged i.e. starting of the line (leftmost side) smallest number is arranged at the rightmost side i.e. end of the line.

ii. Next word as per dictionary is arranged before the last arranged word i.e. leftmost side i.e. and lowest number is arranged left to the last arranged number i.e. second from the last.

iii. The same procedure is to be followed.

Input: height math 23 98 11 ugly and 54 owl 20 67 queen fish 32

Step I: and height math 23 98 ugly 54 owl 20 67 queen fish 32 11

Step II: fish and height math 23 98 ugly 54 owl 67 queen 32 20 11

Step III: height fish and math 98 ugly 54 owl 67 queen 32 23 20 11

Step IV: math height fish and 98 ugly owl 67 queen 54 32 23 20 11

Step V: owl math height fish and 98 ugly queen 67 54 32 23 20 11

Step VI: queen owl math height fish and ugly 98 67 54 32 23 20 11

Step VII: ugly queen owl math height fish and 98 67 54 32 23 20 11

6. So, step VII is the last step.

Therefore, position of "height" in V step is twelfth from the right.

Hence, the correct option is (C).

7. Thus, step VII is the last step.

Hence, the correct option is (B).

8. Thus, step VII is the last step.

Therefore, the position of "98" in Step III is fifth from the left.

Hence, the correct option is (A).

9. So, step VII is the last step.

Therefore, "math height fish and 98 ugly owl 67 queen 54 32 23 20 11" is the fourth step.

Hence, the correct option is (A).

10. Thus, fish is sixth from left in the last step.

Hence, the correct option is (C).

Ques (11-15): The logic followed here is as follows,

1) The rearrangement is taking place from left to right.

2) Words are arranged in a reverse alphabetical order.

3) In each step the next word is placed to the right of previously placed word.

Input: Broom Windex Detergent Towel Napkin Curd

Step 1: Windex Broom Detergent Towel Napkin Curd

Step 2: Windex Towel Broom Detergent Napkin Curd

Step 3: Windex Towel Napkin Broom Detergent Curd

Step 4: Windex Towel Napkin Detergent Broom Curd

Step 5: Windex Towel Napkin Detergent Curd Broom

11. Therefore, 'Windex Towel Broom Detergent Napkin Curd' is the second step.

Hence, the correct option is (B).

12. Therefore, there is one word between "Towel" and "Detergent" in the penultimate step.

Hence, the correct option is (A).

13. Therefore, "Detergent" comes exactly between "Napkin" and "Broom" in the second last step.

Hence, the correct option is (C).

14. Therefore, in the final step "Towel" is the 5th element from the right.

Hence, the correct option is (D).

15. Therefore, "Windex Towel Napkin Detergent Curd Broom" is the final output of the given input.

Hence, the correct option is (B).

Ques (16-20): In the given illustration:

1) In step I, all the words are arranged in ascending order according to the English alphabetical series from left to right.

2) In step II, the words are changed in the format as below.

a) (No of letters) multiplied by 2 → first number

b) Second letter from the left end → middle letter

c) The positional value of the first letter → last number

3) In step III, the two numbers are added and the letter is incremented by two.

4) In step IV, the first letter is the letter that is at the place in the English alphabetical series as the number in step III.

5) Difference between the letters in step IV is taken and the number obtained is assigned the alphabetic letter as per the english alphabetical series.

Similar steps are followed for the given input:

INPUT: Clean clams crammed in clean cans.

Step I: Cans Clams Clean Clean Crammed In

Step II: 8A3   10L3   10L3   10L3   14R3   4N9

Step III: 11C   13N   13N   13N   17T   13P

Step IV: KC   MN   MN   MN   QT   MP

Step V: H   A   A   A   C   C

Step V is the last step.

16. Thus, the term '17T' is present in step III.

Hence, the correct option is (D).

17. QT and MN come together in step IV.

Thus, "none of the above" is the correct answer.

Hence, the correct option is (E).

18. Thus, "MP" is the last term in step IV.

Hence, the correct option is (E).

19. From the above steps "H   A   A   A   C C" is the last step of the given input.

Hence, the correct option is (C).

20. Thus, the term that is second from the right end in step III is "17T".

Hence, the correct option is (E).

Ques (21-25): In the given illustration:

1) In step 1, we arrange the smallest word as per alphabetical order in the left end and the smallest number in the right end. All the words are written with one letter being removed.

2) In step 2, we arrange the pair of the smallest word as per alphabetical order followed by the smallest number from left to right.

3) In step 3, the next pair of the smallest word as per alphabetical order followed by the next smallest number is arranged to the right of the previously arranged pair. One letter is removed from each word.

4) From step 4, step 3 is repeated till a single letter word is reached.

Now given input is:

Input: 20 Rational Trader Particle 41 29 87 Helmet

Step 1: Helme Rationa Trade Particl 41 29 87 20

Step 2: Helme 20 Rationa Trade Particl 41 29 87

Step 3: Helm 20 Partic 29 Ration Trad 41 87

Step 4: Hel 20 Parti 29 Ratio 41 Tra 87

Step 5: He 20 Part 29 Rati 41 Tr 87

Step 6: H 20 Par 29 Rat 41 T 87

21. Therefore, 'He' is on the left end of the arrangement in Step 5.

Hence, the correct option is (E).

22. Fourth from the right end in Step 4 is 'Ratio' and second to the right of 'Ratio' is 'Tra'.

Therefore, 'Tra' is the right answer.

Hence, the correct option is (D).

23. Therefore, following the same pattern, 41 would be related to 87.

Hence, the correct option is (A).

24. Therefore, Step 6 is the last step of the arrangement.

Hence, the correct option is (B).

25. Therefore, "Helm 20 Partic 29 Ration Trad 41 87" is the 3rd step of the rearrangement.

Hence, the correct option is (C).

Ques (26-30): The logic followed is as follows,

In step 1 alphabet is arranged in reverse order (Z→A) in Left end then in Step II word starting with Lowest alphabet that is A→ Z is arranged right side of the word that is arranged in previous step and this process repeated till end.

Apply the same rule on the given input we get,

INPUT: Jack Mango Cat All Nose Base Use Zoo

Step 1: Zoo Jack Mango Cat All Nose Base Use

Step 2: Zoo All Jack Mango Cat Nose Base Use

Step 3: Zoo All Use Jack Mango Cat Nose Base

Step 4: Zoo All Use Base Jack Mango Cat Nose

Step 5: Zoo All Use Base Nose Jack Mango Cat

Step 6: Zoo All Use Base Nose Cat Jack Mango

Step 7: Zoo All Use Base Nose Cat Mango Jack

26. The word 'Mango' is exactly between the word 'jack' and 'cat' in step 3 of the given input.

Hence, the correct option is (A).

27. Step 3 is the given input is 'Zoo All Use Jack Mango Cat Nose Base'.

Hence, the correct option is (C).

28. Jack is the fourth element from the right end of the step 4.

Hence, the correct option is (C).

29. Step 6 is the right output of the given input.

Hence, the correct option is (B).

30. In step 5, 'base' is exactly between the 'use' and 'nose'.

Hence, the correct option is (C).

Ques (1-21):Direction: The following consists of a question and two statements numbered I and II given below it. You have to decide whether the data provided in the statements are sufficient to answer the question.

Q.1 A 7-letter meaningful English word is written somewhere. Find the exactly middle letter of that word?

Statement I: The word comprises of three different vowels and third and seventh letter of the word is same. The word ends with 'N'. T is adjacent to one of the vowels.

Statement II: The word starts with 'C'. One of the vowels used is 'O' and placed at second position from left end. T is adjacent to A.

A. If the data in statement I alone is sufficient to answer the question, while the data in statement II alone is not sufficient to answer the question.

B. If the data in statement II alone is sufficient to answer the question, while the data in statement II alone is not sufficient to answer the question.

C. If the data either in statement I alone or in statement II alone is sufficient to answer the question.

D. If the data in both statement I and II together are not sufficient to answer the question.

E. If the data in both statement I and II together are sufficient to answer the question.

Q.2 Five persons – Mahi, Kona, Ramu, Deva and Jeet, each has a different weight. Who among these persons is the heaviest?

Statement I: Only two persons are heavier than Kona who is heavier than Jeet and Deva.

Statement II: Ramu, who is not the lightest, is heavier than Kona and Deva, but not Mahi.

A. If the data in statement I alone is sufficient to answer the question, while the data in statement II alone is not sufficient to answer the question.

B. If the data in statement II alone is sufficient to answer the question, while the data in statement I alone is not sufficient to answer the question.

C. If the data either in statement I alone or in statement II alone is sufficient to answer the question.

D. If the data in both statement I and II together are not sufficient to answer the question.

E. If the data in both statement I and II together are sufficient to answer the question.

Q.3 Four persons – Arnav, Abdul, Afzal and Azam, are sitting in a straight line facing South then who is sitting adjacent to Arnav?

Statement I: Arnav does not sit next to Azam, who does not sit on the extreme right.

Statement II: No one sit to the right of Arnav and on the left of Abdul, while only one person sits between Afzal and Abdul.

A. If the data in statement I alone is sufficient to answer the question, while the data in statement II alone is not sufficient to answer the question.

B. If the data in statement II alone is sufficient to answer the

question, while the data in statement I alone is not sufficient to answer the question.

C. If the data either in statement I alone or in statement II alone is sufficient to answer the question.

D. If the data in both statement I and II together are not sufficient to answer the question.

E. If the data in both statement I and II together are sufficient to answer the question.

Q.4 Six persons – P, Q, R, S, T and U, each earns a different amount of money. Who earns maximum?

Statement I: R earns more than only two persons. Q earns more than P but not maximum. T earns more than only U.

Statement II: P earns less than only two persons. T earns more than U but less than R. R earns less than P. Q earns less than S.

A. If the data in statement I alone is sufficient to answer the question, while the data in statement II alone is not sufficient to answer the question.

B. If the data in statement II alone is sufficient to answer the question, while the data in statement I alone is not sufficient to answer the question.

C. If the data either in statement I alone or in statement II alone is sufficient to answer the question.

D. If the data in both statement I and II together are not sufficient to answer the question.

E. If the data in both statement I and II together are sufficient to answer the question.

Q.5 In a straight line of twentyfive persons facing north how many persons are sitting between Dev and Han?

Statement I: Ana sits at the extreme left end of the line. Only six persons sit between Ana and Han. Only ten persons sit between Han and Pal. Only four persons sit between Pal and Dev.

Statement II: Mia sits exactly in the middle of the line. Only three persons sit between Ram and Mia. Only six persons sit between Ram and Dev. Ram sits on the left of Dev. Han sits fourth to the left of Mia

A. If the data in statement I alone is sufficient to answer the question, while the data in statement II alone is not sufficient to answer the question.

B. If the data in statement II alone is sufficient to answer the question, while the data in statement I alone is not sufficient to answer the question.

C. If the data either in statement I alone or in statement II alone is sufficient to answer the question.

D. If the data in both statement I and II together are not sufficient to answer the question.

E. If the data in both statement I and II together are sufficient to answer the question.

Q.6 How is Mona related to Shetty?

Statement I: Mona is mother of Jay. Babu is married to Allan. Shetty is daughter of Babu. Allan is brother of Jay.

Statement II: Mona is married to Vida. Vida is father of Jay. Jay is married to Kalu. Jay is uncle of Shetty.

A. If the data in statement I alone is sufficient to answer the question, while the data in statement II alone is not sufficient to answer the question.

B. If the data in statement II alone is sufficient to answer the question, while the data in statement I alone is not sufficient to answer the question.

C. If the data either in statement I alone or in statement II alone is sufficient to answer the question.

D. If the data in both statement I and II together are not sufficient to answer the question.

E. If the data in both statement I and II together are sufficient to answer the question.

Q.7 Five persons – Ankit, Anant, Ankur, Anup and Anwar, each earns a different amount of money. Who among these persons earns second highest?

Statement I: Only Ankur earns more than Anant.

Statement II: Anup and Anwar earns less than Ankit.

A. If the data in statement I alone is sufficient to answer the question, while the data in statement II alone is not sufficient to answer the question.

B. If the data in statement II alone is sufficient to answer the question, while the data in statement I alone is not sufficient to answer the question.

C. If the data either in statement I alone or in statement II alone is sufficient to answer the question.

D. If the data in both statement I and II together are not sufficient to answer the question.

E. If the data in both statement I and II together are sufficient to answer the question.

Q.8 A certain number of persons were sitting in a row facing north then how many persons are there in the row?

Statement I: Manoj is 10th from the left end of the row and 6th to the left of Deepak.

Statement II: Prakas is 14th from the right end of the row and 8th to the right of Deepak.

A. If the data in statement I alone is sufficient to answer the question, while the data in statement II alone is not sufficient to answer the question.

B. If the data in statement II alone is sufficient to answer the question, while the data in statement I alone is not sufficient to answer the question.

C. If the data either in statement I alone or in statement II alone is sufficient to answer the question.

D. If the data in both statement I and II together are not sufficient to answer the question.

E. If the data in both statement I and II together are sufficient to answer the question.

Q.9 What is the code of 'party' in the given code language?

Statement I: In the same code language 'party was great' is coded as 'ar jv cu' and 'that was great' is coded as 'dt jv cu'.

Statement II: In the same code language 'how was the party' is coded as 'ft pd ar lv' and 'when did party start' is coded as 'kl aj rc ar'.

A. If the data in statement I alone is sufficient to answer the question, while the data in statement II alone is not sufficient to answer the question.

B. If the data in statement II alone is sufficient to answer the question, while the data in statement I alone is not

sufficient to answer the question.

C. If the data either in statement I alone or in statement II alone is sufficient to answer the question.

D. If the data in both statement I and II together are not sufficient to answer the question.

E. If the data in both statement I and II together are sufficient to answer the question.

Q.10 How is Tina related to Anu?

Statement I: Anu is the wife of Jai. Anu and Vini are the only children of Dev. Pal is the only daughter of Jai. Tina is the grand-daughter of Dev.

Statement II: Pal is married to Siya. Anu is the mother-in-law of Siya. Anu is the only daughter of Dev and Roy. Tina is the grandchild of Dev.

A. If the data in statement I alone is sufficient to answer the question, while the data in statement II alone is not sufficient to answer the question.

B. If the data in statement II alone is sufficient to answer the question, while the data in statement I alone is not sufficient to answer the question.

C. If the data either in statement I alone or in statement II alone is sufficient to answer the question.

D. If the data in both statement I and II together are not sufficient to answer the question.

E. If the data in both statement I and II together are sufficient to answer the question.

Q.11 Six persons – J, K, L, M, N and O scored different marks in an examination. Who among these persons scored highest?

Statement I: M scored higher than J and O but less than K. N scored higher than M but not the highest scorer. K did not score highest.

Statement II: K scored less than only 2 persons. J scored less than M and K but higher than O. N scored higher than J.

A. If the data in statement I alone is sufficient to answer the question, while the data in statement II alone is not sufficient to answer the question.

B. If the data in statement II alone is sufficient to answer the question, while the data in statement I alone is not sufficient to answer the question.

C. If the data either in statement I alone or in statement II alone is sufficient to answer the question.

D. If the data in both statement I and II together are not sufficient to answer the question.

E. If the data in both statement I and II together are sufficient to answer the question.

Q.12 What is the birth date of Mona's mother?

Statement I: Mona's father remembers that his wife's birthday is after 20th and before 23rd February.

Statement II: Mona's brother remembers that his mother's birthday is after 21st but before 25th February.

A. If the data in statement I alone is sufficient to answer the question, while the data in statement II alone is not sufficient to answer the question.

B. If the data in statement II alone is sufficient to answer the question, while the data in statement I alone is not sufficient to answer the question.

C. If the data either in statement I alone or in statement II alone is sufficient to answer the question.

D. If the data in both statement I and II together are not sufficient to answer the question.

E. If the data in both statement I and II together are sufficient to answer the question.

Q.13 Who is oldest among P, K, J, R, S and T?

Statement I: R is older than P and J. R is younger than K. S is older than only T.

Statement II: S is older than J but younger than P. T is older than only R. P is not the oldest.

A. If the data in statement I alone is sufficient to answer the question, while the data in statement II alone is not sufficient to answer the question.

B. If the data in statement II alone is sufficient to answer the question, while the data in statement I alone is not sufficient to answer the question.

C. If the data either in statement I alone or in statement II alone is sufficient to answer the question.

D. If the data in both statement I and II together are not sufficient to answer the question.

E. If the data in both statement I and II together are sufficient to answer the question.

Q.14 How is 'pant' written in a code language?

Statement I: 'red pant shirt' is written as 'ke ne que' and 'shirt pant black' is written as 'ke joi ne'.

Statement II: 'red is play' is written as 'que yo pa' and 'red is pant play' is written as 'ke que pa yo'.

A. If the data in statement I alone is sufficient to answer the question, while the data in statement II alone is not sufficient to answer the question.

B. If the data in statement II alone is sufficient to answer the question, while the data in statement I alone is not sufficient to answer the question.

C. If the data either in statement I alone or in statement II alone is sufficient to answer the question.

D. If the data in both statement I and II together are not sufficient to answer the question.

E. If the data in both statement I and II together are sufficient to answer the question.

Q.15 There are seven members – A, B, C, D, X, Y and Z in a family such that there are three generations in the family and two married couples. How is D related to B?

Statement I: D is grandson of A. Y is daughter-in-law of C. B is son of C but not married to Y.

Statement II: Y is father of D and son of C. B is brother of X who is daughter of A.

A. If the data in statement I alone is sufficient to answer the question, while the data in statement II alone is not sufficient to answer the question.

B. If the data in statement II alone is sufficient to answer the question, while the data in statement I alone is not sufficient to answer the question.

C. If the data either in statement I alone or in statement II alone is sufficient to answer the question.

D. If the data in both statement I and II together are not sufficient to answer the question.

E. If the data in both statement I and II together are sufficient to answer the question.

Q.16 Six friends – Tipu, Tanu, Tara, Tina, Teja and Titu are sitting around a circular table facing centre. How many persons are sitting between Tanu and Tina?

Statement I: Tipu is sitting third to right of Tanu. Tara is sitting third to the left of Tina. Tara is not sitting adjacent to Tipu.

Statement II: Tina has Tipu and Titu as his immediate neighbours. Tara is not an immediate neighbour of Tipu or Titu.

A. If the data in statement I alone is sufficient to answer the question, while the data in statement II alone is not sufficient to answer the question.

B. If the data in statement II alone is sufficient to answer the question, while the data in statement I alone is not sufficient to answer the question.

C. If the data either in statement I alone or in statement II alone is sufficient to answer the question.

D. If the data in both statement I and II together are not sufficient to answer the question.

E. If the data in both statement I and II together are sufficient to answer the question.

Q.17 Among five persons – A, B, C, D and E each one of different height, who is the tallest?

Statement I: B is taller than C and D but shorter than E who is not the tallest.

Statement II: E is taller than B and C but shorter than A.

A. If the data in statement I alone are sufficient to answer the question, while the data in statement II alone are not sufficient in answer the question.

B. If the data in statement II alone are sufficient to answer the question, while the data in statement I alone are not sufficient to answer the question.

C. If the data in either in statement I alone or in statement II alone are sufficient to answer the question.

D. If the data in both the statements I and II together are not sufficient to answer the question.

E. If the data in both the statements I and II are together sufficient to answer the question.

Q.18 Five persons – P, Q, X, Y and Z are sitting around a circular table with all of them facing towards the center. Who sits to the immediate left of Q?

Statement I: P sits third to right of Q. X sits third to right of P.

Statement II: Q sits immediate left of X who sits second to left of P. Y does not sit adjacent to Q.

A. If the data in statement I alone are sufficient to answer the question, while the data in statement II alone are not sufficient in answer the question.

B. If the data in statement II alone are sufficient to answer the question, while the data in statement I alone are not sufficient to answer the question.

C. If the data in either in statement I alone or in statement II alone are sufficient to answer the question.

D. If the data in both the statements I and II together are not sufficient to answer the question.

E. If the data in both the statements I and II are together sufficient to answer the question.

Q.19 What is the floor number of C in the 5 storey apartment?

Statement I: A's floor, which is adjacent to C, is exactly below E's floor which is fifth floor.

Statement II: C's floor is exactly above F's floor, whose floor is exactly above B's floor which is first.

A. If the data in statement I alone are sufficient to answer the question, while the data in statement II alone are not sufficient in answer the question.

B. If the data in statement II alone are sufficient to answer the question, while the data in statement I alone are not sufficient to answer the question.

C. If the data in either in statement I alone or in statement II alone are sufficient to answer the question.

D. If the data in both statements I and II together are not sufficient to answer the question.

E. If the data in both statements I and II are together sufficient to answer the question.

Q.20 On which day Meena goes to Goa?

Statement I: According to Meena's sister Meena goes to Goa after Tuesday and before Sunday but she did not go to Goa on Thursday.

Statement II: According to Meena's father Meena goes to Goa after Monday and before Saturday.

A. If the data in statement I alone are sufficient to answer the question, while the data in statement II alone are not sufficient in answer the question.

B. If the data in statement II alone are sufficient to answer the question, while the data in statement I alone are not sufficient to answer the question.

C. If the data in either in statement I alone or in statement II alone are sufficient to answer the question.

D. If the data in both the statements I and II together are not sufficient to answer the question.

E. If the data in both the statements I and II are together sufficient to answer the question.

Q.21 How many persons are there in the row if all of them are facing North?

Statement I: P who is tenth from the left end is fifth to the left of Q who is sixteenth from the right end.

Statement II: R is seventh to the left of S who is eleventh from the right end and nineteenth from the left end.

A. If the data in statement I alone are sufficient to answer the question, while the data in statement II alone are not sufficient in answer the question.

B. If the data in statement II alone are sufficient to answer the question, while the data in statement I alone are not sufficient to answer the question.

C. If the data in either in statement I alone or in statement II alone are sufficient to answer the question.

D. If the data in both the statements I and II together are not sufficient to answer the question.

E. If the data in both the statements I and II are together sufficient to answer the question.

Ques (22-30):Direction: The following consists of a question and two statements numbered I and II given below it. You have to decide whether the data provided in the statements are sufficient to answer the question.

Q.22 7 books namely Book 1, Book 2, Book 3, Book 4, Book 5, Book 6 and Book 7 are of different weights. Find the second lightest book?

Statement I: Book 1 is heavier than Book 4, which is just lighter than Book 3. Book 2 is not the lightest. Book 5 is just heavier than Book 3.

Statement II: Book 3 is heavier than only two books. Book 7 is just heavier than Book 1, which is heavier than Book 4. Book 4 is lighter than Book 3.

A. If the data in statement I is sufficient to answer the question.

B. If the data in statement II is sufficient to answer the question.

C. If the data in either statement I or statement II is sufficient to answer the question.

D. If the data in both statement I and statement II is sufficient to answer the question.

E. If the data in neither statement I nor statement II is sufficient to answer the question.

Q.23 Eight persons from A to H sit around a circular table facing towards the centre. What is the position of F with respect to B?

Statement I: E faces A, who is second to the left of D. G and B are immediate neighbors of A. F does not sit adjacent to H.

Statement II: B and D are not adjacent. C is on the immediate right of D. F sits at a gap of two persons from C. H is second to the left of B.

A. If the data in statement I is sufficient to answer the question.

B. If the data in statement II is sufficient to answer the question.

C. If the data in either statement I or statement II is sufficient to answer the question.

D. If the data in both statement I and statement II is sufficient to answer the question.

E. If the data in neither statement I nor statement II is sufficient to answer the question.

Q.24 Find Point D is in which direction from Point A?

Statement I: Point A is in the west of Point B, which is to the north-east of Point D. Point C is in the north of Point D and Point A. Point A is in the middle of Point E and Point C.

Statement II: Point B is to the north of Point F, which is to the east of Point E. Point D is to the west of Point B. Point A is to the north of Point E.

A. If the data in statement I is sufficient to answer the question.

B. If the data in statement II is sufficient to answer the question.

C. If the data in either statement I or statement II is sufficient to answer the question.

D. If the data in both statement I and statement II is sufficient to answer the question.

E. If the data in neither statement I nor statement II is sufficient to answer the question.

Q.25 Certain words are coded in the following manner in a code language. Find the code for "thick tree"?

Statement I : "tree old stem" is coded as '26 84 15' and "stem stand thick" is coded as '10 26 45'.

Statement II : "thick old wine" is coded as '13 84 10' and "tree old stand" is coded as '15 45 84'.

A. If the data in statement I is sufficient to answer the question.

B. If the data in either statement I or statement II is sufficient to answer the question.

C. If the data in both statement I and statement II is sufficient to answer the question.

D. If the data in both statement I and statement II is necessary to answer the question.

E. If the data in neither statement I nor statement II is sufficient to answer the question.

Q.26 A teacher wrote a meaningful English word on the blackboard. Find the exactly middle letter of the 5 letter word?

Statement I: The first and last letter of the word is 'E'. The second and fourth letters of the word are consecutive letters in English alphabet series. R is adjacent to A.

Statement II: The first and last vowel is same. Only one letter is placed between A and E. S is written after R. The vowels are placed at odd numbered positions.

A. If the data in statement I is sufficient to answer the question.

B. If the data in statement II is sufficient to answer the question.

C. If the data in either statement I or statement II is sufficient to answer the question.

D. If the data in both statement I and statement II is sufficient to answer the question.

E. If the data in neither statement I nor statement II is sufficient to answer the question.

Q.27 How is the word 'season' coded?

Statement I: 'Season change by nature' is coded as '4 8 12 9' and 'Change is law nature' is coded as '5 12 24 4'.

Statement II: 'New season came today' is coded as '7 9 51 35' and 'Today change came tomorrow' is coded as '21 35 12 19'.

A. If the data in statement I alone is sufficient to answer the question.

B. If the data in statement II alone is sufficient to answer the question.

C. If the data in statements I and II is sufficient to answer the question.

D. If the data in statements I and II is not sufficient to answer the question.

E. If data in either statement I or II is sufficient to answer the question.

Q.28 8 persons viz. B,D,K,F,H,J,L and N are standing in a linear row facing towards the north. What is the position of H from the right end, if number of persons between H and E are 2?

Statement I: F is second to the left of G, who is on the immediate right of H. No person stands between J and B. B is second to the left of E.

Statement II: E is third to the right of B. J is not an immediate neighbor of L. F and L are not adjacent. H is on the immediate right of F.

A. If the data in statement I alone is sufficient to answer the question.

B. If the data in statement II alone is sufficient to answer the question.

C. If the data in statements I and II is sufficient to answer the

question.

D. If the data in statements I and II is not sufficient to answer the question.

E. If data in either statement I or II is sufficient to answer the question.

Q.29 In a 7 story building where the bottommost floor is numbered as 1 and the topmost floor is numbered as 7, no one lives at floor number 5. Only one person among A,B,C,D,E and F lives at one floor. What is the floor number of D and the difference between the floor numbers of D and B?

Statement I: D lives at a gap of two floors from C. B and E live on adjacent floors where E is above B. Only A lives above F, who is on an even-numbered floor.

Statement II: E lives two floors below the vacant floor. Only one floor is between the floors of D and B. A lives above just above F. B is adjacent to E.

A. If the data in statement I alone is sufficient to answer the question.

B. If the data in statement II alone is sufficient to answer the question.

C. If the data in statements I and II is sufficient to answer the question.

D. If the data in statements I and II is not sufficient to answer the question.

E. If data in either statement I or II is sufficient to answer the question.

Q.30 7 boxes from A to G are placed (not necessarily in same order) in a linear row facing towards north direction. These boxes contain articles like – Ball, Pen, Paper and Cap such that one type of article is contained in two boxes. Only one of the articles is contained in one box only.

If the box containing Cap is placed exactly in the middle of the row then how many boxes are placed between both the boxes containing Balls?

Statement I: Box C, which contains Pen is placed second to the right of Box F. Box B contains Ball and is placed third from the right end. Box E neither contains pen nor placed adjacent to Box A, which has Cap. No other box contains Cap. Box G is on the immediate left of the box which contains Ball.

Statement II: Box E is third to the right of the box that contains cap. Only box A contains cap. Box D is adjacent to Box F, which contains Paper. Box G is placed second from the right end and is adjacent to the box that contains ball. The box containing pen is adjacent to the box containing cap.

A. If the data in statement I alone is sufficient to answer the question.

B. If the data in statement II alone is sufficient to answer the question.

C. If the data in statements I and II is sufficient to answer the question.

D. If the data in statements I and II is not sufficient to answer the question.

E. If data in either statement I or II is sufficient to answer the question.

// Smart Answer Sheet //

Correct   Indicates percentage of students who answered questions correctly.

Skipped   Indicates percentage of students who skipped questions.

Q.	Ans.	Correct / Skipped
1	E	65.91 % / 31.05 %
2	E	56.44 % / 41.03 %
3	B	51.4 % / 39.68 %
4	C	68.79 % / 30.23 %
5	B	20.7 % / 76.16 %
6	C	44.31 % / 48.08 %

Q.	Ans.	Correct / Skipped
7	A	67.89 % / 31.77 %
8	E	51.56 % / 32.56 %
9	C	76.78 % / 10.61 %
10	A	48.35 % / 41.24 %
11	A	42.59 % / 44.27 %
12	E	31.01 % / 68.52 %

Q.	Ans.	Correct / Skipped
13	C	60.02 % / 38.08 %
14	B	56.04 % / 40.4 %
15	A	46.21 % / 39.16 %
16	C	27.6 % / 71.15 %
17	A	57.34 % / 36.35 %
18	B	57.18 % / 34.72 %

Q.	Ans.	Correct / Skipped
19	C	54.9 % / 40.87 %
20	D	65.1 % / 32.88 %
21	C	55.39 % / 40.46 %
22	D	43.7 % / 55.69 %
23	D	64.46 % / 31.18 %
24	A	57.87 % / 41.16 %

Q.	Ans.	Correct / Skipped
25	D	82.59 % / 13.64 %
26	C	61.62 % / 35.65 %
27	C	85.26 % / 12.24 %
28	D	58.66 % / 31.18 %
29	C	44.1 % / 54.92 %
30	A	11.03 % / 74.69 %

Performance Analysis	
Avg. Score (%)	60.0%
Toppers Score (%)	73.33%
Your Score	

//Hints and Solutions//

1. From statement I:

With the given data in statement I, we can find only the third and last letter of the word as 'N', but not the whole word.

Thus, data in statement I alone is not sufficient.

From statement II:

With the data given in statement II, we can have the following inference:

C O _ _ _ _ _

Thus, data in statement II alone is not sufficient.

From both statements I and II:

With statement II we have known the first two letters and statement I, we get to know third and last letters of the word, now let us check the other related hints.

C O N _ _ _ N

T is adjacent to A, this can be used as :

C O N T A _ N

or

C O N _ T A N

or

C O N A T _ N

or

C O N _ A T N

But it has to be a meaningful English word thus between I and U, only vowel 'I' suits the blank and the meaningful English word is "CONTAIN".

Thus, the data in both statement I and II together are sufficient to answer the question.

Hence, the correct option is (E).

2. From Statement I:

Reference:

Only two persons are heavier than Kona who is heavier than Jeet and Deva.

Inference:

After using the above references, we have:

Order of weight:

___ > ___ > Kona > Jeet/Deva > Deva/Jeet

Here, either Mahi or Ramu can be the one who is heaviest.

Clearly, Statement I alone is not sufficient to answer the question.

From Statement II:

Reference:

Ramu, who is not the lightest, is heavier than Kona and Deva but not Mahi.

Inference:

After using the above references, we have:

Order of weight:

Mahi > Ramu > Kona > Deva

Here, we have no information about the weight of Jeet.

Clearly, Statement II alone is also not sufficient to answer the question.

From both Statements II and III together:

Reference 1:

Only two persons are heavier than Kona who is heavier than Jeet and Deva.

Inference 1:

Order of weight:

___ > ___ > Kona > Jeet/Deva > Deva/Jeet

Reference 2:

Ramu, who is not the lightest, is heavier than Kona and Deva but not Mahi.

Inference 2:

After combining the above references with inference 1, we get:

Order of weight:

Mahi > Ramu > Kona > Jeet/Deva > Deva/Jeet

Here, we can say that Mahi is the heaviest among these persons.

Clearly, both statements I and II together are necessary to answer the question.

Hence, the correct option is (E).

3. From Statement I:

Reference:

Arnav does not sit next to Azam, who does not sit on the extreme right.

Inference:

Here, we have no sure information about the position of any of these persons in the row.

Clearly, Statement I alone is sufficient to answer the question.

From Statement II:

Statement II: No one sit to the right of Arnav and on the left of Abdul, while only one person sits between Afzal and Abdul.

Reference:

No one sit to the right of Arnav and on the left of Abdul, while only one person sits between Afzal and Abdul.

Inference:

After using the above references, we can draw a following linear arrangement:

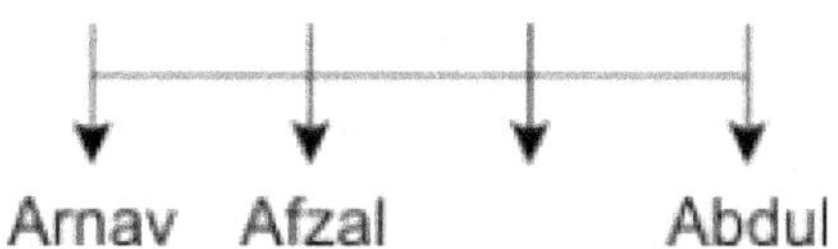

Here, we can say that Afzal sits adjacent to Arnav.

So, the data in Statement II alone is sufficient to answer the question.

Hence, the correct option is (B).

4. From Statement I:

Reference:

R earns more than only two persons.

T earns more than only U.

Q earns more than P but not maximum.

Inference:

After using the above references, we have:

Order of Earnings:

_ > Q > P > R > T > U

Here, we can say that S earns maximum.

Order of Earnings:

S > Q > P > R > T > U

Clearly, Statement I alone is sufficient to answer the question.

From Statement II:

Reference:

T earns more than U but less than R.

R earns less than P.

P earns less than only two persons.

Q earns less than S.

Inference:

After using the above references, we have:

Order of Earnings:

S > Q > P > R > T > U

Here, we can say that S earns maximum.

Clearly, Statement II alone is sufficient to answer the question.

So, the data in either Statement I or II alone is sufficient to answer the question.

Hence, the correct option is (C).

5. From Statement I:

Reference 1:

Ana sits at the extreme left end of the line. Only six persons sit between Ana and Han.

Inference 1:

After using the above references, we have:

Order of persons in the row = Ana + 6 persons + Han + 17 persons

Reference 2:

Only ten persons sit between Han and Pal. Only four persons sit between Pal and Dev.

Inference 2:

Here, we have two possible scenarios in which the above references can be used.

Case 1:

Order of persons in the row = Ana + 6 persons + Han + 10 persons + Pal + 4 persons + Dev + 1 person

Case 2:

Order of persons in the row = Ana + 6 persons + Han + 5 persons + Dev + 4 persons + Pal + 6 persons

Here, we cannot surely say how many persons are sitting between Dev and Han.

Clearly, Statement I alone is not sufficient to answer the question.

From Statement II:

Reference 1:

Mia sits exactly in the middle of the line. Only three persons sit between Ram and Mia. Han sits fourth to the left of Mia.

Inference 1:

After using the above references, we have:

Order of persons in the row = 8 persons + Han + 3 persons + Mia + 3 persons + Ram + 8 persons

Reference 2:

Only six persons sit between Ram and Dev. Ram sits on the left of Dev.

Inference 2:

After using the above references, we have:

Order of persons in the row = 8 persons + Han + 3 persons + Mia + 3 persons + Ram + 6 persons + Dev + 1 person

Here, we can say that 14 persons sit between Han and Dev.

Clearly, Statement II alone is sufficient to answer the question.

So, the data in Statement II alone is sufficient to answer the question.

Hence, the correct option is (B).

6. From Statement I:

Reference:

Mona is mother of Jay.

Babu is married to Allan.

Shetty is daughter of Babu.

Allan is brother of Jay.

Inference:

After using the above references, we can draw a following chart:

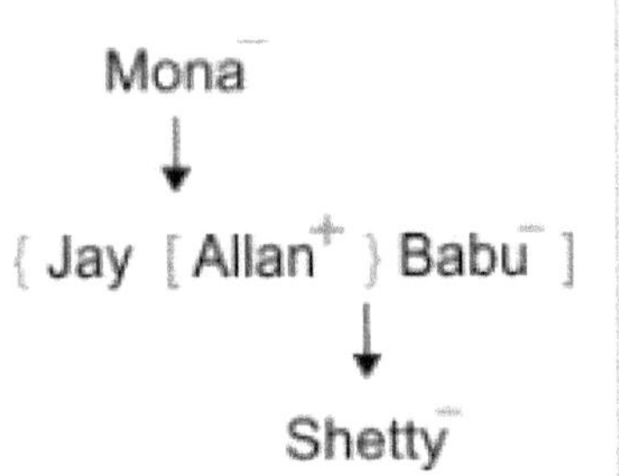

From Statement II:

Reference:

Mona is married to Vida.

Vida is father of Jay.

Jay is married to Kalu.

Jay is uncle of Shetty.

Inference:

After using the above references, we can draw a following chart:

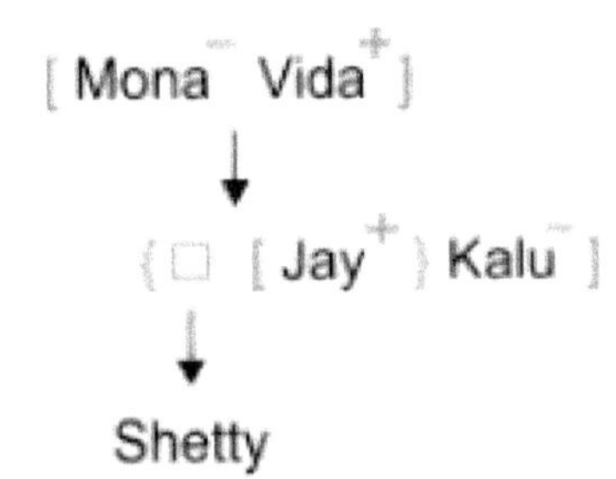

Here, we can say that Mona is grandmother of Shetty.

Clearly, Statement II alone is sufficient to answer the question.

So, the data in either Statement I or II alone is sufficient to answer the question.

Hence, the correct option is (C).

7. From Statement I:

Reference:

Only Ankur earns more than Anant.

Inference:

After using the above references, we have:

Order of Earnings:

Ankur > Anant > ___ > ___ > ___

Here, we can say that Anant earns second highest.

Clearly, Statement I alone is sufficient to answer the question.

From Statement II:

Reference:

Anup and Anwar earns less than Ankit.

Inference:

After using the above references, we have:

Order of Earnings:

Ankit > Anup/Anwar

Here, we have no sure information about the earnings of any of these persons.

Clearly, Statement II alone is not sufficient to answer the question.

So, the data in Statement I alone is sufficient to answer the question.

Hence, the correct option is (A).

8. From Statement I:

Reference:

Manoj is 10th from the left end of the row and 6th to the left of Deepak.

Inference:

Here, we have no information about any of these from right end so we cannot find the total number of persons that were sitting in the row.

Clearly, Statement I alone is not sufficient to answer the question.

From Statement II:

Reference:

Prakas is 14th from the right end of the row and 8th to the right of Deepak.

Inference:

Here, we have no information about any of these from right end so we cannot find the total number of persons that were sitting in the row.

Clearly, Statement II alone is sufficient to answer the question.

From both statements I and II together:

Reference:

Manoj is 10th from the left end of the row and 6th to the left of Deepak.

Prakas is 14th from the right end of the row and 8th to the right of Deepak.

Inference:

After using the above references, we have:

Order of persons in the row = 9 persons + Manoj + 5 persons + Deepak + 7 persons + Prakas + 13 persons

Total number of persons in the row = (9 + 1 + 5 + 1 + 7 + 1 + 13) persons = 37 persons

Clearly, both statements I and II together are necessary to answer the question.

Hence, the correct option is (E).

9. From Statement I:

Reference:

party was great → ar jv cu

that was great → dt jv cu

Inference:

After using the above references, we have:

party → ar

Here, we can say that the code of 'party' is 'ar'.

Clearly, Statement I alone is sufficient to answer the question.

From Statement II:

Reference:

how was the party → ft pd ar lv

when did party started → kl aj rc ar

Inference:

After using the above references, we have:

party → ar

Here, we can say that the code of 'Party' is 'ar'.

Clearly, Statement II alone is sufficient to answer the question.

So, the data in either Statement I or II alone is sufficient to answer the question.

Hence, the correct option is (C).

10. From statement I:

Reference:

Anu is the wife of Jai. Anu and Vini are the only children of Dev.

Pal is the only daughter of Jai.

Tina is the grand-daughter of Dev.

Inference:

After using the above references, we have:

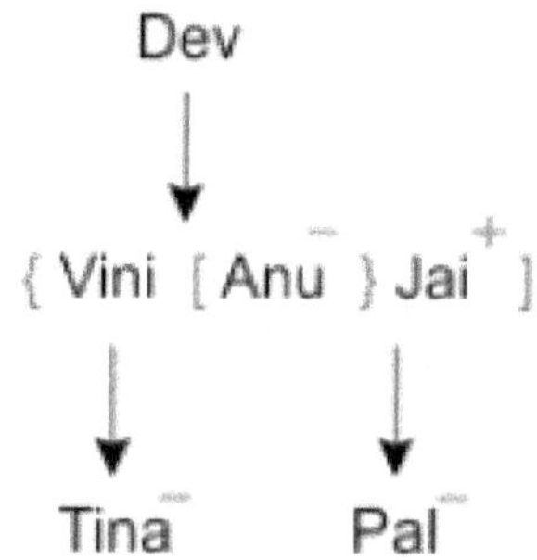

Here, we can say that Tina is the niece of Anu.

Clearly, Statement I alone is sufficient to answer the question.

From statement II:

Reference:

Pal is married to Siya.

Anu is the mother-in-law of Siya.

Anu is the only daughter of Dev and Roy.

Tina is the grandchild of Dev.

Inference:

After using the above references, we have:

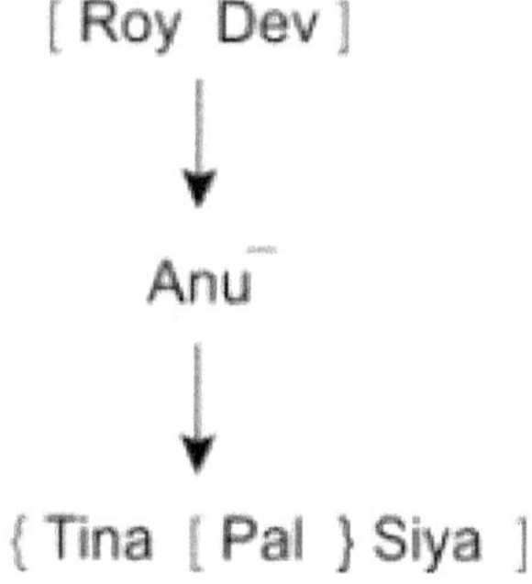

Here, we have no information about the gender of Tina so we cannot find out the relation of Anu and Tina.

Clearly, Statement II alone is not sufficient to answer the question.

So, the data in Statement I alone is sufficient to answer the question.

Hence, the correct option is (A).

11. From statement I:

Reference:

M scored higher than J and O but less than K.

N scored higher than M but not the highest earner.

K did not score highest.

Inference:

After using the above references, we have:

Order of Marks scored:

___ > N/K > K/N > M > J/O > O/J

Here, we can say that L scored highest.

Order of Marks scored:

L > N/K > K/N > M > J/O > O/J

Clearly, Statement I alone is sufficient to answer the question.

From statement II:

Reference:

K scored less than only 2 persons.

J scored less than M and K but higher than O.

N scored higher than J.

Inference:

After using the above references, we have:

Order of Marks scored:

___ > ___> K > M /N> J > O

Here, we cannot surely say anything about the one who scored highest.

Clearly, Statement II alone is not sufficient to answer the question.

So, the data in Statement I alone is sufficient to answer the question.

Hence, the correct option is (A).

12. From statement I:

Reference:

Mona's father remembers that his wife's birthday is after 20th and before 23rd February.

Inference:

In this statement, Mona's mother's birthday is on either 21st or 22nd February.

Clearly, data in statement I alone are not sufficient to reach the answer.

From statement II:

Reference:

Mona's brother remembers that his mother's birthday is after 21st but before 25th February.

Inference:

In this statement, Mona's mother birthday is on 22nd or 23rd or 24th February.

Clearly, data in statement II alone are not sufficient to reach the answer.

From both statements I and II together:

Reference:

Mona's father remembers that his wife's birthday is after 20th and before 23rd February.

Mona's brother remembers that his mother's birthday is after 21st but before 25th February.

Inference:

After using the above references, we can say that Mona's mother birthday is on 22nd February.

Clearly, data in both the statements I and II together are sufficient to answer question.

Hence, the correct option is (E).

13. From statement I:

Reference:

R is older than P and J. R is younger than K. S is older than only T.

Inference:

In this statement:

K > R > P, J and S is older than only T.

Order of age:

K > R > P/J > S > T

Here, we can say that K is oldest among all.

Clearly, data in statement I alone are sufficient to reach the answer.

From statement II:

Reference 1:

T is older than only R.

Inference 1:

After using the above references, we have:

Order of age:

_ > _ > _ > _ > T > R

Reference 2:

S is older than J but younger than P.

P is not the oldest.

Inference 2:

After using the above references, we have:

Order of age:

K > P > S > J > T > R

Here, we can say that K is the oldest.

Clearly, data in statement II alone are sufficient to reach the answer.

So, data in either statement I or statement II alone is sufficient to answer the question.

Hence, the correct option is (C).

14. From statement I:

Reference:

red pant shirt → ke ne que

shirt pant black → ke joi ne

Inference:

In this statement, the code for 'shirt' and 'pant' is either 'ke' or 'ne'.

Clearly, data in statement I alone are not sufficient to reach the answer.

From statement II:

Reference:

red is play → que yo pa

red is pant play → ke que pa yo

Inference:

After using the above references, we have:

pant → ke

Clearly, data in statement II alone are sufficient to reach the answer.

Hence, the correct option is (B).

15. From Statement I:

Reference 1:

D is grandson of A.

Inference 1:

As we know that there are two married couples and either both or none of the parents of a child are alive. Then,

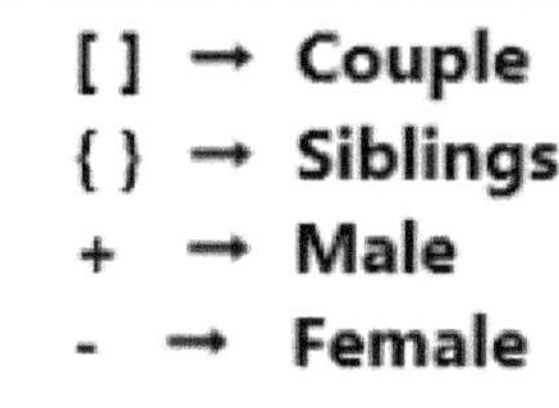

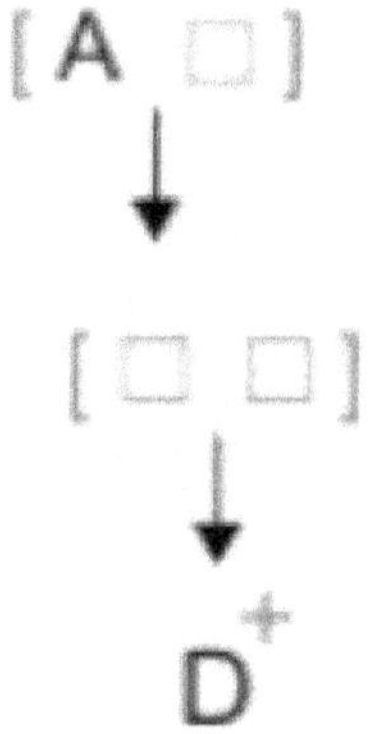

Reference 2:

Y is daughter-in-law of C. B is son of C but not married to Y.

Inference 2:

Using the above references, we have:

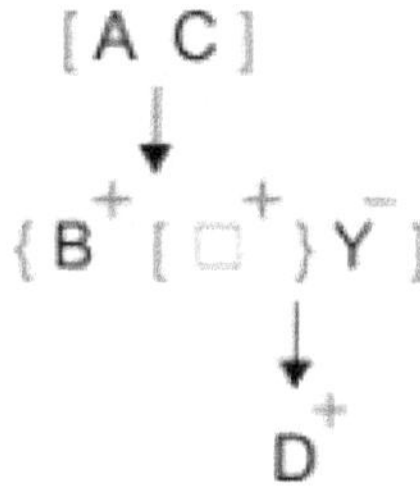

Here, we can surely say that D is the nephew of B.

Clearly, Statement I alone is sufficient to answer the question.

From Statement II:

Reference 1:

Y is father of D and son of C.

Inference 1:

After using the above references, we have:

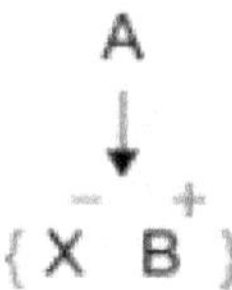

Reference 2:

B is brother of X who is daughter of A.

Inference 2:

After using the above hints, we have:

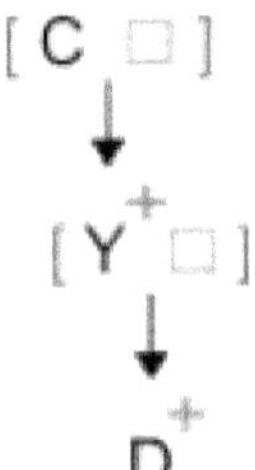

Here, we have no other about the relation of these persons so we cannot find the relation of B and D.

Clearly, Statement II alone is not sufficient to answer the question.

So, Statement I alone is sufficient to answer the question.

Hence, the correct option is (A).

16. From statement I:

Reference 1:

Tipu is sitting third to right of Tanu.

Tara is not sitting adjacent to Tipu.

Inference 1:

Here, we have two possible scenarios in which we can use the above references:

Case 1:

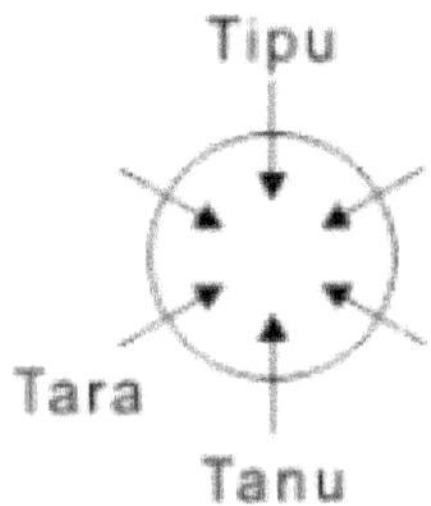

Case 2:

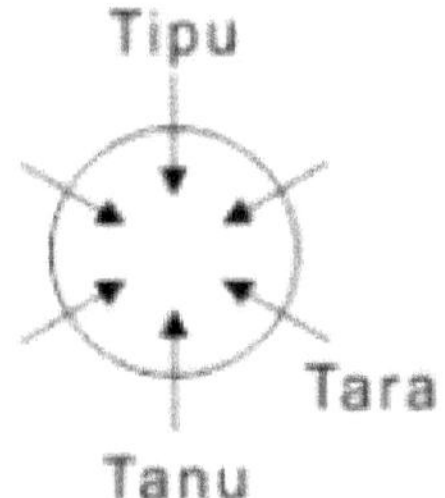

Reference 2:

Tara is sitting third to the left of Tina.

Inference 2:

Using the above references, we have:

Case 1:

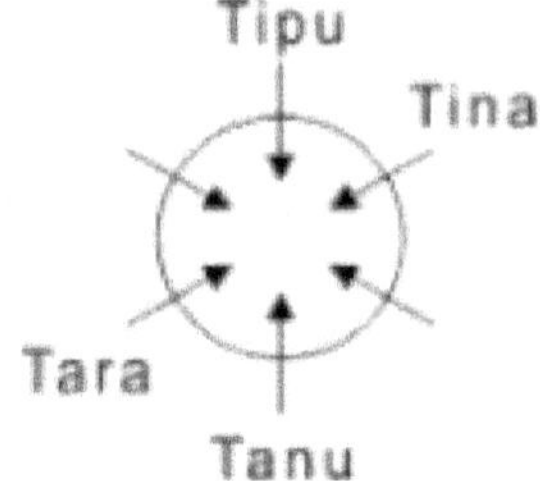

Case 2:

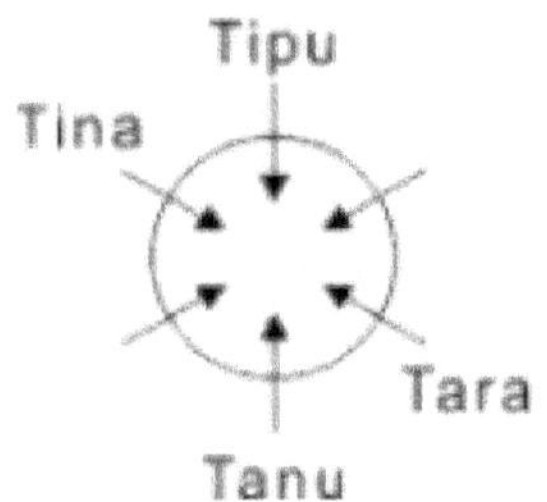

Here, in both of the cases only one person is sitting between Tina and Tanu.

So, we can say that only one person is sitting between Tina and Tanu.

Clearly, Statement I alone is sufficient to answer the question.

From statement II:

Reference 1:

Tina has Tipu and Titu as his immediate neighbours.

Inference 1:

Here, we have two possible scenarios in which we can use the above references:

Case A:

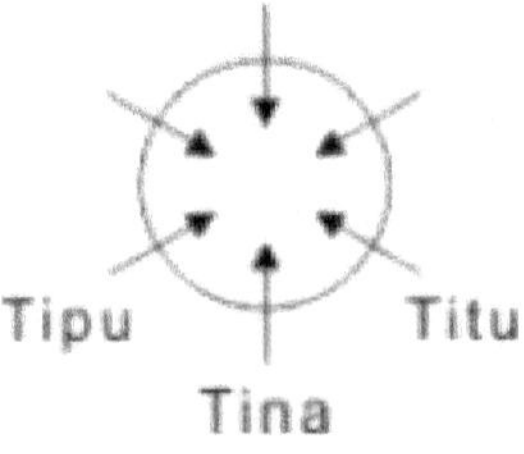

Case B:

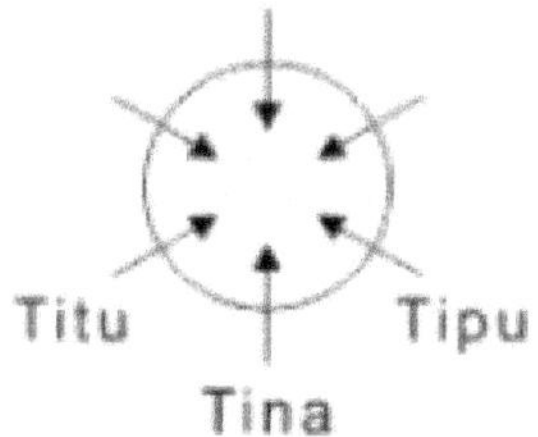

Reference 2:

Tara is not an immediate neighbour of Tipu or Titu.

Inference 2:

After using the above hints, we have:

Case A:

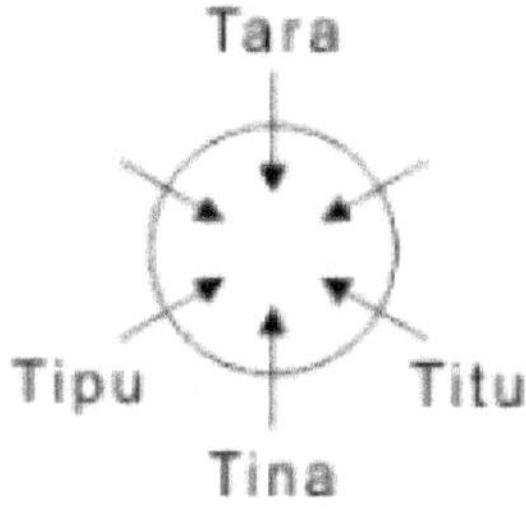

Case B:

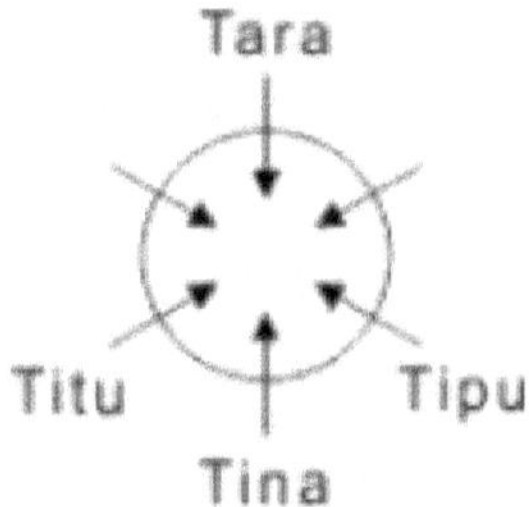

So\, we can fix the position of Tanu and Teja in Case A and B as:

Case A-1:

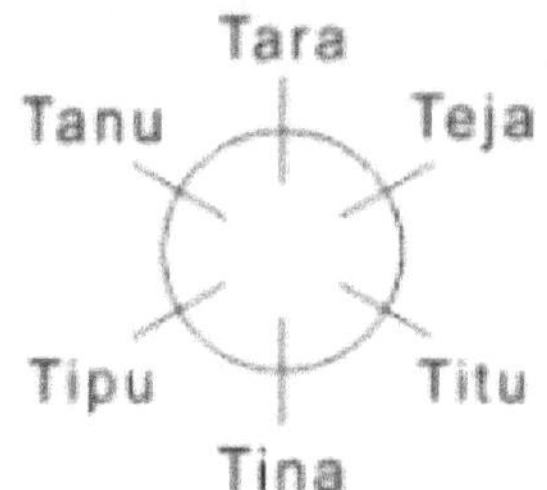

Case A-2:

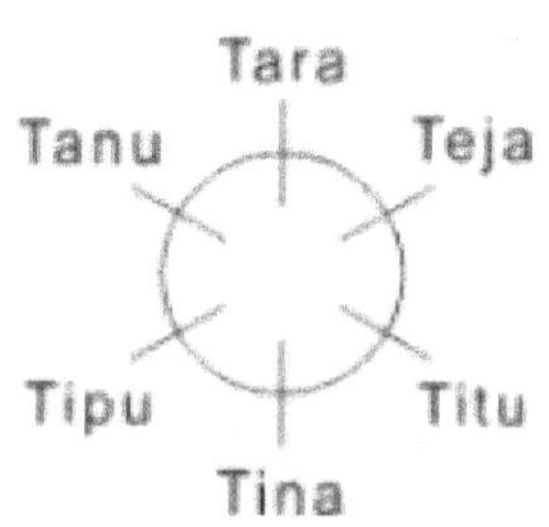

Case B-1:

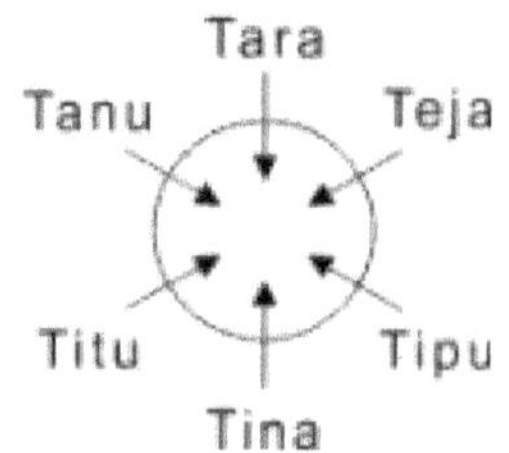

Case B-2:

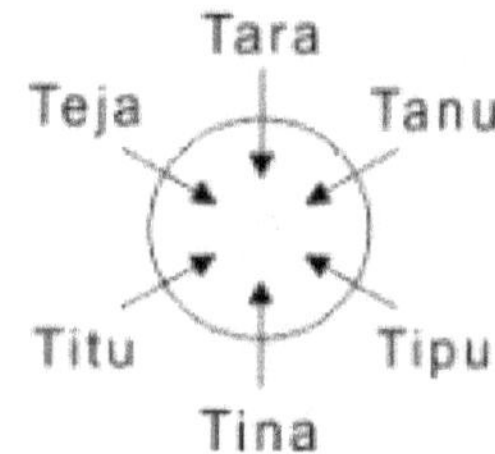

Here, in all four of the cases only one person is sitting between Tina and Tanu.

Thus, we can say that only one person is sitting between Tina and Tanu.

Clearly, Statement II alone is sufficient to answer the question.

So, either Statement I or II alone is sufficient to answer the question.

Hence, the correct option is (C).

17. From Statement I:

Reference:

B is taller than C and D but shorter than E who is not the tallest.

Inference:

Using the given information we can arrange these persons in the decreasing order of their height.

Decreasing order of height → A > E > B > C/D > D/C

Here, in the above arrangement, it is clear that A is the tallest.

So, data in statement I alone is sufficient.

From Statement II:

Reference:

E is taller than B and C but shorter than A.

Inference:

Using the given information we can arrange these persons in the decreasing order of their height.

Decreasing order of height → A > E > B/C > C/B

Here, in the above arrangement we have no information about D.

Thus, data in statement II alone is not sufficient.

So, the data in statement I alone is sufficient to answer the question.

Hence, the correct option is (A).

18. From Statement I:

Reference:

P sits third to right of Q. X sits third to right of P.

Inference:

Using the given information we can create the following circular arrangement.

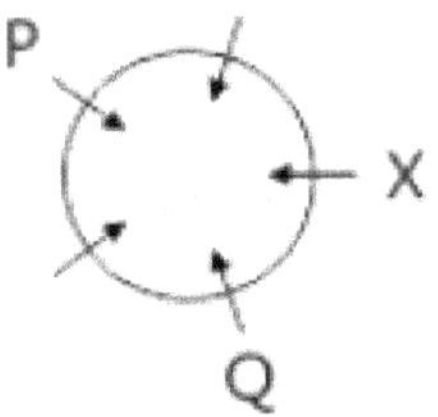

Here, in the above circular arrangement either Y or Z can sit on the immediate left of Q.

So, data in statement I alone is not sufficient.

From Statement II:

Reference:

Q sits immediate left of X who sits second to left of P. Y does not sit adjacent to Q.

Inference:

Using the given information we can create the following circular arrangement.

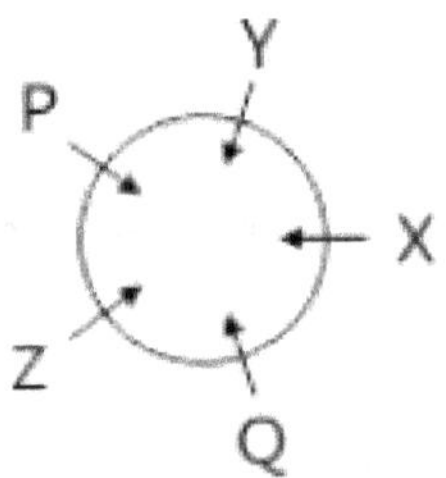

Here, in the above circular arrangement, it is clear that Z sits on the immediate left of Q.

Thus, data in statement II alone is sufficient.

So, the data in statement II alone is sufficient to answer the question.

Hence, the correct option is (B).

19. From Statement I:

Reference:

A's floor, which is adjacent to C, is exactly below E's floor which is fifth floor.

Inference:

Using the given information we can make a floor chart of these persons.

Floor	Person
5	E
4	A
3	C
2	
1	

Here, it is clear that C lives on third floor.

So, data in statement I alone is sufficient.

From Statement II:

Reference:

C's floor is exactly above F's floor, whose floor is exactly above B's floor which is first.

Inference:

Using the given information we can make a floor chart of these persons.

Floor	Person
5	
4	
3	C
2	F
1	B

Here, it is clear that C lives on third floor.

Thus, data in statement II alone is also sufficient.

So, the data in either in statement I alone or in statement II alone are sufficient to answer the question.

Hence, the correct option is (C).

20. From Statement I:

Reference:

According to Meena's sister Meena goes to Goa after Tuesday and before Sunday but she did not go to Goa on Thursday.

Inference:

Using the given information we can say that Meena goes to trip on one of the days among Wednesday, Friday and Saturday.

So, data in statement I alone is not sufficient.

From Statement II:

Reference:

According to Meena's father, Meena goes to Goa after Monday and before Saturday.

Inference:

Using the given information we can say that Meena can go to trip on any of the days among Tuesday, Wednesday, Thursday and Friday.

So, data in statement II alone is also not sufficient.

Combining statement I and II:

From Statement I, we figured out that Meena goes to trip on one of the days among Wednesday, Friday and Saturday.

From Statement II, we figured out that Meena can go to trip on any of the days among Tuesday, Wednesday, Thursday and Friday.

After, compiling the above information we can say that Meena goes to Goa on either Wednesday or Friday.

Thus, data in both statements I and II together are not sufficient.

So, the data in both statements I and II together are not sufficient to answer the question.

Hence, the correct option is (D).

21. From Statement I:

Reference:

P who is tenth from the left end is fifth to the left of Q who is sixteenth from the right end.

Inference:

Using the given information we can say that total persons in the line = 9 persons + P + 4 persons + Q + 15 persons

Total number of persons in the line = 9 + 1 + 4 + 1 + 15 = 30

Thus, data in statement I alone is sufficient.

From Statement II:

Reference:

R is seventh to the left of S who is eleventh from the right end and nineteenth from the left end.

Inference:

Using the given information we can say that total persons in the line = 11 persons + R + 6 persons + S + 10 persons

Total number of persons in the line = 11 + 1 + 6 + 1 + 10 = 29

Thus, data in statement II alone is also sufficient.

So, the data in either in statement I alone or in statement II alone are sufficient to answer the question.

Hence, the correct option is (C).

22. From statement I:

The following arrangement can be prepared with the given hints:

Book 1 > Book 5 > Book 3 > Book 4

But we cannot find the second lightest book because we don't have information for all the books.

Thus data in statement I alone is not sufficient to answer the question.

From statement II:

The following arrangement can be prepared with the given hints:

Book 3> Book 4 > _ or Book 3 > _ > Book 4

Thus Book 4 could be or could not be the second lightest book.

Thus data in statement II alone is not sufficient to answer the question.

From statements I and II:

Book 1 > Book 5 > Book 3 > Book 4

Book 3> Book 4 > _ or Book 3 > _ > Book 4

We can determine Book 4 to be the second lightest book because we get complete information from both the statements together.

Thus, data in both the statements is sufficient to answer the question.

Hence, the correct option is (D).

23. From statement I:

The following arrangement can be prepared with the given hints:

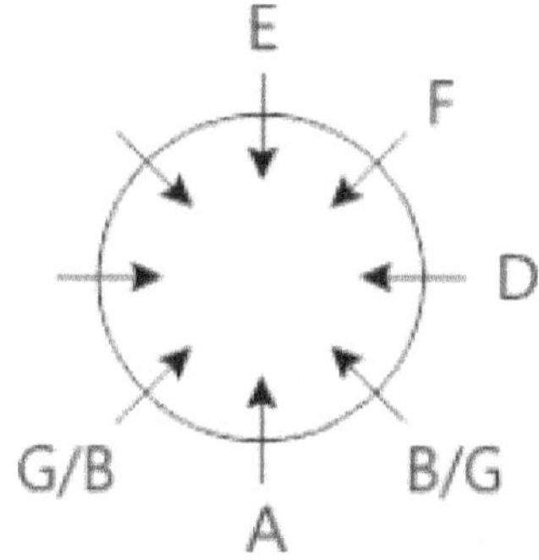

As position of B is not clear, thus we cannot determine the position of F with respect to B.

Thus, data in statement II alone is not sufficient to answer the question.

From statement II:

Following arrangement can be prepared with the given hints:

Case-1:

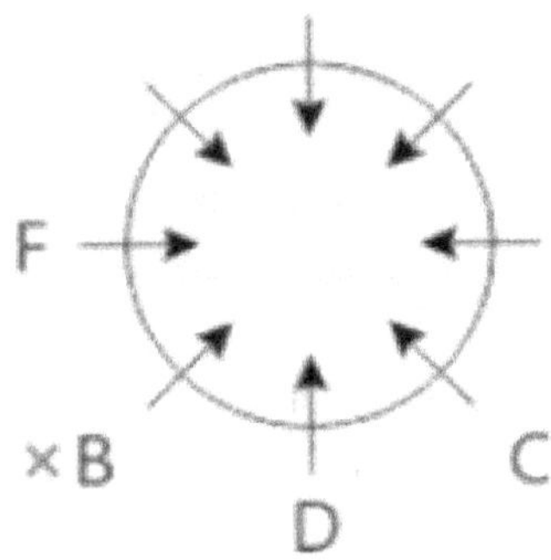

Case-2:

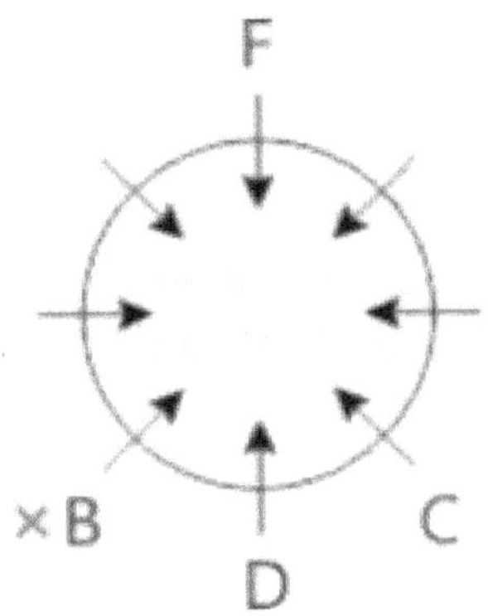

As the position of B is not clear, thus we cannot determine the position of F with respect to B.

Thus, data in statement II alone is not sufficient to answer the question.

From statements I and II:

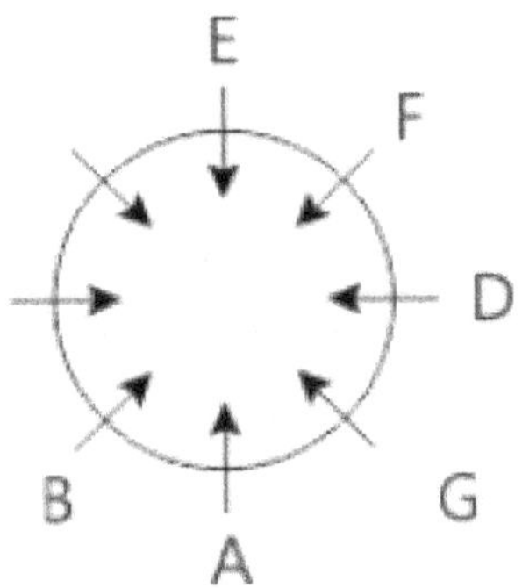

Note- We are not using the other hints deliberately because doing that will make certain hints clash with each other and a single arrangement can not be obtained so.

Thus, F is fourth to the right/left of B.

So, data in both the statements is necessary to answer the question.

Hence, the correct option is (D).

24. From statement I:

The following two cases can be prepared.

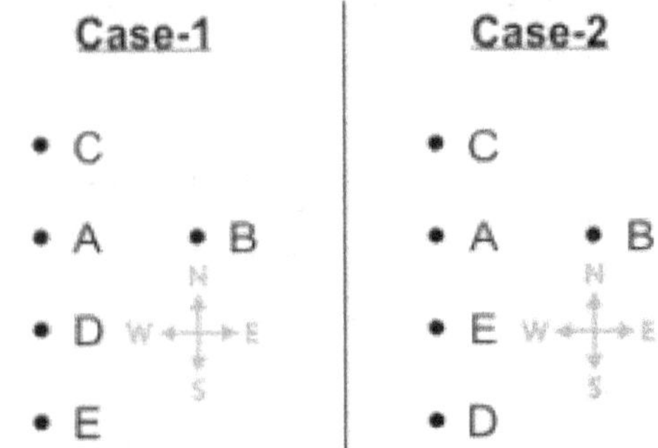

In both the cases point D is in south of Point A.

Thus, data in statement I is sufficient to answer the question.

From statement II:

From statement II following cases can be prepared.

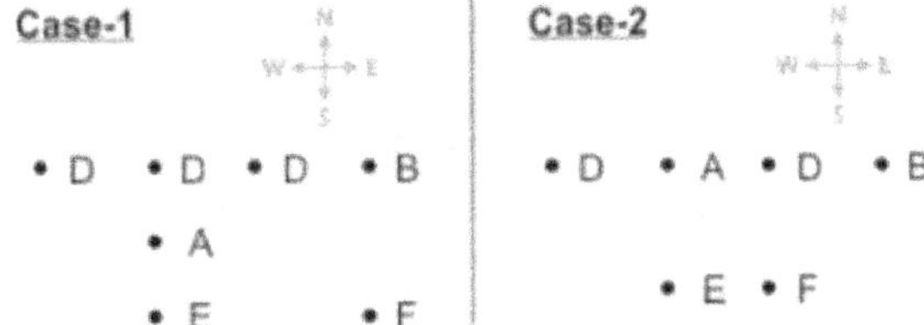

Here, we cannot determine the direction of Point D with respect to Point A, as multiple possibilities arise here.

So, data in statement II is not sufficient to answer the question.

Hence, the correct option is (A).

25. From statement I:

Codes for 'thick and tree' cannot be found out.

Thus, data in statement I is not sufficient.

From statement II:

Codes for 'thick and tree' cannot be found out.

Thus, data in statement II is not sufficient.

From statements I and II:

Code for 'thick' is 10 and code for' tree' is '15'.

Thus, data in statement I and II together is necessary to answer.

Hence, the correct option is (D).

26. From statement I:

E _ _ _ E

The consecutive letters could be A – B or R – S or Q – R.

If we place, A-B then we get no meaningful English word.

EBRAE , EARBE

If we place R-S, then we get one meaningful English word.

ERASE

If we place R-Q, then we get no meaningful English word.

ERAQE , EQARE

Thus, A is placed exactly in the middle.

So, data in statement I is sufficient to answer.

From statement II:

Following two cases can occur.

Case-1: If the letter starts and ends with vowel 'A'.

A R E S A

Case-2: If the letter starts and ends with vowel 'E'.

ERASE

ERASE is meaningful English word. Thus the exactly middle letter is 'A'.

Thus, data in statement II is sufficient to answer.

So, data in either statement I or II is sufficient to answer.

Hence, the correct option is (C).

27. From statement I:

Using this statement, code for the word 'season' cannot be found because the season is not common in both the given signs.

Thus data in statement I is not sufficient.

From statement II:

Using this statement, code for 'season' cannot be found because the season is not common in both the given signs.

Thus data in statement II is not sufficient.

From statements I and II:

Using both the statements, we can say that the code for 'season' is '9'.

Therefore, data in both the statements is necessary to answer the question.

Hence, the correct option is (C).

28. From statement I:

Case-1

Person	J	B	J	E		F	H	G

Case-2

Person	B	J	E		F	H	G	

Thus, we cannot determine whether H is third or second from right end.

So, data in statement I is not sufficient.

From statement II:

Case-1

Person	B			E		F	H	

Case-2

Person		B			E		F	H

Thus, we cannot determine whether H is first or second from right end.

So, data in statement II is not sufficient.

From both the statements:

Hints: "E is third to the right of B" and "B is second to the left of E" clash with each other, thus a single arrangement cannot be obtained using both the statements.

So, the data in statements I and II is not sufficient to answer the question.

Hence, the correct option is (D).

29. From statement I:

Floor number	Persons
7	A
6	F
5	Vacant
4	D/C
3	E
2	B
1	C/D

Here, we cannot determine the floor number of D, thus the required difference cannot be found out.

Thus, data in statement I is not sufficient.

From statement II:

Following three cases are possible with the given hints.

Floor number	Case-1 Pesrons	Case-2 Persons	Case-3 Persons
7	A		A
6	F	D	F
5	Vacant	Vacant	Vacant
4	D	B	B
3	E	E	E
2	B	A	D
1		F	

Thus, data in statement II is not sufficient.

From statements I and II:

Floor number	Persons
7	A
6	F
5	Vacant
4	D
3	E
2	B
1	C

Thus, the difference between the floor numbers of B and D is 2.

So, data in both statements is necessary to answer the question.

Hence, the correct option is (C).

30. From statement I:

As per the given hints, Box E may contain either Paper or Ball and is definitely not placed third from left end.

No other box except Box A contains Cap, thus pens, papers and balls are kept in two boxes.

One of the boxes containing Ball is Box B, but box G can't be placed to its left.

Boxes			Pen	Cap	Ball		Ball
Article	F	E	C	A	B	G	E

Thus, only one box is placed between the two boxes that contain Ball.

So, data in statement I is sufficient.

From statement II:

As per the given hints, it is clear that only one box i.e. Box A contains cap, thus it will be placed exactly in the middle of the row.

Boxes			Pen	Cap	Pen/Ball		Ball
Article				A		G	E

Thus, we cannot determine the second box that contains Ball.

So, data in statement II is not sufficient.

Hence, the correct option is (A).

Ques (1-28):Direction: In the question below a statement is given followed by two courses of action numbered I and II. On the basis of the information given in the statement to be true, then decide which of the suggested courses of action logically follow(s) for pursuing.

Q.1 Statement: It is necessary to adopt suitable measures to prevent repetition of bad debts by learning from the past experiences of mounting non-performing assets of banks.

Courses of action:

I. Before granting loan to customers their eligibility for loan should be evaluated strictly.

II. To ensure the payment of installments of loan, the work, for which loan was granted, should be supervised minutely on a regular basis.

A. Only I follows

B. Only II follows

C. Either I or II follows

D. Neither I nor II follows

E. Both I and II follow

Q.2 Statement: A senior manager does not follow the company protocol while he instructs subordinates to do so.

Course of action:

I. A letter of reprimand should be sent to the manager.

II. A healthy discussion should be made with the senior manager.

A. Only I follows

B. Only II follows

C. Either I or II follows

D. Neither I nor II follows

E. Both I and II follow

Q.3 Statement: Investigations led by the Narcotics Control Bureau lately have unearthed a horrifying picture of the Indian Film industry.

Course of action:

I. Those found guilty must be punished irrespective of their position.

II. Instead of punishing those involved in the dealing of drugs should be counseled and guided about the hazards associated with the drugs.

A. Only I follows

B. Only II follows

C. Either I or II follows

D. Neither I nor II follows

E. Both I and II follow

Q.4 Statement: Relations between India and China have been worsening over the past few months and the two nations are facing off against each other along their disputed border in the Himalayan region.

Course of action:

(I) India should limit and ultimately exclude Chinese involvement in Indian infrastructure.

(II) India should not compromise unless the status quo as on early may is restored.

A. Only (I) follows

B. Only (II) follows

C. Either (I) or (II) follows

D. Neither (I) nor (II) follows

E. Both (I) and (II) follow

Q.5 Statement: Due to inadequate rainfall this monsoon there is a sharp decline in food grain production.

Courses of action:

I. The government should increase the procurement price of food grains to support farmers.

II. The government should subsidize further the prices of seeds and fertilizers for the next season.

A. Only I follows

B. Only II follows

C. Either I or II follows

D. Neither I nor II follows

E. Both I and II follow

Q.6 Statement: Quality education for all can help in reducing poverty.

Courses of action:

I. The focus should be on recruiting, training and supporting teachers to improve the quality of education.

II. The government should provide free education to all girls.

A. Only I follows

B. Only II follows

C. Either I or II follows

D. Neither I nor II follows

E. Both I and II follow

Q.7 Statement: The World Bank estimates that India is one of the highest-ranking countries in the world for the number of children suffering from malnutrition.

Courses of action:

I. Government, People and various NGOs should come together and try to eradicate the problem.

II. Government should take help financial help from foreign countries to eradicate this problem.

A. Only I follows

B. Only II follows

C. Either I or II follows

D. Neither I nor II follows

E. Both I and II follow

Q.8 Statement: Fardeen wants to be the best basketball player in his school.

Courses of action:

I. Fardeen should practice and train regularly.

II. Fardeen should use weekends for playing instead of studying.

A. Only I follows
B. Only II follows
C. Either I or II follows
D. Neither I nor II follows
E. Both I and II follow

Q.9 Statement: Studies have shown that spending too much time on your phone is bad for your focus and mental health.

Courses of action:

I. Most of the push notifications should be turned off.

II. One should get a real alarm clock and avoid taking the mobiles to bed.

A. Only I follows
B. Only II follows
C. Either I or II follows
D. Neither I nor II follows
E. Both I and II follow

Q.10 Statement: Peer pressure in high school is harmful because it can lead to teen depression, high-stress levels and negative behaviour issues.

Courses of Action:

I. Students should avoid making friends in high school.

II. Students should focus on their studies.

A. Only I follows
B. Only II follows
C. Either I or II follows
D. Neither I nor II follows
E. Both I and II follow

Q.11 Statement: Women in general prisons are subject to custodial torture by male staff, denial of health services and lack of clean water and food.

Courses of Action:

I. The Government should provide separate jails for females with female staff.

II. The prisons should be made of bricks.

A. Only I follows
B. Only II follows
C. Either I or II follows
D. Neither I nor II follows
E. Both I and II follow

Q.12 Statement: It is reported that vitamins and minerals in vegetables and fruits are beneficial for the human body. Medicines do not have the same effect on the human body.

Course of Action:

I. People should be encouraged to take fresh fruits and vegetables to meet the human body's requirement of vitamins and minerals.

II. The sale of medicines of vitamins and minerals should be banned.

A. Only I follows
B. Only II follows
C. Either I or II follows

D. Neither I nor II follows
E. Both I and II follow

Q.13 Statement: The Central Bureau of Investigations (CBI) receives the complaint of an officer taking bribes to do the duty he is supposed to.

Courses of action:

I. CBI should try to catch the officer red-handed and then take strict action against him.

II. CBI should wait for some more complaints about the officer to be sure about the matter.

A. Only I follows
B. Only II follows
C. Either I or II follows
D. Neither I nor II follows
E. Both I and II follow

Q.14 Statement: Financial stringency prevented one of the companies from paying salaries to its employees since Lockdown this year.

Courses of action:

I. The company should immediately curtail the staff strength at least by 30%.

II. The company should reduce wasteful expenditure and arrange to pay the salaries of its employees.

A. Only I follows
B. Only II follows
C. Either I or II follows
D. Neither I nor II follows
E. Both I and II follow

Q.15 Statement: A number of school children in the local schools have fallen ill after the consumption of their subsidized tiffin provided by the school authority.

Course of Action:

I. The tiffin facility of all schools should be discontinued with immediate effect.

II. The Government should implement a system to certify the quality of tiffin provided by the school.

A. Only I follows
B. Only II follows
C. Either I or II follows
D. Neither I nor II follows
E. Both I and II follow

Q.16 Statement: A major part of the local market in the city was gutted due to a short circuit causing extensive damage to goods and property.

Courses of action:

I. The Government should issue strict guidelines for all establishments regarding installation and maintenance of electrical fittings.

II. The Government should relocate all the markets to the outskirts of the city.

A. Only I follows
B. Only II follows
C. Either I or II follows

D. Neither I nor II follows

E. Both I and II follow

Q.17 Statement: According to the news, few terrorists are hiding inside an old building in Delhi.

Courses of action:

I. The government should send military forces to Delhi.

II. The government should offer them to shift in the outskirts of Delhi.

A. Only I follows

B. Only II follows

C. Either I or II follows

D. Neither I nor II follows

E. Both I and II follow

Q.18 Statement: Drinking water supply to many parts of the town has been disrupted due to loss of water because of leakage in pipe supplying water.

Courses of action:

I. The Government should order an enquiry into the matter.

II. The civic body should set up a fact-finding team to assess the damage and take effective steps.

A. Only I follows

B. Only II follows

C. Either I or II follows

D. Neither I nor II follows

E. Both I and II follow

Q.19 Statement: Although the Indian economy is still heavily dependent on agriculture, its share in global agricultural trade is less than the share of agricultural exports to total exports.

Courses of action:

I. Efforts should be made to increase our agricultural production.

II. The exports of non-agricultural commodities should be reduced.

A. Only I follows

B. Only II follows

C. Either I or II follows

D. Neither I nor II follows

E. Both I and II follow

Q.20 Statement: A passenger train derailed from its path and many coaches have caught fire.

Course of action:

I. Immediate medical help needs to be sent to the place of the accident.

II. Fire brigade should be sent to the location of an accident so as to stop the burning.

A. Only I follows

B. Only II follows

C. Either I or II follows

D. Neither I nor II follows

E. Both I and II follow

Q.21 Statement: Teachers in India still teach using traditional methods and are not aware of modem methods of teaching.

Course of Action:

I. Orientation programs should be conducted for teachers to change their methods of teaching.

II. There should be a pay hike for teachers who teach using modem methods.

A. Only I follows

B. Only II follows

C. Either I or II follows

D. Neither I nor II follows

E. Both I and II follow

Q.22 Statement: The chairman stressed the need for making the education system more flexible and regretted that the curriculum has not been revised in keeping with the pace of the changes taking place.

Courses of action:

I. Curriculum should be reviewed and revised periodically.

II. System of education should be made more flexible.

A. Only I follows

B. Only II follows

C. Either I or II follows

D. Neither I nor II follows

E. Both I and II follow

Q.23 Statement: Every year, at the beginning or at the end of the monsoon, we have some cases of conjunctivitis, but this year, it seems to be a major epidemic, witnessed after nearly four years.

Courses of action:

I. Precautionary measures should be taken after every four years to check the epidemic.

II. People should be advised to drink boiled water during the monsoon season.

A. Only I follows

B. Only II follows

C. Either I or II follows

D. Neither I nor II follows

E. Both I and II follow

Q.24 Statement: All the central government employees went on strike due to the non-implementation of the 7th pay commission.

Course of Action:

I. 7th pay commission should be implemented immediately.

II. All the central government employees should be suspended.

A. Only I follows

B. Only II follows

C. Either I or II follows

D. Neither I nor II follows

E. Both I and II follow

Q.25 Statement: During natural calamities, many departments blame each other for any wrongdoing due to overlapping functions of these departments.

Course of Action:

I. Only one department should be there to take charge during natural calamities.

II. All departments should be held responsible for wrong-doings and punished.

A. Only I follows
B. Only II follows
C. Either I or II follows
D. Neither I nor II follows
E. Both I and II follow

Q.26 Statement: A recent study shows that children below five die in the cities of developing countries mainly from diarrhoea and parasitic intestinal worms.

Courses of action:

I. Government of the developing countries should take adequate measures to improve the hygienic conditions in the cities.

II. Children below five years in the cities of developing countries need to be kept under constant medication.

A. Only I follow
B. Only II follow
C. Either I or II follows
D. Neither I nor II follows
E. Both I and II follow

Q.27 Statement: Reports of steep and continued decline in the inflows into the Gobind Sagar reservoir of the Bhakra Dam, coupled with a depleted stock of steam coal with the thermal power plants in the North, may lead to a serious power crisis in the region.

Courses of action:

I. The supply of steam coal to the thermal power plants needs to be immediately stepped up by the government.

II. The government should set up hydraulic power plants on other rivers in the region.

A. Only I follow
B. Only II follow
C. Either I or II follows
D. Neither I nor II follows
E. Both I and II follow

Q.28 Statement: Despite enforcement of traffic rules city witnesses regular traffic violations.

Course of actions:

I. Penalty amount for rule violation should be made hefty.

II. Measures should be adopted to involve the citizens, where they get rewarded for reporting a violation.

A. Only I follows
B. Only II follows
C. Either I or II follows
D. Neither I nor II follows
E. Both I and II follow

Ques (29-30):Direction: In the question below a statement is given followed by two courses of action numbered I and II. On the basis of the information given in the statement to be true, then decide which of the suggested courses of action logically follow(s) for pursuing.

Q.29 Statement: There are people who still don't separate wet and dry garbage.

Courses of action:

(I) The waste collectors must not collect their garbage.

(II) People must be made aware of the importance of garbage separation.

A. Only (I) follows
B. Only (II) follows
C. Either (I) or (II) follows
D. Neither (I) nor (II) follows
E. Both (I) and (II) follow

Q.30 Statement: The rate of inflation has significantly reduced in the last 2 years and the economy of the country has been stabilising as well as showing signs of escalation.

Courses of action:

I. The Finance ministry should investigate and modify the economic system of the country.

II. The economic system of the country should be continued as it has been for the past 2 years.

A. Only I follows
B. Only II follows
C. Either I or II follows
D. Neither I nor II follows
E. Both I and II follow

// Smart Answer Sheet //

Correct   Indicates percentage of students who answered questions correctly.

Skipped   Indicates percentage of students who skipped questions.

Q.	Ans.	Correct / Skipped
1	A	79.72 % / 10.48 %
2	E	85.64 % / 12.25 %
3	A	56.56 % / 34.86 %
4	E	60.2 % / 31.99 %
5	E	84.49 % / 15.18 %
6	D	31.71 % / 68.1 %
7	A	41.83 % / 44.78 %
8	A	89.88 % / 10.05 %
9	E	59.23 % / 40.61 %
10	D	82.24 % / 16.93 %
11	A	85.2 % / 11.61 %
12	A	41.38 % / 50.06 %
13	A	80.39 % / 13.8 %
14	B	26.55 % / 68.78 %
15	B	44.25 % / 45.52 %
16	A	41.49 % / 30.63 %
17	A	67.4 % / 31.18 %
18	B	61.25 % / 33.61 %
19	A	85.71 % / 13.78 %
20	E	79.28 % / 13.85 %
21	A	85.74 % / 11.2 %
22	E	47.63 % / 48.94 %
23	B	66.36 % / 33.0 %
24	D	62.76 % / 31.04 %
25	D	62.33 % / 35.43 %
26	E	85.28 % / 12.58 %
27	A	12.18 % / 80.26 %
28	E	50.25 % / 42.56 %
29	B	76.95 % / 22.25 %
30	B	89.87 % / 10.07 %

Performance Analysis	
Avg. Score (%)	56.67%
Toppers Score (%)	60.0%
Your Score	

//Hints and Solutions//

1. The course of action I is advisable because it will reduce the number of defaulters as it will act as a preventive measure. The course of action II does not follow because the bank cannot possibly supervise in a detailed way the work for which loans are granted. Thus, only course of action I follows.

Hence, the correct option is (A).

2. The statement talks about a senior manager not adhering to the company's policies while instructing to do so. If this is known, the top authorities may send him a mail where he is scolded for his behavior. Therefore, course of action I follows. The top authorities may discuss the matter with the manager across the table in an acceptable manner. Therefore, course of action II follows.

Hence, the correct option is (E).

3. The statement talks about the action of a central agency that has led to turmoil in Bollywood because of a deep nexus related to drugs being exposed. Celebrities are icons of society therefore those involved in the illegal consumption/dealing of drugs should be punished regardless of their position or designation to set an example for the rest. Therefore, course of action I follows. Counseling and guiding them will be relevant but those engaged in unlawful drug deals should be punished so that they will learn a lesson and will not do this again in the future. Therefore, course of action II does not follows.

Hence, the correct option is (A).

4. The statement talks about a state of conflict between India and China arising because of cross-border tension. India should try to cut trade ties with China unless the tension is resolved, also China should be excluded from infrastructural pacts for security reasons. Therefore, course of action (I) follows. India should get into no form of settlement unless the original state of affairs during early May is restored. Therefore, course of action (II) follows.

Hence, the correct option is (E).

5. The course of action I is advisable because it will bolster the financial condition of the farmers. The course of action II is also advisable because subsidizing further the price of seeds and fertilizers will act as compensation.

Hence, the correct option is (E).

6. The course of action I does not follow as high-quality trained teachers surely improve the quality of education but just improvement in the education cannot help in reducing poverty. Improved education help in reducing poverty only when it will be available for all levels of people. This course of action could follow if it said: The focus should be on recruiting, training and supporting teachers to improve the quality of education for all. The course of action II also does not follow as providing free education to only girls is not the solution to poverty. Free education should be available for all needy people irrespective of gender.

Hence, the correct option is (D).

7. As the statement talks about India's ranking in the world for the number of children suffering from malnutrition. The course of action I is appropriate because People, government and various NGOs should join their hands and work in a coordinated way to solve this problem. The course of action II is not valid here because in a country like India, to solve such problems there is no need for getting financial aid from foreign countries. A proper budget and planning can solve the problem.

Hence, the correct option is (A).

8. The course of action I follows as practice can help in increasing one's skills. Thus, the course of action I is the correct step taken in accordance with the given statement. Thus, course of action I follows. On the other hand, giving sports more preference than studies at any point of time is not advisable. Thus, course of action II does not follows.

Hence, the correct option is (A).

9. The course of action I follows as the statement tells us about the fact that excessive use of the phone can be bad for our health. Therefore, course of action I provides us a solution to turn off the notifications so that we avoid unnecessary use of the phone. Thus, course of action I follows. At the same time, many people say that they carry mobile phones to bed because they need the alarm. The course of action II follows as it suggests to get a real alarm and avoid taking the phone to bed. This is one of the ways in which we can reduce the use of phones. Therefore, both course of action follows.

Hence, the correct option is (E).

10. From the statement above, we understand the negative effects of peer pressure on a high school student. But the course of action suggested in I is not feasible. Therefore, course of action I does not follow. Similarly, focusing on studies is not a viable course of action for avoiding peer pressure. Therefore, course of action II also does not follows.

Hence, the correct option is (D).

11. From the statement above, we are informed about the wrong treatment of female prisoners in jails. Therefore, in order to prevent it, the Government should provide separate jails for females with female staff. Therefore, course of action I follows. On the other hand, reconstructing prisons is not a viable course of action. Therefore, course of action II does not follows.

Hence, the correct option is (A).

12. As the statement talks about the benefits of taking vegetables and fruit for the human body. It is not talking about the sale of medicines that should be banned. It is just said medicines do not have the same effect on the human body. The course of action I will make people get the benefits of vegetables and fruits. So, the only course I follow. The course of action II is not directly related to the statement. Therefore, course of action II does not follows.

Hence, the correct option is (A).

13. As the complaint is already received by (CBI) for one of his officers. One complaint is enough for wrongdoings like taking a bribe. This should be confirmed by catching the guilty red-handed and then strict action taken against him. So, the course of

action I follow. As the complaint is already received, so waiting for more complaints is not a good course of action for such a prestigious institution. So, course of action II doesn't follows.

Hence, the correct option is (A).

14. As the statement talks about due to financial stringency one of the companies is unable to pay salaries to its employees since Lockdown this year. Curtailing staff strength is not the right solution. There must be no extremity involved in the course of action. Therefore, course of action I does not follows. Curtailing wasteful expenditure is the right step towards making provisions for money to be distributed against pending salaries. Thus, course of action II follows.

Hence, the correct option is (B).

15. As the statement talks about the ill effects of the subsidized tiffin provided by the school authority due to which many children have fallen ill. There should be no extremity involve in the course of action. This will not resolve the problem. So, the course of action I doesn't follow. The course of action II is a good measure to solve the issue which will resolve the quality issues. So, the only course of action II follows.

Hence, the correct option is (B).

16. As the statement talks about the local market in the city which was destroyed due to a short circuit causing extensive damage to goods and property. The course of action I follows as the precautionary measure to be taken to prevent further accidents in the future. The course of action II won't solve the problem and poor electrical fittings would wreak havoc where ever the market be. Thus, the course of action II does not follow.

Hence, the correct option is (A).

17. After knowing the fact that the terrorists are hiding at a certain place the Government should send armed forces as this is a national issue. Therefore, course of action I follows. On the other hand, the course of action II is vague and totally unrealistic. It is practically not possible to achieve such an action. Therefore, offering them to shift somewhere is completely out of question. Thus, course of action II does not follows.

Hence, the correct option is (A).

18. As the statement talks about the disruption in the drinking water supply due to the leakage in pipe supplying water. The course of action I is not the valid solution to the problem. The problem is not so big as to set up a Government inquiry to look into this matter. So, course of action I does not follows. The course of action II is enough that the civic body takes action and assesses the damage and takes the necessary steps. Thus, the course of action II follows.

Hence, the correct option is (B).

19. As the statement talks about the benefits of the Indian economy which is still heavily dependent on agriculture but its share in global agricultural trade is less than the share of agricultural exports to total exports. Only by increasing our agricultural production, we can have a better position in international agricultural trade. So, the course of action I follows. Reduction in non-agricultural commodities will further worsen our position. Therefore, course of action II does not follow.

Hence, the correct option is (A).

20. After a train derails, the first step would be to save the lives of people. Here sending medical help and fire brigade to the location of the accident would be necessary. So, both course of action I and II follow.

Hence, the correct option is (E).

21. In order to make the teachers in India aware of modem methods of teaching, Orientation programs should be conducted to teach them the various method through which they can improve their teaching ability. Therefore, course of action I follows. Just paying more to the teachers who teach using modem methods cannot be a suitable course of action as the existing teachers also need to be brought up to the new standards. Thus, course of action II does not follows.

Hence, the correct option is (A).

22. As the statement talks about the education system problem and the chairman stressed making it more flexible and regretted that the curriculum has not been revised in keeping with the pace of the changes taking place. The statement speaks of inadequacies of the education system and emphasizes the need for flexibility and revision. So, courses of action I and II are right to update the curriculum.

Hence, the correct option is (E).

23. As the statement talks about some cases of conjunctivitis at the beginning or at the end of the monsoon, but this year, it seems to be a major epidemic, witnessed after nearly four years. It is not necessary that such an epidemic occurs after every four years. So, the course of action I does not follows. Prevention during monsoon season is the right step to face the problem of conjunctivitis. So, the course of action II follows.

Hence, the correct option is (B).

24. Here statement says that, all the central government employees went on strike due to non-implementation of 7th pay. Course of Action I does not follow as 7th pay commission cannot be implemented immediately, it will take time as you have to form a committee and a lot of legal paperwork is there to implement it. On the other hand, course of action II also not follows, because you cannot suspend all the central government officers just because they went on strike.

Hence, the correct option is (D).

25. During natural calamities, there is a need for all the departments to function together. Only one department cannot take charge of the whole situation. So, the course of action I does not follow. All the departments cannot be held responsible for the wrongdoing as it will be unfair for those who worked honestly. Only departments which are responsible for the wrongdoings should be punished. So, the course of action II also does not follow.

Hence, the correct option is (D).

26. If the government concentrate to improve the hygienic condition in the cities, definitely reduce the impact of the problem. So, the course of action I follows. A constant medication is another practical feasible step, which would help minimize the

cases of death due to diarrhoea and intestinal worms. Therefore, course of action II also follows.

Hence, the correct option is (E).

27. The statement points out the crisis faced by the power plants and one of the crises is the depletion of the stock of steam coal with the thermal power plants in the North. Therefore, it is the right course of action to supply steam coal to the thermal power plants. So, the course of action I follows. Secondly, since the water inflows into the Gobind Sagar have declined, setting up another hydraulic power plant will be useless. So, the course of action II does not follows.

Hence, the correct option is (A).

28. The statement shares that despite the enforcement of traffic rules there is constant flouting. Course of action I suggest that monetary fine should be increased. Since the loss of money hurts and it will help people gain seriousness. Therefore, course of action I is logical and follows. Course of action II suggests that active involvement of citizens should be sought by rewarding them on any violation reported. This will have a significant impact. Therefore, course of action II is logical and it also follows.

Hence, the correct option is (E).

29. The statement says that people still don't separate wet and dry garbage. Not accepting the waste is not a solution to the given problem. Thus, the course of action (I) does not follow. People, if made aware of the importance of separating wet and dry garbage, might change their ways in the future. Therefore, the course of action (II) follows.

Hence, the correct option is (B).

30. Since the inflation rate has decreased and economic stability has increased, it means that the economic system of the country is working efficiently for the past 2 years. Therefore, the course of action I does not follows and course of action II follows.

Hence, the correct option is (B).

Ques (1-25):Direction: In the question below a statement followed by two assumptions numbered I and II has been given. An assumption is something supposed or taken for granted. You are required to consider the statement and the following assumptions and decide which of the assumptions and decide which of the assumptions is implicit in the statement.

Q.1 Statement: A pen is more powerful than the sword.
Assumptions:

I. Pen is made of metal which is harder than the metal used for making the sword.

II. Mental power is more effective than the physical power.

A. Only assumption I is implicit.
B. Only assumption II is implicit.
C. Either assumption I or assumption II is implicit.
D. Neither assumption I nor assumptions are implicit.
E. Both the assumptions are implicit.

Q.2 Statement: People who play video games are more dexterous than those who don't play such games.
Assumptions:

I. Dexterity develops from playing video games.

II. Pianists are often known to play video games.

A. Only assumption I is implicit.
B. Only assumption II is implicit.
C. Either assumption I or II is implicit.
D. Neither assumption I nor II is implicit.
E. Both the assumptions I and II are implicit.

Q.3 Statement: Most people who stop consuming alcohol gain weight.
Assumptions:

I. If one consumes alcohol, one will lose weight.

II. If one does not stop consuming alcohol, one will not gain weight.

A. Only assumption I is implicit.
B. Only assumption II is implicit.
C. Either assumption I or II is implicit.
D. Neither assumption I nor II is implicit.
E. Both the assumptions I and II are implicit.

Q.4 Statements: "I have not received electricity bills for nine months inspite of several complaints" – A Delhi resident's letter to the editor of a daily.
Assumptions:

I. Every customer has a right to get bills regularly from the electricity department.

II The customer's complaints point to defect in the services which are expected to be corrected.

A. Only assumption I is implicit.
B. Only assumption II is implicit.
C. Either assumption I or II is implicit.

D. Neither assumption I nor II is implicit.
E. Both the assumptions I and II are implicit.

Q.5 Statement: The government has decided to pay compensation to the tune of Rs. 1 lakh to the family members of those who are killed in the earthquake.
Assumptions:

I. The government has enough funds to meet the expenses due to compensation.

II. There may be a reduction in the incidents of deaths caused due to earthquakes in the near future.

A. Only assumption I is implicit.
B. Only assumption II is implicit.
C. Either assumption I or II is implicit.
D. Neither assumption I nor II is implicit.
E. Both the assumptions I and II are implicit.

Q.6 Statement: If you have any problems in studies, consult the teacher.
Assumptions:

I. You have some problems.

II. The teacher can solve any problem.

A. Only assumption I is implicit.
B. Only assumption II is implicit.
C. Either assumption I or II is implicit.
D. Neither assumption I nor II is implicit.
E. Both the assumptions I and II are implicit.

Q.7 Statement: All the employees are unsatisfied with the organization.
Assumptions:

I: The organization does not value the employees and does not give them perks.

II: Employees are mean and greedy and are looking for ways to switch to another organization.

A. Only assumption I is implicit.
B. Only assumption II is implicit.
C. Either assumption I or II is implicit.
D. Neither assumption I nor II is implicit.
E. Both assumptions I and II are implicit.

Q.8 Statement: The safety and health conditions are very bad in construction companies in India.
Assumptions:

I: Safety and health management is better at sectors other than construction companies.

II: Construction companies in other countries provide better safety to its employees.

A. Only assumption I is implicit.
B. Only assumption II is implicit.
C. If either assumption I or II is implicit.
D. If neither I nor II is implicit.

E. If both I and II are implicit.

Q.9 Statement: Marcelo's car broke down and his phone also got fully discharged and just when he started thinking he is having a bad hair day he saw a ray of sunshine.

Assumptions:

I: Everything was going wrong for Marcelo on that particular day.

II: Marcelo was having a bad day because of his dirty hair.

A. Only assumption I is implicit.
B. Only assumption II is implicit.
C. If either assumption I or II is implicit.
D. If neither I nor II is implicit.
E. If both I and II are implicit.

Q.10 Statement: A building was evacuated immediately after they were warned by police of possible terrorist attack.

Assumptions:

I: Police warned the officials of building based on some Intel.

II: Police authorities were threatened by terrorists of attacking on that building.

A. Only assumption I is implicit.
B. Only assumption II is implicit.
C. If either assumption I or II is implicit.
D. If neither I nor II is implicit.
E. If both I and II are implicit.

Q.11 Statement: Security of the building was increased after the incident at the old lady's apartment.

Assumptions:

I: Something dangerous happened at the old lady's apartment.

II: The old lady was an easy target.

A. Only assumption I is implicit.
B. Only assumption II is implicit.
C. Both assumption I and II are implicit.
D. None of the assumptions are implicit.
E. Either I or II is implicit.

Q.12 Statement: During a digging process in a village of country X, a large oil reserve was found. The country X presently lacks in meeting their oil demands and the major portion of the oil is imported by them.

Assumptions:

I. The new oil reserve will help boost the economy of country X.

II. The rates of oil may fall post-discovery of the new oil reserve.

A. Only assumption I is implicit.
B. Only assumption II is implicit.
C. If either assumption I or II is implicit.
D. If neither I nor II is implicit.
E. If both I and II are implicit.

Q.13 Statement: High fly Airline decided to increases the price of the flight ticket.

Assumptions:

I. The number of passengers travelling with High fly airlines increases day by day.

II. They want to earn more profit.

A. If only assumption I is implicit.
B. If only assumption II is implicit.
C. If either assumption I or II is implicit.
D. If neither assumption I nor II is implicit.
E. If both assumption I and II are implicit.

Q.14 Statement: The patient's condition would improve after the operation.

Assumptions:

I. The patient can be operated upon in his condition.

II. The patient cannot be operated upon in his condition.

A. If only assumption I is implicit.
B. If only assumption II is implicit.
C. If either assumption I or II is implicit.
D. If neither assumption I nor II is implicit.
E. If both assumption I and II are implicit.

Q.15 Statement: Misconceptions about HIV cannot be eradicated from our society. We need to create an awareness team for it.

Assumptions:

I: It is impossible to create an awareness team.

II: People do not know about HIV.

A. Only assumption I is implicit.
B. Only assumption II is implicit.
C. Both assumption I and II are implicit.
D. None of the assumptions are implicit.
E. Either I or II is implicit.

Q.16 Statement: The private bus services in the city has virtually collapsed because of the ongoing strike of its employees.

Assumptions:

I. Going on strike has become the right of every employee.

II. People no more require the services of private bus operators.

A. If only assumption I is implicit.
B. If only assumption II is implicit.
C. If either assumption I or II is implicit.
D. If neither assumption I nor II is implicit.
E. If both assumption I and II are implicit.

Q.17 Statement: "Do not lean out of the door of the bus." - a warning in a school bus.

Assumptions:

I. Leaning out of a running bus is dangerous.

II. Children do not pay any heed to such warnings.

A. Only assumption I is implicit.
B. Only assumption II is implicit.
C. Either I or II is implicit.
D. Neither I nor II is implicit.
E. Both I and II are implicit.

Q.18 Statement: "If you are a mechanical engineer, we want you as our supervisor." - an advertisement by company X.

Assumptions:

I. Mechanical engineers are expected to be better performers by company X.

II. The company X needs supervisors.

A. Only assumption I is implicit.
B. Only assumption II is implicit.
C. Either I or II is implicit.
D. Neither I nor II is implicit.
E. Both I and II are implicit.

Q.19 Statement: Be humble even after being victorious.

Assumptions:

I. Many people are humble after being victorious.

II. Generally, people are not humble.

A. Only assumption I is implicit.
B. Only assumption II is implicit.
C. Either I or II is implicit.
D. Neither I nor II is implicit.
E. Both I and II are implicit.

Q.20 Statement: A sentence in the letter to the candidates called for written examinations –'You have to bear your expenses on travel etc.'

Assumptions:

I. If not clarified, all the candidates may claim reimbursement of expenses.

II. Many organisations reimburse expenses on travel to candidates called for written examinations.

A. Only assumption I is implicit.
B. Only assumption II is implicit.
C. Either I or II is implicit.
D. Neither I nor II is implicit.
E. Both I and II are implicit.

Q.21 Statement: One of the opposition leaders said that the time had come for like-minded opposition parties to unite and dislodge the corrupt government.

Assumptions:

I. Like-minded opposition parties should unite only when the have to dislodge a corrupt government.

II. Opposition parties are not corrupt.

A. Only assumption I is implicit.
B. Only assumption II is implicit.
C. Either I or II is implicit.
D. Neither I nor II is implicit.
E. Both I and II are implicit.

Q.22 Statement: Postal rates have been increased to meet the deficit.

Assumptions:

I. The present rates are very low.

II. If the rates are not increased, the deficit cannot be met.

A. Only assumption I is implicit
B. Only assumption II is implicit
C. Either I or II is implicit
D. Neither I nor II is implicit
E. Both I and II are implicit

Q.23 Statement: If degrees are delinked from jobs, boys will think twice before joining college.

Assumptions:

I. Boys join college education to get jobs.

II. A degree is of no use in getting a job.

A. Only assumption I is implicit.
B. Only assumption II is implicit.
C. Either I or II is implicit.
D. Neither I nor II is implicit.
E. Both I and II are implicit.

Q.24 Statement: "Present-day education is in a shambles and the country is going to the dogs."

Assumptions:

I. A good education system is essential for the well-being of a nation.

II. A good education alone is sufficient for the well-being of a nation.

A. Only assumption I is implicit.
B. Only assumption II is implicit.
C. Either I or II is implicit.
D. Neither I nor II is implicit.
E. Both I and II are implicit.

Q.25 Statement: "Computer education should start at schools itself."

Assumptions:

I. Learning computers is easy.

II. Computer education fetches jobs easily.

A. Only assumption I is implicit.
B. Only assumption II is implicit.
C. Either I or II is implicit.
D. Neither I nor II is implicit.
E. Both I and II are implicit.

Ques (26-30):Direction: In the question below a statement followed by two assumptions numbered I and II has been given. An assumption is something supposed or taken for granted. You are required to consider the statement and the following assumptions and decide which of the assumptions and decide which of the assumptions is implicit in the statement.

Q.26 Statement: In today's economic crisis only the ideals of limited family and hard labor in the field of education can lead India towards prosperity.

Assumptions:

I. Ideals of limited family and hard labor in the field of education are correlated with India's prosperity.

II. A large family faces difficulty in bearing the expenses on education.

A. Only assumption I is implicit.
B. Only assumption II is implicit.
C. Either assumption I or assumption II is implicit.
D. Neither assumption I nor assumptions are implicit.
E. Both the assumptions are implicit.

Q.27 Statement: Young boys will think many times before asking for admission in colleges if employment is kept apart from Degree.

Assumptions:

I. Girls do not try to seek employment.

II. Degree is not fundamentally correlated with employment.

A.   Only assumption I is implicit.
B.   Only assumption II is implicit.
C.   Either assumption I or assumption II is implicit.
D.   Neither assumption I nor assumptions are implicit.
E.   Both the assumptions are implicit.

Q.28 Statement: "Neighbor's envy and owner's pride" – an advertisement on television.

Assumptions:

I. People are envious of neighbor's good things.

II. People want to provoke their neighbor's envy.

A.   Only assumption I is implicit.
B.   Only assumption II is implicit.
C.   Either assumption I or assumption II is implicit.
D.   Neither assumption I nor assumptions are implicit.
E.   Both the assumptions are implicit.

Q.29 Statement: We should work hard for success in examination.

Assumptions:

I. It is desirable to be successful in the examination.

II. The fruit of success is tasted by those pupils who work hard.

A.   Only assumption I is implicit.
B.   Only assumption II is implicit.
C.   Either assumption I or assumption II is implicit.
D.   Neither assumption I nor assumptions are implicit.
E.   Both the assumptions are implicit.

Q.30 Statement: "To stop train pull chain. Penalty for use without reasonable and sufficient cause is fine upto Rs. 1,000 and / or imprisonment upto one year."

Assumptions:

I. A few persons are naughty.

II. People travelling in the train want to stop the running train in case of emergency.

A.   Only assumption I is implicit.
B.   Only assumption II is implicit.
C.   Either assumption I or assumption II is implicit.
D.   Neither assumption I nor assumptions are implicit.
E.   Both the assumptions are implicit.

// Smart Answer Sheet //

Correct   Indicates percentage of students who answered questions correctly.

Skipped   Indicates percentage of students who skipped questions.

Q.	Ans.	Correct / Skipped
1	B	58.56 % / 38.09 %
2	A	68.05 % / 30.7 %
3	D	25.68 % / 67.9 %
4	E	77.11 % / 22.21 %
5	A	42.48 % / 51.15 %
6	D	85.6 % / 14.34 %

Q.	Ans.	Correct / Skipped
7	A	50.67 % / 47.84 %
8	D	53.14 % / 46.0 %
9	A	82.76 % / 17.15 %
10	A	43.72 % / 42.11 %
11	A	85.34 % / 10.28 %
12	E	68.67 % / 30.99 %

Q.	Ans.	Correct / Skipped
13	E	14.5 % / 74.71 %
14	A	58.48 % / 37.37 %
15	B	55.3 % / 37.77 %
16	D	62.53 % / 34.46 %
17	A	81.71 % / 11.72 %
18	B	14.25 % / 81.24 %

Q.	Ans.	Correct / Skipped
19	D	65.89 % / 34.08 %
20	E	85.65 % / 12.76 %
21	D	56.66 % / 35.79 %
22	B	27.52 % / 68.96 %
23	A	44.91 % / 33.94 %
24	A	84.12 % / 11.96 %

Q.	Ans.	Correct / Skipped
25	A	58.75 % / 38.99 %
26	A	67.78 % / 30.94 %
27	B	56.16 % / 42.29 %
28	E	43.46 % / 31.25 %
29	E	84.81 % / 10.07 %
30	E	55.56 % / 36.03 %

Performance Analysis	
Avg. Score (%)	**43.33%**
Toppers Score (%)	**70.0%**
Your Score	

//Hints and Solutions//

1. Here, the direct meaning must not be taken. It is assumed that mental power is more effective to physical power and these are compared to the pen and sword respectively because the pen is a tool to write down powerful ideas whereas the sword is a tool to show your physical power.

Hence, the correct option is (B).

2. The statement talks about how video gamers are often nimble with their hands than non-gamers. Thus, assumption I is correct. Again pianists need to have nimble fingers to play the piano perfectly. But we can not assume that pianists play video games very often since no such thing is mentioned in the statement. Thus, assumption II is not correct.

Hence, the correct option is (A).

3. The given statement mentions 'most people'. A generalised statement like in assumption I and II cannot be made because a specific statement cannot be universalised. Moreover, the given statement talks about the after effects of discontinuing the consumption of alcohol. So, it is quite difficult to assume what are the effects of consuming alcohol. Therefore, I is not implicit in the statement. Additionally, it cannot be assumed from the given statement that terminating the consumption of alcohol is the only criterion to gain wait. Also, the given sentence is least concerned about what happens if one does not stop consuming alcohol. So, any assumption in this regard cannot be made. Thus, II is also not implicit.

Hence, the correct option is (D).

4. From the fact that the customer is concerned about not receiving electricity bills, one can assume that every customer has a right to get the bills regularly. Thus I is implicit. II is also implicit as the customer has brought the incident into public by writing about it to the editor of a newspaper daily. This shows that the sheer negligence from the part of the electricity department is expected to be corrected through this means. Hence, both I and II are implicit.

Hence, the correct option is (E).

5. A government cannot fix the compensation to a certain amount unless it has enough funds to bear the expenses. Therefore, I is implicit. II is not implicit because the statement does not refer to reduction of deaths caused due to earthquakes. Moreover, it cannot be ensured that the future occurrences of earthquakes will not cause deaths.

Hence, the correct option is (A).

6. The word 'if' indicates that the 'you' does not necessarily have problems but in case he/she has any, he/she can consult the teacher. So, I is not implicit. Assumption II is not implicit because the statement does not tell us anywhere that any problem can be solved by the teacher, it merely asks to consult the teacher in case there is one. So, assumption II is not implicit.

Hence, the correct option is (D).

7. From the given statement it can be assumed that because the employees do not get their desired perks and respect, they are not satisfied with the organization.

Assumption II, on the other hand, is vague and does not give a concrete assumption regarding the given statement.

Hence, the correct option is (A).

8. There is no comparison made between India and other countries or between the construction sector and other sectors in the statement.

So, neither I nor assumption II.

Hence, the correct option is (D).

9. Concluding both I and II having dirty hair could be one of the reasons but it wasn't the only reason for her bad day.

Therefore, the only assumption I is implicit.

Hence, the correct option is (A).

10. It is clear that police must have informed the building officials only after they had some Intel or information regarding it. Therefore, assumption I is implicit.

But we cannot assume that Intel was the threat by terrorists themselves. Therefore, assumption II is not implicit.

On analyzing the above explanation we can say that only assumption I is implicit.

Hence, the correct option is (A).

11. Increase in security suggests that a crime occurred at the old lady's apartment. So, assumption I is implicit. Nothing is suggested about the living conditions of the old lady. So, assumption II is not implicit.

Hence, the correct option is (A).

12. We are not sure if the new oil reserve will be enough in meeting their demands or not. But it is clear that it will boost their economy because now the import of oil will decrease. Since now they have found an extra source of oil, the oil price may fall. Therefore, both assumptions I and II are implicit.

Hence, the correct option is (E).

13. As we see the statement, it talks about rising in the flight ticket price. The assumption I is implicit here because as we know that if demand increases, then supply increases and it also affects the price. So, the number of passenger traveling with the airline increases, which is profitable for the airline too. So, they want to earn more profit. So, assumption II is also implicit here.

Hence, the correct option is (E).

14. As we see in the statement, the patient requires an operation to improve their condition. The fact that the patient's condition would improve after the operation clearly implies that the patient can be operated upon his condition. So, the assumption I is implicit here. assumption II is in contradiction to assumption I and therefore is not implicit here.

Hence, the correct option is (A).

15. Assumption I is not implicit as statement does not imply that it is impossible to create awareness team. Assumption II is implicit as society does not know much about HIV and have misconceptions about it.

Hence, the correct option is (B).

16. As we see the statement, it talks about private bus services strike. The assumption I is not valid because the statement just because private bus operators have gone on strike does not mean that every employee has a right to go for a strike. Assumption II is totally irrelevant because it never happens that employees strike just because of people no require bus services.

Hence, the correct option is (D).

17. Leaning out of a running bus must be dangerous, otherwise the warning would not have been there. Therefore, I is implicit. But II is not implicit. If the authorities would have assumed that children do not pay any heed to such warning, they would not have put it up there.

Hence, the correct option is (A).

18. I is not implicit. The company wants mechanical engineers. One reason could be that the company expects mechanical engineers to be good performers, as I suggests. But there could be another reason; for example, the company's supervisory job could be such that only a mechanical engineer could perform it. But one thing is certain. The advertisement was for supervisors; this means supervisors are needed. So, II is implicit.

Hence, the correct option is (B).

19. The statement asks a man to be humble even after being victorious. This implies that people are usually not humble after victory. I is just the opposite of it. II is not implicit because it generalises the statement. Generally, people may be humble; the point is if they are humble or not after victory.

Hence, the correct option is (D).

20. If the letter mentions expenses to be borne by candidates, those who sent the letter must have assumed that the candidates may demand for reimbursement if the point is not clarified to them. Also, the candidates would not demand reimbursement if it was not a prevalent practice. So, I and II both are implicit.

Hence, the correct option is (E).

21. To dislodge a corrupt government has been mentioned as the present purpose for the call of unity. But this does not mean that this is the only purpose. So, I is not implicit. Further, the leader asks like-minded parties to unite against the government and not the entire opposition. So, we cannot generalise that (all) opposition parties are non-corrupt. So, II is not implicit.

Hence, the correct option is (D).

22. Postal rates have been increased. The cause : to meet the deficit. This never means that the present rates are low. If the price of goods increases, it is not necessary that the earlier price was low. But the tone of the statement clearly implies that postal rates have been increased out of compulsion : so, II is implicit.

Hence, the correct option is (B).

23. The statement says that if degrees are delinked from jobs, boys will not join colleges. This implies that jobs are a major reason for them to join college. So, I is implicit. Now, if I is implicit, II is not because II is just the opposite of I.

Hence, the correct option is (A).

24. The statement uses a tone that implies that if education is in a shambles, then the country deteriorates. This means that a good education is needed for the well-being of a nation. But this does not mean that a good education alone is sufficient for it. So, I is implicit but II is not.

Hence, the correct option is (A).

25. If one says that computers should be taught at schools he must have assumed that it is an easy subject, because schools are a place of elementary education; tougher things are taught at colleges. But the statement does not say anything about jobs. So I is implied, II is not.

Hence, the correct option is (A).

26. Here, if the sentence talks about prosperity of the nation then the assumption is that only the two factors mentioned can lead to prosperity. Hence, assumption I is implicit. But nothing is mentioned about why larger families will be deterrent to prosperity. While it is common sense that a large family faces difficulty in bearing the expenses on education, it is not implicit in the statement given.

Hence, the correct option is (A).

27. Here, the statement only mentions boys and what girls think is not mentioned so nothing is to be assumed about them. Hence assumption I is not implicit. Since the statement suggests that employment and degree are being kept apart, it can be assumed that it is possible to do so. Thus we can assume that there is no fundamental correlation between degree and employment. So assumption II is implicit.

Hence, the correct option is (B).

28. 'Neighbour's envy' and 'owner's pride' are the two elements to this television advertisement. The advertisement is playing on people's desire of their neighbour's good things. So clearly assumption I is implicit. Also, if simply taking pride in one's good things was enough then the advertisement would simply have stated 'owner's pride'. The fact that the advertisement is targeted at the people who want to provoke their neighbour's envy is clearly stated in assumption II. Thus II is also implicit.

Hence, the correct option is (E).

29. The statement says that we should work hard for success. If it is obligatory for us to work hard for success, then it must be implicit that success in an examination be desirable. The second assumption states the pupils who work hard taste the fruit of success. This assumption is also clearly implict because if there were no reward for working hard in the form of success, then there would be no incentive to work hard. Thus it is evident that both assumptions I and II are implicit.

Hence, the correct option is (E).

30. Let us consider the first statement. In the sentence it is given that 'use without reasonable and sufficient cause'. This indicates that it is implied that some 'people are naughty' and these people pull the chain without sufficient cause. Also, the chain is meant for stopping the train in case of an emergency so it is assumed that everyone would 'want' to stop the train in case of emergency.

Hence, the correct option is (E).

Q.1 Some people still listen only to the radio instead of downloading songs. Apparently, they do not want to miss the thrill of accidentally listening to a song that they did not expect to listen to.

Which of the following is a statement that can be inferred from the facts stated in the above statement?

A. Songs cannot be downloaded from the radio.

B. Unexpected songs are easier to remember.

C. One cannot discover songs by accident when they are downloading them.

D. Downloading is expensive.

E. Songs are better on the radio.

Q.2 What inference can you draw from the following two statements?

I. Hybrid plants are resistant to fungus.

II. Fungus infection reduces the life of plants.

A. Fungus attacks hybrid plants.

B. Yield is more in hybrid plants.

C. All plants are hybrid plants.

D. For a long life-span grow hybrid plants.

E. None of these

Q.3 Studies show that every third woman in the world has been infected by toxoplasma gondii – a virus that is most commonly spread through contact with cats, rats and through consumption of unwashed vegetables. The parasite is successful in that it rarely lets the host know that it has made up residence in her body. It uses very little of her, and for the most part lives out its short life incognito. But sometimes the parasite cause severe problems – the worst of which is pre-eclampsia during pregnancy.

Which of the following is an inference, which can be made from the facts stated in the above paragraph?

A. Toxoplasma gondii is a benign parasite.

B. Toxoplasma gondii is usually asymptomatic.

C. Toxoplasma gondii is spread through consumption of unwashed vegetables.

D. Toxoplasma gondii loves to play dress-up.

E. Toxoplasma gondii is the chief cause of pre-eclampsia in pregnant women.

Q.4 "If a person is rich, he has a lot of influence." What inference can you draw from the above statement?

A. Poor people cannot have influence.

B. Ram has a lot of influence, so he is rich.

C. Govind is not rich, so he does not have a lot of influence.

D. Kamala is rich, so she has a lot of influence.

E. None of these

Q.5 Recent statistics have shown that child labor has increased in urban areas. These children are exploited at a tender age and made to do odd jobs.

Which of the following is a statement that can be inferred from the facts stated in the above statement?

A. Migration to big cities should be checked.

B. Child labor is a problem in urban areas.

C. The plight of the exploitation should be examined properly.

D. None of the above

E. All of these

Q.6 The subway has shaped New York City. More than any other public works program or municipal project, the subway has shaped the city's development and sustained its global competitiveness over the past 100 years. The subway's profound impact on the city's growth and development—particularly in the outer boroughs—surpasses that of the city's other widely acclaimed infrastructure projects, such as the Brooklyn Bridge and Robert Moses' highway network. The innovative, early 20th century transit system still serves the 21st century metropolis well—a tribute to visionary planning and advanced engineering design. The October 2004 centennial of New York's first subway line provides an occasion to look back at how dramatically the city was transformed in the years that the subways were built.

Which of the following is an inference which can be made from the facts stated in the above paragraph?

A. The Subway system in New York is more than 100 years old.

B. The subway system in New York was only needed to connect the outer lying regions to the main city.

C. The subway system in New York was extremely well planned and advanced as even though it's old it still is a viable mode of transport contributing to the growth and development of New York City.

D. The subway system in New York City has been closed down after 100 years of service as it is no longer viable for the betterment and sustainability of the city it serves.

E. The subway system has been expanded with growing population.

Q.7 Till the early 1970s, wetlands were largely unappreciated, rejected and disregarded as ecosystems and viewed as landscapes only. In human terms, they were considered of little or no value, providing breeding grounds for insects such as mosquitoes, obstructing overland and water transportation, curtailing the amount of land available for agriculture and inhibiting the growth of settlements. So they were reclaimed for human use. Since then a deliberate and determined lobby has been arguing for their conservation.

Which of the following is an inference which can be made from the facts stated in the above passage?

A. Even in the 21st Century wetlands are considered to be wastelands and viewed as landscapes only.

B. Conservationists are trying to create more awareness regarding wetlands and their importance in human development.

C. Mosquitoes consider wetlands to be ideal breeding

grounds.

D. Wetlands are often reclaimed for human use by filling up of the said lands with mud and sand taken from other areas.

E. Wetlands need to be conserved for the sustainable development of human kind.

Q.8 Hooghly River is the main source of water for the Kolkata Metropolitan Region. Siltation and reduction in flow pose a problem for Kolkata Port and civic life in the metropolitan area. Groundwater is also not a dependable source due to deterioration in quality and quantity. Rainy season in India, causes flooding in a flat topography, where sporadic and unplanned urbanization has taken place. A well planned, organized and efficient management of water resource and waste disposal is needed for environmental and ecological stability.

Which of the following is an inference which can be made from the facts stated in the above paragraph?

A. Kolkata needs a proper efficient water resource management system if it wants to be sustainable in the near future.

B. The Kolkata Metropolitan area's main source of water is the Hooghly river and other sources of ground water.

C. Efficient water management coupled with proper waste disposal is needed for the sustainable development of any major urban area.

D. Kolkata Port faces a lot of problems due to heavy siltation in the Hooghly river.

E. Urbanization usually takes place on flat topography with a good supply of easily available water resources.

Q.9 The International Council for Engineering and Technology (ICET) has identified the unchecked growth of megacities, particularly in developing countries, as a priority area for its action in the four year period 2002 to 2005. The Council has decided that as a culmination of its activities during this period, it will organise in March 2005 a World Congress on Megacities of the Future, in cooperation with a number of intergovernmental and international non-governmental organisations. The specificity of this Congress will be that it will not limit its forum to engineers and technology experts only but will attempt to be the first ever world congress on megacities to focus on a holistic approach involving all categories of experts concerned including the full range of relevant scientific disciplines (natural and social sciences), and representatives of all stakeholders.

Which of the following is an inference that can be made from the facts stated in the above paragraph?

A. Development of megacities not only depends upon engineers and technology experts but it also needs to engage other experts from both natural and social sciences.

B. Developments of megacities are solely dependent on engineers and technology experts.

C. Megacities have been growing unchecked in the last decade and the Congress should create a framework of policies and laws to curb this growth for the betterment of the world.

D. A World Congress on Megacities of the Future is to be held in March 2005.

E. Intergovernmental and international nongovernment organizations will participate in the march 2005 World Congress.

Q.10 A number of CEOs of various organizations of the country is looking forward to increase the investments in their respective manufacturing units. They have also decided on increasing the number of employers and thus increase the scale of production. There have been a number of studies conducted by such organisations over a period of time that has made them take such steps.

Which among these can be an inference that can be drawn from the passage given?

A. There would be an increase in GDP of around 8 - 9%.

B. The organisations are n risk of great loss.

C. The existing workers would find this unsatisfactory.

D. There would be overall growth in GDP in the next few years.

E. The management before this present management came into force was not efficient.

Q.11 The dominant modern belief is that the soundest foundation of peace would be universal prosperity. One may look in vain for historical evidence that the rich have regularly been more peaceful than the poor but then it can be argued that they have never felt secure against the poor, that their aggressiveness stemmed from fear; and that the situation would be quite different if everybody were rich.

It can be inferred from the above passage that:

A. A lot of aggression in the world stems from the desire of the haves to defend themselves against the have - nots.

B. Universal prosperity as a foolproof measure of peace can no longer be accepted.

C. Peace cannot only be achieved through universal prosperity.

D. Both (A) and (B)

E. Both (B) and (C)

Q.12 We celebrate the birth anniversary of Netaji every year but we do not know about his disappearance. This is a tragedy. An investigation should be started to know the truth about his death.

Which of the following can be a inference based on the above passage?

A. Our country has failed to pay enough respect to Netaji.

B. Netaji's death is a mysterious event about which everyone is clueless.

C. We should not celebrate the birthday of Netaji.

D. Investigations are not encouraged in India.

E. His death is not an important matter to the nation.

Ques (13-22):Direction: Statement is given followed by two inferences I and II. You have to consider the statement to be true even if it seems to be at variance from commonly known facts. You have to decide which of the given inferences, if any, follow from the given statement?

Q.13 Statement: According to experts, the Indian Cricket team has a strong squad in the tournament.

Inferences:

I. India will win the tournament.

II. Rest of the teams have a weak squad.

A. Only I follows.
B. Only II follows.
C. Both I and II follow.
D. Neither I nor II follows.
E. Either I or II follows.

Q.14 Statement: Drinking a glass of water once you get up is quite healthy and beneficial.

Inferences:

I. Our body requires water for the regulation of its various internal and external processes.

II. Drinking water early in the morning can create gas trouble.

A. Only inference I true.
B. Only inference II is true.
C. Both inferences are true.
D. Either of I and II is true.
E. Neither I nor II is true.

Q.15 Statement: WHO declared India a polio free nation.

Inferences:

I. No cases of polio have been reported in the past two decades in India.

II. Vaccine programs for polio should be stopped.

A. Only I follows.
B. Only II follows.
C. Both I and II follow.
D. Neither I nor II follows.
E. Either I or II follows.

Q.16 Statement: Dense smog covered sky of Delhi.

Inferences:

I. People should try to stay indoors.

II. People going out of their house should wear masks.

A. Only I follows.
B. Only II follows.
C. Both I and II follow.
D. Neither I nor II follows.
E. Either I or II follows.

Q.17 Statement: Those who have issues with eyesight need to wear glasses and do the needful as prescribed by the ophthalmologist.

Inferences:

I. Eyesight problems can be cured over time by doing absolutely nothing medically prescribed.

II. On consultation with the doctor, the issue can be easily targeted and worked upon.

A. Only inference I true.
B. Only inference II is true.
C. Both inferences are true.
D. Either of I and II is true.
E. Neither I nor II is true.

Q.18 Statement: Andrew has only a few friends because of his forceful and intolerant attitude.

Inferences:

I. Nobody likes Andrew.

II. There are a few people who still like Andrew despite his attitude.

A. Only I follows.
B. Only II follows.
C. Both I and II follow.
D. Neither I nor II follows.
E. Either I or II follows.

Q.19 Statement: Mental illness is similar to physical disease in its effects on body systems.

Inferences:

I. The effect produced by mental illness on the human body is the same as that produced by physical disease

II. Mental illness and physical diseases are similar.

A. Only I follows.
B. Only II follows.
C. Both I and II follow.
D. Neither I nor II follows.
E. Either I or II follows.

Q.20 Statement: Most of the jobs created by automation pay less than the jobs that were eliminated by automation.

Inferences:

I. The introduction of automation reduced the pay.

II. The workers in the job would have been unhappy with the pay for the job.

A. Only I follows.
B. Only II follows.
C. Both I and II follow.
D. Neither I nor II follows.
E. Either I or II follows.

Q.21 Statement: Many consumers who purchase jogging shoes and they also use it for activities other than jogging.

Inferences:

I. People don't like to jog.

II. People like to utilize things for multiple purpose.

A. Only I follows.
B. Only II follows.
C. Both I and II follow.
D. Neither I nor II follows.
E. Either I or II follows.

Q.22 Statement: The mayor of Greenville city rides the bus to the city hall in the city's midtown area.

Inferences:

I. The mayor does not have a ride of his own.

II. The mayor wants to reach his destination fast.

A. Only I follows.
B. Only II follows.
C. Both I and II follow.
D. Neither I nor II follows.
E. Either I or II follows.

Ques (23-24):Direction: Statement is given followed by two inferences I and II. You have to consider the statement to be true even if it seems to be at variance from commonly known facts. You have to decide which of the given inferences, if any, follow from the given statement?

Q.23 Statement: On the recommendation of the education department, CBSE has been suggested along with the NCERT to cut down the academic curriculum of the students studying in the 10th and 12th and lessening their burden for the board exams.

Inferences:

I: The students will be relieved if this happens.

II: This suggestion is only for government schools.

A. Only inference I follows.

B. Only inference II follows.

C. Both inference I and II follow.

D. None of the inferences follow.

E. Either I or II follows.

Q.24 Statement: For over 80 percent of small businesses in India and Brazil, WhatsApp helps them communicate with customers and grow their business.

Inferences:

I: Without WhatsApp, the majority of small businesses of Brazil and India wouldn't have been successful.

II: People of other countries see WhatsApp strictly as a personal messaging app.

A. Only inference I follows.

B. Only inference II follows.

C. Both inference I and II follow.

D. None of the inferences follow.

E. Either I or II follows.

Ques (25-26):Direction: Statement is given followed by two inferences I and II. You have to consider the statement to be true even if it seems to be at variance from commonly known facts. You have to decide which of the given inferences, if any, follow from the given statement?

Q.25 M.S. Dhoni has resigned from the ODI captaincy of Team India. He said that the pressure was too much and he would like to concentrate on his personal life. He jokingly said that he had started getting white hair prematurely too.

Inferences:

I. He is irritated being a captain of Team India.

II. The stress of captaincy had taken a toll on his family.

A. Only inference I is true.

B. Only inference II is true.

C. Either inference I or II is true.

D. Neither inference I nor II is true.

E. Both the inferences I and II are true.

Q.26 Narendra Modi has announced that India will no longer tolerate any nuisance from across the border. He said that it was high time Pakistan came in line.

Inferences:

I. India will soon wage a war on Pakistan.

II. Pakistan has been given a last warning.

A. Only inference I is true.

B. Only inference II is true.

C. Either inference I or II is true.

D. Neither inference I nor II is true.

E. Both the inferences I and II are true.

Ques (27-28):Direction: Statement is given followed by two inferences I and II. You have to consider the statement to be true even if it seems to be at variance from commonly known facts. You have to decide which of the given inferences, if any, follow from the given statement?

Q.27 Statement: India's population is expected to overtake that of China's in the near future, and the international economists are sweating at the mere thought of it. India does not have the means to even support its current population.

Inferences:

I. Higher population means more number of human resources and therefore, a higher rate of growth.

II. Economists do not want India to progress.

A. Only I follows.

B. Only II follows.

C. Both I and II follow.

D. Neither I nor II follows.

E. Either I or II follows.

Q.28 Statement: In Japan, the incidence of stomach cancer is very high, while that of bowel cancer is very low. But Japanese immigrate to Hawaii, this is reversed - the rate of bowel cancer increases but the rate of stomach cancer is reduced in the next generation. All this is related to nutrition - the diets of Japanese in Hawaii are different than those in Japan.

Inferences:

I. The same diet as in Hawaii should be propagated in Japan also.

II. Bowel cancer is less severe than stomach cancer.

A. Only inference I follows.

B. Only inference II follows.

C. Both the inferences follow.

D. None of the inferences follows.

E. Either I or II inference follows.

Ques (29-30):Directions: In question below, a statement is given followed by inferences I and II. You have to consider the statements to be true even if they seem to be at variance from commonly known facts. You are to decide which of the given inferences, if any, follow from the given statement.

Q.29 Statement: Religions provide the means for attaining eternal peace.

Inferences:

I. Religions ensure prosperous life.

II. Religions help people to eradicate poverty.

A. Only inferences I follows.

B. Only inferences II follows.

C. Both inferences I and II follow.

D. Neither inferences I nor II follow.

E. Either I or II

Q.30 Statement: Government has asked people with sufficient income to give up the subsidy.

Inferences:

I. All citizens do not need the subsidy.

II. Poor people are not getting any subsidy.

A.   Only inference I follows
B.   Only inference II follows
C.   Both the inferences follow
D.   None of the inferences follows
E.   Either I or II follows

// Smart Answer Sheet //

Correct   Indicates percentage of students who answered questions correctly.

Skipped   Indicates percentage of students who skipped questions.

Q.	Ans.	Correct / Skipped	Q.	Ans.	Correct / Skipped	Q.	Ans.	Correct / Skipped	Q.	Ans.	Correct / Skipped	Q.	Ans.	Correct / Skipped
1	A	32.39 % / 67.58 %	7	B	15.98 % / 72.77 %	13	D	60.01 % / 35.03 %	19	A	64.39 % / 33.01 %	25	B	28.51 % / 69.27 %
2	D	86.65 % / 10.99 %	8	A	64.89 % / 33.63 %	14	A	44.02 % / 37.72 %	20	A	79.26 % / 16.86 %	26	B	49.03 % / 38.28 %
3	B	55.97 % / 36.44 %	9	A	81.17 % / 18.56 %	15	D	30.63 % / 67.63 %	21	B	86.96 % / 11.69 %	27	D	17.23 % / 75.94 %
4	D	76.21 % / 21.84 %	10	D	19.46 % / 79.9 %	16	C	85.63 % / 10.15 %	22	D	15.4 % / 75.17 %	28	D	54.08 % / 45.69 %
5	B	62.72 % / 34.18 %	11	A	78.37 % / 19.41 %	17	B	29.81 % / 69.15 %	23	A	68.01 % / 31.88 %	29	D	88.23 % / 11.38 %
6	C	64.62 % / 34.48 %	12	B	46.31 % / 44.43 %	18	B	62.0 % / 32.29 %	24	A	59.85 % / 36.04 %	30	A	56.9 % / 36.88 %

Performance Analysis	
Avg. Score (%)	**60.0%**
Toppers Score (%)	**63.33%**
Your Score	

//Hints and Solutions//

1. We need to find an inference. The passage does not talk about recollecting the song, or the price of the song or the quality of the songs.

That Fact + Assumption = Conclusion (as stated by author)

You can tell the difference between a fact and a conclusion because the former would be the cause and the latter would be the effect.

Here, the Fact → Some people do not want to miss the thrill of accidentally listening to a song that they did not expect to listen to.

Conclusion → Some people still listen only to the radio instead of downloading songs.

The assumption that leads the fact to the conclusion is therefore clearly:

Assumption → One cannot discover songs by accident when they are downloading them.

This statement is the assumption.

We also know that,

Fact + Assumption = Inference (Your understanding of statement, not directly stated by author)

The inference would then clearly be option (A).

Here, Fact → Some people still listen only to the radio instead of downloading songs.

Assumption → If you could download songs from the radio, this would also kill the thrill of listening to an unexpected song.

Inference → Songs cannot be downloaded from the radio.

Hence, the correct option is (A).

2. Hybrid plants are resistant to fungus which cause a reduction in the life of plants. Hence it can be inferred that growing hybrids will give you plants that are not likely to have its life shortened by fungus.

Hence, the correct option is (D).

3. Toxoplasma gondii can cause pre-eclampsia during pregnancy. So, it definitely cannot be considered to be benign. It is also explicitly stated in the passage that Toxoplasma gondii is spread through the consumption of unwashed vegetables. So this is a fact, not an inference. It is stated in the passage that toxoplasma gondii often goes incognito in the body, but you cannot infer from this that it loves to play dress-up. It also cannot be inferred that toxoplasma gondii is the chief cause of pre-eclampsia. It is just mentioned in the passage that it causes pre-eclampsia. So this cannot be an inference either. However, it has been mentioned in the passage that the parasite rarely lets the host know that it has set up residence in her body, which implies that it doesn't usually display any symptoms. Thus we can infer that toxoplasma gondiii is usually asymptomatic.

Hence, the correct option is (B).

4. Kamala is rich, so she has a lot of influence. This option is similar to the given statement, thus this option has to be true.

Hence, the correct option is (D).

5. Since the statement mentions that children are exploited at a tender age and made to do odd jobs in the urban areas we can infer that it is a problem. So, option (B) follows.

Hence, the correct option is (B).

6. The passage talks about the New York City subway system and how it has contributed to the growth and betterment of the city. Option (C) is a better inference as it presents a clear picture and deducts correctly how even well planned old systems can aid us in modern times.

Hence, the correct option is (C).

7. The given passage talks about how wetlands were considered unimportant till 1970s and the change in this conception since then. The last sentence clearly states that a certain group of individuals are campaigning for the protection and conservation of the wetlands. Thus it can be inferred that conservationists are working to create awareness regarding the importance of wetlands. Hence option (B) is the correct inference.

Hence, the correct option is (B).

8. The given passage talks about the sources of water on which the Kolkata metropolitan region is dependent and the problems arising as a result of this dependence. Option (A) is the correct inference as it correctly tells about the need for sustainable water management for the Kolkata Metropolitan Area future betterment.

Hence, the correct option is (A).

9. Option (A) validly states the need for an inclusive approach towards the development issues in megacities and supports the observations in the given paragraph.

Hence, the correct option is (A).

10. If the investments of any organisations are supposed to increase, the most obvious outcome would be an increase in GDP as there would be more production. The passage also suggests that there have been a lot of studies before making such decisions; the probability of loss would decrease.

Hence, the correct option is (D).

11. Option (A) is the correct answer as it has been mentioned that the aggressiveness of the rich against the poor is because of the insecurity.

Hence, the correct option is (A).

12. It can be concluded that Netaji's death has remained a mystery for all of us and an investigation can only clear it.

Hence, the correct option is (B).

13. Having the strong squad has nothing to do with definitely winning the tournament I doesn't follow.

The Indian team is strong doesn't mean that all the teams are weak II doesn't follow.

Hence, the correct option is (D).

14. The statement is regarding the good part of drinking water as soon as one gets up, leading to benefits for health. Out of the inferences provided, only the first one is true and goes along with the statement. The second inference about water causing gas trouble hasn't been talked about in the statement so inference II is not true

Thus, only inference I is true.

Hence, the correct option is (A).

15. As we don't know how many years a nation has to maintain its polio free standard to qualify as a polio free nation and two decades is a long time, we can say that inference I does not follow. Similarly, if we don't want polio to reemerge we should keep our child getting vaccinated. This means vaccine programs for polio should not be stopped. So, neither inference I nor II follows.

Hence, the correct option is (D).

16. As air of Delhi is heavily polluted due to smog, it is advisable to say indoors. If people have to go out on their daily duties they should wear masks. Thus, both inferences I and II follow.

Hence, the correct option is (C).

17. Only inference II is true. The statement talks about how eyesight issues can be cured with proper medical assistance. Out of the inferences provided, the second one says that issues can be easily found out, targeted and made better on consultation with the doctor. As it goes about, it connects and reiterates what has been mentioned in the statement unlike the first inference about natural and gradual healing.

Therefore, Only inference II is true.

Hence, the correct option is (B).

18. From the statement it can inferred that Andrew has few friends. So, he is liked by a few people which makes inference I false. Since Andrew has a few friends, it means that they like him despite of his bad attitude making inference II true.

Hence, the correct option is (B).

19. Inference I is just paraphrasing the statement and hence it is true.

Inference II compares mental illness and physical disease in all aspects and information on that is not provided in the statement making inference II invalid.

Therefore, Only I follows.

Hence, the correct option is (A).

20. Since the jobs created by automation paid less, inference I is true.

Nothing is given about workers happiness in the statement so inference II does not follows

So, only I follows.

Hence, the correct option is (A).

21. The statement does not provide information about people being against jogging. The second inference is true because from the statement it is clear that people use a utility for more than one thing.

Therefore, Only II follows.

Hence, the correct option is (B).

22. From the statement, we can neither draw inference I nor inference II since the information needed for those inferences are not provided.

Therefore, Neither I nor II follows.

Hence, the correct option is (D).

23. If the syllabus is reduced, students will have to study lesser and this will reduce their stress. As a result they'll be relieved.

But the given information is not sufficient to infer if the change is to be implemented across only government schools.

So, only inference I follows.

Hence, the correct option is (A).

24. A business flourishes when the communication with customers is good. 80 percent of small businesses communicate through WhatsApp. Without it majority of them would not have been successful. But this doesn't mean that other countries see it strictly as a personal messaging app. It's just that the amount of small businesses in India and Brazil using it is very high. So, we can say that only I follows.

Hence, the correct option is (A).

25. Personal life obviously refers to his family, and since he already stated that he wants to concentrate on his personal life it is certain that handling such a huge responsibility might take a toll on his personal life earlier and now he wants to give them time. Therefore, (B) is true. But there is no mention of being irritated even if he has white hair.

Hence, the correct option is (B).

26. In no way is it said that India will go on a war for such a reason. And therefore I isn't necessarily true. The fact that he says that India will no longer tolerate means that it is the last warning for Pakistan. So, II is true and Option (B)) is the correct answer.

Hence, the correct option is (B).

27. When India can't support its current population, how will it support even more people? Therefore, they won't become human resources and rather, would be a burden - I doesn't follow. Economists are worried because India won't move forward if the population keeps rising - they want India to grow - II doesn't follow.

Hence, the correct option is (D).

28. The statement does not propagate the diet of the two countries as in either of the cases, people will suffer from one of the cancer's. One can also not compare the severity of the 2 types of cancer as nothing regarding it has been mentioned in the statement. Thus neither of the inferences follow.

Hence, the correct option is (D).

29. The statement says that the religions are the way to achieve long lasting peace which is not related to prosperous or wealthy life. Also it has no relation with poverty.

Therefore, both the inferences don't follow the statement.

Hence, the correct option is (D).

30. We do not know whether the poor people get subsidy or not. Thus this inference does not follow. However, from the statement we can infer that the government has asked people with sufficient income to give up the subsidy. The rationale behind it is that these citizens who are privileged with a sufficient income do not need the subsidy. Thus inference I follows.

Hence, the correct option is (A).

Ques (1-30):Direction: In the following question, the Assertion(s) (A) and Reason(s) (R) have been put forward. Read both the statements carefully and choose the correct alternative from the following:

Q.1 ASSERTION (A): Nuclear demilitarization is essential, to save the future of mankind.

REASON (R): Nuclear weapons are weapons of mass destruction.

A. Both A and R are true and R is the correct explanation of A.
B. Both A and R are true but R is not the correct explanation of A.
C. A is true but R is false.
D. A is false but R is true.
E. Both A and R are false

Q.2 ASSERTION (A): India is one of the world's fastest growing economies.

REASON (R): The agricultural sector is the largest sector of employment, in India.

A. Both A and R are true and R is the correct explanation of A.
B. Both A and R are true but R is not the correct explanation of A.
C. A is true but R is false.
D. A is false but R is true.
E. Both A and R are false

Q.3 Assertion (A): Rabid animals are euthanized by animal control

Reason (R): Rabies is highly contagious, and affects the central nervous system of humans and other mammals.

A. Both (A) and (R) are true and (R) is the correct explanation of (A).
B. Both (A) and (R) are true but (R) is not the correct explanation of (A).
C. (A) is true but (R) is false.
D. (A) is false but (R) is true.
E. Both (A) and (R) are false.

Q.4 Assertion (A): Homeopathy is scientifically accurate.

Reason (R): Homeopathy has been proven to work, for certain cases.

A. Both (A) and (R) are true and (R) is the correct explanation of (A).
B. Both (A) and (R) are true but (R) is not the correct explanation of (A).
C. (A) is true but (R) is false.
D. (A) is false but (R) is true.
E. Both (A) and (R) are false.

Q.5 ASSERTION (A): Cape Town has become the first city in the world to run out of water.

REASON (R): Water scarcity is exacerbated by population growth and poor water resource management.

A. Both A and R are true and R is the correct explanation of A.
B. Both A and R are true but R is not the correct explanation of A.
C. A is true but R is false.
D. A is false but R is true.
E. Both A and R are false.

Q.6 ASSERTION (A): Alexander Graham Bell invented the telephone.

REASON (R): Alexander Graham Bell's wife was deaf.

A. Both A and R are true and R is the correct explanation of A.
B. Both A and R are true but R is not the correct explanation of A.
C. A is true but R is false.
D. A is false but R is true.
E. Both A and R are false.

Q.7 ASSERTION (A): Brazil is one of the world's leading coffee producers.

REASON (R): Coffee plantations cover 27,000 square km, in Brazil.

A. Both A and R are true and R is the correct explanation of A.
B. Both A and R are true but R is not the correct explanation of A.
C. A is true but R is false.
D. A is false but R is true.
E. Both A and R are false.

Q.8 ASSERTION (A): Charcoal grilled, or burnt food is carcinogenic.

REASON (R): Charcoal is poisonous to touch.

A. Both A and R are true and R is the correct explanation of A.
B. Both A and R are true but R is not the correct explanation of A.
C. A is true but R is false.
D. A is false but R is true.
E. Both A and R are false.

Q.9 ASSERTION (A): HIV/AIDS is extremely tough to treat.

REASON (R): HIV/AIDS can be congenital.

A. Both A and R are true and R is the correct explanation of A.
B. Both A and R are true but R is not the correct explanation of A.
C. A is true but R is false.
D. A is false but R is true.
E. Both A and R are false.

Q.10 ASSERTION (A): Police presence on the streets in major cities like New York, has not reduced the crime rate.

REASON (R): The crime in cities like New York, are majorly white collar crimes, and not blue collar crimes.

A. Both A and R are true and R is the correct explanation of A.
B. Both A and R are true but R is not the correct explanation of A.
C. A is true but R is false.

D. A is false but R is true.
E. Both A and R are false.

Q.11 ASSERTION (A): Placebo trials are often used to treat diseases like cancer.

REASON (R): There isn't enough production of cancer medication, to give all cancer patients, and thus placebo's are used.

A. Both A and R are true and R is the correct explanation of A.
B. Both A and R are true but R is not the correct explanation of A.
C. A is true but R is false.
D. A is false but R is true.
E. Both A and R are false.

Q.12 ASSERTION (A): English is the most widely spoken language in the world.

REASON (R): The population of English speakers, far exceeds that of other languages.

A. Both A and R are true and R is the correct explanation of A.
B. Both A and R are true but R is not the correct explanation of A.
C. A is true but R is false.
D. A is false but R is true.
E. Both A and R are false.

Q.13 ASSERTION (A): During the summer season, cotton clothes must be worn.

REASON (R): Cotton clothes absorb sweat and cool down the body.

A. Both A and R are true and R is the correct explanation of A.
B. Both A and R are true but R is not the correct explanation of A.
C. A is true but R is false.
D. A is false but R is true.
E. Both A and R are false.

Q.14 ASSERTION (A): Historically, Andhra Pradesh is called the 'Rice Bowl of India'.

REASON (R): Fields are cultivated in the shape of bowls, in Andhra Pradesh.

A. Both A and R are true and R is the correct explanation of A.
B. Both A and R are true but R is not the correct explanation of A.
C. A is true but R is false.
D. A is false but R is true.
E. Both A and R are false.

Q.15 ASSERTION (A): All bases are alkalis.

REASON (R): Alkalis are water-soluble.

A. Both A and R are true and R is the correct explanation of A.
B. Both A and R are true but R is not the correct explanation of A.
C. A is true but R is false.
D. A is false but R is true.
E. Both A and R are false.

Q.16 ASSERTION (A): The best way to care for nails is to file them and clean them regularly.

REASON (R): Infections can be caused by biting nails.

A. Both A and R are true and R is the correct explanation of A.
B. Both A and R are true but R is not the correct explanation of A.
C. A is true but R is false.
D. A is false but R is true.
E. Both A and R are false.

Q.17 ASSERTION (A): Skipping dinner is healthy.

REASON (R): Skipping dinner helps lose weight and is hence essential to maintaining a good frame.

A. Both A and R are true and R is the correct explanation of A.
B. Both A and R are true but R is not the correct explanation of A.
C. A is true but R is false.
D. A is false but R is true.
E. Both A and R are false.

Q.18 ASSERTION (A): Doors expand during the rainy season.

REASON (R): The moisture is absorbed by the wood, during the rainy season.

A. Both A and R are true and R is the correct explanation of A.
B. Both A and R are true but R is not the correct explanation of A.
C. A is true but R is false.
D. A is false but R is true.
E. Both A and R are false.

Q.19 ASSERTION (A): The male to female sex ratio is less than 1 in India.

REASON (R): Women face a lot of different issues, such as abuse, female infanticide, etc, which affects the sex ratio.

A. Both A and R are true and R is the correct explanation of A.
B. Both A and R are true but R is not the correct explanation of A.
C. A is true but R is false.
D. A is false but R is true.
E. Both A and R are false.

Q.20 ASSERTION (A): Bats are nocturnal animals.

REASON (R): Bats would be vulnerable to raptors like sparrowhawks if they were not nocturnal.

A. Both A and R are true and R is the correct explanation of A.
B. Both A and R are true but R is not the correct explanation of A.
C. A is true but R is false.
D. A is false but R is true.
E. Both A and R are false.

Q.21 ASSERTION (A): Cuckoos steal other birds' nests.

REASON (R): All birds poach nests.

A. Both A and R are true and R is the correct explanation of A.
B. Both A and R are true but R is not the correct explanation of A.
C. A is true but R is false.
D. A is false but R is true.
E. Both A and R are false.

Q.22 ASSERTION (A): When air is blown from mouth into a test tube containing limewater, the limewater turns milky.

REASON (R): The presence of carbon dioxide turns limewater milky.

A. Both A and R are true and R is the correct explanation of A.
B. Both A and R are true but R is not the correct explanation of A.
C. A is true but R is false.
D. A is false but R is true.
E. Both A and R are false.

Q.23 ASSERTION (A): Humans dominate the planet.

REASON (R): Humans are physically superior to animals.

A. Both A and R are true and R is the correct explanation of A.
B. Both A and R are true but R is not the correct explanation of A.
C. A is true but R is false.
D. A is false but R is true.
E. Both A and R are false.

Q.24 ASSERTION (A): People under the age of 18 cannot legally enter into contracts.

REASON (R): It is believed that critical life decisions cannot be made by those under the age of 18.

A. Both A and R are true and R is the correct explanation of A.
B. Both A and R are true but R is not the correct explanation of A.
C. A is true but R is false.
D. A is false but R is true.
E. Both A and R are false.

Q.25 ASSERTION (A): Mitochondria are called the powerhouse of the cell.

REASON (R): Mitochondria release energy on breaking down food.

A. Both A and R are true and R is the correct explanation of A.
B. Both A and R are true but R is not the correct explanation of A.
C. A is true but R is false.
D. A is false but R is true.
E. Both A and R are false.

Q.26 ASSERTION (A): Plastic has been banned in Mumbai.

REASON (R): Plastic is very expensive.

A. Both A and R are true and R is the correct explanation of A.
B. Both A and R are true but R is not the correct explanation of A.
C. A is true but R is false.
D. A is false but R is true.
E. Both A and R are false.

Q.27 ASSERTION (A): Saltwater (saline) is often used to clean open wounds.

REASON (R): Saltwater acts as an antibacterial.

A. Both A and R are true and R is the correct explanation of A.
B. Both A and R are true but R is not the correct explanation of A.
C. A is true but R is false.
D. A is false but R is true.
E. Both A and R are false.

Q.28 ASSERTION (A): Mumbai is prone to flooding, every monsoon.

REASON (R): Many areas have very old drainage sewers.

A. Both A and R are true and R is the correct explanation of A.
B. Both A and R are true but R is not the correct explanation of A.
C. A is true but R is false.
D. A is false but R is true.
E. Both A and R are false.

Q.29 ASSERTION (A): Kerala is called 'God's own country'.

REASON (R): Kerala has a lot of coconut trees.

A. Both A and R are true and R is the correct explanation of A.
B. Both A and R are true but R is not the correct explanation of A.
C. A is true but R is false.
D. A is false but R is true.
E. Both A and R are false.

Q.30 ASSERTION (A): Hindi is the national language of India.

REASON (R): Hindi is the most widely spoken language in the country.

A. Both A and R are true and R is the correct explanation of A.
B. Both A and R are true but R is not the correct explanation of A.
C. A is true but R is false.
D. A is true but R is false.
E. A and R both are false.

// Smart Answer Sheet //

Correct Indicates percentage of students who answered questions correctly.

Skipped Indicates percentage of students who skipped questions.

Q.	Ans.	Correct / Skipped
1	A	54.34 % / 38.56 %
2	B	60.26 % / 34.29 %
3	A	57.39 % / 41.85 %
4	D	48.98 % / 50.63 %
5	A	67.14 % / 31.15 %
6	B	46.99 % / 36.46 %

Q.	Ans.	Correct / Skipped
7	A	46.63 % / 50.87 %
8	C	62.18 % / 31.12 %
9	B	63.22 % / 36.42 %
10	A	64.38 % / 30.22 %
11	C	40.08 % / 44.62 %
12	E	62.86 % / 32.42 %

Q.	Ans.	Correct / Skipped
13	A	51.13 % / 32.01 %
14	C	59.73 % / 37.21 %
15	D	49.15 % / 33.61 %
16	B	49.62 % / 49.84 %
17	E	56.14 % / 39.12 %
18	A	58.88 % / 40.18 %

Q.	Ans.	Correct / Skipped
19	D	62.82 % / 31.83 %
20	A	65.85 % / 33.23 %
21	C	59.02 % / 40.05 %
22	A	68.87 % / 30.56 %
23	C	61.31 % / 31.49 %
24	A	52.36 % / 38.46 %

Q.	Ans.	Correct / Skipped
25	A	54.88 % / 36.86 %
26	C	66.15 % / 33.48 %
27	A	40.55 % / 59.41 %
28	A	54.89 % / 37.71 %
29	B	42.54 % / 43.33 %
30	D	61.31 % / 33.05 %

Performance Analysis

Avg. Score (%)	43.33%
Toppers Score (%)	66.67%
Your Score	

//Hints and Solutions//

1. Both A and R are true and R is the correct explanation of A.

Nuclear weapons are indeed weapons of mass destruction, and their usage can have a very bad impact on mankind, as they are extremely destructive. So, nuclear demilitarization is essential, to save the future of mankind.

Hence, the correct option is (A).

2. Both A and R are true but R is not the correct explanation of A.

The assertion, which states that India is one of the world's fastest-growing economies, is true, In 2018, it overtook China, as the world's fastest-growing economy. The reason is also true, however, it is not an explanation for the assertion, and is merely an independent fact.

Hence, the correct option is (B).

3. Both (A) and (R) are true and (R) is the correct explanation of (A).

Rabies is a virus that affects humans and other mammals very severely, and it is true that these animals are euthanized, for the very same reason.

Hence, the correct option is (A).

4. (A) is false but (R) is true.

Homeopathy is a pseudoscience and is not scientifically accurate, and hence, the assertion is false. However, it has been seen to work on certain cases, and so, the reason is true.

Hence, the correct option is (D).

5. The assertion is a fact which is true, and the crisis has worsened, due to improper management, and a lack of population control. Therefore, Both A and R are true and R is the correct explanation of A.

Hence, the correct option is (A).

6. The assertion Alexander Graham Bell invented the telephone is a true fact, and so is the reason Alexander Graham Bell's wife was deaf, however they are both independent statements, and the reason is not an appropriate explanation for the assertion.

Hence, the correct option is (B).

7. Brazil is known to be the leading producer of coffee in the world, and a major reason for this, is the vast areas of coffee plantations in the country, Hence, both the assertion and the reason are right, with the reason providing enough justification, to prove that the assertion is right.

Hence, the correct option is (A).

8. The assertion is true, as many studies have stated that cooking food over a flame, leads to cancer. The reason for this is that combusting wood, gas, or charcoal emits chemicals known as polycyclic aromatic hydrocarbons. Exposure to these so-called PAHs is known to cause skin, liver, stomach, and several other types of cancer in lab animals.

However, the reason mentioned is false, as charcoal is not poisonous to touch.

Hence, the correct option is (C).

9. The assertion, that HIV/AIDS is very tough to treat, is true, as it is a retroviral disease, and once the retrovirus takes control of the cell, the only hope is to destroy the cell.

The reason mentioned in the question is true, as there are certain cases where HIV is transmitted through the mother to the child, however, it is not the explanation for the assertion that has been made.

Hence, the correct option is (B).

10. Both A and R are true and R is the correct explanation of A.

The assertion is true, as crime rates have not seen a dip, in major cities like New York. The reason is also true, as most of the crime, is a financial crime, such as insider trading, and fraud (White collar crimes), which cannot be controlled by the police presence on the streets. Blue-collar crimes are crimes such as battery, assault, etc, which can be controlled by added police presence.

Hence, the correct option is (A).

11. A is true but R is false.

Placebo's are often used, with the aim to further science, and figure out alternative solutions to diseases such as cancer. However, it is not because of a lack of medication available.

Hence, the correct option is (C).

12. Both A and R are false.

Chinese (Mandarin) is the most widely spoken language in the world, and the population of these Mandarin speakers is 935 million, which outnumbers the English speaking population, which is 365 million.

Hence, the correct option is (E).

13. Both A and R are true and R is the correct explanation of A.

The assertion that cotton clothes must be worn in the summer, is true, and it is so because cotton absorbs sweat, and this process of absorption of sweat does cool down the body.

Hence, the correct option is (A).

14. A is true but R is false.

Andhra Pradesh is the rice bowl of India, however, this is because the ground is extremely fertile, and thus rice is easily grown on it and has nothing to do with the shape of the field.

Hence, the correct option is (C).

15. A is false but R is true.

The assertion is false, as all bases are not alkalis, but all alkalis are bases. The reason is true, as alkalis are indeed water-soluble.

Hence, the correct option is (D).

16. Nails can accumulate dirt, and hence, must be filed and trimmed regularly. Also, infections can definitely be caused by

biting nails, as it could cause the underlying skin to peel, or the nail to break. Hence, both A and R are true.

However, the reason is not an explanation for the assertion.

Hence, the correct option is (B).

17. Both A and R are false.

Skipping meals is not healthy, as the meal skippers have been seen to have elevated fasting glucose levels and delayed insulin response. Conditions that, if they persisted long term, could lead to diabetes.

Hence, the correct option is (E).

18. Both A and R are true and R is the correct explanation of A.

Doors do expand in the rainy season, and this movement in wood occurs because of its unique structure, it constantly expands and contracts as its moisture content changes.

Hence, the correct option is (A).

19. There are more men than women in India, (943 women, to 1000 men, according to a 2011 consensus), and hence, the ratio of men to women is more than one. Hence, the assertion is false. Women do face the issues mentioned in R, and hence R is true.

Hence, the correct option is (D).

20. Both A and R are true and R is the correct explanation of A.

Bats are nocturnal, and if they weren't, they would have to compete with non-nocturnal creatures and could be vulnerable to sparrowhawks, etc.

Hence, the correct option is (A).

21. A is true but R is false.

Cuckoos are known as brood parasites, meaning they hide their eggs in the nests of other species. To avoid detection, the cuckoos have evolved so that their eggs replicate those of their preferred targets. If the host bird doesn't notice the strange egg in its nest, the newly hatched cuckoo will actually take all the nest for itself, taking the other eggs on its back and dropping them out of the nest. However, not all birds do this, and it is unique to the cuckoo.

Hence, the correct option is (C).

22. Both A and R are true and R is the correct explanation of A.

Humans inhale oxygen and exhale carbon dioxide. When we exhale into the test tube the lime water turns milky due to the presence of Carbon dioxide. The products formed in this reaction is Calcium carbonate and water.

Hence, the correct option is (A).

23. A is true but R is false.

Humans do dominate the planet, but it is because humans are mentally superior, and can make decisions that are rational, unlike animals. It is because of their superior judgment, that they dominate the planet.

Hence, the correct option is (C).

24. Both A and R are true and R is the correct explanation of A.

Minors are individuals who are under the age of 18. Minors are not considered to have legal capacity, meaning they do not have the ability to make contracts with other people. The problem, is that the courts will not enforce most contracts involving a minor.

Hence, the correct option is (A).

25. Both A and R are true and R is the correct explanation of A.

Mitochondria are organelles found inside the cell, which helps in the breakdown of food and release of energy. Hence, they are called the 'powerhouse of the cell'.

Hence, the correct option is (A).

26. A is true but R is false.

Plastic has been banned in Mumbai, since 2018. However, it has been banned due to the environmental damage caused by plastic, and not due to its cost.

Hence, the correct option is (C).

27. Both A and R are true and R is the correct explanation of A.

Saltwater helps to clean and promote healing by a process called osmosis. The chemical comprising salt – sodium chloride – forces the liquid in cells to move out of the body when it comes in contact with them. If those liquids are bacterial, they'll be forced out too, effectively helping cleanse the skin.

Hence, the correct option is (A).

28. Both A and R are true and R is the correct explanation of A.

Mumbai is prone to flooding and does get flooded almost every monsoon, and this is due to the old drainage systems put in place, which are unable to cope with repeated floods.

Hence, the correct option is (A).

29. Both A and R are true but R is not the correct explanation of A.

According to Hindu mythology, Kerala was created by Lord Parasurama, to create a land for his devotees, and hence, it is called 'God's own country'. Kerala does have a lot of coconut trees, due to the favorable temperature conditions. But this is not an appropriate explanation for the argument.

Hence, the correct option is (B).

30. A is false but R is true.

As per the Constitution of India, there are 22 official languages followed in India, but no National language. However, R is true, as 43.63% of total population of India speaks Hindi.

Hence, the correct option is (D).

Q.1 Each consonant of the word 'TERMINATION' is changed to the previous letter in the English alphabetical series and each vowel is changed to the next letter in the English alphabetical series. If the new alphabets thus formed are arranged in alphabetical order (from left to right), which of the following will be the sixth letter from the right end?

A. M

B. S

C. P

D. L

E. None of these

Q.2 If in the word 'SEPTUAGENARIAN' first three and then next three letters are written in reverse order and the rest of the letters are written as they appear in English alphabet, the positions of how many letters get changed in the new arrangement?

A. Nil

B. 2

C. 10

D. 12

E. None of these

Q.3 If all the letters of the word 'INTROSPECTION' are arranged in a way that all the vowels are arranged in the beginning in alphabetical order and then all the consonants are arranged in the alphabetical order, then the position of how many letters remains unchanged?

A. Zero

B. One

C. Two

D. More than two

E. None of these

Q.4 In the word 'DOORSTEP' if all the vowels are replaced with the letter immediate next to it in the english alphabet series and all the consonants are replaced with the letter immediate before it in the english alphabet series, then how many vowels are there in the new word so formed?

A. Zero

B. One

C. Two

D. More than two

E. None of these

Q.5 If all the vowels of the word 'FRAGMENT' are changed to the letter immediately succeeding them in the english alphabet series and all the consonants are changed to the letter immediately preceding them in the english alphabet series, then how many letters of the new word are similar to the letters of the old word?

A. Two

B. Three

C. Four

D. More than four

E. None of these

Q.6 If in the word 'FAVOURITE' all the consonants are arranged on the left in reversed alphabetical order after that on the right of these consonants all the vowels are arranged in alphabetical order then how many letters are there in alphabetical series between third letter from right end and fourth letter from left end?

A. 2

B. 5

C. 6

D. 8

E. 9

Q.7 If in the word 'CAPITALIZATION' all the letters are arranged in alphabetic order then how many vowels are replaced by a new vowel?

A. Zero

B. One

C. Two

D. Three

E. More than three

Q.8 If the letter of the words 'FUTURISTIC' are arranged in alphabetic order from left to right then what would be the third letter of the meaningful English word formed using third, fifth, sixth and eighth letter of the word formed after arranging? (If no word is formed mark 'L' as your answer and if more than one word are formed mark 'M' as your answer)

A. R

B. I

C. S

D. L

E. M

Q.9 How many such pairs of letters are there in the word 'ELOQUENT' which has as many letters between them as in the alphabetical series?

A. Zero

B. One

C. Two

D. Three

E. More than three

Q.10 If all the letters of the word 'UNIDENTIFIED' are arranged in the alphabetical order then the position of how many letters will be remain unchanged?

A. Zero

B. One

C. Two

D. Three

E. More than three

Q.11 How many meaningful English words can be formed using the first, third, fourth, and eighth letters of the word 'MAGNIFICENT' after rearranging all the letters in alphabetical order?

A. Zero

B. One

C. Two

D. Three

E. More than three

Q.12 In the word 'MAGNIFICENT', If all the vowels are replaced with their immediate next letter as per the English alphabet series then how many pairs are there in the newly formed word (either forward or backward) which has as many letters between them as they have in the English alphabet series?

A. One

B. Two

C. Three

D. Zero

E. None of these

Q.13 If in the word 'EQUANIMITY' all the letters are arranged in alphabetical order from right to left end then the position of how many alphabets will remain unchanged?

A. One

B. Two

C. Three

D. Four

E. Five

Q.14 If in the word 'EQUANIMITY' all the vowels are changed to their next letter while all the consonants are changed to their

previous letter then the letters of the word thus formed are to be arranged in alphabetic order from left to right end then how many letters are there in alphabetic series between the letters that are fourth from the left end and third from the right end in the newly formed word?

A. Ten   **B.** Thirteen   **C.** Five   **D.** Fifteen
E. Eight

Q.15 What will be the third letter of the meaningful English word formed using 1st, 5th, 6th and 9th letters (each letter to be used once) of 'MASCULINE'? If more than such words can be formed then mark 'X' as your answer and if no such word can be formed then mark 'Y' as your answer.

A. E   **B.** U   **C.** L   **D.** X
E. Y

Q.16 If the letters of the word 'RADIOCHEMIST' are to be arranged in reversed alphabetical order from right to left end then position of how many letters will remain unchanged?

A. More than three   **B.** Two
C. One   **D.** Zero
E. Three

Q.17 How many meaningful English words can be formed with the letters A, D, E and R using all the letters, and each letter only once in each word?

A. Zero   **B.** One   **C.** Two   **D.** Three
E. Four

Q.18 What is the second letter of the meaningful English word that can be formed from the first, third, fourth, and seventh letter of the word 'ONEROUS'? If no such word can be formed then mark your answer as 'N', if more than one word can be formed then mark your answer as 'M'.

A. O   **B.** R   **C.** S   **D.** M
E. N

Q.19 If all the letters of the word 'HARASSMENT' are arranged in alphabetical order then how many letters will retain their original position?

A. Zero   **B.** One
C. Two   **D.** Three
E. More than three

Q.20 If in the word 'RETIREMENT' all the letters are arranged in alphabetical order from left to right end then position of how many letters will remain unchanged?

A. Zero   **B.** One
C. Two   **D.** Three
E. More than three

Q.21 How many such pairs of letters are there in the word 'DISCOVERY' which has as many letters between them as in the alphabetical series?

A. Six   **B.** Five   **C.** Four   **D.** Seven
E. Three

Q.22 Each consonant of the word 'INSURANCE' is changed to the previous letter in the English alphabetical series and each vowel is changed to the next letter in the English alphabetical series. If the new alphabet thus formed are arranged in

alphabetical order (from left to right), which of the following will be the third from the right?

A. M   **B.** B
C. Q   **D.** V
E. None of these

Q.23 How many meaningful English words can be formed using the second, third, fifth and seventh letters of the word 'KITCHEN' using each letter once in each word?

A. One   **B.** Three
C. Two   **D.** Four
E. None of these

Q.24 If the letters in the word 'CREATION' are rearranged as they appear in the English alphabet then the position of how many letters will remain unchanged after the rearrangement?

A. Two   **B.** One   **C.** Three   **D.** Zero
E. Four

Q.25 If it is possible to make only one meaningful word with the first, the third, the fifth and the ninth letters of the word 'FRAGRANCE', which of the following will be second letter of the word? If no such word can be made, give 'Y' as the answer and if more than one such words can be made give 'Z' as the answer.

A. A   **B.** Y   **C.** Z   **D.** E
E. R

Q.26 If the letters in the word 'MOTHERLAND' rearranged as they appear in the English alphabet then the position of how many letter will remain unchanged after the rearrangement?

A. One   **B.** Two
C. Zero   **D.** Three
E. None of these

Q.27 If it is possible to make only one meaningful word with the first, the third, the fifth and the eight letters of the word 'MAXIMIZATION', which of the following will be the second letter of the word? If no such word can be made, give 'Y' as the answer and if more than one such word can be made, give 'Z' as the answer.

A. M   **B.** X   **C.** A   **D.** Y
E. Z

Q.28 Each vowel of the word 'ADJECTIVE' is substituted with the next letter of the English alphabetical series, and each consonant is substituted with the letter preceding it. How many vowels are present in the new arrangement?

A. Zero   **B.** One
C. Two   **D.** Three
E. None of these

Q.29 If a meaningful English word has to be formed using 1st, 4th, 6th, 8th and 9th letters of the word (each letter to be used only once) 'PLASMODIUM' then which of the following will be the 4th letter from the right end? If more than one such word can be formed then mark 'X' as your answer and if no meaningful word can be formed then mark 'Z' as your answer?

A. S   **B.** I   **C.** U   **D.** Z
E. X

Q.30 How many such pairs of letters are there in the word
'HIMALAYAN', each of which has as many letters between them
in the word (both forward and backward direction) as they have
between them in the English Alphabet?

A. One　　　　**B.** Two　　　　**C.** Three　　　　**D.** Four
E. None

// Smart Answer Sheet //

Correct   Indicates percentage of students who answered questions correctly.

Skipped   Indicates percentage of students who skipped questions.

Q.	Ans.	Correct / Skipped
1	A	89.87 % / 10.04 %
2	D	63.01 % / 31.11 %
3	B	88.5 % / 10.28 %
4	B	78.15 % / 10.39 %
5	C	80.52 % / 12.83 %
6	A	10.52 % / 74.47 %

Q.	Ans.	Correct / Skipped
7	C	88.44 % / 10.49 %
8	B	25.88 % / 67.05 %
9	C	64.69 % / 31.38 %
10	B	83.17 % / 13.04 %
11	B	51.42 % / 39.3 %
12	C	52.88 % / 35.03 %

Q.	Ans.	Correct / Skipped
13	B	77.94 % / 13.94 %
14	E	26.99 % / 67.0 %
15	C	57.92 % / 38.84 %
16	E	85.73 % / 12.96 %
17	D	45.94 % / 46.93 %
18	D	54.21 % / 41.54 %

Q.	Ans.	Correct / Skipped
19	C	78.64 % / 16.68 %
20	D	82.12 % / 10.95 %
21	C	25.51 % / 69.31 %
22	C	84.09 % / 15.63 %
23	C	80.66 % / 11.45 %
24	B	82.92 % / 12.3 %

Q.	Ans.	Correct / Skipped
25	C	56.62 % / 38.05 %
26	A	88.32 % / 11.36 %
27	D	57.41 % / 42.34 %
28	C	80.87 % / 13.85 %
29	B	57.73 % / 32.7 %
30	D	78.59 % / 15.22 %

Performance Analysis	
Avg. Score (%)	60.0%
Toppers Score (%)	60.0%
Your Score	

//Hints and Solutions//

1. The given word:

T E R M I N A T I O N

Applying the above condition, we have new word:

S F Q L J M B S J P M

Now, arranging in alphabetical order (from left to right)

B F J J L M M P Q S S

So, M is sixth from the right.

Hence, the correct option is (A).

2. The given word:

SEPTUAGENARIAN

Applying the above condition, we have a new word:

PESAUTAAEGINNR

Now final arrangements of the old and new words are:

S	E	P	T	U	A	G	E	N	A	R	I	A	N
P	E	S	A	U	T	A	A	E	G	I	N	N	R

So clearly, except E and U the positions of all other 12 letters get changed in the new arrangement.

Hence, the correct option is (D).

3. The given word:

INTROSPECTION

Applying the above condition, we have a new word:

EIIOOCNNPRSTT

The final arrangements of the old and new words are:

I	N	T	R	O	S	P	E	C	T	I	O	N
E	I	I	O	O	C	N	N	P	R	S	T	T

Thus the position of only one letter i.e, "O" remains unchanged.

Hence, the correct option is (B).

4. The given word:

DOORSTEP

Applying the above condition, we have new word:

CPPQRSFO

Then the final arrangement of old and new words are:

D	O	O	R	S	T	E	P
C	P	P	Q	R	S	F	O

Thus 'O' is the only vowel in the new arrangement.

Hence, the correct option is (B).

5. The given word:

FRAGMENT

Applying the above condition, we have a new word:

EQBFLFMS

Now, the new arrangement of old and new words are:

F	R	A	G	M	E	N	T
E	Q	B	F	L	F	M	S

Apparently, four letters viz. E, F, F and M of the new word are similar to the letters of the old word.

Hence, the correct option is (C).

6. The given word:

FAVOURITE

After arranging all the consonants on the left in reversed alphabetical order, we get:

VTRF

Now, arranging all the vowels on the right of these consonants, we get:

VTRFAEIOU

Here, the third letter from the right end is I and the fourth letter from the left end is F.

And, we know that there are two letters between F and I in alphabetical series.

Hence, the correct option is (A).

7. The given word:

CAPITALIZATION

After arranging the letters in alphabetic order the word becomes:

AAACIIILNOPTTZ

The final arrangement of new and old words are:

C	A	P	I	T	A	L	I	Z	A	T	I	O	N
A	A	A	C	I	I	I	L	N	O	P	T	T	Z

Here, there are two such vowels which are replaced by a new vowel.

Hence, the correct option is (C).

8. The given word:

FUTURISTIC

After arranging the letters of the word in alphabetic order from left to right, we get:

CFIIRSTTUU

Now, the third, fifth, sixth and eighth letters of the word 'CFIIRSTTUU' are I, R, S and T.

The meaningful English word that can be formed using I, R, S and T is STIR.

Here, the third letter of the word 'STIR' is 'I'.

Hence, the correct option is (B).

9. The given word:

ELOQUENT

Possible pair of letters in the above word which has as many letters between them as in the English alphabetical series:

Pair 1:

Letters in the word	O	Q	U	E	N	T
Letters in the alphabetical series	O	P	Q	R	S	T

Pair 2:

Letters in the word	Q	U	E	N
Letters in the alphabetical series	Q	P	O	N

Here, we can observe that there are two such possible pairs of letters that satisfy the above conditions.

Hence, the correct option is (C).

10. The given word:

UNIDENTIFIED

After arranging the letters in alphabetical order:

DDEEFIIINNTU

The final arrangement of old and new words are:

U	N	I	D	E	N	T	I	F	I	E	D
D	D	E	E	F	I	I	I	N	N	T	U

On comparing both the words we will find that the position of only 1 letter viz. I is unchanged.

Hence, the correct option is (B).

11. The given word:

MAGNIFICIENT

Arranging in alphabetical order:

ACEFGIIMNNT

The first, third, fourth and eighth letters are A, E, F and M.

The meaningful English word that can be formed by using A, E, F and M is FAME.

Thus only one word can be made.

Hence, the correct option is (B).

12. The given word:

MAGNIFICENT

Applying the above condition the new word is:

MBGNJFJCFNT

The two-letter pairs between which there are similar words in alphabetical order are- 'B and F', 'G and N' and 'F and J'.

Hence, the correct option is (C).

13. The given word:

EQUANIMITY

After arranging all the letters in alphabetical order from right to left end, we get:

YUTQNMIIEA

At this point, we have:

Given word	E	Q	U	A	N	I	M	I	T	Y
After Arranging	Y	U	T	Q	N	M	I	I	E	A

Here, we can see that position of two letters is same in both words.

Hence, the correct option is (B).

14. The given word:

EQUANIMITY

After changing all the vowels of the above word to their next letter and all the consonants to their previous letter, we get:

FPVBMJLJSX

After, arranging the letters of the above word in alphabetic order from left to right end, we get:

BFJJLMPSVX

Now, the fourth letter from the left end is J and the third letter from the right end is S.

The letters between 'J' and 'S' in the alphabetic series are:

J, K, L, M, N, O, P, Q, R, S

Finally, there are 8 letters between J and S.

Hence, the correct option is (E).

15. The given word:

MASCULINE

1st, 5th, 6th and 9th letters of MASCULINE are: M, U, L and E.

The meaningful English word formed out of it is "MULE".

Thus the third letter is 'L'.

Hence, the correct option is (C).

16. The given word:

RADIOCHEMIST

After arranging the letters in alphabetical order from right to left end, we get:

Original Word:	R	A	D	I	O	C	H	E	M	I	S	T
After Arrangement:	A	C	D	E	H	I	I	M	O	R	S	T

Here, we have three such letters whose positions are the same in both the words.

Hence, the correct option is (E).

17. The given letters are:

A, D, E and R.

At this point, three meaningful words can be formed using these letters.

DARE, DEAR and READ.

Hence, the correct option is (D).

18. The given word:

ONEROUS

First, third, fourth and seventh letters of ONEROUS are O, E, R and S.

Meaningful English words are:

ROSE and SORE

As two meaningful English words can be formed, thus M would be the answer.

Hence, the correct option is (D).

19. Given word :

HARASSMENT

After arrangements in alphabetical order:

AAEHMNRSST

Thus, there are two letters 'A' and 'T' which retain their original position.

Hence, the correct option is (C).

20. The given word :

RETIREMENT

After arranging all the letters in alphabetical order from left to right end, we get:

EEEIMNRRTT

At this point, we have:

Given word	R	E	T	I	R	E	M	E	N	T
After arranging	E	E	E	I	M	N	R	R	T	T

Here, we can see that position of three letters is same in both words.

Hence, the correct option is (D).

21. The given word:

DISCOVERY

Possible pair of letters in the above word which has as many letters between them as in the English alphabetical series:

Pair 1:

Letters in the word	S	C	O	V
Letters in the alphabetical series	S	T	U	V

Pair 2:

Letters in the word	O	V	E	R
Letters in the alphabetical series	O	P	Q	R

Pair 3:

Letters in the word	V	E	R	Y
Letters in the alphabetical series	V	W	X	Y

Pair 4:

Letters in the word	S	C	O	V	E	R	Y
Letters in the alphabetical series	S	T	U	V	W	X	Y

Here, we can observe that there are four such possible pairs of letters satisfy the above conditions.

Hence, the correct option is (C).

22. The given word:

I N S U R A N C E

Applying the above condition, we have new word:

J M R V Q B M B F

Now, arranging in alphabetical order (from left to right)

B B F J M M Q R V

So, Q is third from the right.

Hence, the correct option is (C).

23. The given word:

KITCHEN

Second, third, fifth and seventh letters of the word are I, T, H and N respectively.

The words formed from the letters:

HINT and THIN

So, two words can be formed from the given letters above.

Hence, the correct option is (C).

24. The given word:

CREATION

After arranging the letters of the given word as they appear in the English alphabet, we have:

ACEINORT

Only 'E' remains at the same position after rearrangement.

Hence, the correct option is (B).

25. The given word:

FRAGRANCE

The first, the third, the fifth and the ninth letters of the above given the word are:

F, A, R, E

While rearranging these letters only once, two meaningful words can be formed:

FARE and FEAR.

Hence, the correct option is (C).

26. The given word:

MOTHERLAND

After, arranging the letters of the given word as they appear in the English alphabet, we have:

ADEHLMNORT

Observing the above arrangement, we can clearly see that its H whose position remain unchanged.

Hence, the correct option is (A).

27. The given word:

MAXIMIZATION

The first, the third, the fifth and the eight letters of the given word above, we have:

M, X, M and A

Here, from the above letter, we cannot make any word that is meaningful.

Hence, the correct option is (D).

28. The given word:

ADJECTIVE

After applying the above condition we have:

BCIFBSJUF

Thus there are two vowels present in the new arrangement.

Hence, the correct option is (C).

29. The given word:

PLASMODIUM

1st, 4th, 6th, 8th and 9th letters are P, S, O, I and U respectively.

The only word which can be formed with these letters is PIOUS.

The 4th letter from the right end is I.

Hence, the correct option is (B).

30.

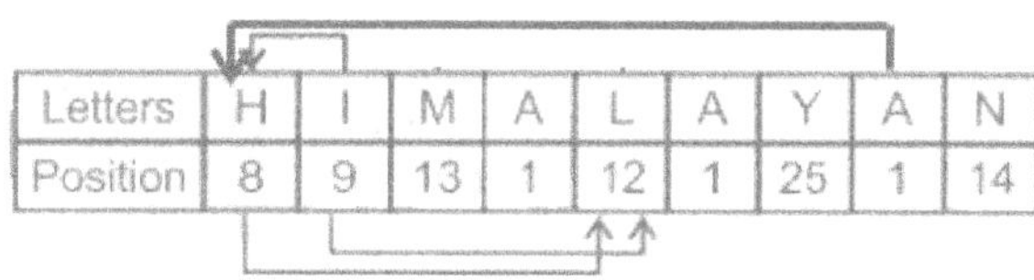

So, four pairs are there in the word 'HIMALAYAN', each of which has as many letters between them in the word (both forward and backward direction) as they have between them in the English Alphabet.

Hence, the correct option is (D).

Reasoning Test 22

Ques (1-30):Direction: In the given question below is given a statement followed by two conclusions numbered I and II. You have to assume everything in the statement to be true, then consider the two conclusions together and decide which of them logically follows the given statement and choose your answer according to that.

Q.1

Statement: In a test cricket match, the total runs made by a team were 400. Out of these 320 runs were made by spinners.

Conclusions:

I. 80% of the team consists of spinners.

II. The opening batsmen were spinners.

A. Only conclusion I follows
B. Only conclusion II follows
C. Either I or II follows
D. Neither I nor II follows
E. Both I and II follow

Q.2 Statement: The old order changed yielding place to new.

Conclusions:

I. Change is the law of nature.

II. Discard old ideas because they are old.

A. Only conclusion I follow
B. Only conclusion II follow
C. Either I or II follows
D. Neither I nor II follows
E. Both I and II follow

Q.3

Statement: The government has spoiled many top-ranking financial institutions by appointing bureaucrats as Directors of these institutions.

Conclusions:

I. Government should appoint Directors of the financial institutes taking into consideration the expertise of the person in the area of finance.

II. The Director of the financial institution should have expertise commensurate with the financial work carried out by the institute.

A. Only conclusion I follow
B. Only conclusion II follow
C. Either I or II follow
D. Neither I nor II follow
E. Both I and II follow

Q.4 Statement: The Government-run company had asked its employees to declare their income and assets but it has been strongly resisted by the employees union and no employee is going to declare his income.

Conclusions:

I. The employees of this company do not seem to have any additional undisclosed income besides their salary.

II. The employees union wants all senior officers to declare their income first.

A. Only conclusion I follows
B. Only conclusion II follows
C. Either I or II follows
D. Neither I nor II follows
E. Both I and II follow

Q.5 Statement: The distance of 900 km by road between Bombay and Jafra will be reduced to 280 km by sea. This will lead to a saving of Rs. 7.92 crores per annum on fuel.

Conclusions:

I. Transportation by sea is cheaper than that by road.

II. Fuel must be saved to the greatest extent

A. Only conclusion I follows
B. Only conclusion II follows
C. Either I or II follows
D. Neither I nor II follows
E. Both I and II follow

Q.6 Statement: The manager humiliated Sachin in the presence of his colleagues.

Conclusions:

I. The manager did not like Sachin.

II. Sachin was not popular with his colleagues.

A. Only conclusion I follows
B. Only conclusion II follows
C. Either I or II follows
D. Neither I nor II follows
E. Both I and II follow

Q.7 Statement: Women's organizations in India have welcomed the amendment of the Industrial Employment Rules 1946 to curb sexual harassment at the workplace.

Conclusions:

I. Sexual harassment of women in the workplace is more prevalent in India as compared to other developed countries.

II. Many organizations in India will stop recruiting women to avoid such problems.

A. Only conclusion I follows
B. Only conclusion II follows
C. Either I or II follows
D. Neither I nor II follows
E. Both I and II follow

Q.8 Statement: Use "Kraft" colours. They add colour to our life. - An advertisement.

Conclusions:

I. Catchy slogans do not attract people.

II. People like dark colours.

A. Only conclusion I follows
B. Only conclusion II follows

C. Either I or II follows

D. Neither I nor II follows

E. Both I and II follow

Q.9 Statement: All those political prisoners were released on bail who had gone to jail for reasons other than political dharnas. Bail was not granted to persons involved in murders.

Conclusions:

I. No political - prisoner had committed murder.

II. Some politicians were not arrested.

A. Only conclusion I follows

B. Only conclusion II follows

C. Either I or II follows

D. Neither I nor II follows

E. Both I and II follow

Q.10 Statement: People who speak too much against dowry are those who had taken it themselves.

Conclusions:

I. It is easier said than done.

II. People have double standards.

A. Only conclusion I follows

B. Only conclusion II follows

C. Either I or II follows

D. Neither I nor II follows

E. Both I and II follow

Q.11 Statement: Money plays a vital role in politics.

Conclusions:

I. The poor can never become politicians.

II. All the rich men take part in politics.

A. Only conclusion I follows

B. Only conclusion II follows

C. Either I or II follows

D. Neither I nor II follows

E. Both I and II follow

Q.12 Statement: Vegetable prices are soaring in the market.

Conclusions:

I. Vegetables are becoming a rare commodity.

II. People cannot eat vegetables.

A. Only conclusion I follows

B. Only conclusion II follows

C. Either I or II follows

D. Neither I nor II follows

E. Both I and II follow

Q.13 Statement: The eligibility for admission to the course is minimum second class Master's degree. However, the candidates who have appeared for the final year examination of Master's degree can also apply.

Conclusions:

I. All candidates who have yet to get their Master's degree will be there in the list of selected candidates.

II. All candidates having obtained second class Master's degree will be there in the list of selected candidates.

A. Only conclusion I follows

B. Only conclusion II follows

C. Either I or II follows

D. Neither I nor II follows

E. Both I and II follow

Q.14 Statement: Only good singers are invited in the conference. No one without sweet voice is a good singer.

Conclusions:

I. All invited singers in the conference have sweet voice.

II. Those singers who do not have sweet voice are not invited in the conference.

A. Only conclusion I follows

B. Only conclusion II follows

C. Either I or II follows

D. Neither I nor II follows

E. Both I and II follow

Q.15 Statement: Applications of applicants who do no fulfil eligibility criteria and/or who do not submit applications before last date will be summarily rejected and will not be called for the written test.

Conclusions:

I. Those who are called for the written test are those who fulfil eligibility criteria and have submitted their applications before last date.

II. Written test will be held only after scrutiny of applications.

A. Only conclusion I follows

B. Only conclusion II follows

C. Either I or II follows

D. Neither I nor II follows

E. Both I and II follow

Q.16 Statement: The standard of education in private schools is much better than Municipal and Zila Parishad-run schools.

Conclusions:

I. The Municipal and Zila Parishad should make serious efforts to improve standard of their schools.

II. All Municipal and Zila Parishad schools should be closed immediately.

A. Only conclusion I follows

B. Only conclusion II follows

C. Either I or II follows

D. Neither I nor II follows

E. Both I and II follow

Q.17

Statement: All the organised persons find time for rest. Sunita, in spite of her very busy schedule, finds time for rest.

Conclusions:

I. Sunita is an organised person.

II. Sunita is an industrious person.

A. Only conclusion I follows

B. Only conclusion II follows

C. Either I or II follows

D. Neither I nor II follows

E. Both I and II follow

Q.18 Statement: Until our country achieves economic equality, political freedom and democracy would be meaningless.

Conclusions:

I. Political freedom and democracy go hand in hand.

II. Economic equality leads to real political freedom and democracy.

A. Only conclusion I follows

B. Only conclusion II follows

C. Either I or II follows

D. Neither I nor II follows

E. Both I and II follow

Q.19 Statement: The best evidence of India's glorious past is the growing popularity of Ayurvedic medicines in the West.

Conclusions:

I. Ayurvedic medicines are not popular in India.

II. Allopathic medicines are more popular in India.

A. Only conclusion I follows

B. Only conclusion II follows

C. Either I or II follows

D. Neither I nor II follows

E. Both I and II follow

Q.20

Statement: Wind is an inexhaustible source of energy and an aerogenerator can convert it into electricity. Though not much has been done in this field, the survey shows that there is vast potential for developing wind as an alternative source of energy.

Conclusions:

I. Energy by wind is comparatively newly emerging field.

II. The energy crisis can be dealt by exploring more in the field of aero-generation.

A. Only conclusion I follows

B. Only conclusion II follows

C. Either I or II follows

D. Neither I nor II follows

E. Both I and II follow

Q.21 Statement: After this amendment to the Constitution, no child below the age of 14 years will be employed to work in any factory or mine or engaged in any other hazardous employment.

Conclusions:

I. Before this amendment, children below 14 years were employed to work in factory or mine.

II. The employers must now abide by this amendment to the Constitution.

A. Only conclusion I follows

B. Only conclusion II follows

C. Either I or II follows

D. Neither I nor II follows

E. Both I and II follow

Q.22 Statement: It has been decided by the Government to withdraw 33% of the subsidy on cooking gas from the beginning of next month. - A spokesman of the Government.

Conclusions:

I. People now no more desire or need such subsidy from Government as they can afford increased price of the cooking gas.

II. The price of the cooking gas will increase at least by 33% from the next month.

A. Only conclusion I follows

B. Only conclusion II follows

C. Either I or II follows

D. Neither I nor II follows

E. Both I and II follow

Q.23 Statement: A large majority of the work force in India is unorganised. Most of them earn either the minimum or uncertain wages while others are engaged in sundry jobs.

Conclusions:

I. The workers in the organised sector get better facilities and stay longer in their jobs.

II. Some workers in the unorganised sector of the work force have a regular and fixed income.

A. Only conclusion I follows

B. Only conclusion II follows

C. Either I or II follows

D. Neither I nor II follows

E. Both I and II follow

Q.24 Statement: Irregularity is a cause for failure in exams. Some regular students fail in the examinations.

Conclusions:

I. All failed students are regular.

II. All successful students are not regular.

A. Only conclusion I follows

B. Only conclusion II follows

C. Either I or II follows

D. Neither I nor II follows

E. Both I and II follow

Q.25 Statement: Today out of the world population of several thousand million, the majority of persons have to live under governments that refuse them personal liberty and the right to dissent.

Conclusions:

I. People are indifferent to personal liberty and the right to dissent.

II. People desire personal liberty and the right to dissent.

A. Only conclusion I follows

B. Only conclusion II follows

C. Either I or II follows

D. Neither I nor II follows

E. Both I and II follow

Q.26 Statement: We should inform all our officers not to read newspapers during office hours - Chief Manager tells.

Conclusions:

I. Reading newspapers during office hours is desirable.

II. Office efficiency will not increase by stopping this.

A. Only conclusion I follows

B. Only conclusion II follows
C. Either I or II follows
D. Neither I nor II follows
E. Both I and II follow

C. Either I or II follows
D. Neither I nor II follows
E. Both I and II follow

Q.27 Statement: This book 'Z' is the only book which focuses its attention to the problem of poverty in India between 1950 and 1980.

Conclusions:

I. There was no question of poverty before 1950.

II. No other book deals with poverty in India during 1950 to 1980.

A. Only conclusion I follows
B. Only conclusion II follows
C. Either I or II follows
D. Neither I nor II follows
E. Both I and II follow

Q.28

Statement: For over three decades Company X has been totally involved in energy conservation, its efficient use and management.

Conclusions:

I. The Company has yet to learn and acquire basic things in this area.

II. It is dedication that is more important than knowledge and expertise.

A. Only conclusion I follows
B. Only conclusion II follows
C. Either I or II follows
D. Neither I nor II follows
E. Both I and II follow

Q.29 Statement: About 50 per cent of the animal by-products - hair, skin, horns etc. is edible protein. American chemists have developed a method of isolating 45 per cent of this protein. They used an enzyme developed in Japan to break down soya protein.

Conclusions:

I. Americans have not been able to develop enzymes.

II. Animal by-products protein has the same composition as soya protein.

A. Only conclusion I follows
B. Only conclusion II follows
C. Either I or II follows
D. Neither I nor II follows
E. Both I and II follow

Q.30 Statement: National Aluminium Company has moved India from a position of shortage to self-sufficiency in the metal.

Conclusions:

I. Previously, India had to import aluminum.

II. With this speed, it can soon become a foreign exchange earner.

A. Only conclusion I follows
B. Only conclusion II follows

// Smart Answer Sheet //

Correct — Indicates percentage of students who answered questions correctly.

Skipped — Indicates percentage of students who skipped questions.

Q.	Ans.	Correct / Skipped
1	D	82.65 % / 15.68 %
2	A	56.09 % / 32.22 %
3	E	25.51 % / 71.24 %
4	D	57.03 % / 42.83 %
5	B	66.96 % / 31.04 %
6	D	76.22 % / 15.17 %

Q.	Ans.	Correct / Skipped
7	D	23.14 % / 75.67 %
8	D	52.7 % / 33.99 %
9	A	20.18 % / 75.79 %
10	E	77.31 % / 18.02 %
11	D	64.31 % / 31.64 %
12	D	53.64 % / 31.17 %

Q.	Ans.	Correct / Skipped
13	D	28.37 % / 67.42 %
14	E	78.41 % / 20.7 %
15	E	56.33 % / 42.26 %
16	A	79.73 % / 10.77 %
17	E	49.71 % / 45.64 %
18	B	64.96 % / 33.26 %

Q.	Ans.	Correct / Skipped
19	D	57.46 % / 41.32 %
20	E	20.23 % / 78.42 %
21	E	31.87 % / 67.64 %
22	D	57.71 % / 31.25 %
23	D	10.53 % / 86.42 %
24	D	79.6 % / 17.72 %

Q.	Ans.	Correct / Skipped
25	B	19.9 % / 75.08 %
26	D	25.4 % / 73.79 %
27	B	78.88 % / 12.24 %
28	D	16.98 % / 75.28 %
29	D	43.57 % / 36.22 %
30	E	49.38 % / 44.84 %

Performance Analysis

Avg. Score (%)	30.0%
Toppers Score (%)	56.67%
Your Score	

//Hints and Solutions//

1. According to the statement, 80% of the total runs were made by spinners. So, I do not follow. Nothing about the opening batsmen is mentioned in the statement. So, II also does not follow.
Hence, the correct option is (D).

2. Clearly, conclusion I directly follow from the given statement. Also, it is mentioned that old ideas are replaced by new ones, as thinking changes with the progressing time. So, II does not follow.
Hence, the correct option is (A).

3. According to the statement, the Government has spoiled financial institutions by appointing bureaucrats as Directors. This means that only those persons should be appointed as Directors who are experts in finance and are acquainted with the financial work of the institute. So, both I and II follow.
Hence, the correct option is (E).

4. Nothing about the details of the employees' income or the cause of their refusal to declare their income and assets, can be deduced from the given statement. So, neither I nor II follows.
Hence, the correct option is (D).

5. According to the statement, sea transport is cheaper than road transport in the case of route from Bombay to Jafra, not in all the cases. So, conclusion I does not follow. The statement stresses on the saving of fuel. So, conclusion II follows.
Hence, the correct option is (B).

6. The manager might have humiliated Sachin not because of his dislike but on account of certain negligence or mistake on his part. So, I does not follow. Also, nothing about Sachin's rapport with his colleagues can be deduced from the statement. So, II also does not follow.
Hence, the correct option is (D).

7. The fact that a certain rule has been more welcomed in a certain country does not imply that the problem is more prevalent there. So, I does not follow. Also, the amendment seeks to discourage only sexual harassment of women and shall in no way discourage employment of women. So, II also does not follow.
Hence, the correct option is (D).

8. The slogan given in the statement is definitely a catchy one which indicates that catchy slogans do attract people. So, the conclusion I do not follow. No conclusion about people's preference for colors can be deduced from the statement. Thus, conclusion II also does not follow.

9. According to the statement, the political prisoners can be divided into two groups - those who were released and those who were put in jail for political dharnas. However, no person involved in murder was released. This means that no political prisoner had committed murder. So, I follows. Clearly, II is not directly related to the statement and does not follow.
Hence, the correct option is (A).

10. The statement clearly implies that it is easier to say than to do something and what people say is different from what they do.

So, both I and II follow.
Hence, the correct option is (E).

11. Neither the poor nor the rich, but only the role of money in politics is being talked about in the statement. So, neither I nor II follows.
Hence, the correct option is (D).

12. The availability of vegetables is not mentioned in the given statement. So, I does not follow Also, II is not directly related to the statement and so it also does not follow.
Hence, the correct option is (D).

13. The statement mentions that the candidates who have obtained second class Master's degree or have appeared for the final year examination of Master's degree, can apply for admission. This implies that both types of candidates may be selected on certain grounds. Thus, some candidates of each type and not all candidates of any one type, may be selected. So, neither I nor II follows.
Hence, the correct option is (D).

14. The statement asserts that a good singer always has a sweet voice and only good singers are invited in the conference. This implies that all those invited in the conference have sweet voice and those who do not have sweet voice are not invited. So, both I and II follow.
Hence, the correct option is (E).

15. The statement clearly mentions that fulfilling the eligibility criteria and submitting the application before the stipulated date are both essential to avoid rejection. So, I follow. Also, since it is given that the candidates whose applications are rejected shall not be called for a written test, so II also follows.
Hence, the correct option is (E).

16. Clearly, the solution to the problem is not to close down the Municipal and Zila Parishad-run schools but to strive to improve the standard of education of these schools. So, only I follows while II does not.
Hence, the correct option is (A).

17. Sunita has a very busy schedule. This means that she is industrious. But still she finds time for rest. This means that she is an organised person. So, both I and II follow.
Hence, the correct option is (E).

18. Nothing about the relation between political freedom and democracy is mentioned in the statement. So, I does not follow. But II directly follows from the given statement.
Hence, the correct option is (B).

19. The popularity of Ayurvedic or allopathic medicines in India is not being talked about in the statement. So, neither I nor II follows.
Hence, the correct option is (D).

20. The phrase 'not much has been done in this field' indicates that wind energy is a comparatively newly emerging field. So, I follow. The expression 'there is vast potential for developing wind as an alternative source of energy' proves II to be true.
Hence, the correct option is (E).

21. The statement mentions that after the amendment, no child below 14 years will be engaged in hazardous employment. This

means that before the amendment, the practice of employing children below 14 years was in vogue. This in turn means that employers will have to abide by the amendment. So, both I and II follow.
Hence, the correct option is (E).

22. The decision to withdraw subsidy has clearly been taken to compensate for the loss and not because people can now afford to pay more for cooking gas. So, I does not follow. Also, the statement talks of withdrawing 33% of the prevailing subsidy and not of reducing 33% of the actual price. So, II also does not follow.
Hence, the correct option is (D).

23. The statement is not talking about workers in the organized sector. So I does not follow. It has been mentioned that some workers in the unorganized sector are engaged in miscellaneous work. This means that their income is not assured. So II also does not follow.
Hence, the correct option is (D).

24. The given statement clearly implies that all irregular and some regular students fail in the examinations. This, in turn, means that all successful students are regular but not all regular students are successful. So, neither I nor II follows.
Hence, the correct option is (D).

25. It is mentioned in the statement that most people are forced to live under Governments that refuse them personal liberty and the right to dissent. This means that they are not indifferent to these rights but have a desire for them. So, only II follows.
Hence, the correct option is (B).

26. Since the given statement talks of an order not to let the officers read newspapers during office hours, it implies that reading newspapers during office hours is undesirable. So, I does not follow. Also, the order has been issued with an intention to prevent harm to office work due to officers' other indulgences. Thus, II also does not follow.
Hence, the correct option is (D).

27. In the statement, the phrase 'book only' implies conclusion II. However, nothing can be concluded from this statement regarding the state of poverty before 1950. So I also does not follow.
Hence, the correct option is (B).

28. Since the company has been working in this area for three decades, it must have the necessary expertise and infrastructure required in this field. So, I do not follow. However, the qualities that have made Company X successful in this field have not been mentioned. So, II also does not follow.
Hence, the correct option is (D).

29. That the American chemists used an enzyme developed in Japan, does not mean that Americans have not been able to develop enzymes. So, I does not follow. Also, nothing about the compositions of animal by products protein and soya protein is mentioned in the statement. So, II also does not follow.
Hence, the correct option is (D).

30. According to the statement, the National Aluminum Company has brought India from a situation of scarcity in the past to self-reliance in the present. This means that earlier India

had to import aluminum. So I follow. At the same time, it can also be concluded that if production increases at this rate, then India can export it in the future. So II also follows.
Hence, the correct option is (E).

Q.1 You have been using a certain computer system to perform your role for years and it has proved to be stable and reliable. Recently, you were informed that it is to be updated next month with new functionality and applications. You are concerned about the time it would take to have a trouble-free system as the current system took six months to become trouble-free. You now need to decide your response to this news.

What would be the least effective answer?

A. Find out all you can about the system and volunteer to be the first to trail run it.

B. Voice your concern to your superior and recommend that all possible upgrades be delayed until all possible issues have been identified and resolved.

C. Ask All other colleagues to run the new systems for errors so that the quality of your work is not compromised, but seek their reviews.

D. Believe that the appropriate checks have been carried out and wait for the introduction of the upgrade so that you can assess its functionality.

E. None of these

Q.2 As a relatively small part of your role, you are responsible for the maintenance of a database of statistical information regarding meteorological data and its link to road traffic levels at the Indian met department. This is drawn upon every three months for analysis, although for the past few years the results have been consistent and predictable and some people have questioned the need for such detailed data. In order to compile the information, you rely on daily input of information from a number of people in different localities. One day, one of these individuals comes to you to request that data be submitted on a weekly rather than daily basis, to save time. Your boss is on holiday and you are left to take the decision. Which of the given options must not be considered by the employee?

A. Inform them that you cannot authorize it until your boss is back from leave.

B. Make the change as it seems more sensible, and inform your boss when he returns.

C. Inform him that there is no chance of any change in the reporting pattern.

D. Ask the other person involved in it and what is their take and tell this to your boss once he comes back.

E. None of these

Q.3 You are new to your department and your boss has handed you a brief for a presentation that covers what you should tell your department about the new IT system that is being introduced. Your boss would have done it himself, but he has annual leave for the next few days. It contains a lot of facts and you are aware that your boss prefers a more factual dry presentation style. However, you are concerned that the audience would find the content dull and you want to make a good first impression on them. What would be the least effective answer?

A. Respect the approach that your superior would have taken and present just the facts, but try to do so quickly so that the audience doesn't get too bored.

B. Introduce a range of interactive, entertaining elements to the briefing that increase audience engagement with the content prepared by your boss, but might not reflect the style of your boss.

C. Send a brief around in email form prior to the meeting and then engage in a two way discussion with the audience about the system.

D. Suggest to your boss that he may like to present the content when he returns, as this will ensure that it is delivered in the way he intended.

E. None of these

Q.4 You have been asked by your boss to meet with a representative from another unit to present the findings from your team's latest piece of research. After giving you the briefing, your boss advises you to 'tone down' your 'usual style' as she thinks this will work better. You are not quite sure what she meant by this and feel a little offended: your style has always worked well in the past. How would you respond? What would be the most effective answer?

A. Make your boss understand that your tone is good for the presentation.

B. Ask your boss for more detail on what they meant by the comment.

C. Ask your colleagues what they meant by the comment.

D. Self-reflect upon what your boss meant then change your behaviour accordingly.

E. None of these

Q.5 The public sector where you are working for is to be included for a major restructure. Some posts will vanish, some roles will change and there will be some new opportunities created. The announcement has created some concern within the PSU, especially as it has been performing well up to this point. Your CMD has arranged for a one on one meeting with everyone to discuss the restructure. You need to decide how best to prepare for the meeting. Which of the given statements must definitely be followed with reference to the information?

A. Properly express your strengths in the meeting so that your position within the firm is protected.

B. Plan to ask questions about what new opportunities are available and how you can position yourself to take advantage of it.

C. Aim to get as much information from your CMD about the restructure: timescale and impact.

D. Prepare a convincing case concerning why the company should not be included in the restructuring.

E. None of these

Q.6 You work in an office where the work being carried out in different departments is visible. You have noticed that an engineering trainee in another department spends most of the time 'lost' with little work to do. You have already brought this issue to the notice of your head of the department but nothing seems to have happened to solve the situation. In addition, the boss is often out of office so does not see it himself. What would be the least effective answer?

A. Go over to the person in question and set them tasks to complete for your department.

B. Speak to someone else in the department and ask them if there is any work the person could complete for them.

C. Speak to the person in question and tell him to find some work to do as they are currently giving a bad impression.

D. Schedule a meeting for tomorrow with the person's head of the department where you can suggest some work for him.

E. None of these

Q.7 You have sent a survey to multiple units in order to gauge levels of job satisfaction as part of a wide internal survey across the organization. When the results arrive back, you see that by far the biggest cause of dissatisfaction seems to be the pay levels. However, your manager has suggested that in reality staff are content with their pay: this survey is just seen as an opportunity to ask for more. There is no time or budget to repeat the survey and you need to decide how to proceed. What would be the most effective answer?

A. Conduct some online research into other surveys of this nature to see whether this is a common pattern: include this observation in the report and recommendations.

B. Accept your manager's views and highlight this in your summary report and recommendations.

C. Accept the original data and avoid including your manager's interpretation when collating the summary report and recommendations.

D. Declare the results of the survey around pay levels to be 'ambiguous' and instead concentrate on the second most important area of the survey.

E. None of these

Q.8 A new director was recently appointed to manage your directorate after being managed by the previous person for a couple of years. In her introductory speech, the new director states that there will be a number of changes to be made now she has arrived: some will happen quickly and others will be introduced over the next few months. She does not give more detail than this but reassures everyone that people will be informed as soon as possible about the changes. Which of the following is the best step that any employee working under her must take?

A. Request a meeting straight away with the new director and say that you need to know more about the planned changes.

B. Wait a few weeks and then request a meeting with the new director and find out more about the planned changes.

C. Be alert to the news about the changes, but continue to work as usual until more is announced.

D. Try to find out more about the changes that the new director made in other parts of the organization in order to gain an insight into what she might be planning for your area.

E. None of these

Q.9 You are working on a complex project when one of the members of your department gives you some negative feedback about your way of working that comes as a complete

surprise to you. You have never received feedback on this area before and you had previously considered it a moderate strength of yours. It has been playing on your mind for the past week as you are keen to be seen in a positive way by others. Choose the most effective answer.

A. Try to improve your image in the eyes of the person who gave you the feedback by describing to them why you acted in the way you did and how it has brought you success in the past.

B. Ask the person who provided the original feedback for more detail about why they think the way they do.

C. Ask a section of other people for feedback on the area concerned to see if this corroborates the original negative feedback.

D. Self reflect some more, and read up on how to develop in the area identified.

E. None of these

Q.10 You are in the middle of speaking to an audience about some work that had a successful outcome and that you are very proud of about ten minutes into your speech, you notice that a couple of the audience members are yawning and looking at their watches. Choose the most effective answer.

A. Pause at an appropriate point and ask for audience feedback on what you have covered so far.

B. Look directly at them and ask 'am I keeping you awake?' in order to embarrass them and make them pay more attention.

C. Speed up your pace of talking and vary your tone in order to re-engage your interest.

D. Make greater use of visual aids and props in order to stimulate their interest.

E. None of these

Q.11 You have been given two weeks in which to review a large body of data, spot certain types of errors and inconsistencies and then produce a corrected and improved version as a result. Your superior has asked to meet with you after four days to review your progress. Three days into your review you realize that there are also several other types of errors and inconsistencies in the data and you will not have the time to review it all in two weeks, let alone in time for your meeting with yours superior tomorrow. You feel a more realistic timescale would be four weeks. However, you know that a lot of people are awaiting the outcome of your review and corrections and if it is delayed this will hold up the work of other units. Pick the least effective answer.

A. Use the two weeks to focus on correcting those types of errors that the original assignment called for and complete the assignment on time.

B. Use the meeting with your superior to argue for an extension of the deadline so that you can correct the further errors you discovered as well.

C. Start correcting all discovered errors and complete as much as you can in two weeks.

D. Start correcting all discovered errors but arrange to feed the results of your review through in stages to other units so that they can begin work.

E. None of these

Q.12 You have differences of opinion regarding the final report prepared by your subordinate that is to be submitted urgently.

The subordinate is justifying the information given in the report. You would:

A. Convince the subordinate that he is wrong

B. Tell him to reconsider the results

C. Revise the report on your own

D. Tell him not to justify the mistake

E. None of these

Q.13 You are competing with your batch-mate for the prestigious award to be decided based on an oral presentation. You have been asked by the committee to finish on time. Your friend however, is allowed more than the stipulated time period. At this point what will be your response?

A. Lodge a complaint to chairperson against the discrimination

B. Not listen to any justification from the committee

C. Ask for withdrawal of your name

D. Protest and leave the place

E. None of these

Q.14 You are handling a time bound project. During the project review meeting, you find that project is likely to get delayed due to lack of cooperation of the team members. You would:

A. Warn the team members for their non-cooperation

B. Look into the reasons for non-cooperation

C. Ask for the replacement of the team members

D. Ask for the extension of time citing reasons

E. None of these

Q.15 You are a chairperson of a state sports committee. You have received a complaint and later it was found that an athlete in the junior age category who has won a medal has crossed the age criteria by 5 days. You would:

A. Ask the screening committee for a clarification

B. Ask the athlete to return the medal

C. Ask the athlete to get an affidavit from the court declaring his/her age

D. Ask the members of the committee for their views

E. None of these

Q.16 You are handling a priority project and have been meeting all the deadlines and planning your leave during the project. Your immediate boss does not grant leave citing the urgency of the project. You would:

A. Proceed on leave without waiting for the sanction

B. Pretend to be sick and take leave

C. Approach higher authority to reconsider the leave application

D. Tell the boss that it is not justified

E. None of these

Q.17 You are involved in setting up a water supply project in remote area. Full recovery of cost is impossible in any case. The income levels in the area are low and 25% of the population is below poverty line (BPL). When a decision has to be taken on pricing you would:

A. Recommended that the supply of water be free of charge in all respects

B. Recommended that the users pay a one time fixed sum for installation of taps and the usage of water be free

C. Recommended that a fixed monthly charges be levied on the non-BPL families and for BPL families water should be free

D. Recommended that the users pay a charge based on the consumption of water with differentiated charges for Non-BPL and BPL families

E. None of these

Q.18 As a citizen you have some work with a government department. The official calls you again and again; and without directly asking you, sends out feelers for a bribe. You want to get your work done. You would:

A. Give a bribe

B. Behave as if you have not understood the feelers and persist with your application

C. Go to the higher officer for help verbally complaining about feelers

D. Send in a formal complaint

E. None of these

Q.19 You have been asked to give an explanation for not attending an important official meeting. Your immediate boss who has not informed you about the meeting is now putting pressure on you not to place an allegation against him/her. You would:

A. Send a written reply explaining the fact

B. Seek an appointment with the top boss to explain the situation

C. Admit your fault to save the situation

D. Put the responsibility on the coordinator of the meeting for not informing

E. None of these

Q.20 A local thug (bad element) has started illegal construction on your vacant plot. He has refused your request to vacate and threatened you of dire consequences in case you do not sell the property at a cheap price to him. You would:

A. Sell the property at a cheap price to him.

B. Go to the police for necessary action.

C. Ask for help from your neighbours.

D. Negotiate with the goon to get a higher price.

E. None of these

Q.21 You have to accomplish a very important task for your Headquarters within the next two days. Suddenly you meet with an accident. Your office insists that you complete the task. You would:

A. Ask for an extension of deadline.

B. Inform headquarters of your inability to finish on time.

C. Suggest alternate person to headquarters who may do the needful.

D. Stay away till you recover.

E. None of these

Q.22 You are an officer-in-charge for providing basic medical facilities to the survivors of an earthquake-affected area. Despite your best possible effort, people put allegations against you for making money out of the funds given for relief. You would:

A. Let an enquiry be set up to look into the matter.

B. Ask your senior to appoint some other person in your place.

C. Not pay attention to allegations.

D. Stop undertaking any initiative till the matter is resolved.

E. None of these

Q.23 You have been made responsible to hire boats at a short notice to be used for an area under flood. On seeing the price mentioned by the boat owners you found that the lowest price was approximately three times more than the approved rate of the Government. You would:

A. Reject the proposal and call for a fresh price.

B. Accept the lowest price.

C. Refer the matter to the Government and wait.

D. Threaten the boat owners about a possible cancellation of the licence.

E. None of these

Q.24 You are the officer-in-charge of a village administering distribution of vaccines in an isolated epidemic-hit village, and you are left with only one vaccine. There is a requirement of that vaccine from the Gram Pradhan and also a poor villager. You are being pressurized by Gram Pradhan to issue the vaccine to him. You would:

A. Initiate the procedure to expedite the next supply without issuing the vaccine to either.

B. Arrange vaccine for the poor villager from the distributor of another area.

C. Ask both to approach a doctor and get an input about the urgency.

D. Arrange vaccine for the Gram Pradhan from the distributor of another area.

E. None of these

Q.25 You have taken up a project to create night-shelters for homeless people during the winter season. Within a week of establishing the shelters, you have received complaints from the residents of the area about the increase in theft cases with a demand to remove the shelters. You would:

A. Ask them to lodge a written complaint at the police station.

B. Assure residents of an inquiry into the matter.

C. Ask residents to consider the humanitarian effort made.

D. Continue with the project and ignore their complaint.

E. None of these

Q.26 You are the head of your office. There are certain houses reserved for the allotment to the office staff and you have been given the discretion to do so. A set of rules for the allotment of the houses has been laid down by you and has been made public. Your personal secretary, who is very close to you, comes to you and pleads that as his father is seriously ill, he should be given priority in the allotment of a house. The office secretariat that examined the request as per the rules turns down the request and recommends the procedure to be followed according to the rules. You do not want to annoy your personal secretary in such circumstances, what would you do?

A. Call him over to your room and personally explain why the allotment cannot be done.

B. Allot the house to him to win his loyalty.

C. Agree with the office note to show that you are not biased and that you do not indulge in favoritism.

D. Keep the file with you and not pass any orders.

E. None of these

Q.27 While traveling in a Delhi-registered commercial taxi from Delhi to an adjacent city (another State), your taxi driver informs you that as he has no permit for running the taxi in that city, he will step at it Transport Office and pay the prescribed fee of Rs. forty for a day. While paying the fee at the counter you find that the transport clerk taking an extra fifty rupees for which no receipt is being given. You are in a hurry for your meeting. In such circumstances, what would you do?

A. Go up to the counter and ask the clerk to back the money which he has illegally taken.

B. Do not interfere at all as this it a matter between the taxi driver and the tax authorities.

C. Take note of the incident and subsequently report the matter to the concerned authorities.

D. Treat it as a normal affair and imply forget about it.

E. None of these

Q.28 You are a teacher in a University and are setting a question paper on a particular subject. One of your colleagues, whose son is preparing for the examination on that subject, comes to you and informs you that it is his son's last chance to pass that examination and whether you could help him by indicating what questions are going to be in the examination. In the past, your colleague had helped you in another matter. Your colleague informs you that his son will suffer from depression if he fails in this examination. In such circumstances, what would you do?

A. In view of the help, he had given you, extend your help to him.

B. Regret that you cannot be of any help to him.

C. Explain to your colleague that this would be violating the trust of the University authorities and you are not in a position to help him.

D. Report the conduct of your colleague to the higher authorities.

E. None of these

Ques (29-30):Directions: Analyse the information given below about an election campaign strategy and answer the following question:

You are supposed to prepare a strategy for election campaigning which is going to start in 6 months time. This is to be done at multiple constituencies involving many agencies. There would be a huge amount of logistical support which would be required once the format has been decided. The Minister has called for a meeting to hear your action plan and you need to be prepared for it.

Q.29 What would be the most effective answer?

A. Concentrate on coordinating with the different agencies and having them approve the strategy.

B. Concentrate on setting deadlines, targets, and checkpoints in order to meet the deadlines.

C. Concentrate on getting an immediate feel for the contents design and layout of the strategy.

D. Concentrate on logistics: how to move people and

equipments from one place to another smoothly.

E. None of these

Q.30 What would be the least effective answer?

A. Concentrate on coordinating with the different agencies and having them approve the strategy.

B. Concentrate on setting deadlines, targets and checkpoints in order to meet the deadlines.

C. Concentrate on getting an immediate feel for the contents design and layout of the strategy.

D. Concentrate on logistics: how to move people and equipment from one place to another smoothly.

E. None of these

// Smart Answer Sheet //

Correct — Indicates percentage of students who answered questions correctly.

Skipped — Indicates percentage of students who skipped questions.

Q.	Ans.	Correct / Skipped
1	D	65.56 % / 31.55 %
2	B	63.35 % / 35.12 %
3	D	65.59 % / 32.61 %
4	D	41.69 % / 53.15 %
5	A	49.4 % / 38.48 %
6	A	57.62 % / 32.29 %
7	A	40.14 % / 57.48 %
8	C	47.63 % / 48.65 %
9	C	89.94 % / 10.04 %
10	D	14.02 % / 80.74 %
11	C	12.23 % / 71.26 %
12	C	87.49 % / 10.4 %
13	A	57.33 % / 31.2 %
14	B	85.56 % / 10.04 %
15	A	67.58 % / 31.36 %
16	C	55.83 % / 37.75 %
17	D	26.11 % / 68.55 %
18	D	78.0 % / 16.34 %
19	A	10.53 % / 77.41 %
20	B	80.86 % / 15.48 %
21	C	63.26 % / 35.59 %
22	A	17.12 % / 68.56 %
23	B	42.9 % / 37.9 %
24	C	47.02 % / 33.36 %
25	B	25.91 % / 69.5 %
26	A	82.19 % / 15.19 %
27	C	53.3 % / 36.53 %
28	C	31.18 % / 68.01 %
29	C	10.39 % / 78.53 %
30	D	43.26 % / 46.91 %

Performance Analysis

Avg. Score (%)	43.33%
Toppers Score (%)	66.67%
Your Score	

//Hints and Solutions//

1. The least effective answer would be believe that the appropriate checks have been carried out and wait for the introduction of the upgrade so that you can assess its functionality.

First the existing work needs to be reviewed to secure the data and only then the new upgrades can be enjoyed.

Hence, the correct option is (D).

2. As suggested the data should be submitted weekly instead of daily to save time but it should not be changed immediately by the employee. Since the boss is on leave, the boss should not make quick decisions without informing him.

Hence, the correct option is (B).

3. Since the boss has given an opportunity to the employee to make a presentation and you are new to your department. So you should make the most of this opportunity. The least effective answer in such a situation would be to tell the boss that you will wait for them to come and perform only after they arrive.

Hence, the correct option is (D).

4. Since the boss has spoken for a presentation regarding the findings of the research and he commented that you should tone down your tone. Behind which they have argued that it will work better. So your most effective response in such a situation should be to self-analyze so that you can understand the implications of the boss's comment and present accordingly.

Hence, the correct option is (D).

5. Since the situation has been given that after the restructuring, some positions will be abolished, some roles will change and some new opportunities will be created. Therefore, properly express your strengths in the meeting so that your position within the firm is protected.

Hence, the correct option is (A).

6. The least effective answer would be go over to the person in question and set them tasks to complete for your department. Without the Manger's approval you cannot go to a person from another department and assign him work.

Hence, the correct option is (A).

7. The most effective answer would be to conduct some online research into other surveys of this nature to see whether this is a common pattern: include this observation in the report and recommendations. This will ensure that both, the Manager and the employee's point is presented to the organisation.

Hence, the correct option is (A).

8. "Be alert to the news about the changes but continue to work as usual until more is announced" is the best step that any employee working under her must take.

Since the information is given clearly states that when any further changes shall be introduced, people shall be informed. Thus, employees must continue to work as usual and stay updated with any new information.

Hence, the correct option is (C).

9. The most appropriate response would be to ask a few others for feedback on the relevant field to see if this confirms the original negative feedback.

Ideas may differ and asking others will help the employee get a better idea whether the idea is more common among more people or just one person's opinion.

Hence, the correct option is (C).

10. The most effective answer make greater use of visual aids and props in order to stimulate their interest.

Visual aids most attract the people around. So, visual aids and props will distract the audience and make them a bit more interested in the speech.

Hence, the correct option is (D).

11. In the given situation when we know that errors are there and it may take four weeks to complete them accurately. In this case, the least effective option would be to start correcting all discovered errors and complete as much as you can in two weeks.

Hence, the correct option is (C).

12. Since the final report has to be submitted immediately, it may take time to reconsider the report. On the other hand, if subordinates are justifying the information given in the report, then time will be wasted to convince them. In such a situation, the best option is to revise the report yourself on points where there are differences of opinion.

Hence, the correct option is (C).

13. Because in the same competition your friend is being given more time than you. Therefore, there is a direct discrimination being done by the committee here. The most appropriate response in such a situation would be to lodge a complaint to chairperson against the discrimination.

Hence, the correct option is (A).

14. You notice that the project is getting delayed due to lack of cooperation from the team members. Therefore, first of all you will look into the reasons for non-cooperation, after that it will be appropriate to take some other step.

Hence, the correct option is (B).

15. As the Screening Committee is responsible for checking the eligibility of the athlete in the junior age group. Therefore, once the complaint is received and confirmed, you will first seek clarification from the Screening Committee regarding the eligibility of that particular athlete.

Hence, the correct option is (A).

16. Since you are handling a priority project and meeting all the deadlines means that on your part you are sure that the project will be completed on time. In such a situation, after the cancellation of the leave by the adjacent boss, you are left with the option of contacting the higher authority to reconsider the leave application.

Hence, the correct option is (C).

17. You are involved in setting up a water supply project in a remote area. In any case, full recovery of the cost is impossible. The income level in the area is low and 25% of the population is below poverty line (BPL). In such a situation, such a way should be adopted so that maximum recovery can be done without putting additional burden on the people below the poverty line. So the most appropriate option would be that the users pay the charges based on the water consumption with separate charges for non-BPL and BPL households.

Hence, the correct option is (D).

18. As we know that both taking and giving bribe are illegal. Therefore, as a citizen, you should file a formal complaint if a signal of bribe is received by a government department.

Hence, the correct option is (D).

19. You have been asked to give an explanation for not attending an important official meeting. Your immediate boss didn't inform you about the meeting and is now pressuring you not to accuse him. In such a situation, a better option would be that you send a written reply explaining the facts.

Hence, the correct option is (A).

20. Since the local thug (bad element) has started illegal construction on your vacant plot and threatens you with dire consequences. This is an outright criminal act. In such a situation the proper option would be to go to police for necessary action.

Hence, the correct option is (B).

21. As the situation has been given that within two days the important work of the headquarters is to be done and you are being pressurized by the office to complete the work. But due to your accident, you are unable to do the work yourself. Therefore, in such a situation, it would be most appropriate that you suggest an alternate person in relation to the headquarters, who can complete the required work on time.

Hence, the correct option is (C).

22. Since you are the officer in charge for providing basic medical facilities to the survivors in the earthquake affected area. But despite your best efforts, people accused you of making money from the relief money. Since you are discharging your duties with utmost sincerity on your part, then you will allow inquiry to be set up to look into this matter and till then you will continue with your work.

Hence, the correct option is (A).

23. As given the situation that you need a boat for use in the area under flood but after looking at the price quoted by the boat owners you found that the lowest price was almost three times more than the government sanctioned rate. On the other hand the situation is such that relief work should not be hampered, so the most appropriate choice among the most given options would be that you accept the lowest price and rent the boat.

Hence, the correct option is (B).

24. Since the situation is given that you have only one vaccine left and two people need it. In such a situation, it would be most appropriate that both of you will be asked to both to approach a doctor and will provide the vaccine to the one who needs more.

Hence, the correct option is (C).

25. Since within a week of the start of the project, there have been complaints of theft and removal of shelter sites. In such a situation, you will assure the residents that the matter will be thoroughly investigated.

Hence, the correct option is (B).

26. As the situation is given that the Office Secretariat does not find the request made by your Private Secretary as per the rules and rejects the request. But you don't want to annoy your personal secretary, then the best option among the given options would be to invite him to your room and explain personally why the allotment cannot be done.

Hence, the correct option is (A).

27. Since the incident given here seems to be related to illegal recovery or bribery. In such a situation, it is your responsibility to pay attention to this incident and later report the matter to the concerned officer.

Hence, the correct option is (C).

28. Since here the situation is given that your colleague had helped you in some other matter in the past but the university authorities have asked you to prepare the question paper by showing confidence, in such a situation if you help him then it is breaking the rules of the university and there will be irresponsibility on your part. In such a situation, the best thing would be to explain to your colleague that this would be a breach of trust of the university authorities and you are not in a position to help him.

Hence, the correct option is (C).

29. The most effective answer would be to concentrate on getting an immediate feel for the design and layout of the strategy.

The question clearly states that the logistics team needs to contact after the format has been decided, thus eliminating the fourth option. Only when the strategy is ready the agencies can be contacted and then deadlines can be set, thus eliminating the first and second options.

Hence, the correct option is (C).

30. The least effective answer would be concentrate on logistics: how to move people and equipment from one place to another smoothly.

Moving the equipment is the last step. Only once the entire strategy is set and the agencies agree to the strategy, then based on the deadlines the equipment shall be moved from one place to another.

Hence, the correct option is (D).

Ques (1-5):Direction: Answer the question based on the information given below.

9 movies (A, B, C, D, E, F, G, H and I) are released on 4th, 17th and 25th during June, July and August. Neither H nor E is released in June and 3 movies are released between H and E. F is released immediately after E but not on 17th of any month. 2 movies are released between F and G. 3 movies are released between G and D. C and B are released in the same month. C is not the first movie to be released. I is released neither before A nor immediately before H.

Q.1 Movie I is released on _____.

A. 17th July
B. 4th August
C. 4th July
D. 25th June
E. None of the above

Q.2 Movie A is released immediately before movie __.

A. E
B. H
C. G
D. B
E. None of these

Q.3 How many movies are released between E and B?

A. 2
B. 4
C. 3
D. 6
E. None of these

Q.4 ___ is released on 17th August.

A. Movie I
B. Movie E
C. Movie A
D. Movie D
E. None of these

Q.5 Number of movies released before G is equal to the number of movies released after ____.

A. H
B. D
C. A
D. F
E. None of these

Ques (6-10):Direction: Answer the question based on the information given below.

Nine students A, B, C, D, E, F, G, H and K are born on 1st of different months among January, February, April, May, June, August, September, October and December in the same year. Students, who were born in months with only 30 days, have different ranks among 1st, 2nd and 3rd.

B was born immediately after the 3rd rank holder. K was born two months after B, who was not born in May. One student was born before D. Two students were born between K and G. A was born immediately before F. E was born after C, who was born after H. A is not 1st rank holder. E doesn't have any rank.

Q.6 How many students are elder than E?

A. Six
B. Four
C. Five
D. Eight
E. None of the above

Q.7 Who was born immediately after 2nd rank holder?

A. E
B. H
C. B
D. F
E. None of the above

Q.8 Find the odd one out.

[LIC AAO (Generalist), 2021]

A. H
B. F
C. D
D. B
E. K

Q.9 Who is four months elder than C?

A. G
B. F
C. H
D. A
E. None of the above

Q.10 Which among the following statements is/are true?

A. F was born after G
B. C was born in August
C. F was born two months after D
D. H is not the eldest
E. None of the above statements is true

Ques (11-15):Direction: Answer the question based on the information given below:

Seven kids A, B, C, D, E, F and G were born in different months among January, February, April, May, July, August and November in different years among 1998, 2003, 2006, 2008, 2010, 2014 and 2015 not necessarily in the same order.

Note: If a person is n (=1, 2, 3, 4, so on) years elder than another person, consider only the years. F was born in 2003. C, who was born in July, is five years elder than D. D was born in a month, which consists of only 30 days. A is at most two years elder than the one, who was born in February. B is elder than E, who was not born in 2014. G was not born immediately before the one, who was born in April. The kid, who was born in January, is elder than the one, who was born in April. The kid, who was born in May is not elder than the one, who was born in April. Kid, who was born in 1998, was not born in January.

Q.11 __ is three years elder than ___.

A. B, F
B. A, E
C. C, G
D. F, A
E. None of the above

Q.12 Who was born in the month of May?

A. G
B. A
C. F
D. B
E. None of the above

Q.13 The eldest child was born in ___ while the youngest child was born in ___.

A. August, May
B. April, November
C. April, August
D. August, November

E. None of the above

Q.14 Kid, who was born in May, is ___ years younger than F.

A. 11 **B.** 2
C. 9 **D.** 16
E. None of the above

Q.15 Which among the following statements is/are true?

A. B was born in May
B. F was born in a leap year
C. 2nd eldest kid was born in January
D. G was born in a month, which has only 30 days
E. None of the given statements is true

Ques (16-20):Direction: Answer the question based on the information given below.

Seven persons: I, J, K, L, M, N, and O have their birthdays in different months - January, March, April, June, July, September, and December, but not necessarily in the same order.

I's birthday falls in a month having 31 days. J's birthday month is after I's birthday month. N's birthday falls in month having 31 days. J's birthday month comes after N's birthday month. L has a birthday in a month having 30 days. K has a birthday in a month having 31 days but not in July and March. M's birthday fall in a month having 30 days but before September. O's birthday month is not after J's birthday month. J's Birthday is not in December. M birthday falls before O but not in the month of June. Only three persons have birthdays between N and L.

Q.16 Whose birthday is in the month of January?

A. O **B.** I
C. M **D.** N
E. Either N or I

Q.17 How many persons have birthday between I and K?

A. 2 **B.** 3
C. 4 **D.** More than Four
E. None of these

Q.18 How many persons have birthday after M?

A. 1 **B.** 2
C. 3 **D.** 4
E. None of these

Q.19 Four of the following five are alike in a certain way based on their positions in the above arrangement and so form a group. Which is the one that does not belong to that group?

A. O **B.** I **C.** J **D.** N
E. K

Q.20 Which of the following statement is true?

A. J has birthday immediately after O
B. K has birthday in the last month of the year
C. No one has birthday between I and N
D. M's birthday falls immediately before O
E. All are true

Ques (21-25):Direction: Answer the question based on the information given below:

Eight friends Amit, Arun, Aarzoo, Alok, Ajay, Ashish, Aakash and Ankit have their wedding anniversary in the different months of the year viz. May, July, September and November but not necessarily in the same order. They have an anniversary on either 12 or 27 of the month. No two persons have the same anniversary date.

Amit's anniversary is in the month which has 30 days but not on an odd-numbered date. Only three persons have their anniversary between Amit's and Aruns'. Arun's anniversary is on an even-numbered date. Ajay and Alok have their anniversary in one particular month that has 31 days. Alok does not have his anniversary before Ajay's. Besides, both of them did not have their anniversary in the month of May. Only one person has his anniversary between Ashish and Ankit. Aarzoo does not have his anniversary on an even-numbered date. Ankit has his anniversary just after Aakash's.

Q.21 Whose anniversary is on 27th of July?

A. Alok **B.** Ashish
C. Arun **D.** Amit
E. None of these

Q.22 How many persons' anniversaries are falling between Aakash's and Ajay's?

A. 5 **B.** 2
C. 3 **D.** 4
E. None of these

Q.23 Four of the following five are alike in a certain way and so form a group. Which one does not belong to that group?

A. Amit **B.** Ashish **C.** Aakash **D.** Ankit
E. Aarzoo

Q.24 Whose anniversary is falling earlier than that of anyone else in the group?

A. Alok **B.** Arun
C. Aarzoo **D.** Ankit
E. None of these

Q.25 How many anniversary dates are falling between Arun's and Ankit's?

A. 6 **B.** 2
C. 3 **D.** 4
E. None of these

Ques (26-30):Direction: Read the following information carefully and answer the question given beside.

7 actors viz. S, A, L, M, O, N and K won the Best Actor award during the years 2010 and 2016 such that in one year only one actor received the award and none of the actors received the award twice. They won the award for 7 different films that they were part of such that one actor was part of one film only.

Further, it is known that L received the award for 'Barfi' in a leap year. A received award just before K for '2 States'. K received an award for 'Fan' after the award received by L. 2 actors received an award between the awards received by A and S, who won it for 'Sultan'. S was not the last person to receive the award. M received the award for 'Kites' in an odd-numbered year. O was awarded for 'Fitoor' before M but O was not the

first one to receive the award. N received the award for
'Andhadhun'.

Q.26 Which actor was awarded in year 2016?

A. M	**B.** K
C. N	**D.** S

E. None of these

Q.27 In which of the following years, award was given for 2
States?

A. 2012	**B.** 2013
C. 2011	**D.** 2015

E. None of these

Q.28 Who among the following was part of the film which got
awarded just before 'Kites'?

A. L	**B.** A
C. S	**D.** K

E. None of these

Q.29 Find the odd one out?

A. Andhadhun	**B.** Sultan
C. Barfi	**D.** Fan

E. Fitoor

Q.30 How many actors were awarded after M?

A. 1	**B.** 2
C. 3	**D.** 5

E. None of these

// Smart Answer Sheet //

Correct Indicates percentage of students who answered questions correctly.

Skipped Indicates percentage of students who skipped questions.

Q.	Ans.	Correct / Skipped
1	B	50.68 % / 47.48 %
2	C	42.97 % / 44.19 %
3	D	54.58 % / 31.97 %
4	B	58.19 % / 39.81 %
5	A	44.77 % / 48.87 %
6	D	69.85 % / 30.05 %

Q.	Ans.	Correct / Skipped
7	D	42.36 % / 44.22 %
8	C	69.7 % / 30.3 %
9	B	44.54 % / 33.1 %
10	E	11.95 % / 83.98 %
11	D	18.84 % / 76.16 %
12	A	54.66 % / 39.99 %

Q.	Ans.	Correct / Skipped
13	D	59.77 % / 38.44 %
14	A	42.25 % / 54.01 %
15	C	12.61 % / 70.52 %
16	B	10.49 % / 71.5 %
17	D	48.3 % / 45.84 %
18	D	65.24 % / 31.31 %

Q.	Ans.	Correct / Skipped
19	A	16.16 % / 67.21 %
20	E	56.24 % / 39.93 %
21	A	60.24 % / 37.62 %
22	C	46.98 % / 42.43 %
23	E	47.86 % / 49.53 %
24	B	53.74 % / 44.76 %

Q.	Ans.	Correct / Skipped
25	A	62.54 % / 36.25 %
26	C	58.66 % / 33.7 %
27	B	58.56 % / 40.54 %
28	D	68.66 % / 30.1 %
29	E	69.84 % / 30.12 %
30	A	51.98 % / 37.39 %

Performance Analysis	
Avg. Score (%)	33.33%
Toppers Score (%)	60.0%
Your Score	

//Hints and Solutions//

Ques (1-5):1. Neither H nor E is released in June and 3 movies are released between them.

2. F is released immediately after E but not on 17th of any month.

3. 2 movies are released between F and G, so the possible cases are:

Months	Case I			Case II		
	4th	17th	25th	4th	17th	25th
June						G
July	H		G		E	F
August		E	F			H

4. 3 movies are released between G and D.

5. C and B are released in the same month.

Months	Case I			Case II		
	4th	17th	25th	4th	17th	25th
June	B/C	D	C/B	B/C	C/B	G
July	H		G		E	F
August		E	F	D		H

6. C is not the first movie to be released.

7. I is released neither before A nor immediately before H, so case II is rejected. The final table is given below:

Months	Case I		
	4th	17th	25th
June	B	D	C
July	H	A	G
August	I	E	F

1. So, Movie I is released on 4th August.

Hence, the correct option is (B).

2. So, Movie A is released immediately before movie G.

Hence, the correct option is (C).

3. So, 6 movies are released between E and B.

Hence, the correct option is (D).

4. So, Movie E is released on 17th August.

Hence, the correct option is (B).

5. So, the Number of movies released before G is equal to the number of movies released after H.

Hence, the correct option is (A).

Ques (6-10):1. One student was born before D.

2. B was born immediately after the 3rd rank holder.

3. K was born two months after B, who was not born in May.

4. Two students were between K and G.

So, B was born in either August or October. K was born in either October or December. G was born in either June or August.

Case I: B was born in August:

Month	Student	Rank
January		
February	D	
April		
May		
June	G	3rd
August	B	
September		
October	K	
December		

Case II: B was born in October:

Month	Student	Rank
January		
February	D	
April		
May		
June		
August	G	
September		3rd
October	B	
December		

Month	Student	Rank
January	H	
February	D	
April	A	2nd
May	F	
June	G	3rd
August	B	
September	C	1st
October	K	
December	E	

5. K was born two months after B, this is not possible in case II, so case II is rejected.

6. A was born immediate before F.

7. E was born after C, who was born after H.

8. A is not 1st rank holder. E doesn't have any rank.

So, E was born in December. C was born in September and H is born in January. C is 1st rank holder and A is 2nd rank holder.

The final table is given below:

6. So, Eight students are elder than E

Hence, the correct option is (D).

7. So, F was born immediately after 2nd rank holder.

Hence, the correct option is (D).

8. So, H, F, B, and K were born in January, May, August, and October month respectively which has 31 days but D was born in February.

Hence, the correct option is (C).

9. So, F is four months elder than C.

Hence, the correct option is (B).

10. So, None of the above statements is true.

Hence, the correct option is (E).

Ques (11-15):1. F was born in 2003. C, who was born in July, is five years elder than D.

		1998
F		2003
		2006
		2008
C	July	2010
		2014
D		2015

So, B was born in 1998. E was born in 2008. G was born in 2014 and D was born in November.

B		1998
F		2003
A		2006
E	February	2008
C	July	2010
G		2014
D	November	2015

2. D was born in a month, which consists of only 30 days.

3. A is at most two years elder than the one, who was born in February.

So, D was born either in April or November. A was born in 2006 and the one, who is born in February, is born in 2008.

		1998
F		2003
A		2006
	February	2008
C	July	2010
		2014
D	April/November	2015

4. B was elder than E, who was not born in 2014.

5. G was not born immediately before the one, who was born in April.

6. The kid, who was born in January, is elder than the one, who was born in April.

7. The kid, who was born in May is not elder than the one, who was born in April.

8. Kid, who was born in 1998, was not born in January.

So, F was born in January. A was born in April. G was born in May. B was born in August.

The final table is given below:

B	August	1998
F	January	2003
A	April	2006
E	February	2008
C	July	2010
G	May	2014
D	November	2015

11. F is three years elder than A.

Hence, the correct option is (D).

12. So, G was born in the month of May.

Hence, the correct option is (A).

13. The eldest child was born in August while the youngest child was born in November.

Hence, the correct option is (D).

14. So, Kid, who was born in May, is 11 years younger than F.

Hence, the correct option is (A).

15. So, the true statement is 2nd eldest kid was born in January

Hence, the correct option is (C).

Ques (16-20): 1. N's birthday falls in month having 31 days.

2. I's birthday falls in month having 31 days and J's birthday month is after I's birthday month

3. J's birthday month comes after N's birthday month.

4. J's Birthday is not in December

From the above references, it is clear that I and N birthday will be before N and either in January or March month as J birthday cannot be in the month of December.

Month	Person
January (31)	I/N
March (31)	I/N
April (30)	
June (30)	
July (31)	J
September (30)	
December (31)	

5. K has birthday in a month having 31 days but not in July and March.

6. M birthday falls before O but not in the month of June.

7. O's birthday month is not after J's birthday month.

From the reference, it is clear that K birthday will be in December only.

It is given that M birthday falls before O but not in the month of June and O's birthday month is not after J's birthday month. So, M birthday will fall in April and O birthday will fall in June.

Month	Person
January (31)	I/N
March (31)	I/N
April (30)	M
June (30)	O
July (31)	J
September (30)	
December (31)	K

8. L has birthday in a month having 30 days.

9. Only three persons have birthday between N and L.

L has birthday in a month having 30 days. So, L birthday will fall in September.

As only three persons have birthday between N and L. So, N birthday falls in March.

Month	Person
January (31)	I
March (31)	N
April (30)	M
June (30)	O
July (31)	J
September (30)	L
December (31)	K

16. So, I birthday falls in January.

Hence, the correct option is (B).

17. So, five persons have their birthdays between I and K.

Hence, the correct option is (D).

18. So, 4 persons have their birthday after M.

Hence, the correct option is (D).

19. So, Except O all have their birthdays in the months having 31 days.

Hence, the correct option is (A).

20. So, All the given statements are true.

Hence, the correct option is (E).

Ques (21-25):1. Amit's anniversary in the month has 30 days but not on the odd-numbered date.

2. Only three persons have anniversaries between Amit and Arun who are born on an even-numbered date but not in the month of July.

So, it is clear that Amit's Anniversary is on 12th September and Arun's Anniversary is on the 12th of May.

Month	Date	Person
May	12	Arun
May	27	
July	12	
July	27	
September	12	Amit
September	27	
November	12	
Novemeber	27	

3. Ajay and Alok have their anniversary in the month has 31 days.

4. Alok does not have his anniversary before Ajay also both of them did not have their Anniversary in the month of May.

5. Ajay's anniversary is before Alok's Anniversary.

It is clear that Ajay and Alok have their anniversary in the month of July where Ajay's anniversary is on 12th July and Alok's anniversary is on 27th July.

Month	Date	Person
May	12	Arun
May	27	
July	12	Ajay
July	27	Alok
September	12	Amit
September	27	
November	12	
Novemeber	27	

6. Only one person has his anniversary between Ashish and Ankit.

7. Aarzoo doesn't have his anniversary on the even-numbered date.

8. Ankit has his anniversary just after Aakash.

So, Ankitis's anniversary is on 27 November and Ashish's anniversary is on 27th September. As Aarzoo doesn't have his anniversary on an even-numbered date so Aarzoo's anniversary is on 27th May. So, Ankit and Aakash both have their anniversary in the month of November.

Month	Date	Person
May	12	Arun
May	27	Aarzoo
July	12	Ajay
July	27	Alok
September	12	Amit
September	27	Ashish
November	12	Aakash
Novemeber	27	Ankit

21. So, Alok's anniversary is on 27 july.

Hence, the correct option is (A).

22. So, we can see that 3 persons have their anniversaries between Aakash's and Ajay's.

Hence, the correct option is (C).

23. So, Among all, only Aarzoo has his anniversary in a month that has 31 days.

Hence, the correct option is (E).

24. So, we can observe that Arun's anniversary is falling on 12th May which is earlier than anyone else's anniversary date.

Hence, the correct option is (B).

25. So, clearly, 6 persons' anniversary dates are falling between Arun's and Ankit's.

Hence, the correct option is (A).

Ques (26-30):1. 7 actors viz. S, A, L, M, O, N and K won the Best Actor award during the years 2010 and 2016 such that in one year only one actor received the award and none of the actors received the award twice.

2. Further it is known that L received the award for 'Barfi' in a leap year.

3. A received award just before K for '2 States'.

4. K received the award for 'Fan' after the award received by L.

5. 2 actors received awards between the awards received by A and S, who won it for 'Sultan'.

6. S was not the last person to receive the award.

As L received the award in a leap year, so only two possible years are 2012 and 2016, but as per the third hint K received an award after L, thus the only possibility is that L received the award in 2012.

The following two cases are possible with respect to the last hint.

Hence, the correct option is (E).

30. So, Only one actor was awarded after M.

Hence, the correct option is (A).

Case-1		
Year	Actor	Film
2010	S	Sultan
2011		
2012	L	Barfi
2013	A	2 States
2014	K	Fan
2015		
2016		

Case-2		
Year	Actor	Film
2010		
2011	S	Sultan
2012	L	Barfi
2013		
2014	A	2 States
2015	K	Fan
2016		

7. M received the award for 'Kites' in an odd-numbered year.

8. O was awarded for 'Fitoor' before M but O was not the first one to receive the award.

9. N received the award for 'Andhadhun'.

Case-2 gets eliminated as the given hints cannot be fulfilled.

Case-1		
Year	Actor	Film
2010	S	Sultan
2011	O	Fitoor
2012	L	Barfi
2013	A	2 States
2014	K	Fan
2015	M	Kites
2016	N	Andhadhun

26. So, N was awarded in 2016.

Hence, the correct option is (C).

27. So, The award for 2 States was given in 2013.

Hence, the correct option is (B).

28. So, K was part of the film which got awarded just before 'Kites'.

Hence, the correct option is (D).

29. So, Fitoor is the odd one out as the actor part of the rest films were awarded in even-numbered years.

Q.1 Direction: When the following figure is folded to form a cube, find the symbol on the face opposite the face showing the symbol

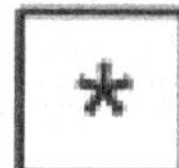

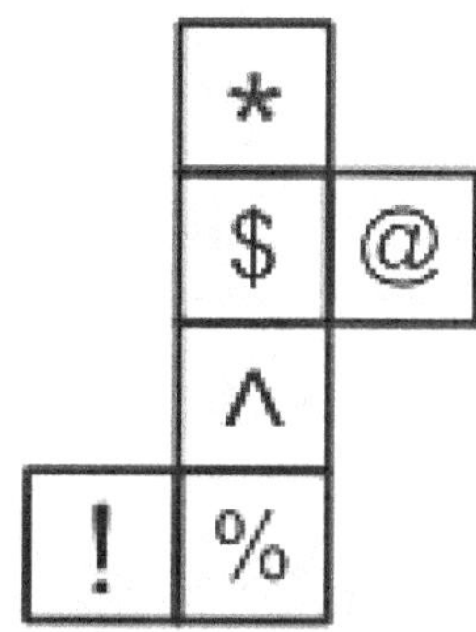

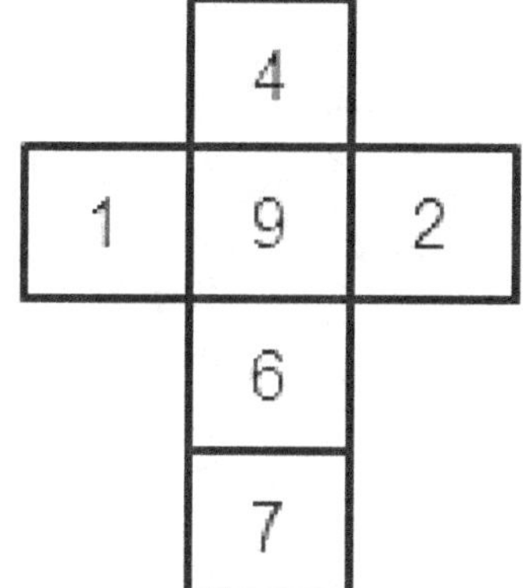

A. %   **B.** !   **C.** $ **D.** ^
E. @

Q.2 Direction: From the given options, choose the cube that is similar to the cube formed from the given sheet of paper?

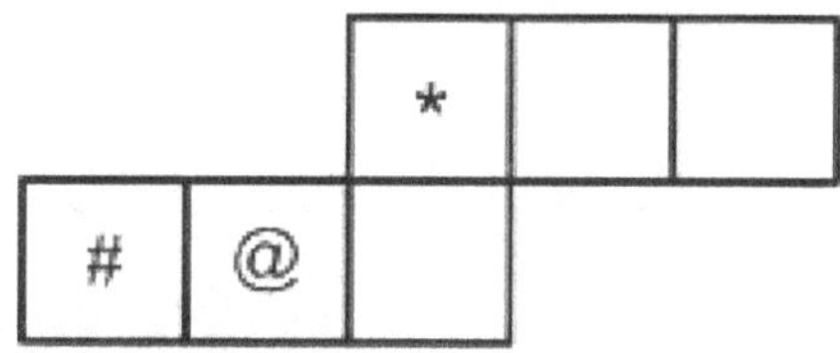

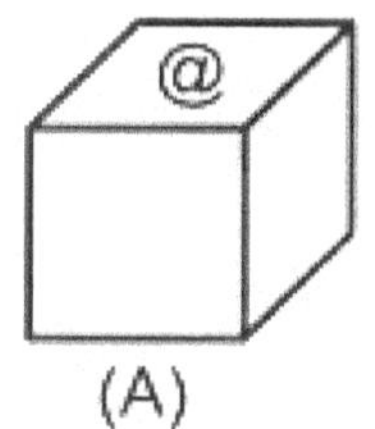

(A)   (B)   (C)

A. Only (A)   **B.** Only (B)
C. Both (A) and (C)   **D.** Both (B) and (C)
E. All of the above

Q.3 Direction: The following figure is folded to form a cube. Which representations of the cube in the given option is the correct one?

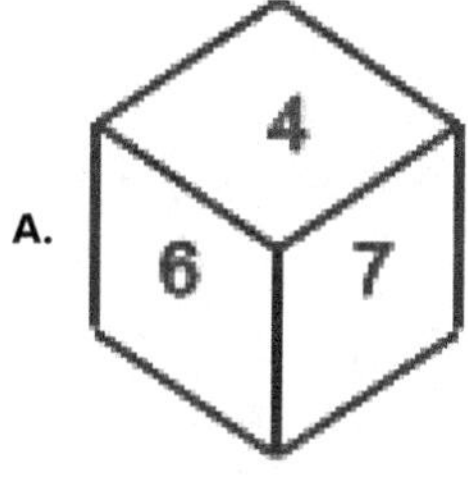

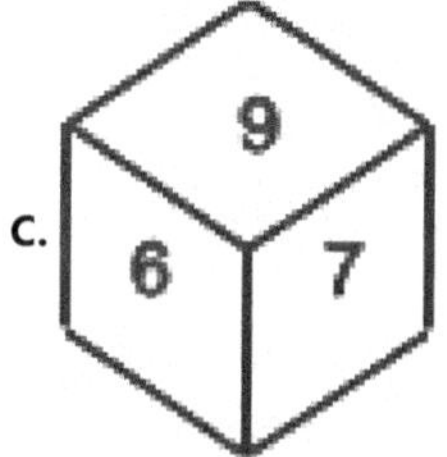

A.   **B.**

C.   **D.**

E. None of these

Q.4 Direction: Which of the following cube in the answer figure cannot be made based on the unfolded cube in the question figure?

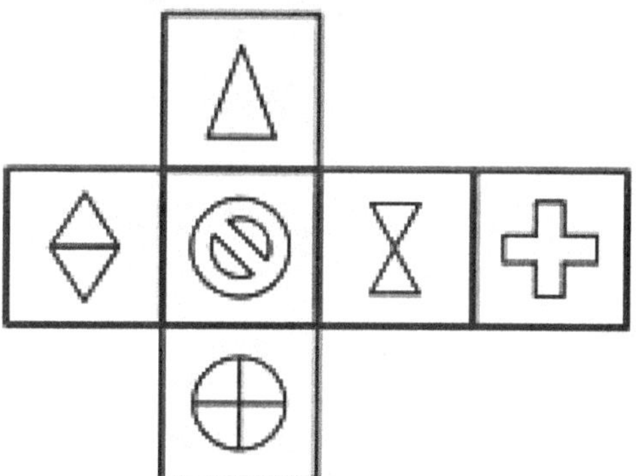

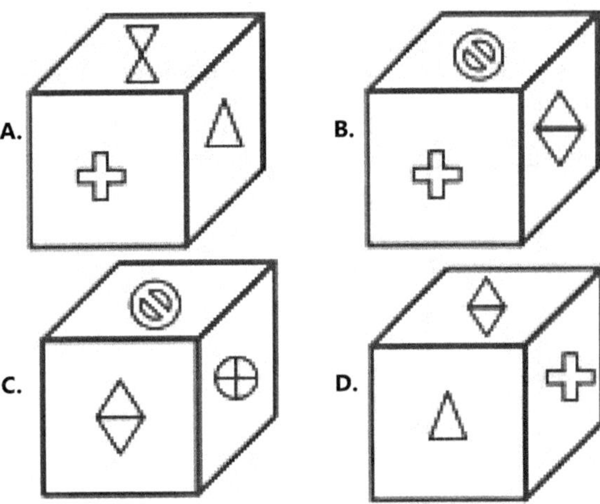

E. None of these

Q.5 Direction: Which of the following cubes in the answer figure can be made based on the unfolded cube in the question figure?

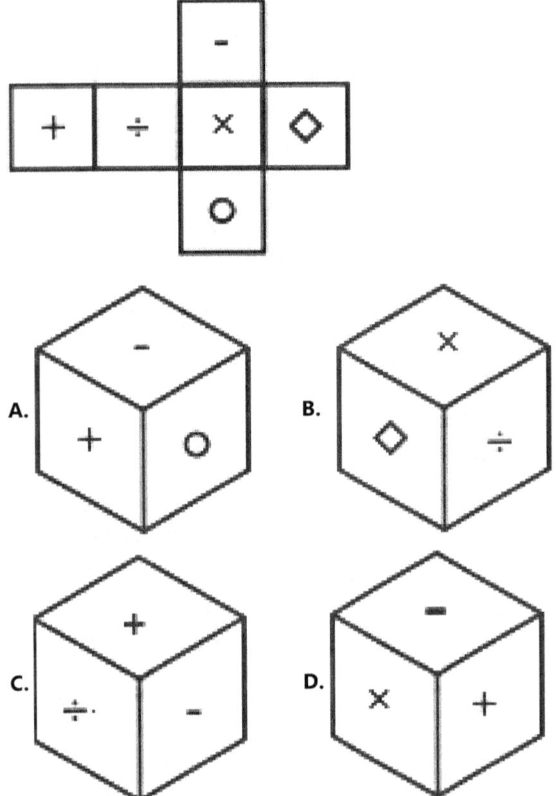

E. None of these

Q.6 Direction: If a mirror is placed on the line AB, then which of the answer figures is the right image of the given figure?

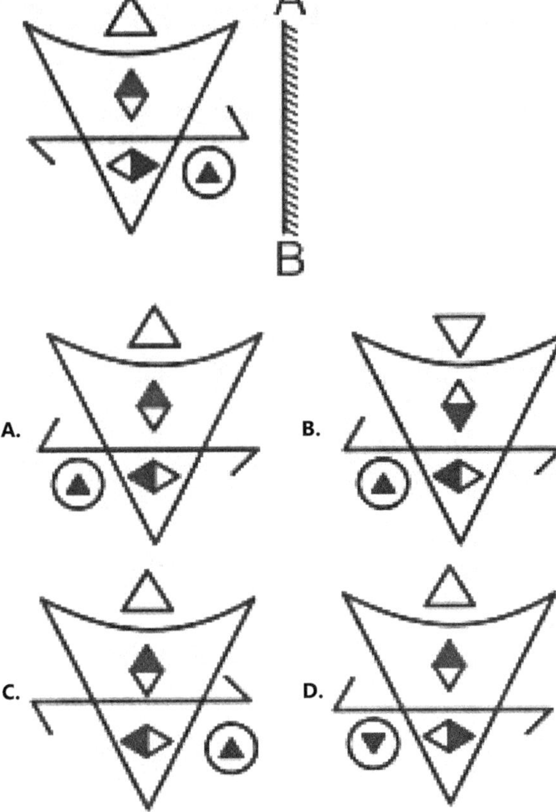

E. None of these

Q.7 Direction: If a mirror is placed on the line AB, then which of the answer figures is the correct image of the given figure?

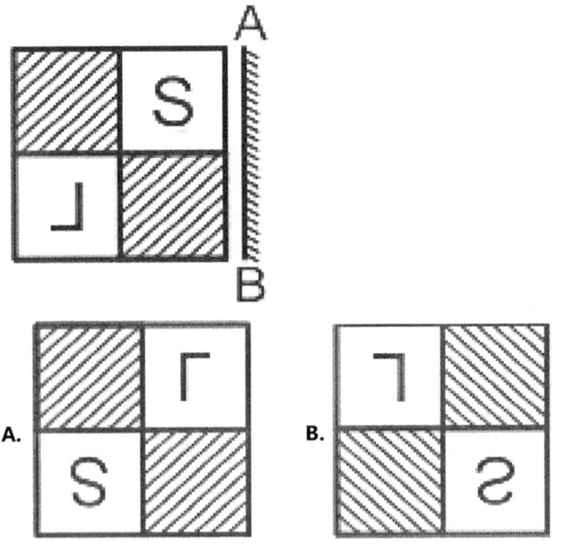

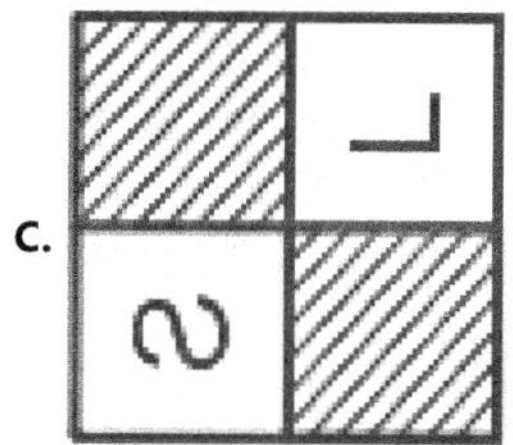

C.

D.

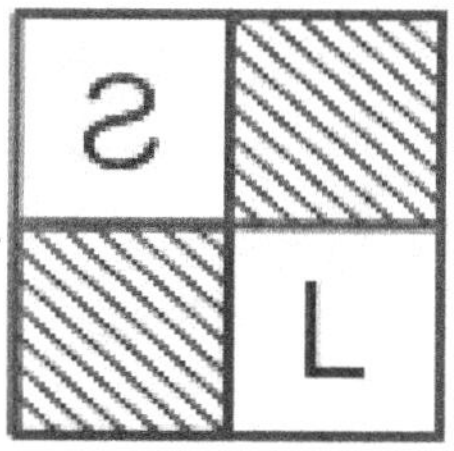

E. None of these

Q.8 Direction: Choose the mirror image of the following figure along the XY axis.

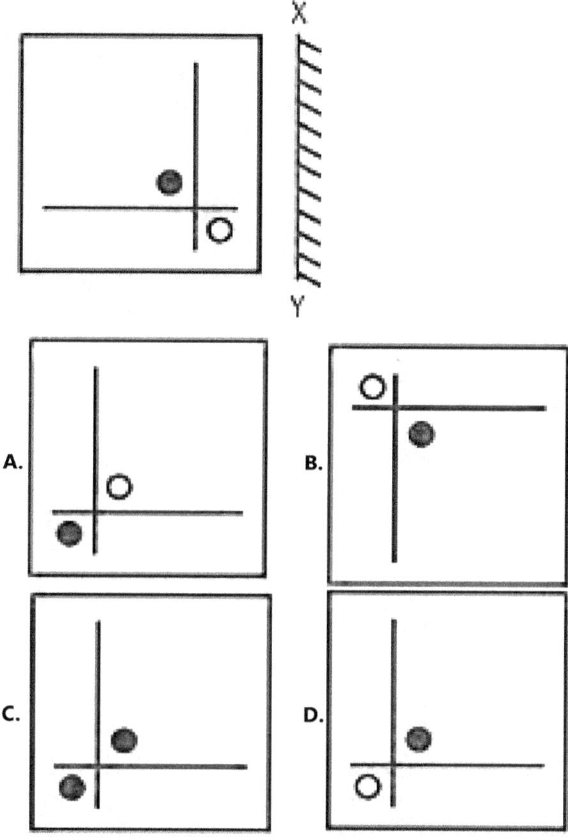

A.

B.

C.

D.

E. None of these

Q.9 Direction: Select the correct mirror image of the given image, when the mirror is placed at right side.

A.  ꓭ ꟻ ꓤ I 9 5 u h

B.  ꓱ ꓞ ꓤ I 9 5 u h

C.  ꓱ ꓞ ꓤ I 9 5 u h

D.  ꓱ ꓞ ꓤ I 9 5 u h

E. None of these

Q.10 Direction: If a mirror is placed on the line AB, then which of the answer figure is the right mirror image of the given figure?

247593

A. 395742   B. 392457

C.    D.

E. None of these

Q.11 Find the minimum number of straight lines required to make the given figure.

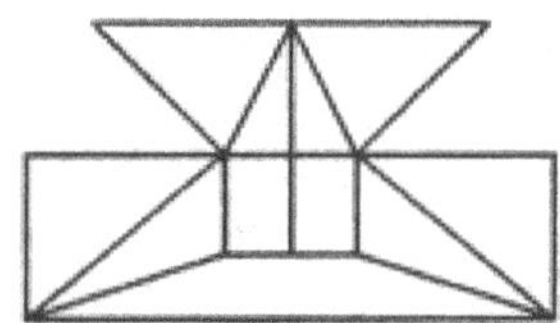

[Intelligence Bureau Security Assistant, 2017]

A. 16   **B.** 17   **C.** 18   **D.** 19
E. 21

Q.12 Find the number of triangles in the given figure.

A. 22   **B.** 24   **C.** 26   **D.** 28
E. 30

Q.13 Find the number of triangles in the given figure.

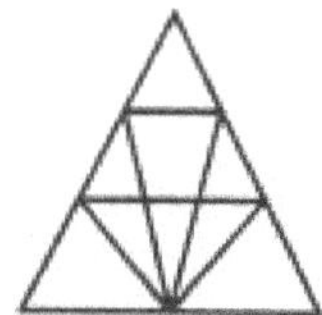

A. 12   **B.** 18   **C.** 22   **D.** 26
E. 30

Q.14 Find the number of triangles in the given figure.

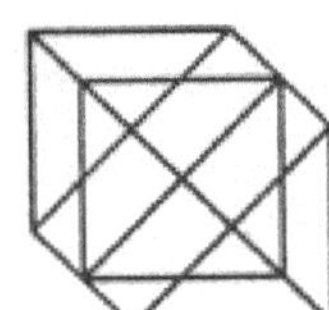

[Intelligence Bureau Security Assistant, 2017]

A. 18   **B.** 20   **C.** 24   **D.** 27
E. 29

Q.15 Find the minimum number of straight lines required to make the given figure.

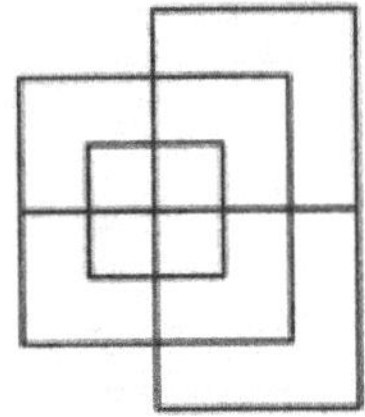

A. 13   **B.** 15   **C.** 17   **D.** 19
E. 21

Q.16 Find the number of triangles in the given figure.

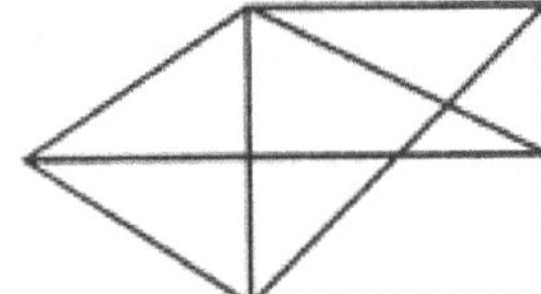

A. 12   **B.** 13   **C.** 14   **D.** 15
E. 17

Q.17 Find the number of triangles in the given figure.

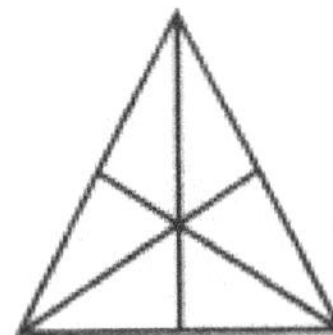

A. 16   **B.** 13   **C.** 9   **D.** 7
E. 5

Q.18 Find the number of triangles in the given figure.

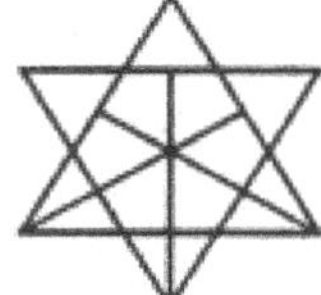

A. 21   **B.** 23   **C.** 25   **D.** 27
E. 29

Q.19 Find the number of triangles in the given figure.

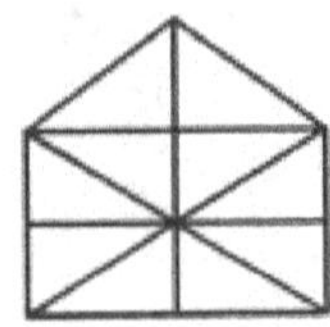

A. 10   **B.** 19   **C.** 21   **D.** 23
E. 25

Q.20 Find the minimum number of straight lines required to make the given figure.

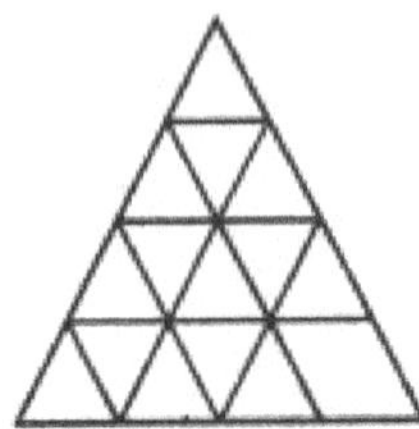

A. 9   **B.** 11   **C.** 15   **D.** 16
E. 18

Q.21 Find the number of triangles in the given figure.

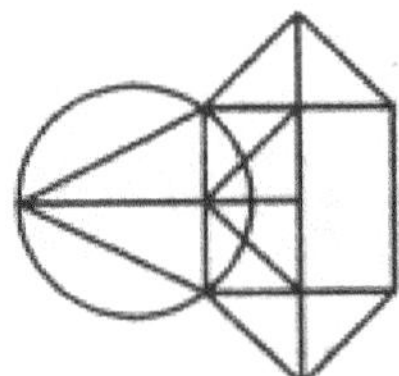

A. 10   **B.** 12   **C.** 14   **D.** 16
E. 18

Q.22 Find the number of triangles in the given figure.

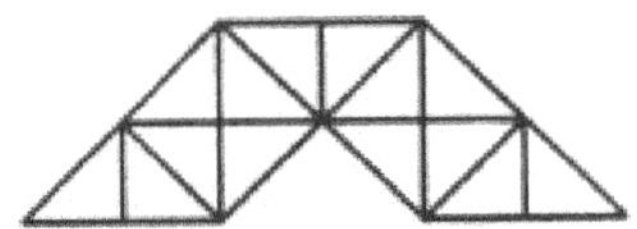

A. 23   **B.** 27   **C.** 29   **D.** 31
E. 33

Q.23 Find the number of triangles in the given figure.

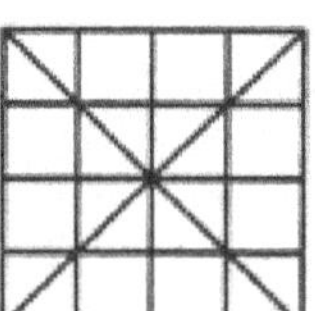

A. 36   **B.** 40   **C.** 44   **D.** 48
E. 52

Q.24 Find the number of triangles in the given figure.

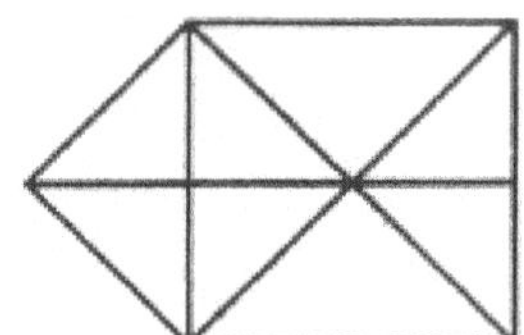

A. 15 **B.** 16 **C.** 17 **D.** 18
E. 19

Q.25 Find the number of triangles in the given figure.

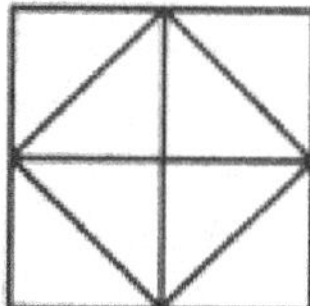

A. 8 **B.** 10 **C.** 12 **D.** 14
E. 16

Q.26 Find the number of triangles in the given figure.

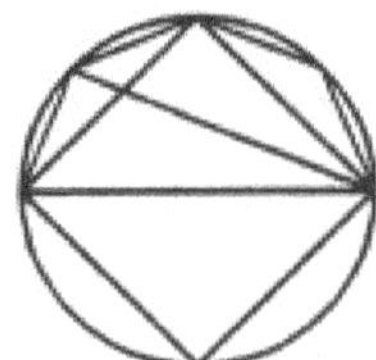

A. 8 **B.** 10 **C.** 11 **D.** 12
E. 14

Q.27 If a mirror is placed on line AB, which of the following answer figures is the right image of the given figure?

A. XAЯ **B.** RAX
C. XAR **D.** ЯAX

E. None of the above

Q.28 Two different positions of the same dice are shown below, the six faces of which are numbered 1 to 6. Which number is on the face opposite the face showing '1'?

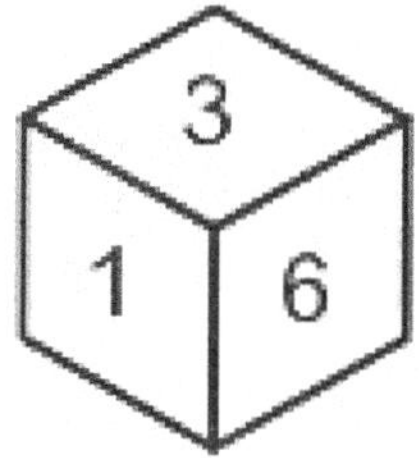 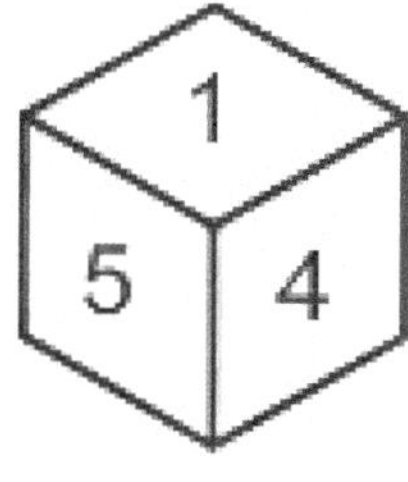

A. 4 **B.** 2 **C.** 5 **D.** 3
E. 6

Q.29 From the given answer figures, select the one in which the Question image is hidden/embedded (Rotation not allowed)?

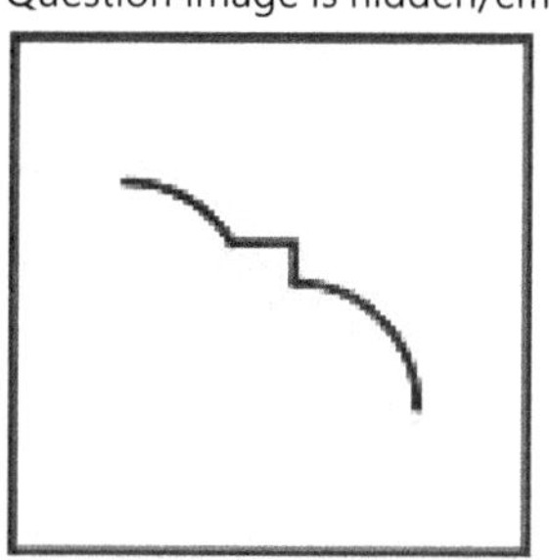

A.

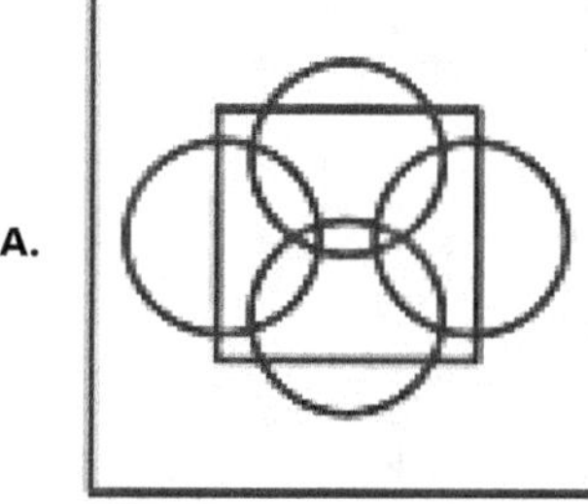

B.

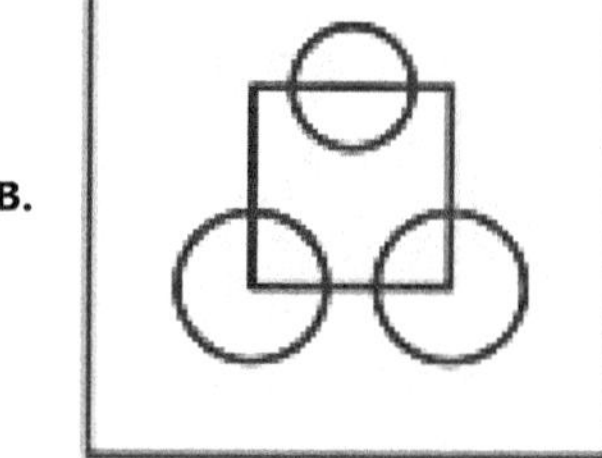

C.

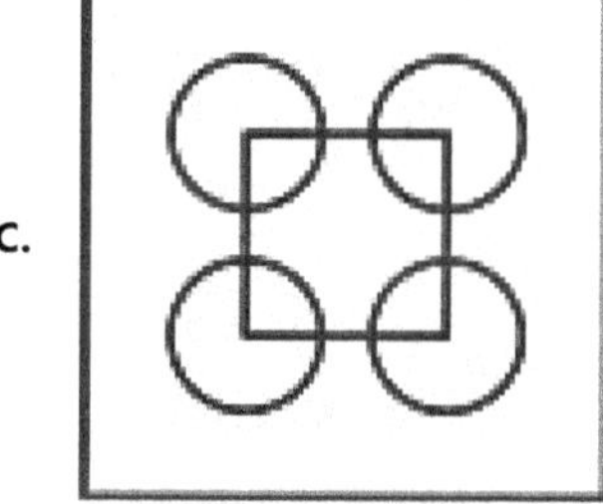

D.

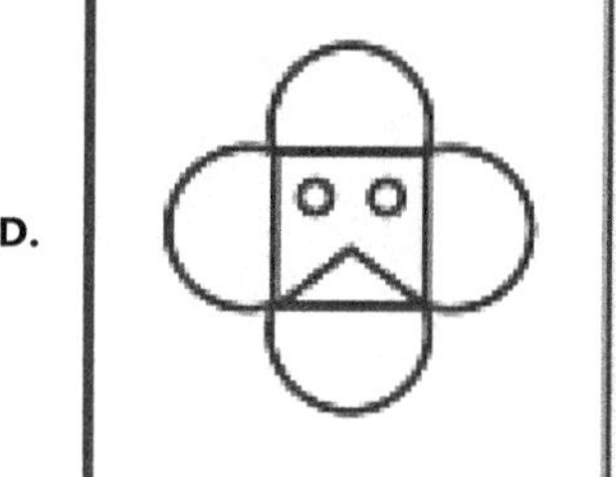

E. None of these

Q.30 The following figure is folded to form a cube. Which representation of the cube in the given options cannot be formed from the figure?

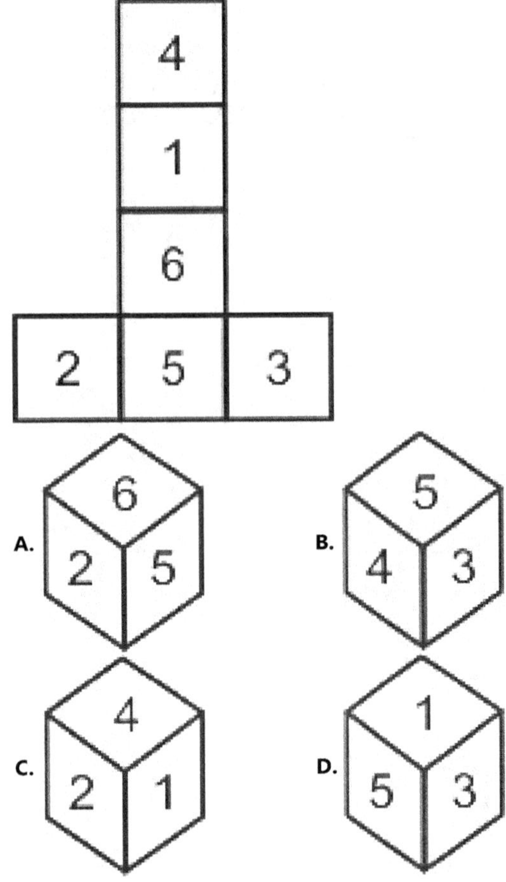

E. None of these

// Smart Answer Sheet //

Correct — Indicates percentage of students who answered questions correctly.

Skipped — Indicates percentage of students who skipped questions.

Q.	Ans.	Correct / Skipped
1	D	69.53 % / 30.31 %
2	E	62.52 % / 36.02 %
3	D	55.45 % / 37.15 %
4	B	16.21 % / 74.39 %
5	C	42.84 % / 30.64 %
6	A	40.5 % / 35.69 %
7	D	77.62 % / 17.17 %
8	D	76.23 % / 13.04 %
9	C	68.21 % / 30.43 %
10	C	76.97 % / 15.07 %
11	B	60.27 % / 37.94 %
12	D	40.53 % / 39.81 %
13	B	42.13 % / 52.71 %
14	C	54.33 % / 38.76 %
15	A	64.9 % / 33.56 %
16	D	44.04 % / 32.72 %
17	A	47.34 % / 38.34 %
18	D	29.84 % / 67.56 %
19	C	60.08 % / 35.05 %
20	B	49.7 % / 42.72 %
21	C	15.29 % / 81.51 %
22	C	69.36 % / 30.03 %
23	D	55.32 % / 33.9 %
24	C	51.26 % / 40.85 %
25	C	60.05 % / 37.62 %
26	B	42.16 % / 45.27 %
27	A	87.44 % / 10.64 %
28	B	54.86 % / 43.41 %
29	A	40.13 % / 34.26 %
30	D	55.15 % / 41.35 %

Performance Analysis	
Avg. Score (%)	50.0%
Toppers Score (%)	73.33%
Your Score	

//Hints and Solutions//

1. After folding the given figure, following will be opposite to each other:

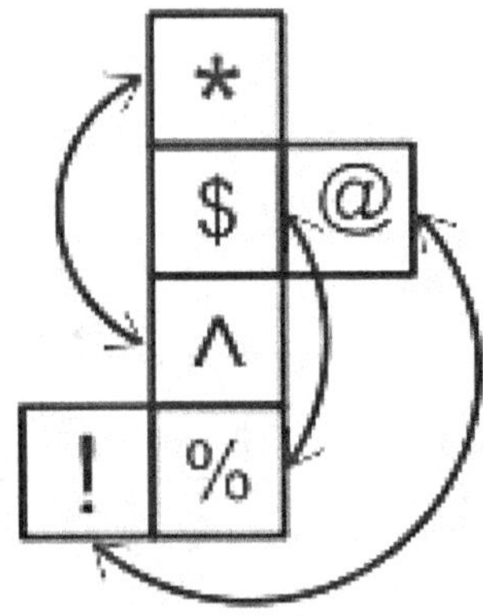

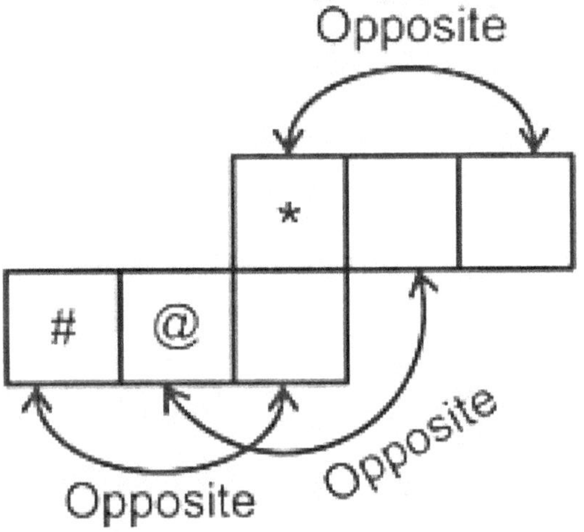

Clearly, the symbol opposite to is .

Hence, the correct option is (D).

2. In the given figure, opposite faces are:

Here, all the cubes can be formed as no face is placed adjacent to the face which is its opposite.

So, all cubes can be formed.

Hence, the correct option is (E).

3. When the unfolded cube is folded, the following pairs of faces will be opposite to each other:

$$1 \longrightarrow 2$$

$$4 \longrightarrow 6$$

$$9 \longrightarrow 7$$

Option (A), (B) and (C) contradict this.

Hence, the correct option is (D).

4. The opposite faces of the cube are:

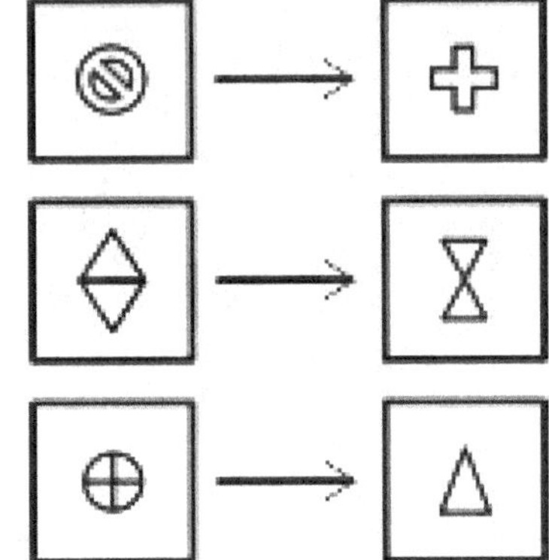

The opposite faces cannot become adjacent faces.

Hence, the correct option is (B).

5. When the unfolded cube is folded, the following pairs of faces will be opposite to each other.

$\times \longrightarrow +$

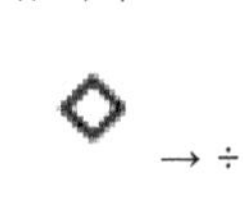

$\longrightarrow \div$

$o \longrightarrow -$

Options (A), (B) and (D) contradict this.

Hence, the correct option is (C).

6. The mirror image will be:

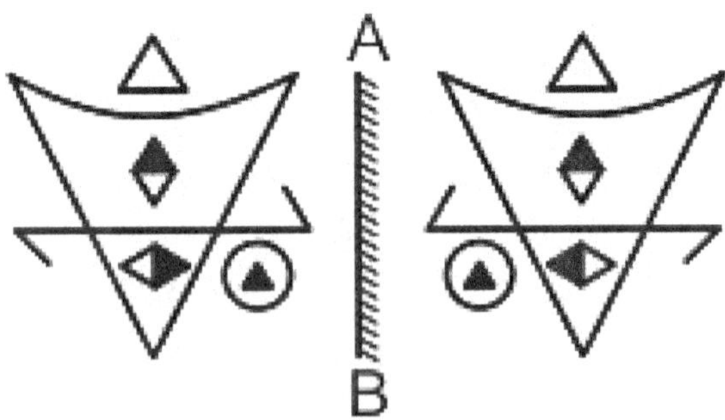

Hence, the correct option is (A).

7. The mirror image will be:

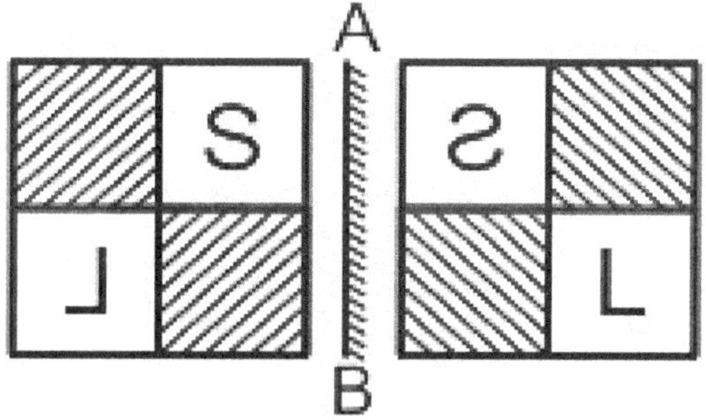

Hence, the correct option is (D).

8. The correct mirror image of question figure is shown below:

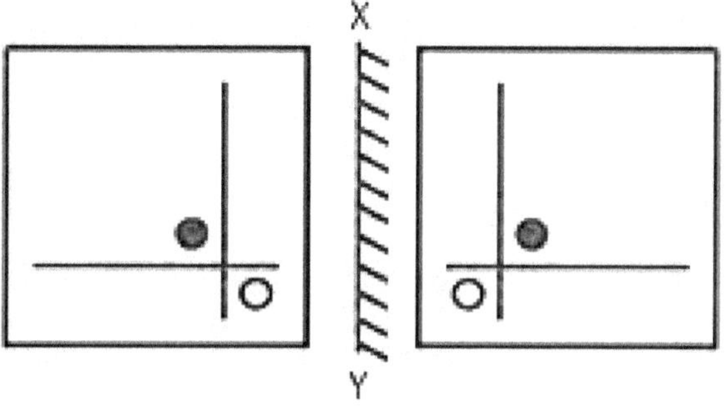

So, option (D) is the correct mirror image of the given image.

Hence, the correct option is (D).

9.

So, option (C) is the correct mirror image of the given question figure.

Hence, the correct option is (C).

10. If a mirror is placed on the line AB, then we will get this mirror image:

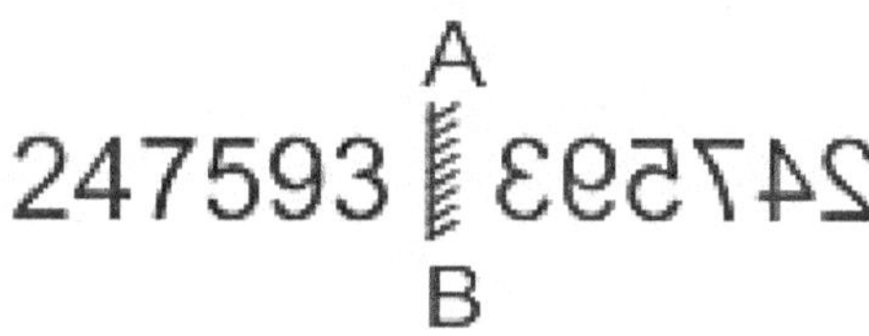

Hence, the correct option is (C).

11. The figure may be labelled as shown.

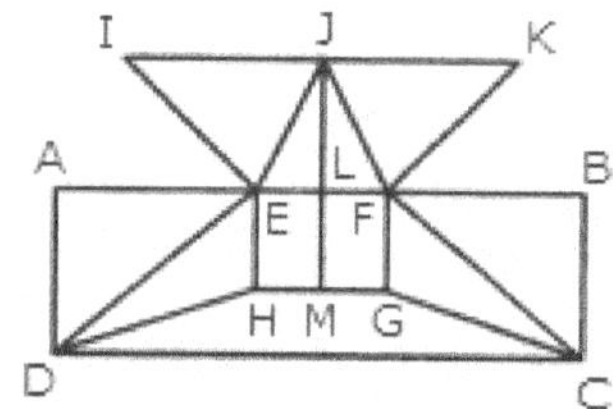

The horizontal lines are IK, AB, HG and DC i.e. 4 in number.

The vertical lines are AD, EH, JM, FG and BC i.e. 5 in number.

The slanting lines are IE, JE, JF, KF, DE, DH, FC and GC i.e. 8 is number.

Thus, there are 4 + 5 + 8 = 17 straight lines in the figure.

Hence, the correct option is (B).

12. The figure may be labelled as shown.

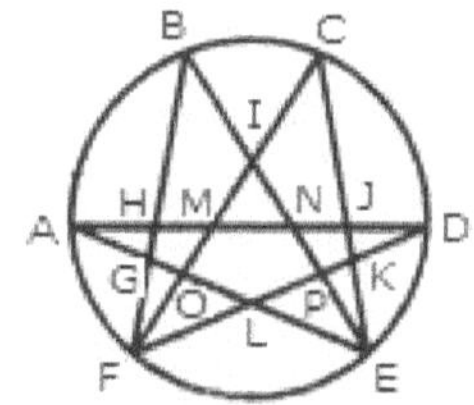

The simplest triangles are AGH, GFO, LFO, DJK, EKP, PEL and IMN i.e. 7 in number.

The triangles having two components each are GFL, KEL, AMO, NDP, BHN, CMJ, NEJ and HFM i.e. 8 in number.

The triangles having three components each are IOE, IFP, BIF and CEI i.e. 4 in number.

The triangles having four components each are ANE and DMF i.e. 2 in number.

The triangles having five components each are FCK, BGE and ADL i.e. 3 in number.

The triangles having six components each are BPF, COE, DHF and AJE i.e. 4 in number.

Total number of triangles in the figure = 7 + 8 + 4 + 2 + 3 + 4 = 28.

Hence, the correct option is (D).

13. The figure may be labelled as shown.

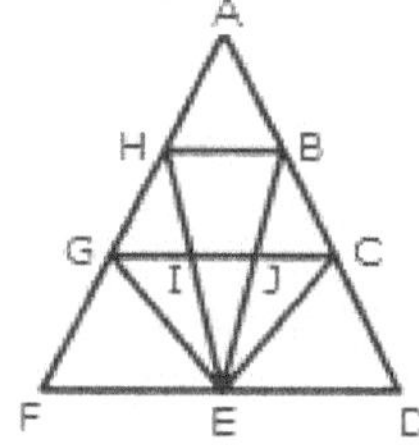

The simplest triangles are AHB, GHI, BJC, GFE, GIE, IJE, CEJ and CDE i.e. 8 in number.

The triangles composed of two components each are HEG, BEC, HBE, JGE and ICE i.e. 5 in number.

The triangles composed of three components each are FHE, GCE and BED i.e. 3 in number.

There is only one triangle i.e. AGC composed of four components.

There is only one triangle i.e. AFD composed of nine components.

Thus, there are 8 + 5 + 3 + 1 + 1 = 18 triangles in the given figure.

Hence, the correct option is (B).

14. The figure may be labelled as shown.

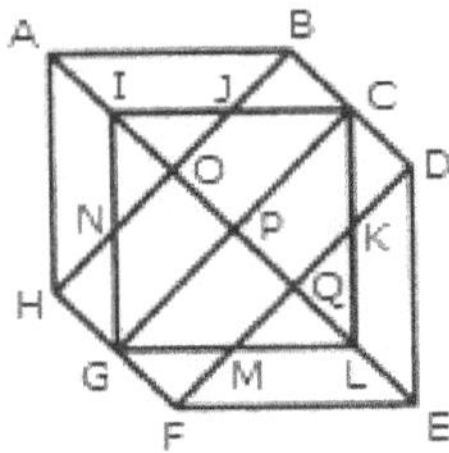

The simplest triangles are IJO, BCJ, CDK, KQL, MLQ, GFM, GHN and NIO i.e. 8 in number.

The triangles composed of two components each are ABO, AHO, NIJ, IGP, ICP, DEQ, FEQ, KLM, LCP and LGP i.e.10 in number.

The triangles composed of four components each are HAB, DEF, LGI, GIC, ICL and GLC i.e. 6 in number.

Total number of triangles in the figure = 8 + 10 + 6 = 24.

Hence, the correct option is (C).

15. The figure may be labelled as shown.

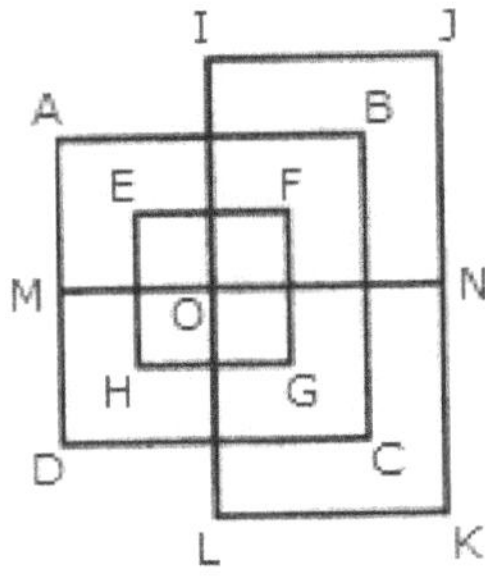

The horizontal lines are IJ, AB, EF, MN, HG, DC and LK i.e. 7 in number.

The vertical lines are AD, EH, IL, FG, BC and JK i.e. 6 in number.

Thus, there are 7 + 6 = 13 straight lines in the figure.

Hence, the correct option is (A).

16. The figure may be labelled as shown.

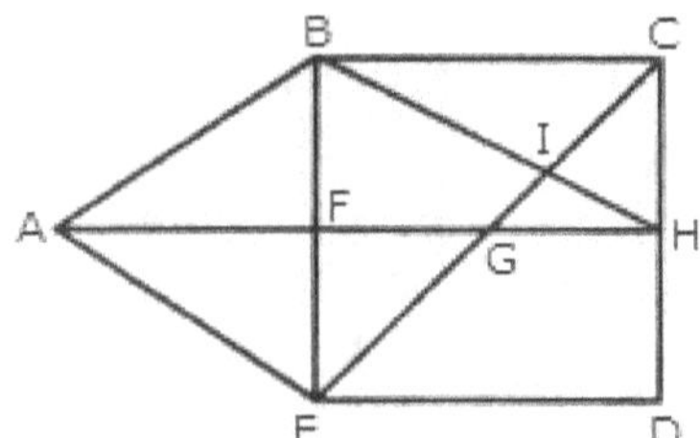

The simplest triangles are ABF, BIC, CIH, GIH, FGE and AFE i.e. 6 in number.

The triangles composed of two components each are ABE, AGE, BHF, BCH, CGH and BIE i.e. 6 in number.

The triangles composed of three components each are ABH, BCE and CDE i.e. 3 in number.

So, the total number of triangles in the figure = 6 + 6 + 3 = 15.

Hence, the correct option is (D).

17. The figure may be labelled as shown.

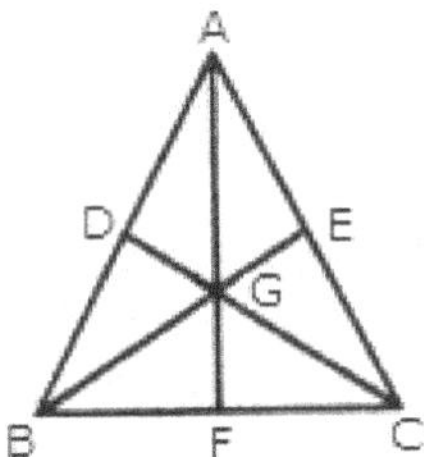

The simplest triangles are AGE, EGC, GFC, BGF, DGB and ADG i.e. 6 in number.

The triangles composed of two components each are AGC, BGC and ABG i.e. 3 in number.

The triangles composed of three components each are AFC, BEC, BDC, ABF, ABE and DAC i.e. 6 in number.

There is only one triangle i.e. ABC composed of six components.

Thus, there are 6 + 3 + 6 + 1 = 16 triangles in the given figure.

Hence, the correct option is (A).

18. The figure may be labeled as shown.

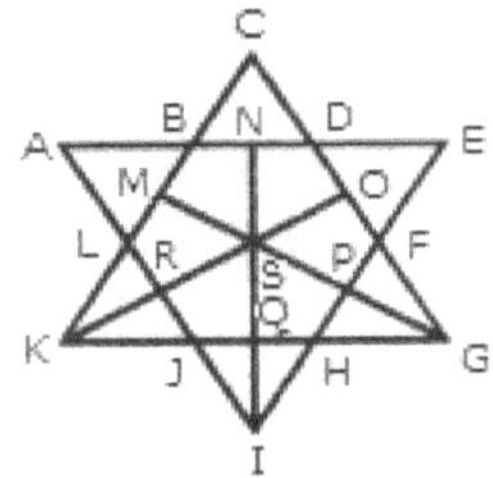

The simplest triangles are ABL, BCD, DEF, FGP, PGH, QHI, JQI, KRJ and LRK i.e. 9 in number.

The triangles composed of two components each are OSG, SGQ, SPI, SRI, KSQ, KMS, FGH, JHI and JKL i.e. 9 in number.

There is only one triangle i.e. KSG which is composed of four components.

The triangles composed of five components each are NEI, ANI, MCG and KCO i.e. 4 in number.

The triangles composed of six components each are GMK and KOG i.e. 2 in number.

There is only one triangle i.e. AEI composed of ten components.

There is only one triangle i.e. KCG composed of eleven components.

Therefore, Total number of triangles in the given figure = 9 + 9+1 + 4 + 2+1 + 1 = 27.

Hence, the correct option is (D).

19. The figure may be labelled as shown.

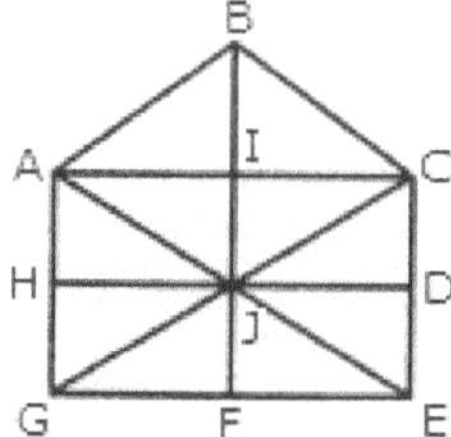

The simplest triangles are ABI, BIC, AIJ, CIJ, AHJ, CDJ, JHG, JDE, GJF and EJF i.e. 10 in number.

The triangles composed of two components each are ABC, BCJ, ACJ, BAJ, AJG, CJE and GJE i.e. 7 in number.

The triangles composed of four components each are ACG, ACE, CGE and AGE i.e. 4 in number.

Total number of triangles in the figure =10+ 7 + 4 = 21.

Hence, the correct option is (C).

20. The figure may be labelled as shown.

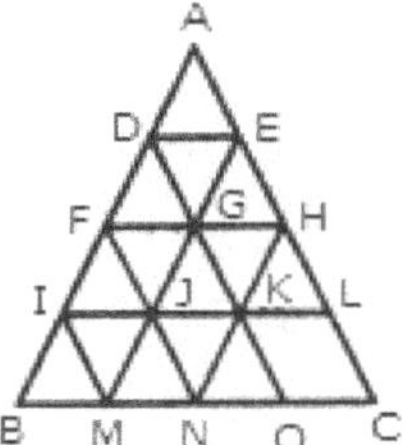

The horizontal lines are DE, FH, IL and BC i.e. 4 in number.

The slanting lines are AC, DO, FN, IM, AB, EM and HN i.e. 7 in number.

Thus, there are 4 + 7 = 11 straight lines in the figure.

Hence, the correct option is (B).

21. The figure may be labelled as shown.

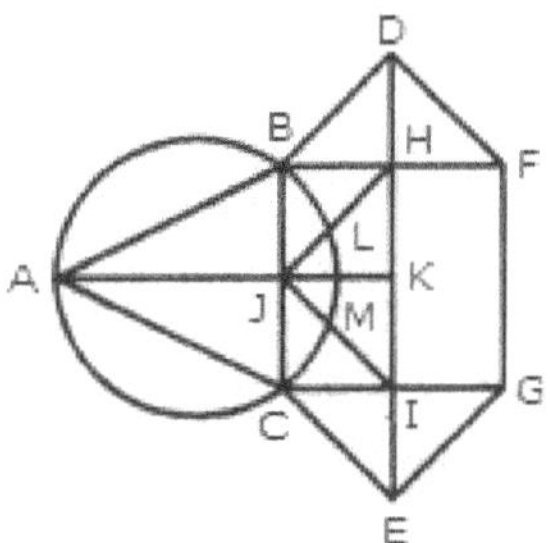

The simplest triangles are ABJ, ACJ, BDH, DHF, CIE and GIE i.e. 6 in number.

The triangles composed of two components each are ABC, BDF, CEG, BHJ, JHK, JKI and CJI i.e. 7 in number.

There is only one triangle JHI which is composed of four components.

Thus, there are 6 + 7 + 1 = 14 triangles in the given figure.

Hence, the correct option is (C).

22. The figure may be labelled as shown.

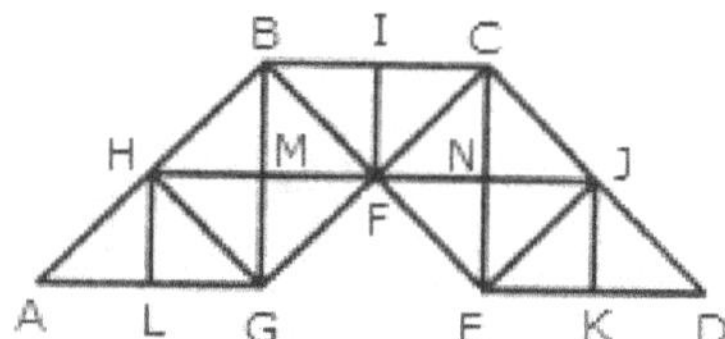

The simplest triangles are AHL, LHG, GHM, HMB, GMF, BMF, BIF, CIF, FNC, CNJ, FNE, NEJ, EKJ and JKD i.e. 14 in number.

The triangles composed of two components each are AGH, BHG, HBF, BFG, HFG, BCF, CJF, CJE, JEF, CFE and JED i.e. 11 in number.

The triangles composed of four components each are ABG, CBG, BCE and CED i.e. 4 in number.

Total number of triangles in the given figure = 14 + 11 + 4 = 29.

Hence, the correct option is (C).

23. The figure may be labelled as shown.

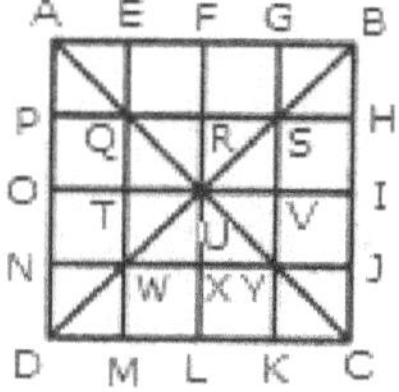

The simplest triangles are APQ, AEQ, QTU, QRU, BGS, BHS, RSU, SUV, TUW, UWX, NWD, WDM, UVY, UXY, JCY and YKC i.e. 16 in number.

The triangles composed of two components each are QUW, QSU, SYU and UWY i.e. 4 in number.

The triangles composed of three components each are AOU, AFU, FBU, BIU, UIC, ULC, ULD and OUD i.e. 8 in number.

The triangles composed of four components each are QYW, QSW, QSY and SYW i.e. 4 in number.

The triangles composed of six components each are AUD, ABU, BUC and DUC i.e. 4 in number.

The triangles composed of seven components each are QMC, ANY, EBW, PSD, CQH, AGY, DSK and BJW i.e. 8 in number.

The triangles composed of twelve components each are ABD, ABC, BCD and ACD i.e. 4 in number.

Thus, there are 16 + 4 + 8 + 4 + 4 + 8 + 4 = 48 triangles in the figure.

Hence, the correct option is (D).

24. The figure may be labelled as shown.

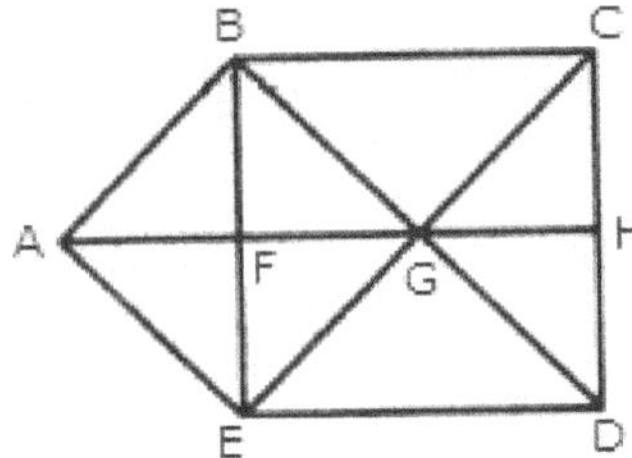

The simplest triangles are ABF, BFG, BCG, CGH, GHD, GED, EFG and AFE i.e. 8 in number.

The triangles composed of two components each are ABG, BGE, AGE, ABE and GCD i.e. 5 in number.

The triangles composed of three components each are BCD, CDE, BED and BCE i.e. 4 in number.

Thus, there are 8 + 5 + 4 = 17 triangles in the figure.

Hence, the correct option is (C).

25. The figure may be labelled as shown.

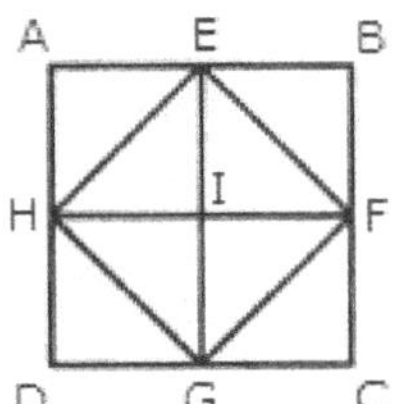

The simplest triangles are AEH, EHI, EBF, EFI, FGC, IFG, DGH and HIG i.e. 8 in number.

The triangles composed of two components each are HEF, EFG, HFG and EFG i.e. 4 in number.

Thus, there are 8 + 4 = 12 triangles in the figure.

Hence, the correct option is (C).

26. The figure may be labeled as shown.

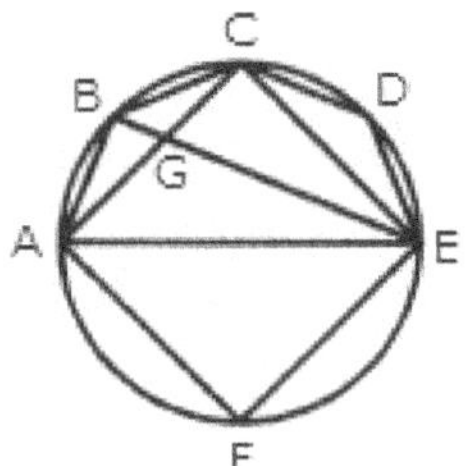

The simplest triangles are ABG, BCG, CGE, CDE, AGE and AEF i.e. 6 in number.

The triangles composed of two components each are ABE, ABC, BCE and ACE i.e. 4 in number.

There are 6 + 4 = 10 triangles in the figure.

Hence, the correct option is (B).

27. The mirror image of the question figure is shown below:

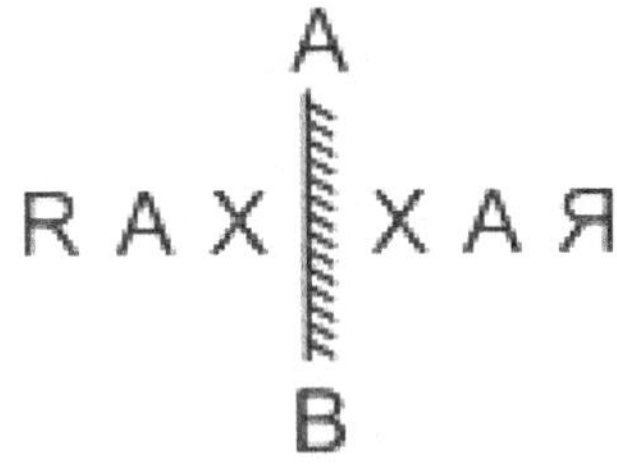

Hence, the correct option is (A).

28. Given

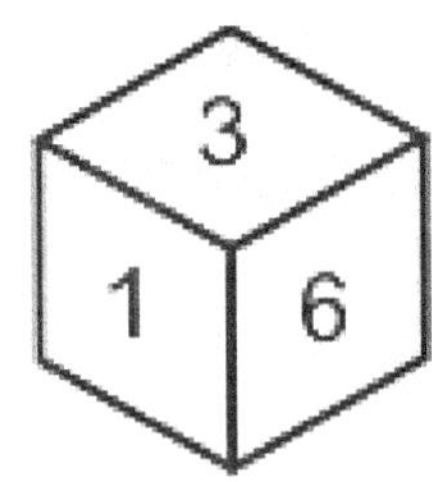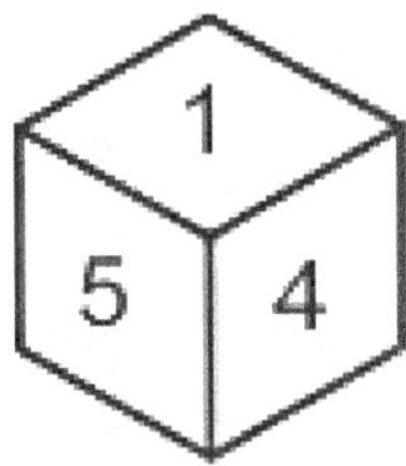

The opposite faces are,

1	3	6
2	4	5

Here we see 2 is on the face opposite face showing 1.

Hence, the correct option is (B).

29. The question figure is hidden/Embedded in figure (A).

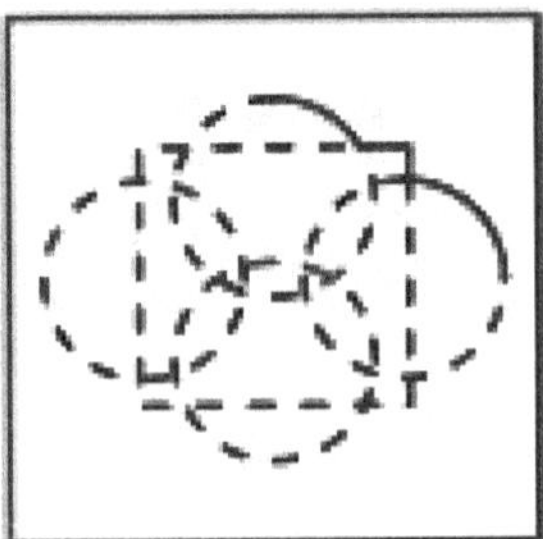

Hence, the correct option is (A).

30. The faces opposite to each other is shown below:

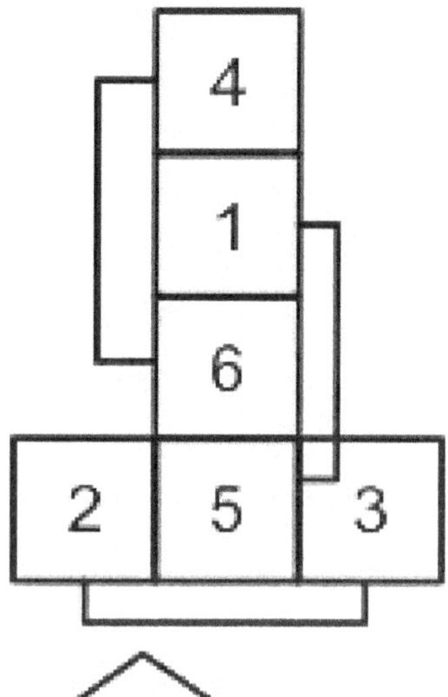

1) → This cube can be formed as no two opposite faces appear together on the same dice.

2) → This cube can be formed as no two opposite faces appear together on the same dice.

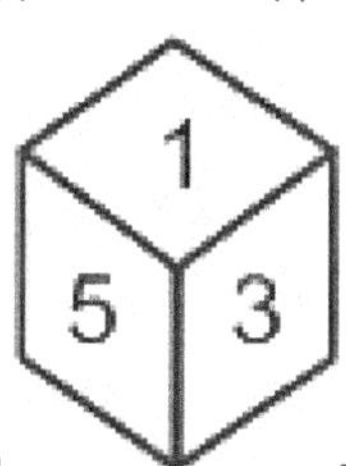

3) → This cube can be formed as no two opposite faces appear together on the same

4) → This cube cannot be formed as '1' and '5' faces are opposite faces and no two opposite faces can appear together on the same dice.

Hence, the correct option is (D).

// Notes //

// Notes //